चण्डीपाठः

Caṇḍīpāṭhaḥ

incorporating
Śrīdurgāsaptaśatī (*Devīmāhātmyam*)
and the associate Hymns

चण्डीपाठः

श्रीदुर्गासप्तशती (देवीमाहात्म्यम्)
अन्यानि सहयोगीस्तोत्राणि च

मूलपाठः देवनागरीरोमनलिपिभ्याम् समुपेताः
आङ्ग्लानुवादपरिचयात्मकलेखौ
भावनापंकजायाः सहयोगेन

इलाहाबादिया प्राणनाथ पंकजेन

मोतीलाल बनारसीदास
दिल्ली, मुम्बई, चेन्नई, कोलकाता,
बंगलूरू, वाराणसी, पटना

Caṇḍīpāṭhaḥ

incorporating
Śrīdurgāsaptaśatī (*Devīmāhātmyam*)
and the associate Hymns

with text in *Devanāgarī* and Roman,
Translation and Introductory Essay by

ALLAHABADIA PRAN NATH PANKAJ
in association with Bhavana Pankaj

MOTILAL BANARSIDASS PUBLISHERS
PRIVATE LIMITED • DELHI

Revised and Corrected Edition: Delhi, 2018
First Edition: Delhi, 2013

ISBN: 978-81-208-3557-3 (Cloth)
ISBN: 978-81-208-3619-8 (Paper)

MOTILAL BANARSIDASS

41 U.A. Bungalow Road, Jawahar Nagar, Delhi 110 007
1 B, Jyoti Studio Compound, Kennedy Bridge, Nana Chowk, Mumbai 400 007
203 Royapettah High Road, Mylapore, Chennai 600 004
236, 9th Main III Block, Jayanagar, Bengaluru 560 011
Sanas Plaza, 1302 Baji Rao Road, Pune 411 002
8 Camac Street, Kolkata 700 017
Ashok Rajpath, Patna 800 004
Chowk, Varanasi 221 001

Printed in India

by RP Jain at NAB Printing Unit,
A-44, Naraina Industrial Area, Phase I, New Delhi–110028
and published by JP Jain for Motilal Banarsidass Publishers (P) Ltd,
41 U.A. Bungalow Road, Jawahar Nagar, Delhi-110007

Scheme of Transliteration

स्वर (*svaras*/vowels)

अ	आ	इ	ई	उ	ऊ	ऋ	ॠ	लृ	ए	ऐ	ओ	औ
a	ā	i	ī	u	ū	ṛ	ṝ	ḷ	e	ai	o	au

अनुस्वार (anusvāra/nasal)	विसर्ग (visarga)
अं (˙)	अः (:)
ṁ	ḥ

व्यञ्जन (vyañjanas/consonants)

कण्ठ्य (kaṇṭhya/gutturals) –	क्	ख्	ग्	घ्	ङ्
	k	kh	g	gh	ṅ
तालव्य (tālavya/palatals) –	च्	छ्	ज्	झ्	ञ्
	c	ch	j	jh	ñ
मूर्धन्य (mūrdhanya/cerebrals) –	ट्	ठ्	ड्	ढ्	ण्
	ṭ	ṭh	ḍ	ḍh	ṇ
दन्त्य (dantya/dentals) –	त्	थ्	द्	ध्	न्
	t	th	d	dh	n
ओष्ठ्य (oṣṭhya/labials) –	प्	फ्	ब्	भ्	म्
	p	ph	b	bh	m

अन्तःस्थ (antaḥstha/semivowels) –	य्	र्	ल्	व्
	y	r	l	v
ऊष्म (ūṣma/sibilants) –	श्	ष्	स्	
	ś	ṣ	s	
महाप्राण (mahāprāṇa/aspirate) –	ह्			
	h			

क्ष्	त्र्	ज्ञ्
kṣ	tr	jñ
ऽ		

With Salutations to
Jagadambā

From a son and a brother
to the memory of
his mother and sister.

From a husband to his wife
and
from a father to his daughter.

Contents

Preface to the Second Edition

With the blessings of the Divine Mother, we are glad to present the second edition of *Caṇḍīpāṭhaḥ* which was originally published in the year 2013 and very well received.

The contents of the Book required some additions and minor corrections. These have been carried out and a thorough revision made in the present edition. This, we hope, will enhance the value of the Book.

A.P.N. Pankaj
Bhavana Pankaj

Invocation from the *Vinaya Patrikā*

जय जय जगजननि देवि सुर-नर-मुनि-असुर-सेवि,
भुक्ति-मुक्ति-दायिनि भय-हरणि कालिका ।
मंगल-मुद-सिद्धि-सदनि पर्वशर्वरीश-वदनि,
ताप-तिमिर-तरुण-तरणि-किरणमालिका ।।

jaya jaya jagajanani devi sura-nara-muni-asura-sevi,
bhukti-mukti-dāyini bhaya-haraṇi kālikā ।
maṅgala-muda-siddhi-sadani parvaśarvarīśa-vadani,
tāpa-timira-taruṇa-taraṇi-kiraṇamālikā ।।

Glory to the Divine Mother of the Universe, whom the gods, the men, the ascetics and the demons serve; who grants the worldly joys and final beatitude; who is *Kālī*, the Controller of Time, the Destroyer of Fear, the Power of Death and Transformation; the Abode of Auspiciousness, Delight and Accomplishments; whose face is beautiful like the full-moon, who is like a garland of the sun's rays for rooting out physical, mental and supernatural afflictions that, like darkness, engulf the beings.

बर्म, चर्म, कर कृपाण, शूल-शेल-धनुषबाण-
धरणि, दलनि दानव-दल, रण-करालिका ।
पूतना-पिशाच-प्रेत-डाकिनि-शाकिनि समेत,
भूत-ग्रह-बेताल-खग-मृगालि-जालिका ।।

barma, carma, kara, kṛpāṇa, śūla-śela-dhanuṣabāṇa-
dharaṇi, dalani dānava-dala, raṇa-karālikā ।
pūtanā-piśāca-preta-ḍākini-śākini sameta,
bhūta-graha-betāla-khaga-mṛgāli-jālikā ।।

O Mother! in your hands you hold the shield and sword, pike, dagger, bow and arrows and on your body, wear an armour. You are the slayer of the troops of demons. In the battleground, you are the Tongue of Flames for the enemy. For the forces of evil – demonesses, hell-hounds, goblins, witches, fairies along with ghosts, planetary calamities and spirits – you are the Snare that catches birds and beasts.

गोस्वामी तुलसीदास
विनय पत्रिका १६.१–२
GOSVĀMĪ TULASĪDĀSA
Vinaya Patrikā 16.1–2

A Personal Statement

This is the acknowledgement of a debt which does not get time-barred on account of the law of limitation. Only incidentally, it is also a preface to this book.

The Mother plays.

She rocks the boat, giving an impression that She is tilting it. Sometimes She does tilt it; on other occasions, She stops short. But all the while She holds it. She plays unceasingly. And She does so in Her own discipline. She pushes a person to the precipice and then decides to bring him back so that, as Her instrument, he may perform the task that She has chosen him for.

In both, pushing and pulling back, She only dispenses Her grace. Blinded by false ego, when an individual assumes the arrorgance of learning and wisdom and, like a fool, believes that it is he who is the doer – *ahaṅkāra vimūḍhātmā kartāhamiti manyate*[1] – She, deciding to restore to him his essential humility, pushes him gently but firmly enough to send him to the precipice. Since, however, She still has Her work for him, She brings him back leaving with him the realization that he is just the instrument – *nimittamātra*[2]. Even in assigning the tasks, She identifies the priorities, taking upon Herself the burden of decision.

In the autumn of 2009, when I was deeply involved in writing a treatise on *Śrīrāmacaritamānasa* of Gosvāmī Tulasīdāsa, I suddenly suffered from an ailment serious enough to shatter all plans and activities. I was completely bed-ridden, partly in hospital but mostly at home. The kind physician who, patiently, painstakingly and over a long period, treated me, had told my wife and daughter that I had almost reached a point of no return. The Mother had obviously chosen him as Her instrument to

[1] Gītā III.27
[2] Ibid., XI.33

bring me back. His name is Dr. Arvind Sahni. And I am indebted to him.

At that time, however, I had no idea of what plans the Mother had for me. Even as I was still convalescing, my good friends since the college days, Narendra and Jainendra Jain of Motilal Banarsidass, who had been in close touch with me all through those days, asked me if I would undertake to do the English rendering of the *Caṇḍīpāṭha*, complete with the original text in *Devanāgarī* and its Roman transliteration. They were willing to wait till I had recovered enough to take up the work. There was, however, an unspoken understanding that priority was to be accorded to this work once I resumed my normal functions. Even as I accepted it as the Mother's command, it turns out that despite my having completed the work fairly early, its publication, due to some unavoidable technical reasons, has been inordinately delayed and it is, finally, coming out now. I wonder if this too is a part of Her Play!

Obviously, the Mother had chosen them as Her instruments, even perhaps without their knowing it, to reach out to me, to do Her work. My grateful thanks to both the brothers.

In the period of my suffering, a period which was rather long and exhausting—Karuna, my wife and Bhavana, my daughter, silently suffered and prayed, maintaining all the while a cheerful and encouraging demeanour. As a student of Behavioral Science, I had, at length, read, written and spoken on the meanings of the term empathy. They became the living illustrations of the term. Karuna, though herself in fragile health, put her own worries on hold and centralised all her attentions to me.

I have mentioned Bhavana's name in the by line of this book. This is for two reasons. She has, of course, actively assisted me in this work and, as a professional editor, edited it. More than that, she kept my spirits up even when my health was low and I felt physically and mentally exhausted. From Delhi, when she was there with Vivek, her husband, who kept cheering me up, or from here, when she was with us which most of the time she was, she kept reminding me that I was doing the Mother's work and it had to be accomplished. *Daughter, indeed, is the Mother.*

All three of them, to me, were and are the Mother's chosen instruments through whom She operated so that I could begin, continue and complete this work. They are, however, too close to me to be thanked. It is only the Mother's love and grace which I experience that I can share with them. And I do.

I Personally owe a debt of gratitude to Shri Vinay Jain, an eminent graphic-designer and a valued friend who took time and pains to do the cover design of the book.

There have been a number of friends, relatives and well wishers who lent moral and active support to us during those difficult days. It is not possible to mention all of them here by name. I would, however, like to specially mention Shrimati Sudarshan Kukreja, Karuna's elder sister; Shri K.D. Sharma, Bhavana's father-in-law; Shri Shyam Sundar Gupta, Shri Shashi Gupta, Shri Brahm Puri and Shrimati Vinod Gupta, my dear friends since my days in State Bank of India and Shri Darhsan Kumar Vashishth, a devotee of the Divine Life Society and a frequent visitor to Ramakrishna Mission Ashrama, Chandigarh and another very dear friend. To them all, I am beholden.

Many passages from our religious literature can be cited – and I, for one have, since childhood, experienced their truth – that say that saints are God's apostles on earth. The Mother blessed me with one such apostle in Śraddheya Swami Brahmeshananda Ji, Secretary, Rama-

Krishna Mission Ashrama, Chandigarh[3] and by qualification a physician. He proverbially held my hand as I took faltering steps and gently, gradually, restored my faith and will and mental health. I can never, ever, be adequately grateful to him.

But all these expressions of gratitude, are to be seen in a specific context. I am thankful to them all not because they facilitated my return to health. Frankly, I shall have no regrets if I depart today though I may not be asking for it. I am thankful because as the Mother's instruments, all of them, each in her/his own assigned role, helped me do the job She had chosen me for.

When I was a toddler, I used to see my parents, Shrimati Ram Pyari and Shri Gopinath, starting their day with the worship of *Śrī Sītā-Rāmacandra. Śrīrāmacaritamānasa* of Gosvāmī Tulasīdāsa was the holy book at our Amritsar home where, after early morning ablutions, the day began in a small in-house shrine with *pūjā* and the recitation of *Mānasa.* In the shrine, there was also an image of the Mother *Mahiṣāsuramardinī.* My mother would tell me the stories from the *Caṇḍīsaptśatī* (or *Durgāsaptśatī* as she called it) and their symbolic significance. I attentively listened and asked for more. My father once told me that they were the devotees of the Mother and it was at Her implicit command that *Śrī Sītā-Rāmacandra* were placed alongside Her and, *Śrī Rāmacaritamānasa,* on a pedestal in the shrine.

All this went deep into my psyche and stays. I cannot claim even an iota of the devotion they had for the Divine Mother and *Śrī Sītā-Rāmacandra* but, without doubt, I love *Them.* I look to *Them* as my living, loving and caring parents and can feel *Their* presence around me. It is this inspiring feeling of proximity of the Divine Mother and *Śrī Sītā-Rāmacandra* that has enabled me to go on with this work and complete it.

[3] Swami Ji has since retired and settled in Varanasi,

In a very tangible sense, my biological parents were my spiritual parents too and the debt of gratitude I owe to them can never he repaid.

This, then, is a work of *śraddhā* and love, neither of scholarship nor erudition. There is no claim to orginality in this work. Since childhood, I have read many religious, spiritual and philosophic works some of which I have consciously or unconsciously absorbed. They keep, as they do in this work, appearing again and again through my writings and speeches. Coming to think of it, even the words used by me are not mine for they are all available in the lexicons. I have reproduced them mostly from memory and occasionally from those lexicons. Even as I further think, thoughts, emotions and words and expressions are all Hers and they return to Her when I use them here. In the final analysis, the Mother as *Vāgdevatā*, is the creator, controller, retainer and consumer of all thought and speech. To their partakers, the authors and creators – known, unknown and not in the memory-box – of those works, I owe a deep debt of gratitude and pay obeisance : ***pranavaun sabahin kapaṭa saba tyāgein***[4]. Can I even claim my feelings of love and reverence as my own original feelings? From an ocean of Her love and the pervasive feelings of reverence in this vast universe, She has blessed me with a few tiny drops thereof. I call them my own: *my feelings of love and reverence* for Her. If these touch the devout readers as they go through the following passages, it will only mean that these tiny drops travel down to join the other similar ones eventually to become a part of the expanse of the Mother's love.

In January 1947, the famous Hindi Journal, '*Kalyāṇa*' of the Gita Press, Gorakhpur, had brought out the special annual issue, the *Mārkaṇḍeya-Brahmapurāṇāṅka*. A year

[4] Rāmacaritamānasa I.14.3

later, a compact Hindi publication of *Śrīdurgāsaptaśatī*, was also brought out by them. The *Devīmāhātmya*, or the *Caṇḍīpāṭha*, including the *Saptaśatī* and the associate preceding and succeeding texts were incorporated in these publications. In this present work, I have mainly followed those texts and even otherwise been greatly influenced by those publications. I am deeply indebted to the publishers thereof.

Apart from the *Devanāgarī* text, Roman transliteration, English translation and an introductory essay, some other additions have also been made herein. Names, adjectives and epithets of the Mother appearing in the text have been arranged in the alphabetical order. Weapons used by the fighting forces on both sides have been listed and brief explanation thereof given. A glossary of main Sanskrit terms/words has been provided. Firstline Index of Sanskrit verses has been added hymn/chapter wise. All these appear as appendices.

All said, it is still a work of the human mind and hands – and I do not here refer to the original text of the *mantradraṣṭā* seers, but what I and my daughter have attempted. If the discerning readers – scholars and devotees – find here any errors, omissions and weaknesses, and I am sure there would be many, they, I pray, would bear with them and us:

chamihahin sajjana mori ḍhiṭhāī
sunihahin bāla bacana mana lāī[5]

Noble persons will please pardon our impudence and, with indulgence, attend to our childish prattle.

Karuṇāyatana A.P.N. PANKAJ
1064/1, Sector-39-B, Chandigarh
September 30th, 2012

---

[5] Ibid., I.8.4

Important Instructions/Suggestions

Śrīdurgāsaptaśatī is one of the holiest texts of the Hindu religion. For devotees, it is the *Śabdāvatāra* – incarnation in words – of the Mother. The book should therefore, be handled and treated with reverence. Following discipline is recommended to be observed before and during the recitation:

1. After the morning ablutions and performing daily worship *or sandhyā*, one should sit on a clean and pure *āsana* facing east or north.
2. The book should be placed on an elevated stand, preferably in a copper plate.
3. Pūjā – the worship – of the Book should be performed with the following two *mantras*:

ॐ नमो देव्यै महादेव्यै शिवायै सततं नमः ।
नमो प्रकृत्यै भद्रायै नियताः प्रणताः स्म ताम् ॥

Oṁ namo devyai mahādevyai śivāyai satataṁ namaḥ ।
namo prakṛtyai bhadrāyai niyatāḥ praṇatāḥ sma tām ॥

ध्यात्वा देवीं पञ्चपूजां[1] कृत्वा योन्या प्रणम्य च।
आधारं स्थाप्य मूलेन स्थापयेत्तत्र पुस्तकम्॥

dhyātvā devīṁ pañcapūjāṁ[1] *kṛtvā yonyā praṇamya ca* ।
ādhāraṁ sthāpya mūlena sthāpayettatra pustakam ॥

4. After meditating upon the Mother and worshipping the Book, *yoni-mudrā* should be shown, obeisance should be paid and worship of the *pīṭha* – seat – should be performed with the *mūla* – *navārṇa mantra* (given in the beginning of the *Navārṇavidhiḥ)* – and the book placed thereon.

[1] *Pañcapūjā* or *Pañcopāsanā* is the worship of *pañcamahābhūtas* – five elements – Earth, Water, Fire, Air and Ether representing their presiding deities : *Śiva, Gaṇesa, Śakti* (Māheśvarī), Sun, and *Viṣṇu* respectively.

5. Bells should be sounded in the beginning and at the end of each chapter.
6. Eighth, ninth and fourteenth dates of each fortnight of the Indian lunar month and Tuesday, Friday and Saturday of every week are considered auspicious for recitation of the *Saptāśatī*.
7. There are three Acts (*prathama carita* – First Act – Chapter One; *madhyama carita* – Middle Act – Chapters Two to Four; and *uttara* or *uttama carita* – Final or the Foremost Act – Chapters Five to Thirteen). If it is not possible to recite the entire *Saptaśatī* in a single day, one should read the *madhyama carita* on the first day, and the *prathama* and the *uttara carita* on the second day.
8. For those who perform daily recitation but cannot complete it in one day, it is enjoined that they should complete it in the following order: First day – One chapter; Second day – Two chapters; Third day – One Chapter; Fourth day – Four Chapters; Fifth day – Two chapters; Sixth day – one chapter; Seventh day – Two chapters.
9. One should recite the *mantras* with deliberate concentration of mind meditating upon the Goddess, in soft tones, pronouncing the letters clearly, at a pitch which is neither too low nor too high, clearly separating the lines and quarters of each verse.
10. Recitation should not be closed or discontinued before completing the chapter. If for some reason or inadvertently it is discontinued, one should start the chapter from the beginning and complete it.
11. Recitation should not be done speechlessly (mentally) but vocally. It should not be done very loudly and one should not be in a hurry to finish.

12. Recitation may be done from the Book if the text is not committed to memory. One should not, however, read from the manuscript written in one's own hand.
13. For performing the *anuṣṭhāna* – the systematic observance of the prescribed austerities connected with the recital of the *Saptaśatī*, for attainment of a specific objective – it is necessary to get initiated by a qualified *Guru* belonging to the lineage of preceptors who have been traditionally performing and are well-versed in the rites of worship.

Prakṛti and *Puruṣa*

रामं विद्धि परं ब्रह्म सच्चिदानन्दमद्वयम् ।
सर्वोपाधिविनिर्मुक्तं सत्तामात्रमगोचरम् ॥

rāmaṁ viddhi paraṁ brahma saccidānandamadvayam ।
sarvopādhivinirmuktaṁ sattāmātramagocaram ॥

Know *Rāma* as the Supreme *Brahman*; Truth, Consciousness and Bliss; without a second; without attributes; Pure Existence, Inaccessible through senses.

मां विद्धि मूलप्रकृतिं सर्गस्थित्यन्तकारिणीम् ।
तस्य सन्निद्धिमात्रेण सृजामीदमतन्द्रिता ॥

māṁ viddhi mūlaprakṛtiṁ sargasthityantakāriṇīm ।
tasya sannidhimātreṇa sṛjāmīdamatandritā ॥

Know *Me* as *Mūla Prakṛti*, the Primary Nature*, the cause of creation, sustenance and dissolution. By virtue of His proximity alone, I am actively engaged in creation.

रामो न गच्छति न तिष्ठति नानुशोचत्याकाङ्क्षते त्यजति नो न करोति किञ्चित् ।
आनन्दमूर्तिरचलः परिणामहीनो मायागुणाननुगतो हि तथा विभाति ॥

rāmo na gacchati na tiṣṭhati nānuśocatyākāṅkṣate
tyajati no na karoti kiñcit ।
ānandamūrtiracalaḥ pariṇamahīno māyāguṇānanugato
hi tathā vibhāti ॥

Rāma neither goes, nor stays; neither grieves nor desires; neither quits nor does anything. He is the form of Pure Bliss, without change. Attended by the attributes of *Māyā*, He seems to appear like all that.

Sītā to *Hanumān*
(in the *Adhyātma Rāmāyaṇa*, I.i.32,34,43)

---

* *Pradhāna* of the *Sāṅkhya* Philosophy

Introductory Essay

1. The Timeless Mother

Since when has India been worshipping the Mother Goddess? Scholars trace it back to the days of the Harappā culture and say that the Āryans adopted her from there. Put this question to a devout Hindu and see him raise his brow. 'Since eternity'; he will retort, 'if its evidence is available in the pre-Vedic or Vedic ages, it only means that we may not have archaeological or literary evidence prior to those times. Divine Power and her manifestations in several forms and names have been the mainstay of humans ever since there have been human beings. And the Mother Goddess as one manifestation of the Supreme Power has stood by humans as much as the father figure – perhaps more – representing that Power.'

In the *Ṛgveda*[1], the Mother is eulogised as 'the support and substratum of earth, living in heaven' and 'embodiment of Power.' She is the intrinsic Nature and true Power of God whom we call *Śaktimān,* as his potential as well as kinetic energy. In the unmanifest *Brahman, Śakti* remains its inherent and all-pervasive power. *Brahmā, Viṣṇu* and *Śiva,* the agents of the unmanifest *Brahman,* who respectively create, sustain or preserve and dissolve the *prapañca jagat* – the phenomenal world – function only through their respective *Śaktis* – *Sarasvatī, Lakṣmī* and *Durgā.* She is the *prakṛti* of the *Sāṅkhya* school and *māyā* of the *Vedānta.* We may say that while *Śakti* and *Śaktimān* are not separate from each other, devotees according to their faith and reverence, lay greater emphasis on one or the other aspect of the same Supreme Reality. That they are, indeed, inseparable is highlighted in the

[1] *Ṛgveda* I.136.3

ardhanārīśvara, the deity as half *Śiva* and half *Pārvatī*: the concept of Ultimate Reality. The *ṛṣis* – seers – of the Vedic hymns experienced the grandeur, glory, beauty and awe of the Almighty in Nature, in its many splendoured manifestations and just as they celebrated one Supreme Reality in many forms of the gods, they also envisioned the same Reality expressing itself in various goddesses, e.g., *Pṛthvī,* the Earth personified; *Aditi,* the Great Mother of the gods; *Uṣas,* the Goddess of Dawn; *Rātri,* the Goddess of Night[2] and *Araṇyānī,* the Goddess of Forest, etc. It is significant that the Sanskrit term *devatā* is applied to both, the gods and the goddesses.

In the *Atharvaveda,* we come across the hymn, *Devyatharvaśīrṣaṁ* (which has been reproduced in this book). The term means 'the highest meaning of the Goddess.' *Atharvaśīrṣa* also means the highest part of the *Atharvaveda.* Vedas are notionally divided into three parts – *Saṁhitās, Brāhmaṇas* and *Āraṇyakas.* The *Upaniṣads* are mainly a part of the *Āraṇyakas. Atharvaśīrṣas* too are the *Upaniṣads.* There are five principal *Atharvaśīrṣas* and the *Devyatharvaśīrṣa* is considered to be the most exalted of them all, since by reciting this alone, one reaps the fruit of reciting all the five. *Upaniṣads* are known as *Brahmavidyā,* the knowledge of *Brahman. Devyatharvaśīrṣa* is, therefore, *Brahmavidyā.* The Goddess herself declares in it that she is *Brahmasvarūpiṇī,* the female principle of *Brahman,* and that this entire universe of *Prakṛti* and

---

[2] As part of Hymns preceding the *Saptaśatī,* we have given the *Rātri Sūkta* – the Hymn of Night – of the *Ṛgveda* in this book. An allusion to it is obvious in the first chapter of the *Saptaśatī* where Lord *Viṣṇu* is depicted in deep sleep under the spell of his *Yoganidrā,* the cosmic sleep, when the world had dissolved as one great ocean. In the famous *Nāsadīya Sūkta* of the *Ṛgveda,* we have the statement of that phenomenon of night : *tama āsīttamasā gūvhamagre* (X.129.3).

Puruṣa is born from her.[3] She also says there (in the fifth *mantra*) that she moves about as *Rudras* and *Vasus*, as *Ādityas* and *Viśvedevas*, that she nourishes and nurtures both *Mitra* and *Varuṇa*, that she is *Agni* and *Aśvins*.

In the *Upaniṣadic* literature, the *bahuśobhanā* – the most beautiful – *Umā Haimavātī* of the golden hue, the daughter of *Hīmālaya*, reveals the *Upaniṣadic* idealism to the gods.[4] She is revered as the powerful *Gāyatrī* and *Sāvitrī* with fire as her mouth.[5] She is all that has come to be, whatever there is – *idaṁ sarvaṁ bhūtaṁ yadidaṁ kiñca*. Verily, she is what this earth is, for on it everything that has come to be, is established – *sā yeyaṁ pṛthivī, asyāṁ hīdaṁ sarvaṁ bhūtaṁ pratiṣṭhitam*.[6] She is *Devātmaśakti* – self-power of God, hidden by her own qualities – *svaguṇairnigūḍhā*.[7] She is *Parāśakti*, the kinetic power, from whom all the gods and semi-gods, material for consumption and enjoyment, all living beings including humans and inanimates, were born.[8] In the Bhagavadgītā, *Śrī Kṛṣṇa* says that among women, he is '*Kīrti* (fame), *Śrī* (fortune), *Vāk* (speech), *Smṛti* (memory) *Medhā* (intelligence), *Dhṛti* (fortitude) and *Kṣamā* (forbearance)'.[9]

In the *Paurāṇic* literature she is *Yogamāyā*, the sister of Lord *Kṛṣṇa*.[10] *Gopikās* worship her as the Goddess *Kātyāyanī*.[11] In the *Brahmavaivarta Purāṇa*,[12] Śrī Kṛṣṇa says:

---

[3] *Devyatharvaśīrṣam* 2; also *Ṛgveda Aṣṭaka* VIII.7.11.

[4] *Kenopaniṣad* III.12

[5] *Bṛhadāraṇyaka Upaniṣad* V.14.6

[6] *Chāndogya Upaniṣad* III.12.2

[7] *Śvetāśvataropaniṣad* I.3

[8] *Bahvṛcopaniṣad*

[9] *Gītā* X.34. Śrī Kṛṣṇa also says (IV.6) that he, resorting to his *Prakṛti*, comes into being through his own Inscrutable Power (*Māyā*).

[10] *Śrīmadbhāgavata* X.4.9

[11] Ibid., X.22.1–4

[12] *Brahmavaivarta Purāṇa, Prakṛtikhaṇḍa* II.66.7–10. (Three modes

You are the Mother of all, the primal nature (*Pradhāna* of the *Sāṅkhya school*), the Supreme Sovereign. In the beginning of creation, you are the primeval energy and voluntarily incorporate the three modes in yourself. Although you are, in truth, without attributes, yet for functional purposes, you imbibe them. You are intrinsically *Brahman*, the infinite ultimate being; you are truth, eternity, primeval, of the nature of effulgence, ultimate reality and for your devotees, the ultimate grace. You are the essential nature of all, ruler of all, substratum of all and the Supreme Being. You are the seed of all creation, worshipped by all, requiring no substratum for yourself. You are omniscient, resting place for all and abode of all auspiciousness.

In order to have *Sītā* released from *Rāvaṇa*'s captivity, *Rāma*, himself the incarnation of *Viṣṇu*, worships and observes *navarātryupāsanā* (nine-days' vow during autumn months – September/October – preceding *vijayādaśamī*) to propitiate the Mother Goddess. She appears before him, saddled on the lion, her mount, and grants him the boon of victory. Following this, *Rāma* performs *Vijayā-pūjā* – the worship of the Victory Goddess – and, accompanied by the army of *vānaras*, marches towards the sea.[13] In the *Kṛttivāsa* (Bengali) Rāmāyaṇa, *Śrī Rāma* requires 108 blue lotuses to offer to the Goddess to propitiate her. One of them is playfully stolen by the Goddess and *Rāma* ventures to offer her one of his 'lotus-eyes' (*rājīvanayana*) when the Goddess appears and blesses him with victory.[14] The famous Hindi poet Sūrya Kānta Tripāṭhī Nirālā has

---

mentioned here are *sāttvika*, *rājasika* and *tāmasika*. Also see *Rāmacaritamānasa* (I.235, 2–4 to 236) where *Sītā* goes to *Gaurī* for worship and is blessed by the Mother that the former would get the husband of her choice (*Rāma*).

[13] *Devībhāgavata Purāṇa* III.28–30. In the *Mahābhāgavata Purāṇa* (Chs. 44, 46–47), *Bṛhaddharma Purāṇa* (Ch. 22) and *Kālikāpurāṇa* (Ch. 62), Lord Brahmā worships the Goddess for Rāma's victory.

[14] Ibid., 92–102

also narrated this episode beautifully in his long poem *Rāma-Kī-Śaktipūjā.*

'यह है उपाय,' कह उठे राम ज्यों मन्द्रित घन-
'कहती थीं माता मुझे सदा राजीवनयन !
दो नील कमल हैं शेष अभी, यह पुरश्चरण
पूरा करता हूँ देकर मातः एक नयन।'
कह कर देखा तूणीर ब्रह्मशर रहा झलक,
ले लिया हस्त, लक-लक करता वह महाफलक;
ले अस्त्र वाम कर, दक्षिण कर दक्षिण लोचन
ले अर्पित करने को उद्यत हो गए सुमन
जिस क्षण बँध गया बेधने को दृग दृढ़निश्चय
काँपा ब्रह्माण्ड, हुआ देवी का तुरत उदयः-
'साधु, साधु, साधक धीर, धर्म-धन-धान्य राम !'
कह, लिया भगवती ने राघव का हस्त थाम
देखा राम ने सामने श्री दुर्गा...........

('yaha hai upāya' kaha uṭhe rāma jyon mandrita ghana –
'kahatī thīn mātā mujhe sadā rājīvanayana !
do nīla kamala hain śeṣa abhī, yaha puraścaraṇa
pūrā karatā hūṁ dekar mātaḥ eka nayana.'
kaha kara dekhā tūṇīra brahmaśara rahā jhalaka,
le liyā hasta, laka-laka karatā vaha mahāphalaka;
le astra vāma kara, dakṣiṇa kara dakṣina locana
le arpita karane ko udyata ho gaye sumana
jisa kṣaṇa bandha gayā bedhane ko dṛga dṛḍha niścaya
kānpā brahmāṇḍa, huā devī kā turata udaya: –
'sādhu, sādhu, sādhaka dhīra, dharma-dhana dhānya rāma !'
kaha, liyā bhagavatī ne rāghava kā hasta thāma
dekhā rāma ne sāmane śrī durgā.....)

'Here', exclaimed Rāma in deep delighful voice, 'is the remedy. My mother used always to call me *Rājīvanayana*', the one with the blue-lotus-eyes. Two blue lotuses are there still, O Mother! and by offering one of them I shall complete the ritual worship. Saying this, he looked at the *Brahma-bāṇa* (Brahmā's arrow) jetting out of the quiver. He took that great dazzling weapon in his left hand and with his right hand, he proceeded to offer the flower of his right eye.

The moment he made the irrevocable resolution to pierce his eye, the universe shook and, immediately, the Goddess appeared 'Bravo! Rāma, you are a great, resolute devotee for whom *Dharma* – righteousness – is the ultimate wealth', saying this, the Goddess held his hand. *Rāma* beheld *Śrī Durgā* in front of him...

Following hundred years of penance by *Svāyambhū Manu,* the Mother Goddess grants him the boon of unobstructed rule and continued lineage.[15] Cursed by the sage *Gautama,* when a thousand female genital organs grow on *Indra*'s body, the latter propitiates the Goddess and with her blessing, the organs become a thousand eyes on the eve of *Śrī Rāma*'s marriage to *Sītā. Indra,* thereby, is enabled to see the beautiful rites of the marriage with them.[16] In the beginning of his famous *Saundaryalaharī, Ācārya Śaṅkara* says that *Śiva,* when united with *Śakti* is able to create, otherwise he is incompetent to move.[17] In the *Adhyātma Rāmāyaṇa, Sītā,* the incarnation of the Mother Goddess, tells *Hanumān* that '*Rāma* neither goes nor stays; neither grieves nor desires; neither gives up nor engages in any activity. From being born in *Ayodhyā* to his return there after slaying *Rāvaṇa* and being coronated as king, all these activities

---

[15] *rājyaṁ niṣkaṇṭakaṁ te 'stu putrā vaṁśkarā api* (*Devībhāgavata* X.2.3)

[16] *Padma Purāṇa* (V.51.48), read with *Rāmacaritamānasa* (I.317.3) of Gosvāmī Tulasīdāsa

[17] *Śivaḥ Śaktyā yukto yadi bhavati Śaktaḥ prabhavitum/na cedevaṁ devo na kuśalaḥ spanditumapi* ||

are indeed mine. I am the *Mūla-Prakṛti*, the primeval Nature'.[18]

2. *Śāktaism* and *Āgamas*

Literature relating to *Śiva* and *Śakti* (and, for that matter the *Vaiṣṇava* literature also) is included in the *āgamas*. The *Śaiva āgamas* and *Śākta āgamas* or *tantra*, celebrate the power of women and are famous, apart from other things, for reverence to them. *Āgamas* rank equal to the *Nigamas* (*Vedas*). The former are special inasmuch as they are for everyone. Men and women without distinction of caste and status can recite them, imbibe them and worship their chosen deity with their help. Following their path, one attains to *bhoga* (worldly pleasures) as well as *mokṣa* (final liberation), *preya* (pleasant) and *śreya* (good) unlike the Vedic path which makes it necessary for its followers to shun *bhoga* and *preya* to attain to the final liberation. Orthodox Hindus also sometimes reserve the right to the Vedic studies only to certain classes of men only but there is no such restriction for the study of the *āgamas*. There are seventy-seven *Śākta Āgamas* enunciating practices that lead to knowledge and liberation, sixty-four *kaulāgamas* which teach practices intended to develop magical powers, and eight *miśrāgamas* which aim at both[19] or *tantras*. According to V. Raghavan, '*The Tantras* are usually enumerated as 64 but actually there are no less than 327 subsidiary texts, designated as *Upatantras*'.[20]

---

[18] *Adhyātma Rāmāyaṇa* I.1. 34–43.

[19] See Radhakrishnan S., *Indian Philosophy*, Vol. II (New York: The Macmillan Co., Indian Edition, 1956) p. 735.

[20] See Raghavan V., *The Indian Heritage* (Bangalore: The Indian Institute of World Culture, 1958), p. xxi.

According to *Śāktaism, Śiva* is the *Paramatattva*, the Supreme Reality or *Prakāśa*, Pure Consciousness. He is *Akhilānugata*, Omnipresent; *Akartṛka*, Impersonal; and *Akriya*, Non-Active. He is *Sampūrṇa*, Absolute; *Nirapekṣa*, devoid of relativity and *Sat*, Pure Being. *Śakti* is the active personal being and includes all individual souls: *tvayaikayā pūritamambayaitat.*[21] She is related to *Śiva* as *Vimarśa* to *Prakāśa. Vimarśa* has been defined as the spontaneous vibration – *svābhāvika sphuraṇa* – of the Ultimate Reality.[22] *Vimarśa* is *Śakti* and when it comes in contact with *Prakāsa*, the Absolute as it were, the world of *nāma* and *rūpa* – name and form – comes into existence. In other words, when *Śakti* as the impulse creates vibration in *Prakāśa*, the dormant and latent consciousness springs into action and there is creation. When Consciousness (*Śiva*) passes over Vibration (*Śakti*) as *tejas*, the virile seed, it takes the shape of *vindu* (or *bindu*) – the drop – the male principle and when *Śakti* enters *Śiva, nāda* – the sound, the female principle – is manifested. When the two – *nāda* and *vindu* – are united, we have the *Ardhanārīśvara* – *Pārvatī* and *Śiva* in unison. They are, as Kālidāsa would say, *vāgarthāviva saṁpṛktau...pārvatī parameśvarau,*[23] connected, even blended together. Hence, if *Śiva* is *Trinetra*, three-eyed, so is *Pārvatī*. Together they are reverenced as *Ardhāmbikeśa*, i.e., half *Ambikā*, half *Śiva*.[24] This is the essential *kāma*-principle, the original seed of desire and creation. The entire object-world potentially exists in *Śakti* and *Śiva*.

3. She, of Many Names, Forms and Functions

For meditation and worship, the great *Śakti* has ten forms : known as *Daśa Mahāvidyās*, the Ten Wisdom

[21] *Śrīdurgāśaptaśatī* XI.6

[22] *Bhāskararāya* : *Lalitāsahasranāma*, under *Vimarśarūpiṇī*

[23] *Raghuvaṁśa* I.I. Also see Tulasī, *Rāmacaritamānasa* I.18

[24] *Śrīdurgāsaptaśatī* IX. Meditation.

Goddesses : *Mahākālī, Ugratārā, Ṣoḍaśī* (*Tripurasundarī*), *Bhuvaneśvarī, Bhairavī, Chinnamastā, Dhūmāvatī, Bagalāmukhī, Mātaṅgī* and *Kamalā.*[25]

These ten forms of the Mother have been divided into two *Kulas*—families : terrible and benign. These are : (i) *Kāli-kula* and (ii) *Śrīkula.* The former comprises *Mahākālī, Bhairavī, Chinnamastā, Bagalāmukhī* and *Dhūmāvatī* while the latter consists of *Ṣoḍaśi* (*Tripurasundarī*), *Bhuvaneśvarī, Mātaṅgī* and *Kamalā. Ugratārā* of dark-blue and of white forms is placed in between. She is both baneful (in dark-blue form) and blissful (in white form). These two forms remind us of the nature being propitiated in the Vedas both as awful and beautiful. Both these forms, terrible as well as benign, are complementary. While the former annihilates the evil of *moha* – ignorance – the latter bestows knowledge – *vidyā.*

Of the ten goddesses mentioned above, *Mahākālī,* representing power (*śakti*), *Tārā* representing wisdom (*prajñā*) and *Tripurasundarī,* representing beauty (*saundarya*) are considered more important. They relate to *Śiva,* the destroyer; *Brahmā,* the creator and *Viṣṇu,* the sustainer or preserver, respectively. They are also, in that order, *sat, cit* and *ānanda,* Being, Consciousness and Bliss. We may reiterate that these are the different forms of one and the same Supreme Goddess and they represent her different functions and roles. It also needs to be added that these ten forms are not the only ones in which the Mother manifests herself. Countless are her names, countless forms and countless functions. While she manifests herself in all female forms, she is the imperceptible, implicit energy in all the male forms. In

[25] Their male counterparts are *Mahākāla/Akṣobhya, Puruṣa, Pañcavaktra Rudra, Tryambaka, Kabandha, Dakṣiṇāmūrti, Ekavaktra Rudra, Mataṅga* and *Viṣṇu. Dhūmāvatī* is considered to be a widow.

fact, as the *Śvetāśvatara Upaniṣad* (I.3) says, she as the self-power of the Divine, is seen by those who meditate upon her even though she is hidden in her own attributes.

The five functions attributed to the Mother are: *ābhāsa* (light), *rakti* (charmingness), *vimarśana* (examination), *bījāvasthāna* (planting the seed) and *vilapanatā* (lamentation). In her is also incorporated the non-conscious matter corresponding to *prakṛti* of *Sāṅkhya* school. The Goddess has also been described as *sāmyāvasthā guṇopādhikā brahmasvarūpiṇī* – *Brahman* in the state of equanimity endowed with qualifying modes. In her womb, *māyā* or *prakṛti* remain potential in *pralaya* and active in creation. She is the presiding deity in all animate and inanimate objects. Like heat, light and inflammatory powers in the fire and like virility in man, she abides as the essential nature in all. She is energy, power, nature and the *Ātmaśakti* – intrinsic will – which when awakened, makes all terrestrial and transcendental accomplishments possible.

During the first three days of *Navarātras,* worship of *Mahākālī* is advised. By doing so, we rid ourselves of evil orientations, evil propensities and demoniac attitudes by fighting against them. This is the first stage.

In the middle three days, *Mahālakṣmī* is worshipped. She bestows upon her devotees the impossible transcendental qualities. She is the *Sāttvika* – good/ positive – energy; *Tuṣṭi* – gratification; and *Puṣṭi* – nurturance and strength. When demoniac propensities and evil urges decay and inherent goodness ascends, man becomes worthy of attaining *Jñāna* – knowledge – and, thus, moves to the worship of *Mahāsarasvatī* in the last three days. She is *Brahmavidyā,* personified knowledge of *Brahman.* She plays her *vallakī* – lute – which helps develop concentration of mind and the devotee is thereby rendered ready for self-realization. With her grace, the devotee sheds his *jīva-bhāva* or matter-centred attitude and experiences unity with Brahman: *so 'haṁ* – I am That – and, thus, attains to liberation in this very life – *jīvanmukti*.

The above are only functional differences. All the three forms are essentially one, manifesting as many.

Mantra, yantra and *mudrā* are important modes of the *tāntrika* worship. A *mantra* is a mystic formula. The entire alphabet is the Goddess herself embodied in the syllables and every syllable has a mystic significance. It is neither possible nor desirable to try and interpret them intellectually. Only with the Mother's grace and reverential worship in deep contemplation does a devotee discover them within his mind. This is the proverbial opening of the third eye. These *mantras* must, however, be learnt from a qualified and practising teacher in person. Their abuse can prove very harmful, even disastrous.

A *yantra* or *cakra* is a diagram or a chart in which the mystic syllables are inscribed in the prescribed niches. A *cakra* is drawn on a surface or made in relief in geometrical patterns. A fully blossomed lotus is enclosed within it. *Śrī cakra* is considered to be the abode of the Mother Goddess and is of highest symbolic significance. It also represents one's own being.

Mudrās (literally, seals) are gestures or signs, also with mystic import – call them body language if you like – accompanying the utterance of *mantras* or meditation or worship.

4. Śrīdurgāsaptaśati

Śrīdurgāsaptaśatī (seven hundred verses to Durgā), also called the *Devīmāhātmya* (glory or majesty of the Goddess) or *Caṇḍīsaptaśatī* or just *Caṇḍīpāṭha*, forms the most important part of the *Mārkaṇḍeya Purāṇa*. It has thirteen chapters dealing comprehensively with the nature, form, acts, character and characteristics, means and methods of meditation and worship of the Mother Goddess. For the Mother's devotees, every *śloka,* even each letter or syllable of a *śloka* is a *mantra* which bears great mystic and spiritual significance. Its recitation with *śraddhā, viśvāsa* and *bhakti* – reverence, faith and loving devotion – yields fortune, fame, glory, progeny and all kinds of happiness in worldly life and, ultimately, leads to final liberation. In other words, all the four objectives of an individual's life, i.e., *dharma, artha, kāma* and *mokṣa* can be attained if it is recited religiously. All afflictions, diseases, impediments, obstructions, calamities and evil designs of adversaries are thwarted and negated by its recitation.

This *Saptaśatī* has three acts : *Prathama carita* (First Act), *Madhyama carita* (Middle Act) and *Uttara* or *Uttama carita* (Final or the Foremost Act). In all, there are thirteen chapters in the *Saptaśatī* which are covered under the forementioned Acts as follows :

First Act : Chapter One
Middle Act : Chapters Two to Four
Final Act : Chapters Five to Thirteen

There are several accompanying and associate hymns preceding and succeeding the main text of seven hundred verses and they vary from edition to edition compiled by different devotees and scholars depending upon their preference. There are, however, some more important texts which form an integral part of the main text and have been incorporated in this book as follows:

Before the Saptaśatī

1. *Saptaślokī Durgā* (Hymn of Seven Verses to *Durgā*)
2. *Śrīdurgāṣṭottaranāmastotram* (Hymn of One Hundred and Eight Names of *Śrīdurgā*)

3. *Devyāḥ Kavacam* (Armour of the Goddess)
4. *Argalāstotram* (Hymn of the Bolt)
5. *Kīlakam* (Hymn of the Pin)
6. *Vedoktaṁ Rātrisūktam* (Hymn of the Night from the *Veda*)
7. *Tantroktaṁ Rātrisūktam* (Hymn of the Night from *Tantra*)
8. *Śrīdevyatharvaśīrṣam* (Hymn of the Goddess according to the *Atharvaveda*)
9. *Navārṇavidhiḥ* (The System of Worship).

Succeeding the Saptaśatī

1. *Upasaṁhāraḥ* (Conclusion) (Repetition of *Navārṇavidhiḥ*)
2. *Ṛgvedoktaṁ Devīsūktam* (*Ṛgvedic* Hymn to the Goddess).
3. *Tantroktaṁ Devīsūktam* (Hymn to the Goddess from *Tantra*)
4. *Rahasyatrayam* (Trilogy of Secrets)
   (i) *Prādhānikaṁ Rahasyam* (Pre-eminent Secret)
   (ii) *Vaikṛtikaṁ Rahasyam* (Modified Secret)
   (iii) *Mūrti Rahasyam* (Secret of Personifications)
5. *Durgādvātriṁśannāmamālā* (Rosary of Thirty-two Names of Durgā)
6. *Devyaparādhakṣamāpanastotram* (Hymn Seeking Pardon of the Goddess for Committing Offences)
7. *Siddhakuñjikāstotram* (Hymn of the Key to Accomplishment)
8. *Kṣamā Prārthanā* (Seeking Forgiveness).

As the name suggests, the *Durgāsaptaśatī* has seven hundred *ślokas* dedicated to the Impassable Mother Goddess. Not all of these seven hundred *ślokas* are, however, complete verses. In fact, some of them are not even half verses but are only the author's interventions stating who spoke or said – *uvācamantras*, e.g., *Ṛṣiruvāca* (the seer said), or *Mārkaṇḍeya uvāca* (Mārkaṇḍeya said),

Devyuvāca (Goddess said), etc. Each of them has, however, been treated as one *mantra.* Half *mantras* are one-liners but each is treated as a complete *mantra.* In the fifth chapter, verses from number 14 to 76 and 78 to 80 are *tripānmantras* (*mantras* of three divisions) and every division has been counted as one *mantra.* For example,

yā devī sarvabhūteṣu viṣṇumāyeti śabditā I
namastasyai II4II *namastasyai* II5II *namastasyai namo namaḥ* II6II

Counted thus, we have seven hundred *ślokas* made up as under:

Chapter No.	Uvāca mantras	Half ślokas	Tripānmantras	Ślokas	Total
1.	14	24	00	66	104
2.	01	00	00	68	69
3.	03	00	00	41	44
4.	05	02	00	35	42
5.	09	00	66	54	129
6.	04	00	00	20	24
7.	02	00	00	25	27
8.	01	01	00	61	63
9.	02	00	00	39	41
10.	04	01	00	27	32
11.	04	01	00	50	55
12.	02	02	00	37	41
13.	06	11	00	12	29
Total	57	42	66	535	700

The *Saptaśatī* begins in the First Act, First Chapter, with the king *Suratha* and the trader *Samādhi* approaching the sage *Medhā* with their respective problems. Thereafter the sage, referring to the impact of *Mahāmāyā*, the Illusive Great Mother, due to which the entire universe, including persons of spiritual wisdom, is bewildered, narrates how the Supreme Goddess as *Yoganidrā* – the Cosmic Divine Sleep – had put Lord *Viṣṇu* in deep sleep at the time of the dissolution of universe and *Brahmā*, the Creator, seated on *Viṣṇu's* navel-lotus, was tormented by the demons *Madhu* and *Kaiṭabha*. *Brahmā* thereupon propitiates *Yoganidrā* to cause Lord *Viṣṇu* to rise from his sleep. Pleased, the Goddess releases Lord *Viṣṇu* and the latter slays the two demons.

In the Second Act, there is the demon *Mahiṣa* who has usurped the powers and functions of all the gods. The latter, led by *Brahmā*, seek refuge in Lord *Viṣṇu* whose anger, joined by that of all the other collected gods exudes great energy and lustre which, getting focused, takes the form of a Goddess of incomparable effulgence. All the gods present, from their respective stocks, the weapons to her to fight *Mahiṣa* and his army. A great battle ensues in which the demoniac forces are completely decimated and the gods celebrate.

In the Final Act, the gods propitiate and pray to the Mother to slay *Śumbha* and *Niśumbha* and then from the body of *Pārvatī* emerges *Śakti* who, accompanied by her divine associates and others, slays the demons *Dhūmralocana, Caṇḍa* and *Muṇḍa, Raktabīja* and finally, *Niśumbha* and *Śumbha.*

Intermittently, there are panegyrics extolling the Mother, sung by the gods for protecting them and the universe from the high-handedness of the demoniac forces. In Act One, *Brahmā* eulogises the Goddess as *Yoganidrā*, the Cosmic Divine sleep of Lord *Viṣṇu*. This invocation is known as the *Tāntrika Rātrisūkta* – Hymn of the Night from the *Tantra* (I.73–87). In Act Two, the gods propitiate the Mother following the death of *Mahiṣāsura* (IV.3–27). Then they pay obeisance to her addressing her by more than fifty names and epithets (V.9–80). This is the same as the *Tantrokta Devīsūkta*. Inevitably, for all these names, feminine gender has been used but the important point here is one of their pervasive character. These epithets – indicate good as well as not good, auspicious as well as inauspicious attributes – observed in all beings in some way and measure or the other. While the gods rever the Mother as *Māyā* who is the embodiment of all types of attributes, they invoke her grace and seek her blessings for auspiciousness and goodness even while praying to protect them from evil and demoniac forces. The last invocation (XI.3–35) comes after the death of *Śumbha.* These panegyrics are laced with feelings of gratitude for the Mother for taking care of her children and for promising to keep doing so in future. Although repetitive at times, these verses are poetically of great lyrical beauty and when recited, a treat to the listener. Full of deeper mystic connotations as they are, for connoisseurs, they are also full of deep meaning and substance. For devotees, they are the expressions of their hearts' sincerest sentiment voiced by an equally sincere and a blessed poet.

There is also a reference to the future incarnations of the Mother whenever forces of evil might raise their head. This reminds us of Lord *Kṛṣṇa*'s promise of *saṁbhavāmi yuge yuge.*[26]

Some salient symbolic messages and inherent factors that we observe in the study of the *Saptaśatī* are as follows :

(i) It is imperative that we identify, activate and realize the latent and potential energy that each one of us possesses. Every individual is blessed with tremendous potential. Very little of it is, however, explored and put to use by most of us. A major part thereof remains dormant. Of the small portion that is put to use, the larger chunk is wasted in negative, even evil action. It is necessary to explore and maximise our potential and channelise it in the direction of good and positive endeavour by overcoming the demoniac propensities within us.

---

[26] *Gītā* IV.8

(ii) As long as this energy remains asleep, it is not possible to achieve any of the objectives of human life whether of this world or of *mokṣa.* What can one say of the mortals when even Lord *Viṣṇu,* the preserver and sustainer of the universe, is incapable of doing anything if his intrinsic energy is not awakened? Once that sleep (symbolically) leaves him and the awareness of his potential is restored to him, he rises up to fight brute forces.

(iii) Brute force may vanquish and rule over the forces of righteousness for a while but eventually it is the power of intelligence that attains an edge over the evil, the physical-animal might : *buddhiryasya balaṁ tasya.* Those who are devoted to God and serve Him with love are granted the boon of *buddhi-yoga,* concentration of intelligence.[27] *Madhu-Kaiṭabha* fought with Lord *Viṣṇu* for a long time but the combat remained inconclusive. It was then their foolish arrogance that invited their death when they offered Lord *Viṣṇu* to seek a boon of his choice and the latter intelligently sought their death. We should seek and pray for the boon of *buddhi-yoga* from the Goddess in order to succeed in our righteous efforts.

(iv) Incidents and stories of conflict between *Śāktas* and *Vaiṣṇavas* are legion. *Śakti* or the Divine Mother is considered by the *Śāktas* to be the Supreme Power. And they are not wrong. But *Śakti* is here the power of *Viṣṇu* and between the two, there is no conflict. In fact, they are not separate from each other. *Śakti* is the intrinsic nature of *Viṣṇu* and *Viṣṇu* performs his functions only through, or with the help of, *Śakti.* Where then is any room for conflict between the *Śāktas* and the *Vaiṣṇavas*? The same thing can be said about *Śaivas* and *Vaiṣṇavas.* *Śiva* and *Viṣṇu* are simultaneously related mutually as

[27] Ibid. X.10

servitors, masters and friends of each other.[28] Looking at the Divine family-tree as described in the *Prādhānika Rahasya* – the pre-eminent secret[29] – we observe that *Mahālakṣmī* of the three modes, *sāttvika, rājasika* and *tāmasika,* is the basic source of both *Viṣṇu* and *Śiva* and the two are connected with each other as kin. In fact, one lesson we learn on reading different *Purāṇas* as well as the Vedic literature, is that all the deities, performing their respective functions, are the manifestations of the same primeval force and devotees, depending upon their attitude, inclination and choice, place any one of them on the highest pedestal. While there is nothing wrong in it, we have to bear in mind their essential oneness and should not over-zealously denigrate or undermine the position of the others because this so-called 'otherness' is only the kinetic energy manifesting itself in different names and forms of one and the same God.

(v) That unity is strength and the power unleashed by the team-synergy has no parallel is apparent from the *Madhyama Carita.* Singlehandedly, none of the gods is in a position to challenge the might of *Mahiṣa* and his armies. In fact, defeated and dethroned from their respective positions by *Mahiṣa*'s forces, they are desperately hoping to be rescued when their common calamity climaxes in them making a common cause. Incidentally, here too, Lord *Viṣṇu* is seen as their rallying point. Seething with anger they unleash their respective energies which, in concentrated form, is manifested as the Supreme Energy, the Mother Goddess. The gods then present their weapons to her. This again represents the pooling of resources. More than once, we see the energies of various gods and divine incarnations appearing in female forms,

---

[28] Tulasī : *Rāmacaritamānasa* : *sevaka svāmi sakhā siya pīke* (I.15.2)

[29] First of the three secrets – *rahasya-traya* – in this book

coordinating their actions under the command of one supreme leader and destroying the demoniac forces. These episodes place emphasis on the importance on concentrated, focused and united action.

(vi) Some critics have satirically or derisively commented upon the Mother Goddess imbibing *madhu* and getting intoxicated. Others, in defence, have said that this *madhu* cannot be interpreted as an alcoholic drink or liquor but some form of processed honey drinking which results in but a mild after-effect. This, in turn, rouses the fighting spirit. Be that as it may, the fact is that the Mother and her associates have been represented here as heroes in the battlefield who, on the eve of launching an offence, prepare themselves in several ways. This should, however, not be the pretext for the devotees who worship the Mother, not in a battlefield but in a sacred sanctum or in a similar place, to consume alcohol. Some scholars see a symbolic meaning in this act of the Mother. *Madhu* here is an external facilitating means for raising the fighting spirit. Such facilitating means or devices keep the morale of the fighter high. They, like the beat of drums, sound of conches and slogans of victory, rejuvenate a soldier's spirit and ensure that the determination to defeat the enemy is redoubled and slackness in effort does not become an intrusion. In the left-handed *tāntrika sādhanā* (*vāmācāra*), however, the use of alcohol which is called *sudhā* or *kāraṇavāri*, the original water produced at the beginning of the creation, is considered to be a part of their rituals and they drink it from *kapāla*, the skull used as container. There are two different interpretations to it. First is that in the *vāmācāra*, the objective of such practices is to rise above the baser emotions of good or bad. There are several other practices followed by them with the objective of transcending the feelings of like and dislike; attachment and revulsion; infatuation and abhorrence, etc. In fact, it is a very difficult path which even *yogis* find inaccessible – *vāmo mārgaḥ paramagahano yogināmapyagamyaḥ.*

According to the other interpretation, *brahmarandhra* – the aperture in the crown of the head – also called the *daśamadvāra* or *sahasrāra* is the *kapāla* or skull from which flows *sudhā*, the nectar of realization of the Supreme and the *Yogīs* drink it through the *kulakuṇḍalinī.*[30] With this drink, they rise above the mundane wants and, drunk in ecstasy, attain to a state of bliss. The Mother, herself the Divine Energy, symbolically drinks *madhu* and warns *Mahiṣāsura* that he can only growl till she has not finished her drink and that once she kills him, it is the gods who would roar and rejoice.[31] This is a warning served on the forces of evil by the power of righteousness.

(vii) War is but the last option. This is the tradition followed by those who believe in righteous action. *Śrī Rāma* sends his ambassadors – *Hanumān* and *Aṅgada* – twice to *Rāvaṇa* in a bid to persuade the demon king to return *Vaidehī Jānakī*. *Śrī Kṛṣṇa* himself goes to *Hastināpura* to convince *Duryodhana* that war is not in the interest of either side and even agrees to accept just five villages for the *Pāṇḍavas* to avoid war. In the *Saptaśatī*, the goddess

---

[30] The term is made up of two words – *Kula* and *Kuṇḍalinī*. *Kulī*, literally means clan or family and contextually refers to the *Kaula* school of *Tantra*. *Kuṇḍalinī*, often translated as serpent power, is the coiled-up energy that abides in a *kuṇḍa*, a basin or a cave. It is the power or the energy of the Mother Goddess that remains dormant in an individual, close to the *mulādhāra*, the root-base. By intense devotion, meditation or the prescribed *yogic* techniques, its arousal is attained. When it rises, it reaches *sahasrāra*, the thousand pettled lotus. In the *Kaula* school or the *Vāmācāra*, attainment results in the realization of the ultimate bliss.

[31] *Saptaśatī* III.38

Śivadūtī deputes *Sadāśiva* who epitomises auspiciousness, renunciation and pacification, as her ambassador of peace to *Śumbha-Niśumbha* to tell them to revert to their rightful kingdom of *pātāla* and return *Indra*'s kingdom to him.[32] It is only when this offer is spurned and war becomes inevitable that the fierce fighting ensues.

(viii) The *Durgāsaptaśatī* celebrates female power. In this scripture, while we do have occasional visions of the beauty, delicacy, slender frame, and tenderness of the Mother in different forms and see her grace, boons and blessings being showered on the gods and her devotees, the ruling rasa – mood – is of a fighter engaged in a fight-to-finish-combat against ruthless and unscrupulous enemies. Talking of *rasas* – the poetic sentiments – in the *Saptaśatī*, the major ones are *vīra* (heroic), *raudra* (wrath), *bhayānaka* (terrible), even *bībhatsa* (loathsome). We do not have here a dumb beautiful doll, a meek, pliant woman who can be cowed down. She is a volcano of power and if her devotees or children are threatened and their survival is in jeopardy, her power and energy explode and she wreaks havoc on those who dare challenge her might or try to fiddle with her dignity and honour. She is *Durgā*, the Impassable; *Kālī*, the Ferocious Face of Death and *Śakti*, Energy, in kinetic and manifest form. The *Saptaśatī*, by declaring that the women the world over are but her personfications, emphasizes not only the Mother in a woman who loves and is loved by her children but also serves a warning that to cast an evil eye on her or threaten those protected by her is to invite annihilation.

(ix) And yet, a woman is not separate from man. Both are inseparable, incomplete without each other. She is *Ardhāmbikā* and Śiva is *Ardheśa.* It is in the functional sense that there is separation. The *Bṛhadāraṇyaka Upaniṣad* says

[32] Ibid., VIII.24–26

that a man and a woman are like two halves of a split pea (*ardhabṛgala*) and are essentially united.[33] The Hindus do not believe in the Biblical enunciation that the 'Lord God....took one of his (man's) ribs and ....made (it) into a woman',[34] which implies that she is just a small fraction of the man's body. No, says the Hindu sage. She has no reason to be subservient to her male counterpart and does not have to play second fiddle to him. In harmony and happiness the two should live together, discharging their natural and social duties and functions. It is in the interest of smooth and effective performance of their respective roles that they are different from each other so that the process of creation may go on unabated. It is a travesty that women, in practically all religions including Hinduism which swears by *yatra nāryastu pūjyante ramante tatra devatāḥ,* have for long suffered and cast in an inferior position and that woman – *Śakti* herself – should have to seek empowerment. The *Durgāsaptaśatī* does not approve of it.

(x) From *Śakti*'s blessings, come both – *bhukti* and *mukti* worldly fortunes and pleasures and the final liberation. In philosophical terms too, the storyline, the Acts and episodes have an important message. The king *Suratha* is, after worshipping the Mother, blessed with invincible power to rule the world and enjoy all luxuries while the trader *Samādhi* attains to *mokṣa* as he desires. *Madhu* and *Kaiṭabha* are the contaminating evil that pollute the mind. One has to exercise temperance over the senses and habits of eating and indulging in order to remain mentally unpolluted. *Mahiṣāsura* is delusion – the blinding force of darkness – which is a powerful enemy within. It has to be tamed if life is to be saved from falling into the abyss

[33] *Bṛhadāraṇyaka Upaniṣad* I.43

[34] *The Holy Bible,* Genesis 2.21–22

of confusion and bewilderment. *Śumbha* and *Niśumbha* are egoity and anger. *Dhūmralocana, Caṇḍa-Muṇḍa* and *Raktābīja,* as commanders of *Śumbha-Niśumbha's* army, represent sloth, infatuation and aversion and desires respectively. They have all to be slayed for the successful accomplishment of the ultimate endeavour of human-life, i.e., Self-realization, God-realization or *mokṣa.* It is necessary to invoke the *Ātma-śakti* – self-power or strong will power – to conquer these formidable foes.

(xi) While the Mother ruthlessly annihilates the demoniac forces, she does not nurture hatred for them. On the contrary, she has compassion for them – *citte kṛpā samaranisṭhurtā*[35] – even as she delivers them from the confinement in the body steeped in evil, so that, on one hand the world may heave a sigh of relief and, on the other, they attain to the celestial abodes.

(xii) When *Śumbha* challenges the Mother to fight him alone without the assistance of the other goddesses, she says, *ekaivāhaṁ jagatyatra dvitīyā kā mamāparā*[36] – 'only one am I here in this world, who else is there other than me?' Read it with the statements of the sage *Medhā* in the first chapter where he says that this world is bewildered under the reeling impact of *Mahāmāyā,* the Great Deluding Power. The consciousness even of men of knowledge is drawn away by her forcefully. She pervades the entire universe of the animates and inanimates. It is she to whom this world owes its existence and it is she who, when she dispenses her grace, delivers people from *bondage.*[37] This verily is also the *māyā* of the advaitins.

(xiii) The lion is the mount of the Mother Goddess. He is the king of beasts, the ultimate symbol or

---

[35] *Saptaśatī* IV.22

[36] Ibid., X.5

[37] Ibid., I.55–57

representative of animal power. But the Mother has tamed him and he submits to her diktat. The lion also represents power, will and determination. The Mother riding the lion symbolizes her mastery over all the above qualities. For the devotee, it means to possess all these qualities to get over the demon of ego. This lion is her companion as she goes on the spree to kill other beasts and brutes. In her victory he rejoices. In the battlefield, he slays the demoniac forces alongside the Mother and her associates. In the same manner, if we are in a position to tame our powerful passions and control them, they can become a positive, enabling force.

(xiv) The Mother wields a variety of weapons, including the water empowered by *mantras*. Her arms and visages are many and spread in all directions. They represent her omnipotence and omnipresence. Her third eye is the eye of knowledge. Knowledge itself is power and it also sublimates the physical and animal power. Without knowledge, *viveka* – discriminatory wisdom – power is like an unbridled horse and only destroys indiscriminately. At the same time, the third eye is also fire. It burns. An individual endowed with knowledge is aware of his potential to burn and destroy but uses it with discrimination. If the Self is the *lord* of the chariot, which is the body, and the mind, the *reins*, then, the *Upaniṣad* says, the intellect – *buddhi* – is the charioteer.[38] Going by this analogy, *Śrī Kṛṣṇa*, the charioteer of *Arjuna*, the lord of the chariot, represents the discriminating intellect of *Arjuna*, the self or the *jīva*, who, on the crossroads of life's challenges has to decide whether to fight or run away. *Buddhi* – *Kṛṣṇa* – guides him to slay the forces of unrighteousness without harbouring doubt, and feeling

---

[38] *Kaṭha Upaniṣad* I.3.3

remorse or contrition. This is the proverbial use of the third eye. When *Kāma* attempts to dominate *Śiva*, the latter opens the third eye and reduces him to ashes.[39] The Mother is extremely gentle, but she is at the same time, extremely ferocious – *atisaumyātiraudrā.*[40] To the question whether non-violence is a credo in all situations and at all times, *Patañjali*'s reply may be that it has to be practised without reservations as to time, purpose or caste rules,[41] *Saptaśatī* says that the forces of unrighteousness – be they in the external battlefield or in the mind – must be wiped out. That is the message of the *Gītā* also, notwithstanding its commitment to non-violence otherwise.[42] The third eye of knowledge is also the instrument of decision making. With it we can protect as well as destroy. The Mother does both – she protects her devotees, the pilgrims of righteousness and slays the brutes, the representatives of unbridled passion.

Given above are but a few of the aspects which we observe as we go through the *Saptaśati.* One recitation or reading may, however, not reveal the intrinsic and deeper meanings of this great text. As one reads the *Saptaśatī,* it may apear, to begin with, that there are metaphysical paradoxes, even contradictions. However, as one persists with its study, a resolution of these so-called contradictions is seen. Just as this whole creation of the Mother is full of contradictions and so is an individual's life itself, there are several dimensions to the Mother's acts which may appear irreconcilable. This has been symbolically indicated in the fact of her having several visages and hands spread in different directions. But just as an

---

[39] *Rāmacaritamānasa* I.87.3

[40] *Saptaśatī* V.13

[41] *Yoga sūtras* II.30–31.

[42] Gītā XIII.8., XVI.2

individual as well as this universe have to be seen in their respective holistic forms, actions and events, the varying forms, names and acts of the Mother have to be seen in totality as many in one for all contradictions are ultimately resolved in her.

While intellect is helpful in covering some distance, it does not, by itself, take us very far. We have to transcend the realm of intellect – *yo buddheḥ paratastu saḥ*[43] – and enter the realm of experience. Our sages have used the term *aparokṣānubhūti* – direct cognition – for that state. Just as by *dhyāna-yoga* the sages see the *devātmaśakti*, similarly for the revelation of the hidden meanings of a text like *Durgāsaptaśatī* which is full of mystic allusion and import, meditation and concentration are required.

True as it is, it may also not by itself be enough. Ultimately, it is with the Mother's grace, her compassion, that the authentic meanings of such a text are revealed to a devotee. Then, in the depth of his heart, are discovered the jewels and pearls of meanings and they give him joy unspeakable. These jewels and pearls, however, are also her property and must be placed at her feet with humility. Those who cherish *preya* and *abhyudaya* – the worldly fortune and material ascendance, including heavenly bliss – reverential recitation or hearing of this book ensures these for them. Those whose devotion for the Mother is without motive, there is the ever growing experience of her loving grace and *sannidhi* – proximity.[44] That is the *śreya* or *niḥśreyasa* – the highest good : her hand of benediction – *varada hasta* – on the devotee's *mastaka*, and the devotee's *mastaka* in her feet, in obeisance.

***

---

[43] Ibid., III.42

[44] Saptaśatī XII.13–20

सप्तश्लोकी दुर्गा

1. *Saptaślokī Durgā*

Hymn of Seven Verses to *Durgā*

शिव उवाच

śiva uvāca

देवि त्वं भक्तसुलभे सर्वकार्यविधायिनी ।
कलौ हि कार्यसिद्ध्यर्थमुपायं ब्रूहि यत्नतः ॥

devi tvaṁ bhaktasulabhe sarvakāryavidhāyinī ।
kalau hi kāryasiddhyarthamupāyaṁ brūhi yatnataḥ ॥

Śiva said

You, O Divine Goddess! are easily accessible to your devotees and bless all their endeavours with success. Kindly describe, with due deliberation, the means for achieving accomplishment in their efforts in this *Kaliyuga.*

देव्युवाच

devyuvāca

शृणु देव प्रवक्ष्यामि कलौ सर्वेष्टसाधनम् ।
मया तवैव स्नेहेनाप्यम्बास्तुतिः प्रकाश्यते ॥

śṛṇu deva pravakṣyāmi kalau sarveṣṭasādhanam ।
mayā tavaiva śnehenāpyambāstutiḥ prakāśyate ॥

The Goddess said

Listen, O Lord! I shall describe the best means to accomplish all desires in *Kaliyuga.* Since you ardently love me, I shall reveal this *Ambāstuti*, the panegyric to the Mother.

ॐ अस्य श्रीदुर्गासप्तश्लोकीमन्त्रस्य नारायणऋषिः, अनुष्टुप् छन्दः
श्रीमहाकालीमहालक्ष्मीमहासरस्वत्यो देवताः, श्रीदुर्गाप्रीत्यर्थं
सप्तश्लोकीदुर्गापाठे विनियोगः ।

oṁ asya śrīdurgāsaptaślokīmantrasya nārāyaṇarṣiḥ,
anuṣṭup chandaḥ, śrīmahākālīmahālakṣmīmahāsarasvatyo
devatāḥ, śrīdurgāprītyarthaṁ saptaślokī
durgāpāṭhe viniyogaḥ ।

Of this *mantra* comprising seven verses of homage to *Śrī Durgā, Lord Nārāyaṇa* is the seer, *Anuṣṭup* is the metre, *Śrī Mahākālī Mahālakṣmī Mahāsarasvatī* are the deities; for pleasing *Śrī Durgā*, the Goddess who redeems from misery, this *mantra* of seven verses is here presented.

ॐ ज्ञानिनामपि चेतांसि देवी भगवती हि सा ।
बलादाकृष्य मोहाय महामाया प्रयच्छति ।।१।।

1. *oṁ jñānināmapi cetāṁsi devī bhagavatī hi sā* ।
balādākṛṣya mohāya mahāmāyā prayacchati ।।

Even of the persons endowed with the knowledge of *Brahman*, that *Māhāmāyā*, the Great Deluding Force, forcibly attracts the consciousness and deludes them.

दुर्गे स्मृता हरसि भीतिमशेषजन्तोः
स्वस्थैः स्मृता मतिमतीवशुभां ददासि ।
दारिद्र्यदुःखभयहारिणी का त्वदन्या
सर्वोपकारकरणाय दयार्द्रचित्ता ।।२।।

2. *durge smṛtā harasi bhītimaśeṣajantoḥ*
svasthaiḥ smṛtā matimatīva śubhāṁ dadāsi ।
dāridryaduḥkhabhayahāriṇi kā tvadanyā
sarvopakārakaraṇāya dayārdracittā ।।

On being remembered, O *Durgā*, you dispel the fears of all beings. On being remembered by those whose minds are settled in the Self, you bless them with felicific intelligence. Who but you, with your heart flowing with compassion, destroy indigence, misery and fear for the beneficence of all?

सर्वमङ्गलमङ्गल्ये शिवे सर्वार्थसाधिके ।
शरण्ये त्र्यम्बके गौरि नारायणि नमोऽस्तु ते ॥३॥

3. *sarvamaṅgalamaṅgalye śive sarvārthasādhike* ।
śaraṇye tryambake gauri nārāyaṇi namo 'stu te ॥

O *Nārāyaṇī,* the consort of *Nārāyaṇa,* protector and preserver of the universe! you are the embodiment of all auspiciousness. O *Śivā,* the consort of *Śiva,* the dispenser of all felicity! you are the accomplisher of all intents. O *Gaurī,* the fair complexioned Goddess! O *Tryambakā,* the three-eyed Goddess! You are the refuge of all. Our obeisance to you.

शरणागतदीनार्तपरित्राणपरायणे ।
सर्वस्यार्तिहरे देवि नारायणि नमोऽस्तु ते ॥४॥

4. *śaraṇāgatadīnārtaparitrāṇaparāyaṇe* ।
sarvasyārtihare devi nārāyaṇi namo 'stu te ॥

You, O *Nārāyaṇī* ! are forever engaged in protecting the destitute, the indigent and those who surrender themselves unto you. You destroy the misery of all. O Divine Goddess! our obeisance to you.

सर्वस्वरूपे सर्वेशे सर्वशक्तिसमन्विते ।
भयेभ्यस्त्राहि नो देवि दुर्गे देवि नमोऽस्तु ते ॥५॥

5. *sarvasvarūpe sarveśe sarvaśaktisamanvite* ।
bhayebhyastrāhi no devi durge devi namo 'stu te ॥

You are the true self of all. You are the ruler of all. You are endowed with all powers. Deliver us, O Goddess! from all fears. Our obeisance to you, O *Durgā*!

रोगानशेषानपहंसि तुष्टा ।
रुष्टा तु कामान् सकलानभीष्टान् ।
त्वामाश्रितानां न विपन्नराणां
त्वामाश्रिता ह्याश्रयतां प्रयान्ति ॥६॥

6. *rogānaśeṣānapahaṁsi tuṣṭā*
ruṣṭā tu kāmān sakalānabhīṣṭān ।
tvāmāśritānāṁ na vipannarāṇāṁ
tvāmāśritā hyāśrayatāṁ prayānti ॥

Pleased, you destroy all afflictions. Angry, you render all desires sterile. Those who have obtained refuge in you do not suffer misfortune. Having obtained refuge in you they become the refuge of others.

सर्वबाधाप्रशमनं त्रैलोक्यस्याखिलेश्वरि ।
एवमेव त्वया कार्यमस्मद्वैरिविनाशनम् ॥७॥

7. *sarvabādhāpraśamanaṁ trailokyasyākhileśvari* ।
evameva tvayā kāryamasmadvairivināśanam ॥

O the Sovereign of this entire universe! Please keep alleviating all the miseries of the three worlds and continue to annihilate our enemies in this very manner.

इति सप्तश्लोकी दुर्गा सम्पूर्णा ।

Iti saptaślokī durgā sampūrṇā ।

Saptaślokī Durgā concluded.

ॐ

श्री दुर्गायै नमः

śrī durgāyai namaḥ

Salutations to *Śrīdurgā*

श्री दुर्गाष्टोत्तरशतनामस्तोत्रम्

2. *Śrīdurgāṣṭottaraśatanāmastotram*

Hymn of One Hundred and Eight Names of *Śrīdurgā*

ईश्वर उवाच

īśvara uvāca

शतनाम प्रवक्ष्यामि शृणुष्व कमलानने ।
यस्य प्रसादमात्रेण दुर्गा प्रीता भवेत् सती ॥१॥

1. *śatanāma pravakṣyāmi śṛṇuṣva kamalānane* ।
yasya prasādamātreṇa durgā prītā bhavet satī ॥

Īśvara (*Śiva*) said

Listen O Lotus Faced (*Pārvatī*)! I shall narrate one hundred (and eight) names. Just by hearing or uttering them, one earns the blessings of the Virtuous *Durgā*.

ॐ सती साध्वी भवप्रीता भवानी भवमोचनी ।
आर्या दुर्गा जया चाद्या त्रिनेत्रा शूलधारिणी ॥२॥

2. *oṁ satī sādhvī bhavaprītā bhavānī bhavamocanī* ।
āryā durgā jayā cādyā trinetrā śūladhāriṇī ॥

Chastity, Righteousness, Lover of *Śiva*, Consort of *Śiva*, Redeemer from metempsychosis, Noble, Invincible or Redeemer from misery, Victory, Primordial, Three Eyed, Wielder of Pike. (1–11)

पिनाकधारिणी चित्रा चण्डघण्टा महातपाः ।
मनोबुद्धिरहंकारा चित्तरूपा चिता चितिः ॥३॥

3. *pinākadhāriṇī citrā caṇḍaghaṇṭā mahātapāḥ* ।
manobuddhirahaṅkārā cittarūpā citā citiḥ ॥

Wielder of a Bow, Characterised by Variegation, Impetuously Sounding the Battle Bell, Great Ascetic, Faculty of Cogitation, Faculty of Comprehension, Substratum of Ego, Form of Cognizance, Funeral Pyre (or the Final Resting Place of All Bodies) or Recollection of All, Consciousness of All. (12–21)

सर्वमन्त्रमयी सत्ता सत्यानन्दस्वरूपिणी ।
अनन्ता भाविनी भाव्या भव्याभव्या सदागतिः ॥४॥

4. *sarvamantramayī sattā satyānandasvarūpiṇī* ।
anantā bhāvinī bhāvyā bhavyābhavyā sadāgatiḥ ॥

Embodiment of All *Mantras*, Pure Being, True Nature of Truth and Bliss, Infinite, Progenitor of All, Worthy of Meditation and Devotion, True Nature of Welfare, Matchless in Magnificence, Ever the Resort of All. (22–30)

शाम्भवी देवमाता च चिन्ता रत्नप्रिया सदा ।
सर्वविद्या दक्षकन्या दक्षयज्ञविनाशिनी ॥५॥

5. *śāmbhavī devamātā ca cintā ratnapriyā sadā* ।
sarvavidyā dakṣakanyā dakṣayajñavināśinī ॥

Beloved of *Śiva*, Mother of the Gods, Reflection, Fond of Jewels (or a Lovable Jewel), Embodiment of All Knowledge, Daughter of *Dakṣa*, Destroyer of *Dakṣa*'s Sacrifice. (31–37)

अपर्णानेकवर्णा च पाटला पाटलावती ।
पट्टाम्बरपरीधाना कलमञ्जीररञ्जिनी ॥६॥

6. *aparṇānekavarṇā ca pāṭalā pāṭalāvatī* ।
paṭṭāmbaraparīdhānā kalamañjīra rañjinī ॥

Forsaker of Eating (even) Leaves during Penance, Of Multiple Hues, Of Red Complexion, Adorned with Red Flowers. Wearing Silk Garments, Enjoying Wearing the Sonorous Sounding Anklets. (38–43)

अमेयविक्रमा क्रूरा सुन्दरी सुरसुन्दरी ।
वनदुर्गा च मातङ्गी मतङ्गमुनिपूजिता ॥७॥

7. *ameyavikramā krūrā sundarī surasundarī* ।
vanadurgā ca mātaṅgī mataṅgamunipūjitā ॥

Of Immeasurable Valour, Merciless (for the demons), Beautiful, Most Beautiful Among the Gods, *Durgā* of the Forest (Presiding Deity of the inaccessible forests), Greatest of all Women, Worshipped by the sage *Mataṅga*. (44–50)

ब्राह्मी माहेश्वरी चैन्द्री कौमारी वैष्णवी तथा ।
चामुण्डा चैव वाराही लक्ष्मीश्च पुरुषाकृतिः ॥८॥

8. *brāhmī māheśvarī caindrī kaumārī vaiṣṇavī tathā* ।
cāmuṇḍā caiva vārāhī lakṣmīśca puruṣākṛtiḥ ॥

Brahmā's Consort (as *Mahāsarasvatī*), *Śiva*'s Consort (as *Mahākālī*), *Indra*'s Consort (as *Śacī*), *Kumārī* (*Kārtikeya's Consort*) or ever the Virgin, Consort of *Viṣṇu* (as *Mahālakṣmī*), Of the Terrific Form, Consort of *Varāha* (*Viṣṇu* in the Boar Incarnation) Goddess of Wealth, Personified Primordial *Puruṣa* in Feminine Form. (51–59)

विमलोत्कर्षिणी ज्ञाना क्रिया नित्या च बुद्धिदा ।
बहुला बहुलप्रेमा सर्ववाहनवाहना ॥९॥

9. *vimalotkarṣiṇī jñānā kriyā nityā ca buddhidā* ।
bahulā bahulapremā sarvavāhanavāhanā ॥

Unblemished, Bestower of Eminence, Knowledge, Action, Eternity, Bestower of Wisdom, Abundance, Abundance of Love (Fond of *Kṛṣṇapakṣa*, the Dark Half of a Lunar Month), Carrier of All Carriers. (60–68)

निशुम्भशुम्भहननी महिषासुरमर्दिनी ।
मधुकैटभहन्त्री च चण्डमुण्डविनाशिनी ।।१०।।

10. *niśumbhaśumbhahananī mahiṣāsuramardinī* ।
madhukaiṭabhahantrī ca caṇḍamuṇḍavināśinī ।।

Slayer of *Niśumbha* and *Śumbha*, Killer of *Mahiṣāsura*, Annihilator of *Madhu* and *Kaiṭabha* and Destroyer of *Caṇḍa* and *Muṇḍa*. (69–72)

सर्वासुरविनाशा च सर्वदानवघातिनी ।
सर्वशास्त्रमयी सत्या सर्वास्त्रधारिणी तथा ।।११।।

11. *sarvāsuravināśā ca sarvadānavaghātinī* ।
sarvaśāstramayī satyā sarvāstradhāriṇī tathā ।।

Killer of all demons, Killer of all evil forces, Soul of all Scriptures, Truth and Wielder of All Weapons. (73–77)

अनेकशस्त्रहस्ता च अनेकास्त्रस्य धारिणी ।
कुमारी चैककन्या च कैशोरी युवती यतिः ।।१२।।

12. *anekaśastrahastā ca anekāstrasya dhāriṇī* ।
kumārī caikakanyā ca kaiśorī yuvatī yatiḥ ।।

Holding Several Weapons in Hands, Wielding Many a Weapon, Ever Pure (Virgin), Sole Daughter, Youthful Maiden, Young Woman, Ascetic. (78–84)

अप्रौढा चैव प्रौढा च वृद्धमाता बलप्रदा ।
महोदरी मुक्तकेशी घोररूपा महाबला ।।१३।।

13. *apraudhā caiva praudhā ca vṛddhamātā balapradā* ।
mahodarī muktakeśī ghorarūpā mahābalā ।।

Never Maturing, Ever Mature, Aged Mother (or the Mother of the Aged), Bestower of Strength, Of Enormous Midriff, Of Flowing Tresses, Of Terrible Form, Of Gigantic Prowess. (85–92)

अग्निज्वाला रौद्रमुखी कालरात्रिस्तपस्विनी ।
नारायणी भद्रकाली विष्णुमाया जलोदरी ।।१४।।

14. *agnijvālā raudramukhī kālarātristapasvinī* ।
nārāyaṇī bhadrakālī viṣṇumāyā jalodarī ॥

Fireflame, Of Frightful Visage, Dark Night of Dissolution, Performer of Severe Penance, Consort of *Nārāyaṇa*, Auspicious *Kālī*, Inscrutable Power of *Viṣṇu*, Risen from Water. (93–100)

शिवदूती कराली च अनन्ता परमेश्वरी ।
कात्यायनी च सावित्री प्रत्यक्षा ब्रह्मवादिनी ।।१५।।

15. *śivadūtī karālī ca anantā parameśvarī* ।
kātyāyanī ca sāvitrī pratyakṣā brahmavādinī ॥

She Who Deputed *Śiva* as Ambassador, Formidable, Infinite, Sovereign Ruler, Daughter of the Sage *Kātyāyana* (or the Mother of *Kārtikeya*), Ray of Light, Manifest and Exponent of the *Vedas* (or One who Propounds *Brahman*). (101–108)

य इदं प्रपठेन्नित्यं दुर्गानामशताष्टकम् ।
नासाध्यं विद्यते देवि त्रिषु लोकेषु पार्वति ।।१६।।

16. *ya idaṁ prapaṭhennityaṁ durgānāmaśatāṣṭakam* ।
nāsādhyaṁ vidyate devi triṣu lokeṣu pārvati ॥

For him, O Goddess *Pārvatī* ! who regularly recites this Hymn of one Hundred and Eight Names of *Durgā*, there is nothing unfeasible in the three worlds.

धनं धान्यं सुतं जायां हयं हस्तिनमेव च ।
चतुर्वर्गं तथा चान्ते लभेन्मुक्तिं च शाश्वतीम् ।।१७।।

17. *dhanaṁ dhānyaṁ sutaṁ jāyāṁ hayaṁ hastinameva ca* ।
caturvargaṁ tathā cānte labhenmuktiṁ ca śāśvatīm ॥

He achieves wealth and food, children and wife, horses and elephants, four objectives of huṃan endeavour, i.e., *dharma, artha, kāma* and *mokṣa* and, finally, eternal liberation.

कुमारीं पूजयित्वा तु ध्यात्वा देवीं सुरेश्वरीम् ।
पूजयेत् परया भक्त्या पठेन्नामशताष्टकम् ।।१८।।

18. *kumārīṁ pūjayitvā tu dhyātvā devīṁ sureśvarīm* ।
pūjayet parayā bhaktyā paṭhennāmaśatāṣṭakam ।।

After worshipping the Virgin Goddess and meditating upon the Empress of the gods, let one worship her with supreme devotion and recite One Hundred and Eight Names.

तस्य सिद्धिर्भवेद् देवि सर्वैः सुरवरैरपि ।
राजानो दास्यतां यान्ति राज्यश्रियमवाप्नुयात् ।।१९।।

19. *tasya siddhirbhaved devi sarvaiḥ suravarairapi* ।
rājāno dāsyatāṁ yānti rajyaśriyamavāpnuyāt ।।

He shall be blessed, O Goddess! with superior powers by all the exalted gods also, kings will become his slaves and he shall attain to the stature of royalty.

गोरोचनालक्तककुङ्कुमेन सिन्दूरकर्पूरमधुत्रयेण ।
विलिख्य यन्त्रं विधिना विधिज्ञो भवेत् सदा धारयते पुरारिः ।।२०।।

20. *gorocanālaktaka kuṅkumena*
sindūrakarpūramadhutrayeṇa ।
vilikhya yantraṁ vidhinā vidhijño
bhavet sadā dhārayate purāriḥ ।।

Well versed in the procedure, he who draws the *yantra* (a diagrammatic representation) hereof, following the due process, with the unguent made up of cow's urine, red resin, saffron, red lead, camphor and *madhutraya* (honey, sugar and milk) and wears it, becomes equal to *Śiva* (the Liberated One).

भौमावस्यानिशामग्रे चन्द्रे शतभिषां गते ।
विलिख्य प्रपठेत् स्तोत्रं स भवेत् सम्पदां पदम् ।।२१।।

21. *bhaumāvasyāniśāmagre candre śatabhiṣāṁ gate ।*
vilikhya prapaṭhet stotraṁ sa bhavet sampadāṁ padam ॥

He who writes this Hymn on the first midnight of the new moon of a Tuesday when the moon is in *Śatabhiṣā* asterism and recites it, becomes wealthy.

इति श्रीविश्वसारतन्त्रे दुर्गाष्टोत्तरशतनामस्तोत्रं समाप्तम् ।

itī śrīviśvasāratantre durgāṣṭottaraśatañama-stotraṁ samāptam ।

Durgā's Hymn of One Hundred and Eight Names of *śrīviśvasāra-tantra* concluded.

अथ देव्याः कवचम्

3. *Atha Devyāḥ Kavacam*

Armour of the Goddess

ॐ अस्य श्रीचण्डीकवचस्य ब्रह्मा ऋषिः, अनुष्टुप् छन्दः,
चामुण्डा देवता, अङ्गन्यासोक्तमातरो बीजम्, दिग्बन्धदेवतास्तत्त्वम्,
श्री जगदम्बाप्रीत्यर्थे सप्तशतीपाठाङ्गत्वेन जपे विनियोगः ।

oṁ asya śrīcaṇḍīkavacasya brahmā ṛṣiḥ, anuṣṭup chandaḥ,
cāmuṇḍā devatā, aṅganyāsoktamātaro bījam,
digbandhadevatāstattvam, śrījagadambā prītyarthe
saptaśatīpāṭhāṅgatvena jape viniyogaḥ ।

Oṁ. Of this *Śrīcaṇḍīkavaca, Brahmā* is the seer, *Anuṣṭup* is the metre, *Cāmuṇḍā* is the deity; as described in the *aṅganyāsa* (the assignation of limbs), the Mother is the seed, the force that binds the gods of all directions is the principle. This is presented here as the limb of the recitation of the *Durgāsaptaśatī*, for felicitating the Mother of the Universe.

ॐ नमश्चण्डिकायै ॥

Oṁ namaścaṇḍikāyai ॥

Oṁ. Obeisance to the Formidable One.

मार्कण्डेय उवाच

mārkaṇḍeya uvāca

ॐ यद्गुह्यं परमं लोके सर्वरक्षाकरं नृणाम् ।
यन्न कस्यचिदाख्यातं तन्मे ब्रूहि पितामह ॥१॥

1. *oṁ yadguhyaṁ paramaṁ loke sarvarakṣākaraṁ nṛṇām* ।
yanna kasyacidākhyātaṁ tanme brūhi pitāmaha ॥

Mārkaṇḍeya said

Oṁ. O Great Father! narrate to me that ultimate secret in this world which affords protection to all but has not been shared by you hitherto with anyone.

ब्रह्मोवाच

brahmovāca

अस्ति गुह्यतमं विप्र सर्वभूतोपकारकम् ।
देव्यास्तु कवचं पुण्यं तच्छृणुष्व महामुने ।।२।।

2. *asti guhyatamaṁ vipra sarvabhūtopakārakam* ।
devyāstu kavacaṁ puṇyaṁ tacchṛṇuṣva mahāmune ।।

Brahmā said

There is, O wise sage! this greatest secret which grants beneficence to all the beings. Listen, O great ascetic! it is the holy Armour of the Goddess.

प्रथमं शैलपुत्री च द्वितीयं ब्रह्मचारिणी ।
तृतीयं चन्द्रघण्टेति कूष्माण्डेति चतुर्थकम् ।।३।।

3. *prathamaṁ śailaputrī ca dvitīyaṁ brahmacāriṇī* ।
tritīyaṁ candraghaṇṭeti kūṣmāṇḍeti caturthakam ।।

The first is the Daughter of *Himālaya*, the second is the Observer of the Vow of Chastity, the third is the One in Possession of the Moon Shaped Bell and the fourth, in Whose Belly Resides the Universe.

पञ्चमं स्कन्दमातेति षष्ठं कात्यायनीति च ।
सप्तमं कालरात्रीति महागौरीति चाष्टमम् ।।४।।

4. *pañcamaṁ skandamāteti ṣaṣṭhaṁ kātyāyanīti ca* ।
saptamaṁ kālarātrīti mahāgaurīti cāṣṭamam ।।

The fifth is the Mother of *Skanda*; the sixth, the (foster) Daughter of the sage *Kātyāyana*; the seventh is the Goddess of the Night of Death and the eighth, the Great Fair Complexioned One.

नवमं सिद्धिदात्री च नवदुर्गा प्रकीर्तिताः ।
उक्तान्येतानि नामानि ब्रह्मणैव महात्मना ।।५।।

5. *navamaṁ siddhidātrī ca navadurgā prakīrtitāḥ* ।
uktānyetāni nāmāni brahmaṇaiva mahātmanā ।।

The ninth is the Bestower of All Accomplishments. These are known as the Nine Forms of the Goddess *Durgā,* the Slayer of the demon *Durga* and the One who Redeems from Misery. These names have been mentioned by the noble *Brahmā* himself.

अग्निना दह्यमानस्तु शत्रुमध्ये गतो रणे ।
विषमे दुर्गमे चैव भयार्ताः शरणं गताः ॥६॥

6. *agninā dahyamānastu śatrumadhye gato raṇe* ।
viṣame durgame caiva bhayārtāḥ śaraṇaṁ gatāḥ ॥

न तेषां जायते किञ्चिदशुभं रणसंकटे ।
नापदं तस्य पश्यामि शोकदुःखभयं न हि ॥७॥

7. *na teṣāṁ jāyate kiñcidaśubhaṁ raṇasaṅkaṭe* ।
nāpadaṁ tasya paśyāmi śokaduḥkhabhayaṁ na hi ॥

Being burnt by fire, surrounded by enemies in the battlefield, caught in the most adverse crisis or paralysed by fear, if people seek refuge in the Goddess, nothing inauspicious will happen to them even in the most critical circumstances of battle nor do I see any calamity, grief or distress visiting them.

यैस्तु भक्त्या स्मृता नूनं तेषां वृद्धिः प्रजायते ।
ये त्वां स्मरन्ति देवेशि रक्षसे नात्र संशयः ॥८॥

8. *yaistu bhaktyā smṛtā nūnaṁ teṣāṁ vṛddhiḥ prajāyate* ।
ye tvāṁ smaranti deveśi rakṣase nātra saṁśayaḥ ॥

O Supreme Goddess! those who, with devotion, remember you, will certainly be on ascendance. There is no doubt that you protect those who remember you.

प्रेतसंस्था तु चामुण्डा वाराही महिषासना ।
ऐन्द्री गजसमारूढा वैष्णवी गरुडासना ॥९॥

9. *pretasaṁsthā tu cāmuṇḍā vārāhī mahiṣāsanā* ।
aindrī gajasamārūḍhā vaiṣṇavī garuḍāsanā ॥

The Slayer of *Caṇḍa* and *Muṇḍa* is seated on a ghost. The seat of the Consort of *Varāha*, the Great Boar (Incarnation of *Viṣṇu*), is *Mahiṣa* (buffalo). *Indra*'s Consort rides the elephant and the Consort of *Viṣṇu* is seated on Garuḍa, the Golden Eagle.

माहेश्वरी वृषारूढ़ा कौमारी शिखिवाहना ।
लक्ष्मी: पद्मासना देवी पद्महस्ता हरिप्रिया ।।१०।।

10. *māheśvarī vṛṣārūḍhā kaumārī śikhivāhanā* ।
lakṣmīḥ padmāsanā devī padmahastā haripriyā ।।

The Consort of the Supreme Lord (*Śiva*) rides a bull. The Consort of *Kumāra* (*Kārtikeya*) has a peacock for her vehicle. *Lakṣmī*, the beloved of *Hari*, sits on a lotus with a lotus in her hand.

श्वेतरूपधरा देवी ईश्वरी वृषवाहना ।
ब्राह्मी हंससमारूढा सर्वाभरणभूषिता ।।११।।

11. *śvetarūpadharā devī īśvarī vṛṣaavāhanā* ।
brāhmī haṁsasamārūḍhā sarvābharaṇabhūṣitā ।।

The Supreme Goddess with white complexion moves on a bull. The Consort of *Brahmā*, embellished with all ornaments, rides a swan.

इत्येता मातर: सर्वा: सर्वयोगसमन्विता: ।
नानाभरणशोभाढ्या नानारत्नोपशोभिता: ।।१२।।

12. *ityetā mātaraḥ sarvāḥ sarvayogasamanvitāḥ* ।
nānābharaṇaśobhāḍhyā nānāratnopaśobhitāḥ ।।

In this way, all these Mothers, endowed with the powers of *yoga*, are radiant with many ornaments and many jewels.

दृश्यन्ते रथमारूढा देव्य: क्रोधसमाकुला: ।
शङ्खं चक्रं गदा शक्तिं हलं च मुसलायुधम् ।।१३।।

13. *dṛśyante rathamārūḍhā devyaḥ krodhasamākulāḥ* ।
śaṇkhaṁ cakraṁ gadā śaktiṁ halaṁ ca musalāyudhaṁ ।।

खेटकं तोमरं चैव परशुं पाशमेव च ।
कुन्तायुधं त्रिशूलं च शार्ङ्गमायुधमुत्तमम् ॥१४॥

14. *kheṭakaṁ tomaraṁ caiva paraśuṁ pāśameva ca* ।
kuntāyudhaṁ triśūlaṁ ca śārṅgamāyudhamuttamam ॥

दैत्यानां देहनाशाय भक्तानामभयाय च ।
धारयन्त्यायुधानीत्थं देवानां च हिताय वै ॥१५॥

15. *daityānāṁ dehanāśāya bhaktānāmabhayāya ca* ।
dhārayantyāyudhānītthaṁ devānāṁ ca hitāya vai ॥

These Goddesses, sitting in their chariots, are seething with anger. For slaying the bodies of the demons, for instilling fearlessness among devotees and for ensuring welfare of the gods, they can be seen wielding the conch, discus, mace, missile, plough, pestle, shield, club, battle-axe, noose, lance, trident and the excellent bow *śārṅga.*

नमस्तेऽस्तु महारौद्रे महाघोरपराक्रमे ।
महाबले महोत्साहे महाभयविनाशिनि ॥१६॥

16. *namaste 'stu mahāraudre mahāghoraparākrame* ।
mahābale mahotsāhe mahābhayavināśini ॥

O the Formidable One! of the Fierce Prowess! we pay obeisance to you. You are the Mightiest, the Great Energy and the Great Allayer of Fear.

त्राहि मां देवि दुष्प्रेक्ष्ये शत्रूणां भयवर्धिनि ।
प्राच्यां रक्षतु मामैन्द्री आग्नेय्यामग्निदेवता ॥१७॥

17. *trāhi māṁ devi duṣprekṣye śatrūṇāṁ bhayavardhini* ।
prācyāṁ rakṣatu māmaindrī āgneyyāmagnidevatā ॥

दक्षिणेऽवतु वाराही नैर्ऋत्यां खड्गधारिणी ।
प्रतीच्यां वारुणी रक्षेद् वायव्यां मृगवाहिनी ॥१८॥

18. *dakṣiṇe 'vatu vārāhī nairṛtyāṁ khaḍgadhāriṇī* ।
pratīcyāṁ vāruṇī rakṣed vāyavyāṁ mṛgavāhinī ॥

उदीच्यां पातु कौमारी ऐशान्यां शूलधारिणी ।
ऊर्ध्वं ब्रह्माणि मे रक्षेदधस्ताद् वैष्णवी तथा ।।१६।।

19. *udīcyāṁ pātu kaumārī aiśānyāṁ śūladhāriṇī* ।
ūrdhvaṁ brahmāṇi me rakṣedadhastād vaiṣṇavī tathā ।।

It is difficult, O Goddess! to behold you (for such is your dazzling effulgence). You spell terror among the enemies. Please protect me. May the Consort of *Indra* protect me in the East. May the Goddess Fire protect me in the South-east.

In the South, may the Consort of the Great Boar protect me. May the Wielder of the Sword protect me in the South-west. In the West, may the Consort of *Varuṇa* (the Lord of Oceans) protect me. May the Goddess, whose mount is a deer, protect me in the North-west.

May the Consort of *Kumāra* (Kārtikeya) protect me in the North. In the North-east, may the Wielder of Pike protect me. May I be protected from above by the Consort of *Brahmā* and from below by the Consort of *Viṣṇu*.

एवं दश दिशो रक्षेच्चामुण्डा शववाहना ।
जया मे चाग्रतः पातु विजया पातु पृष्ठतः ।।२०।।

20. *evaṁ daśa diśo rakṣeccāmuṇḍā śavavāhanā* ।
jayā me cāgrataḥ pātu vijayā pātu pṛṣṭhataḥ ।।

Likewise, may the Slayer of *Caṇḍa* and *Muṇḍa* astride a corpse protect me in all the ten directions. May the Conqueror protect me from the front and the Triumphant from the rear.

अजिता वामपार्श्वे तु दक्षिणे चापराजिता ।
शिखामुद्योतिनी रक्षेदुमा मूर्ध्नि व्यवस्थिता ।।२१।।

21. *ajitā vāmapārśve tu dakṣiṇe cāparājitā* ।
śikhāmudyotinī rakṣedumā mūrdhni vyavasthitā ।।

मालाधरी ललाटे च भ्रुवौ रक्षेद् यशस्विनी ।
त्रिनेत्रा च भ्रुवोर्मध्ये यमघण्टा च नासिके ॥२२॥

22. *mālādharī lalāṭe ca bhruvau rakṣed yaśasvinī* ।
trinetrā ca bhruvormadhye yamaghaṇṭā ca nāsike ॥

शङ्खिनी चक्षुषोर्मध्ये श्रोत्रयोर्द्वारवासिनी ।
कपोलौ कालिका रक्षेत्कर्णमूले तु शाङ्करी ॥२३॥

23. *śaṅkhinī cakṣuṣormadhye śrotrayordvāravāsinī* ।
kapolau kālikā rakṣet karṇamūle tu śāṅkarī ॥

नासिकायां सुगन्धा च उत्तरोष्ठे च चर्चिका ।
अधरे चामृतकला जिह्वायां च सरस्वती ॥२४॥

24. *nāsikāyāṁ sugandhā ca uttaroṣṭhe ca carcikā* ।
adhare cāmritakalā jihvāyāṁ ca sarasvatī ॥

दन्तान् रक्षतु कौमारी कण्ठदेशे तु चण्डिका ।
घण्टिकां चित्रघण्टा च महामाया च तालुके ॥२५॥

25. *dantān rakṣatu kaumārī kaṇṭhadeśe tu caṇḍikā* ।
ghaṇṭikāṁ citraghaṇṭā ca mahāmāyā ca tāluke ॥

कामाक्षी चिबुकं रक्षेद् वाचं मे सर्वमङ्गला ।
ग्रीवायां भद्रकाली च पृष्ठवंशे धनुर्धरी ॥२६॥

26. *kāmākṣī cibukaṁ rakṣed vācaṁ me sarvamaṅgalā* ।
grīvāyāṁ bhadrakālī ca pṛṣṭhavaṁśe dhanurdharī ॥

नीलग्रीवा बहिः कण्ठे नलिकां नलकूबरी ।
स्कन्धयोः खड्गिनी रक्षेद् बाहू मे वज्रधारिणी ॥२७॥

27. *nīlagrīvā bahiḥ kaṇṭhe nalikāṁ nalakūbarī* ।
skandhayoḥ khaḍginī rakṣed bāhū me vajradhāriṇī ॥

May the Invincible Goddess protect me from the left and the Unconquerable One from the right. May the Ever Alert Goddess protect the knotted tuft of the hair of my head and, settled in my head, may *Umā*, the Splendid Consort of Śiva, protect it.

May the Goddess holding the Rosary in Her Hand protect me in my forehead and the Eminent One in my eyebrows. May the Three-Eyed Goddess protect me in the middle of my brows and the Bell of Death, in my nostrils.

In the centre of my eyes, may the Bearer of the Conch protect me and my ears, the Dweller at the Door. May the Controller of Time protect my cheeks and the Bestower of Felicity, the bases of my ears.

May the Fragrant One, dwelling in my nostrils, protect them and Reflection settled on my upper lip, protect it. May the Digit of Ambrosia protect my lower lip and the Goddess of Speech, my tongue.

May the Energy of *Kārtikeya* protect my teeth, the Impetuous Goddess, the region of my throat, the Wielder of Variegated Bell, my uvula and may the Great Deluding Power, by staying in my palate, protect it.

May the Goddess with Love Inspiring-Eyes, protect my chin and the Bestower of Universal Auspiciousness, my speech. May the Gentle *Kālī* settle in my neck and protect it. In the spinal column, may the Wielder of the Bow, protect me.

May my outer throat be protected by the Goddess with the Blue Throat and my throat-pipe by the Offspring of *Kubera*. May my shoulders be protected by the Wielder of the Sword and my arms by the Wielder of the Thunderbolt.

हस्तयोर्दण्डिनी रक्षेदम्बिका चाङ्गुलीषु च ।
नखाञ्छूलेश्वरी रक्षेत्कुक्षौ रक्षेत्कुलेश्वरी ॥२८॥

28. *hastayordaṇḍinī rakṣedambikā cāṅgulīṣu ca* ।
nakhāñchūleśvarī rakṣetkukṣau rakṣetkuleśvarī ॥

स्तनौ रक्षेन्महादेवी मनः शोकविनाशिनी ।
हृदये ललितादेवी उदरे शूलधारिणी ॥२९॥

29. *stanau rakṣenmahādevī manaḥ śokavināśinī* ।
hṛdaye lalitādevī udare śūladhāriṇī ॥

नाभौ च कामिनी रक्षेद् गुह्यं गुह्येश्वरी तथा ।
पूतना कामिका मेढ्रं गुदे महिषवाहिनी ॥३०॥

30. *nābhau ca kāminī rakṣed guhyaṁ guhyeśvarī tathā* ।
pūtanā kāmikā meḍhraṁ gude mahiṣavāhinī ॥

कट्यां भगवती रक्षेज्जानुनी विन्ध्यवासिनी ।
जङ्घे महाबला रक्षेत्सर्वकामप्रदायिनी ॥३१॥

31. *kaṭyāṁ bhagavatī rakṣejjānunī vindhyavāsinī* ।
jaṅghe mahābalā rakṣetsarvakāmapradāyinī ॥

गुल्फयोर्नारसिंही च पादपृष्ठे तु तैजसी ।
पादाङ्गुलीषु श्री रक्षेत्पादाधस्तलवासिनी ॥३२॥

32. *gulphayornārasiṃhī ca pādapṛṣṭhe tu taijasī* ।
pādāṅgulīṣu śrī rakṣetpādādhastalavāsinī ॥

नखान् दंष्ट्राकराली च केशांश्चैवोर्ध्वकेशिनी ।
रोमकूपेषु कौबेरी त्वचं वागीश्वरी तथा ॥३३॥

33. *nakhān daṁṣṭrākarālī ca keśāṁścaivordhvakeśinī* ।
romakūpeṣu kauberī tvacaṁ vāgīśvarī tathā ॥

May the Wielder of Staff protect my hands and the Mother, my fingers. May the Pike-Wielding Goddess protect my nails. May the Goddess of Progeny protect my belly.

May my breasts be protected by the Great Goddess and my mind by the Alleviator of Grief. May the Comely Goddess protect my heart and the Wielder of Pike my stomach.

May the Goddess of Beauty protect my navel by staying there and the Ruler of Secrets, my private parts. May the Desirable Goddess riding a corpse protect my penis and the Rider of *Mahiṣa* my anus.

May the Supreme Goddess by staying in my waist, protect it and the Dweller of *Vindhya* Mountain my two knees. May the Goddess of Immense Might who fulfils all desires protect both of my shanks by staying there.

May the Energy of the Man-Lion protect my two ankles and the Embodiment of Energy, by staying in the surface of my two feet, protect them. May the Prosperity of the Powerful stay in and protect my two toes and the Dweller of Lower Regions my two soles.

May the One with Frightful Fangs protect my nails and the One with the Raised Hair, my hair. May the Consort of *Kubera* protect the pores of my skin and the Ruler of Speech, my skin.

रक्तमज्जावसामांसान्यस्थिमेदांसि पार्वती ।
अन्त्राणि कालरात्रिश्च पित्तं च मुकुटेश्वरी ॥३४॥

34. *raktamajjavasāmāṁsānyasthimedāṁsi pārvatī* ।
antrāṇi kālarātriśca pittaṁ ca mukuṭeśvarī ॥

पद्मावती पद्मकोशे कफे चूडामणिस्तथा ।
ज्वालामुखी नखज्वालामभेद्या सर्वसंधिषु ॥३५॥

35. *padmāvatī padmakośe kaphe cūḍāmaṇistathā* ।
jvālāmukhī nakhajvālāmabhedyā sarvasandhiṣu ॥

शुक्रं ब्रह्माणि मे रक्षेच्छायां छत्रेश्वरी तथा ।
अहंकारं मनोबुद्धिं रक्षेन्मे धर्मधारिणी ॥३६॥

36. *śukraṁ brahmāṇi me rakṣecchāyāṁ chatreśvarī tathā* ।
ahaṅkāraṁ manobuddhiṁ rakṣenme dharmadhāriṇī ॥

प्राणापानौ तथा व्यानमुदानं च समानकम् ।
वज्रहस्ता च मे रक्षेत्प्राणं कल्याणशोभना ।।३७।।

37. *prāṇāpānau tathā vyānamudāṇaṁ ca samānakam* ।
vajrahastā ca me rakṣetprāṇaṁ kalyāṇaśobhanā ।।

May the Daughter of *Himālaya* protect the blood, the marrow of bones, lymphs, flesh, bones and fat. May the Night Heralding Death guard my intestines and the Goddess who Protects the Crowns of rulers, my bile.

May the Goddess Abiding in Lotus protect my lungs and the Crest Jewel of Divinities my phlegm. May She with Flaming Face protect the lustre of my nails and the Impenetrable One, dwelling in all my joints, protect them.

May the Energy of the Creator protect my semen and my shadow the Wielder of the Umbrella. May the Holder of Righteousness protect my ego, mind and intellect.

May the Wielder of the Thunderbolt protect my inhaling, exhaling, diffusing, rising and equalizing breaths and the Goddess Shining in Auspiciousness my life.

रसे रूपे च गन्धे च शब्दे स्पर्शे च योगिनी ।
सत्त्वं रजस्तमश्चैव रक्षेन्नारायणी सदा ।।३८।।

38. *rase rūpe ca gandhe ca śabde sparśe ca yoginī* ।
sattvaṁ rajastamaścaiva rakṣennārāyaṇī sadā ।।

May the Goddess who Unites, dwell in and protect the taste, form, smell, speech and touch. May the Energy of *Nārāyaṇa* always protect the modes of goodness, passion and dullness (or knowledge, action and desire).

आयू रक्षतु वाराही धर्मं रक्षतु वैष्णवी ।
यशः कीर्तिं च लक्ष्मीं च धनं विद्यां च चक्रिणी ।।३६।।

39. *āyū rakṣatu vārāhī dharmaṁ rakṣatu vaiṣṇavī* ।
yaśaḥ kīrtiṁ ca lakṣmīṁ ca dhanaṁ vidyāṁ ca cakriṇī ।।

May the span of my life be protected by the Energy of the Great Boar and the righteousness by the Consort of *Viṣṇu.* May the Wielder of the Disc protect my glory, prestige, prosperity, wealth and wisdom.

गोत्रमिन्द्राणि मे रक्षेत्पशून्मे रक्ष चण्डिके ।
पुत्रान्रक्षेन्महालक्ष्मीर्भार्यां रक्षतु भैरवी ॥४०॥

40. *gotramindrāṇi me rakṣetpaśūnme rakṣa caṇḍike* ।
putrānrakṣenmahālakṣmīrbhāryāṁ rakṣatu bhairavī ॥

May the Consort of *Indra* preserve my race. Protect, O Impetuous Goddess, my cattle. May the Great *Lakṣmī* protect my children and protect *O Bhairavī*, the Formidable Goddess, my wife.

पन्थानं सुपथा रक्षेन्मार्गं क्षेमकरी तथा ।
राजद्वारे महालक्ष्मीर्विजया सर्वतः स्थिता ॥४१॥

41. *panthānaṁ supathā rakṣenmārgaṁ kṣemakarī tathā* ।
rājadvāre mahālakṣmīrvijayā sarvataḥ sthitā ॥

रक्षाहीनं तु यत्स्थानं वर्जितं कवचेन तु ।
तत्सर्वं रक्ष मे देवि जयन्ती पापनाशिनी ॥४२॥

42. *rakṣāhīnaṁ tu yatsthānaṁ varjitaṁ kavacena tu* ।
tatsarvaṁ rakṣa me devi jayantī pāpanāśinī ॥

May the Guide on the Path of Righteousness protect my path and the Conferror of Security my ways. In the king's court may the Great *Lakṣmī* protect me and may the Omnipresent Triumpher protect me on all sides.

O Ever Victorious Annihilator of Evil! protect me in all those places which have not been covered by this armour and are unprotected.

पदमेकं न गच्छेत्तु यदीच्छेच्छुभमात्मनः ।
कवचेनावृतो नित्यं यत्र यत्रैव गच्छति ॥४३॥

43. *padamekaṁ na gacchettu yadīcchecchubhamātmanaḥ* ।
kavacenāvṛto nityaṁ yatra yatraiva gacchati ॥

तत्र तत्रार्थलाभश्च विजयः सर्वकात्मिकः।
यं यं चिन्तयते कामं तं तं प्राप्नोतिनिश्चितम्।
परमैश्वर्यमतुलं प्राप्स्यते भूतले पुमान् ।।४४।।

44. *tatra tatrārthalābhaśca vijayaḥ sarvakātmikaḥ* ।
yaṁ yaṁ cintayate kāmaṁ taṁ taṁ prāpnoti niścitam ।
paramaiśvaryamatulaṁ prāpsyate bhūtale pumān ।।

If a person wishes his welfare, he should not take even a single step out without being covered by the Armour. Always covered by the Armour, wherever a person goes, he is financially benefited, gains victory on all fronts and certainly achieves whatever desires he has in his mind. Such a person attains to the highest glory and riches on this earth.

निर्भयो जायते मर्त्यः संग्रामेष्वपराजितः।
त्रैलोक्ये तु भवेत्पूज्यः कवचेनावृतः पुमान् ।।४५।।

45. *nirbhayo jāyate martyaḥ saṅgrāmeṣvaparājitaḥ* ।
trailokye tu bhavetpūjyaḥ kavacenāvṛtaḥ pumān ।।

Though a mortal, he becomes fearless and remains invincible in battles. He, if covered with the Armour, is respected in the three worlds.

इदं तु देव्याः कवचं देवानामपि दुर्लभम्।
यः पठेत्प्रयतो नित्यं त्रिसन्ध्यं श्रद्धयान्वितः ।।४६।।

46. *idaṁ tu devyāḥ kavacaṁ devānāmapi durlabham* ।
yaḥ paṭhetprayato nityaṁ trisandhyaṁ śraddhayānvitaḥ ।।

दैवी कला भवेत्तस्य त्रैलोक्येष्वपराजितः।
जीवेद् वर्षशतं साग्रमपमृत्युविवर्जितः ।।४७।।

47. *daivī kalā bhavettasya trailokyeṣvaparājitaḥ* ।
jīved varṣaśataṁ sāgramapamṛtyuvivarjitaḥ ।।

He who recites this Armour of the Goddess which is not easily accessible even to the gods, with reverential faith three times everyday in the morning, noon and evening hours of prayer, is blessed with divine power, remains invincible in three worlds and lives for a hundred years untouched by untimely death or death caused by fire, floods, lightning or snakebite, etc.

नश्यन्ति व्याधयः सर्वे लूताविस्फोटकादयः ।
स्थावरं जङ्गमं चैव कृत्रिमं चापि यद्विषम्* ।।४८।।

48. *naśyanti vyādhayaḥ sarve lūtāvisphoṭakādayaḥ* ।
*sthāvaraṁ jaṅgamaṁ caiva kṛtrimaṁ cāpi yadviṣam** ।।

अभिचाराणि सर्वाणि मन्त्रयन्त्राणि भूतले ।
भूचराः खेचराश्चैव जलजाश्चोपदेशिकाः ।।४९।।

49. *abhicārāṇi sarvāṇi mantrayantrāṇi bhūtale* ।
bhūcarāḥ khecarāścaiva jalajāścopadeśikāḥ ।।

सहजा कुलजा माला डाकिनी शाकिनी तथा ।
अन्तरिक्षचरा घोरा डाकिन्यश्च महाबलाः ।।५०।।

50. *sahajā kulajā mālā ḍākinī śākinī tathā* ।
antarikṣacarā ghorā ḍākinyaśca mahābalāḥ ।।

ग्रहभूतपिशाचाश्च यक्षगन्धर्वराक्षसाः ।
ब्रह्मराक्षसवेतालाः कूष्माण्डा भैरवादयः ।।५१।।

51. *grahabhūtapiśācāśca yakśagandharvarākṣasāḥ* ।
brahmarākṣasavetālāḥ kūṣmāṇḍā bhairavādayaḥ ।।

नश्यन्ति दर्शनात्तस्य कवचे हृदि संस्थिते ।
मानोन्नतिर्भवेद् राज्ञस्तेजो वृद्धिकरं परम् ।।५२।।

52. *naśyanti darśanāttasya kavace hṛdisaṁsthite* ।
mānonnātir bhaved rājñastejo vṛddhikaraṁ param ।।

All types of afflictions including skin-infections, eruptions, etc., vanish and poisons, natural as well as man-made, remain ineffective on him.*

* Poison of oleander, opium, hemp, datura stramonium, etc., is known

All magical spells, incantations and amulets in this world, all the semi-gods roaming on the earth, in the sky and those born in water, all the lower forms of the gods who are felicitated by the others with inducements; all those who appear along with the individual at the time of his birth, the family deities, scrofula, imps and demonesses, the frightful spirits roaming in the space, the mighty witches, possessive spirits, ghosts, goblins, tribes of semi-gods, e.g., *yakṣas* and *gandharvas*, demons, *brāhmaṇa*-ghosts, vampires, terrifying females with pot bellies, *Bhairava*, the frightful form of *Rudra*; all of them disappear at the very sight of the one in whose heart this Armour abides. His prestige ascends in the eyes of the kings and his lustre increases manifold.

यशसा वर्धते सोऽपि कीर्तिमण्डितभूतले ।
जपेत्सप्तशतीं चण्डीं कृत्वा तु कवचं पुरा ।।५३।।

53. *yaśasā vardhate so 'pi kīrtimaṇḍitabhūtale* ।
japetsaptaśatīṁ caṇḍīṁ kṛtvā tu kavacaṁ purā ।।

यावद्भूमण्डलं धत्ते सशैलवनकाननम् ।
तावत्तिष्ठति मेदिन्यां संततिः पुत्रपौत्रिकी ।।५४।।

54. *yāvad bhūmaṇḍalaṁ dhatte saśailavanakānanam* ।
tāvattiṣṭhati medinyāṁ santatiḥ putrapautrikī ।।

देहान्ते परमं स्थानं यत्सुरैरपि दुर्लभम् ।
प्राप्नोति पुरुषो नित्यं महामायाप्रसादतः ।।५५।।

55. *dehānte paramaṁ sthānaṁ yatsurairapi durlabham* ।
prāpnōti puruṣo nityaṁ mahāmāyāprasādataḥ ।।

---

as *sthāvara*, stable; that caused by snakebite or scorpion sting is *jaṅgama*, moving; and the concoction of opium and oil is the *kṛtrima*, artificial or man made poison.

लभते परमं रूपं शिवेन सह मोदते ॥ॐ॥५६॥

56. *labhate paramaṁ rūpaṁ śivena saha modate* ॥*oṁ*॥

He who first recites the Armour and then recites the Seven Hundred Verses of *Caṇḍī* (*Saptaśatī*), rises in fame and is adorned with glory on earth.

As long as exists this earth, including hills, forests and woods, his progeny of children and grandchildren will continue to flourish.

On relinquishing his body, he shall, with the grace of the Supreme Illusive Power, attain for eternity to the highest abode which is difficult even for the gods.

He acquires the most beautiful form, and shares the highest bliss with Lord Śiva. Oṁ

देव्याः कवचं सम्पूर्णम् ॥

devyāḥ kavacaṁ sampūrṇam

Armour of the Goddess concluded.

अथार्गलास्तोत्रम्

4. *Atha Argalāstotram*

Hymn of the Bolt

ॐ अस्य श्री अर्गलास्तोत्रमन्त्रस्य विष्णुर्ऋषिः, अनुष्टुप् छन्दः,
श्रीमहालक्ष्मीर्देवता, श्रीजगदम्बाप्रीतये सप्तशतीपाठाङ्गत्वेन
जपे विनियोगः ।

oṁ. asya śrī argalāstotramantrasya viṣnurṛṣiḥ, anuṣṭup chandaḥ, śrīmahālakṣmīrdevatā, śrījagadambāprītaye saptaśatīpāṭhāṅgatvena jape viniyogaḥ ।

Oṁ. Of this *argalā stotra mantra*, the Hymn of the Bolt, *Viṣṇu* is the seer, *Anuṣṭup* is the metre, *Śrīmahālakṣmī* is the deity. Here presented is this, as a limb of the *Saptaśatī*.

ॐ नमश्चण्डिकायै ॥

oṁ namaścaṇḍikāyai ॥

Oṁ. Obeisance to *Caṇḍikā*

मार्कण्डेय उवाच

mārkaṇḍeya uvāca

ॐ जयन्ती मङ्गला काली भद्रकाली कपालिनी ।
दुर्गा क्षमा शिवा धात्री स्वाहा स्वधा नमोऽस्तु ते ॥१॥

1. *oṁ. jayantī maṅgalā kālī bhadrakālī kapālinī* ।
durgā kṣamā śivā dhātrī svāhā svadhā namo 'stu te ॥

Mārkaṇḍeya said

O Ever Triumphant, Auspicious, Controller of Time, Gentle Goddess of Dark Complexion, Holder of Skull in the Hand and Wearer of a Garland of Skulls around the Neck, Attainable after Performing Difficult Processes of Worship, Forgiveness, Abode of Felicity, Substratum of the Universe, Receiver of Oblations in Sacrifice on behalf of the gods and Acceptor of Libations on behalf of the manes! Obeisance to you.

जय त्वं देवि चामुण्डे जय भूतार्तिहारिणी ।
जय सर्वगते देवि कालरात्रि नमोऽस्तु ते ॥२॥

2. *jaya tvaṁ devi cāmuṇḍe jaya bhūtārtihāriṇī* ।
jaya sarvagate devi kālarātri namo 'stu te ॥

Victory O Goddess! to you who slayed *Caṇḍa* and *Muṇḍa.* Victory to you who takes away the miseries of all the beings. O Goddess! victory to you who abides in all. Obeisance to you, O Night of Death!

मधुकैटभविद्राविविधातृवरदे नमः ।
रूपं देहि जयं देहि यशो देहि द्विषो जहि ॥३॥

3. *madhukaiṭabha vidrāvividhātṛvarade namaḥ* ।
rūpaṁ dehi jayaṁ dehi yaśo dehi dviṣo jahi ॥

O Liquidator of *Madhu-Kaiṭabha*! We reverence you. We reverence you, O Bestower of Boons on the Creator! Grant me elegance, grant me victory, grant me glory, slay my enemies.

महिषासुरनिर्णाशि भक्तानां सुखदे नमः ।
रूपं देहि जयं देहि यशो देहि द्विषो जहि ॥४॥

4. *mahiṣāsuranirṇāśi bhaktānāṁ sukhade namaḥ* ।
rūpaṁ dehi jayaṁ dehi yaśo dehi dviṣo jahi ॥

Obeisance to you, O Annihilator of *Mahiṣāsura*! Obeisance to you, O Bestower of Joy on Devotees! Grant me elegance, grant me victory, grant me glory, slay my enemies.

रक्तबीजवधे देवि चण्डमुण्डविनाशिनि ।
रूपं देहि जयं देहि यशो देहि द्विषो जहि ॥५॥

5. *raktabījavadhe devi caṇḍamuṇḍavināśini* ।
rūpaṁ dehi jayaṁ dehi yaśo dehi dviṣo jahi ॥

O Slayer of *Raktabīja,* O Destroyer of *Caṇḍa-Muṇḍa,* O Goddess! grant me elegance, grant me victory, grant me glory, slay my enemies.

शुम्भस्यैव निशुम्भस्य धूम्राक्षस्य च मर्दिनि ।
रूपं देहि जयं देहि यशो देहि द्विषो जहि ॥६॥

6. *śuṁbhasyaiva niśuṁbhasya dhūmrākṣasya ca mardini* ।
rūpaṁ dehi jayaṁ dehi yaśo dehi dviṣo jahi ॥

O Trampler of the demons *Śumbha, Niśumbha* and *Dhūmrākṣa*! grant me elegance, grant me victory, grant me glory, slay my enemies.

वन्दिताङ्घ्रियुगे देवि सर्वसौभाग्यदायिनि ।
रूपं देहि जयं देहि यशो देहि द्विषो जहि ॥७॥

7. *vanditāṅghriyuge devi sarvasaubhāgyadāyini* ।
rūpaṁ dehi jayaṁ dehi yaśo dehi dviṣo jahi ॥

O Goddess, Dispenser of All Fortunes! your two feet are reverenced by all. Grant me elegance, grant me victory, grant me glory, slay my enemies.

अचिन्त्यरूपचरिते सर्वशत्रुविनाशिनि ।
रूपं देहि जयं देहि यशो देहि द्विषो जहि ॥८॥

8. *acintyarūpacarite sarvaśatruvināśini* ।
rūpaṁ dehi jayaṁ dehi yaśo dehi dviṣo jahi ॥

O Goddess of Incomprehensible Form and Acts! O Destroyer of All Enemies! grant me elegance, grant me victory, grant me glory, slay my enemies.

नतेभ्यः सर्वदा भक्त्या चण्डिके दुरितापहे ।
रूपं देहि जयं देहि यशो देहि द्विषो जहि ॥९॥

9. *natebhyaḥ sarvadā bhaktyā caṇḍike duritāpahe* ।
rūpaṁ dehi jayaṁ dehi yaśo dehi dviṣo jahi ॥

O *Caṇḍikā*! You are the remover of all the sins of your devotees who, with loving devotion, always bow before you. Grant me elegance, grant me victory, grant me glory, slay my enemies.

स्तुवद्भ्यो भक्तिपूर्वं त्वां चण्डिके व्याधिनाशिनि ।
रूपं देहि जयं देहि यशो देहि द्विषो जहि ॥१०॥

10. *stūvadbhyo bhaktipūrvaṁ tvāṁ caṇḍike vyādhināśini* ।
rūpaṁ dehi jayaṁ dehi yaśo dehi dviṣo jahi ॥

O *Caṇḍikā*! Annihilator of all Ailments! to them who eulogise you with loving devotion, grant elegance, grant victory, grant glory, slay their enemies.

चण्डिके सततं ये त्वामर्चयन्तीह भक्तितः ।
रूपं देहि जयं देहि यशो देहि द्विषो जहि ॥११॥

11. *caṇḍike satataṁ ye tvāmarcayantīha bhaktitaḥ* ।
rūpaṁ dehi jayaṁ dehi yaśo dehi dviṣo jahi ॥

To them, O *Caṇḍikā*! who unfailingly worship you here with devotion, grant elegance, grant victory, grant glory, slay their enemies.

देहि सौभाग्यमारोग्यं देहि मे परमं सुखम् ।
रूपं देहि जयं देहि यशो देहि द्विषो जहि ॥१२॥

12. *dehi saubhāgyamārogyaṁ dehi me paramaṁ sukham* ।
rūpaṁ dehi jayaṁ dehi yaśo dehi dviṣo jahi ॥

Bless me with good fortune and freedom from disease. Bless me with the highest bliss. Grant me elegance, grant me victory, grant me glory, slay my enemies.

विधेहि द्विषतां नाशं विधेहि बलमुच्चकैः ।
रूपं देहि जयं देहि यशो देहि द्विषो जहि ॥१३॥

13. *vidhehi dviṣatāṁ nāśam vidhehi balamuccakaiḥ* ।
rūpaṁ dehi jayaṁ dehi yaśo dehi dviṣo jahi ॥

Destroy those who are jealous of me. Augment my strength. Grant me elegance, grant me victory, grant me glory, slay my enemies.

विधेहि देवि कल्याणं विधेहि परमां श्रियम् ।
रूपं देहि जयं देहि यशो देहि द्विषो जहि ॥१४॥

14. *vidhehi devi kalyāṇaṁ vidhehi paramāṁ śriyaṁ* ।
rūpaṁ dehi jayaṁ dehi yaśo dehi dviṣo jahi ॥

O Goddess! bless me with auspiciousness. Bless me with the highest fortune. Grant me elegance, grant me victory, grant me glory, slay my enemies.

सुरासुरशिरोरत्ननिघृष्टचरणेऽम्बिके ।
रूपं देहि जयं देहि यशो देहि द्विषो जहि ॥१५॥

15. *surāsuraśiroratnanighṛṣṭacaraṇe 'mbike* ।
rūpaṁ dehi jayaṁ dehi yaśo dehi dviṣo jahi ॥

O Mother! both the gods and the demons rub their crest jewels in your feet. Grant me elegance, grant me victory, grant me glory, slay my enemies.

विद्यावन्तं यशस्वन्तं लक्ष्मीवन्तं जनं कुरु ।
रूपं देहि जयं देहि यशो देहि द्विषो जहि ॥१६॥

16. *vidyāvantaṁ yaśasvantaṁ lakṣmīvantaṁ janaṁ kuru* ।
rūpaṁ dehi jayaṁ dehi yaśo dehi dviṣo jahi ॥

I am your servitor. Make me wise, eminent and wealthy. Grant me elegance, grant me victory, grant me glory, slay my enemies.

प्रचण्डदैत्यदर्पघ्ने चण्डिके प्रणताय मे ।
रूपं देहि जयं देहि यशो देहि द्विषो जहि ॥१७॥

17. *pracaṇḍadaityadarpaghne caṇḍike praṇatāya me* ।
rūpaṁ dehi jayaṁ dehi yaśo dehi dviṣo jahi ॥

O *Caṇḍikā*! you are the destroyer of the fiercest demons' pride. To me, who has taken refuge in you, grant elegance, grant victory, grant glory, slay my enemies.

चतुर्भुजे चतुर्वक्त्रसंस्तुते परमेश्वरि ।
रूपं देहि जयं देहि यशो देहि द्विषो जहि ॥१८॥

18. *caturbhuje caturvaktrasaṁstute parameśvari* ।
rūpaṁ dehi jayaṁ dehi yaśo dehi dviṣo jahi ॥

O Sovereign Goddess! you are eulogised by *Brahmā* of Four Faces. Grant me elegance, grant me victory, grant me glory, slay my enemies.

कृष्णेन संस्तुते देवि शश्वद्भक्त्या सदाम्बिके ।
रूपं देहि जयं देहि यशो देहि द्विषो जहि ॥१९॥

19. *kṛṣṇena saṁstute devi śaśvadbhaktyā sadāmbike* ।
rūpaṁ dehi jayaṁ dehi yaśo dehi dviṣo jahi ॥

O Mother! you are eternally eulogised by Lord *Viṣṇu* of the Dark Complexion. Grant me elegance, grant me victory, grant me glory, slay my enemies.

हिमाचलसुतानाथसंस्तुते परमेश्वरि ।
रूपं देहि जयं देहि यशो देहि द्विषो जहि ॥२०॥

20. *himācalasutānāthasaṁstute parameśvari* ।
rūpaṁ dehi jayaṁ dehi yaśo dehi dviṣo jahi ॥

O Supreme Goddess! you are eulogised by *Śiva,* the Consort of the Daughter of *Himālaya.* Grant me elegance, grant me victory, grant me glory, slay my enemies.

इन्द्राणीपतिसद्भावपूजिते परमेश्वरि ।
रूपं देहि जयं देहि यशो देहि द्विषो जहि ॥२१॥

21. *indrāṇīpatisadbhāvapūjite parameśvari* ।
rūpaṁ dehi jayaṁ dehi yaśo dehi dviṣo jahi ॥

O Sovereign Ruler! *Indra,* the Consort of *Indrāṇī,* worships you with noble intent. Grant me elegance, grant me victory, grant me glory, slay my enemies.

देवि प्रचण्डदोर्दण्डदैत्यदर्पविनाशिनि ।
रूपं देहि जयं देहि यशो देहि द्विषो जहि ।।२२।।

22. *devi pracaṇḍadordaṇḍadaityadarpavināśini* ।
rūpaṁ dehi jayaṁ dehi yaśo dehi dviṣo jahi ।।

O Goddess! you have decimated the arrogance of the demons of mighty arms. Grant me elegance, grant me victory, grant me glory, slay my enemies.

देवि भक्तजनोद्दामदत्तानन्दोदयेऽम्बिके ।
रूपं देहि जयं देहि यशो देहि द्विषो जहि ।।२३।।

23. *devi bhaktajanoddāmadattānandodaye 'mbike* ।
rūpaṁ dehi jayaṁ dehi yaśo dehi dviṣo jahi ।।

O Mother Goddess! you keep bestowing boundless bliss upon your devotees. Grant me elegance, grant me victory, grant me glory, slay my enemies.

पत्नीं मनोरमां देहि मनोवृत्तानुसारिणीम् ।
तारिणीं दुर्गसंसारसागरस्य कुलोद्भवाम् ।।२४।।

24. *patnīṁ manoramāṁ dehi manovṛttānusāriṇīm* ।
tāriṇīṁ durgasaṁsārasāgarasya kulodbhavām ।।

Give me an attractive wife who accords with my disposition, who may liberate me from the impervious metempsychosis and is of a noble family.

इदं स्तोत्रं पठित्वा तु महास्तोत्रं पठेन्नरः ।
स तु सप्तशतीसंख्यावरमाप्नोति सम्पदाम् ।।ॐ।।२५।।

25. *idam stotraṁ paṭhitvā tu mahāstotraṁ paṭhennaraḥ* ।
sa tu saptaśatīsaṅkhyāvaramāpnoti sampadām ।।*oṁ*।।

He, who recites this hymn before reciting the Great Hymn of Seven Hundred Verses (*Saptaśatī*), achieves, along with abundant wealth, the best of boons. Oṁ.

इति देव्या अर्गलास्तोत्रं सम्पूर्णम् ।

iti devyā argalā stotraṁ sampūrṇam ।

The Hymn of Bolt to the Goddess concluded.

अथ कीलकम्

5. *Atha Kīlakam*

Hymn of the Pin

ॐ अस्य श्रीकीलकमन्त्रस्य शिव ऋषिः, अनुष्टुप् छन्दः,
श्रीमहासरस्वती देवता, श्रीजगदम्बाप्रीत्यर्थं सप्तशतीपाठाङ्गत्वेन
जपे विनियोगः ।

oṁ asya śrīkīlaka mantrasya śiva ṛṣiḥ, anuṣṭup chandaḥ ,
śrimahāsarasvatī devatā, śrījagadambāprītyarthaṁ saptaśatī-
pāṭhāṅgatvena jape viniyogaḥ ।

Oṁ. Of this *śrīkīlaka mantra, Śiva* is the seer, *Anuṣṭup* is the metre, *Śrī Mahāsarasvatī* is the deity. Here is this recitation presented as a limb of the *Saptaśatī.*

ॐ नमश्चण्डिकायै

oṁ namaścaṇḍikāyai

Oṁ. Obeisance to *Caṇḍikā*

मार्कण्डेय उवाच

mārkaṇḍeya uvāca

ॐ विशुद्धज्ञानदेहाय त्रिवेदीदिव्यचक्षुषे ।
श्रेयः प्राप्तिनिमित्ताय नमः सोमार्धधारिणे ।।१।।

1. *oṁ viśuddhajñānadehāya trivedīdivyacakṣuṣe* ।
śreyaḥ prāptinimittāya namaḥ somārdhadhāriṇe ।।

Mārkaṇḍeya said

I reverence *Śiva* for attaining to the Highest Bliss. He is the Embodied Pure Knowledge. Three *Vedas* are his Three Eyes. On his crest he supports the Crescent Moon.

सर्वमेतद्विजानीयान्मन्त्राणामभिकीलकम् ।
सोऽपि क्षेममवाप्नोति सततं जाप्यतत्परः ।।२।।

2. *sarvametadvijānīyānmantrāṇāmabhikīlakam* ।
so 'pi kṣemamavāpnoti, satataṁ jāpyatatparaḥ ।।

One should fully understand the *mantras* (of the *Saptaśatī*) which remove the Pin that causes obstruction in their recitation. He, too, who is perpetually intent upon their recitation attains to felicity.

सिद्धयन्त्युच्चाटनादीनि वस्तूनि सकलान्यपि ।
एतेन स्तुवतां देवी स्तोत्रमात्रेण सिद्धयति ॥३॥

3. *siddhyantyuccāṭanādīni vastūni sakalānyapi ।*
etena stuvatāṁ devī stotramātreṇa siddhyati ॥

All his objectives and desires, including (incantations for) extirpation (of enemies), too are accomplished. The Goddess is won over just by being eulogised with this Hymn.

न मन्त्रो नौषधं तत्र न किञ्चिदपि विद्यते ।
विना जाप्येन सिद्धयेत सर्वमुच्चाटनादिकम् ॥४॥

4. *na mantro nauṣadhaṁ tatra na kiñcidapi vidyate ।*
vinā jāpyena siddhyeta sarvamuccāṭanādikam ॥

There is neither a *mantra* nor a medicament that would be necessary for a person who recites *Saptaśatī* along with the Hymn of Pin. All his acts of incantations, etc., succeed even without the quiet recital of the other *mantras.*

समग्राण्यपि सिद्धयन्ति लोकशङ्कामिमां हरः ।
कृत्वा निमन्त्रयामास सर्वमेवमिदं शुभम् ॥५॥

5. *samagrāṇyapi siddhyanti lokaśaṅkāmimāṁ haraḥ ।*
kṛtvā nimantryāmāsa sarvamevamidaṁ śubham ॥

All the other desires too are accomplished. Doubt of the people as to which (recitation with other *mantras* or recitation of *Saptaśatī*) is better if both can fulfil the desires, was removed by Lord *Śiva.*

स्तोत्रं वै चण्डिकायास्तु तच्च गुप्तं चकार सः ।
समाप्तिर्न च पुण्यस्य तां यथावन्नियन्त्रणाम् ।।६।।

6. *stotraṁ vai caṇḍikāyāstu tacca guptaṁ cakāra saḥ* ।
samāptirna ca puṇyasya tāṁ yathāvanniyantraṇām ।।

He ordained the Hymn to *Caṇḍikā* (i.e., *Durgāsaptaśatī*) to be a secret. He prescribed restraint considering that this virtuous act of a person who recites it will yield undiminishing virtuous effects.

सोऽपि क्षेममवाप्नोति सर्वमेवं न संशयः ।
कृष्णायां वा चतुर्दश्यामष्टम्यां वा समाहितः ।।७।।

7. *so 'pi kṣemamavāpnoti sarvamevaṁ na saṁśayaḥ* ।
kṛṣṇāyāṁ vā caturdaśyāmaṣṭamyāṁ vā samāhitaḥ ।।

ददाति प्रतिगृह्णाति नान्यथैषा प्रसीदति ।
इत्थंरूपेण कीलेन महादेवेन कीलितम् ।।८।।

8. *dadāti pratigṛhṇāti nānyathaiṣā prasīdati* ।
itthaṁrūpeṇa kīlena mahādevena kīlitam ।।

There is no doubt that even he who, along with the recitation of the other *mantras*, recites the Hymn of *Saptaśatī* and repeats the *mantras*, attains to felicity. That devotee alone who, on the eighth or the fourteenth day of the dark fortnight of a lunar month, surrenders everything to the Mother Goddess and receives it back from her as her leavings, pleases her. There is no other way to please her; this is how the Great God (*Śiva*) has pinned it down (subjected to it the accomplishment of the desired objective).

यो निष्कीलां विधायैनां नित्यं जपति संस्फुटम् ।
स सिद्धः स गणः सोऽपि गन्धर्वो जायते नरः ।।९।।

9. *yo niṣkīlāṁ vidhāyaināṁ nityaṁ japati saṁsphuṭam* ।
sa siddhaḥ sa gaṇaḥ so 'pi gandharvo jāyate naraḥ ।।

He who, after removing the pin (i.e., after the recital of *kīlaka*), always chants it (i.e., *Saptaśatī*) in a clear and correct manner, is endowed with supernatural powers, becomes an attendant of the Goddess and becomes a *gandharva.*

न चैवाप्यटतस्तस्य भयं क्वापीह जायते ।
नापमृत्युवशं याति मृतो मोक्षमवाप्नुयात् ॥१०॥

10. *na caivāpyaṭatastasya bhayaṁ kvāpīha jāyate* ।
nāpamṛtyuvaśaṁ yāti mṛto mokṣamavāpnuyāt ॥

He shall have no fear of any kind wherever he may go about nor shall he have premature or unnatural death. When he dies, he shall attain to the final beatitude.

ज्ञात्वा प्रारभ्य कुर्वीत न कुर्वाणो विनश्यति ।
ततो ज्ञात्वैव सम्पन्नमिदं प्रारभ्यते बुधैः ॥११॥

11. *jñātvā prārabhya kurvīta na kurvāṇo vinaśyati* ।
tato jñātvaiva saṁpannamidaṁ prārabhyate budhaiḥ ॥

Only after having understood (and removed) it (the Pin), one should commence recitation (of the *Saptaśatī*). If that is not done, one would perish. Therefore, the wise commence its recitation only after understanding (and removing) it (the Pin).*

सौभाग्यादि च यत्किञ्चिद् दृश्यन्ते ललना जने ।
तत्सर्वं तत्प्रसादेन तेन जाप्यमिदं शुभम् ॥१२॥

12. *saubhāgyādi ca yatkiñcid dṛsyante lalanā jane* ।
tatsarvaṁ tatprasādena tena jāpyamidaṁ śubham ॥

---

* This has been stated just to emphasise the imperative requirement of the removal of Pin. Recitation of *Caṇḍīpātha* in any manner, however, yields beneficial results. The only conditions are faith and loving devotion. This is implicit in the other statements of this book. (e.g., see *Śrīdurgāsaptaśatī* XII. 11)

Whatever good fortune (beauty, knowledge, happiness, good family life, etc.) is witnessed among women, is all due to the grace of the Goddess. This felicific Hymn should, therefore, be regularly recited.

शनैस्तु जप्यमानेऽस्मिन् स्तोत्रे सम्पत्तिरुच्चकैः ।
भवत्येव समग्रापि ततः प्रारभ्यमेव तत् ॥१३॥

13. *śanaistu japyamāne 'smin stotre saṁpattiruccakaiḥ* ।
bhavatyeva samagrāpi tataḥ prārabhyameva tat ॥

If recited in soft tones, it results in limited prosperity. If recited in a higher tone, it will yield abundant riches. The commencement of recitation of this auspicious Hymn should, therefore, be done (in a high tone).

ऐश्वर्यं यत्प्रसादेन सौभाग्यारोग्यसम्पदः ।
शत्रुहानिः परो मोक्षः स्तूयते सा न किं जनैः ॥ॐ॥१४॥

14. *aiśvaryaṁ yatprasādena saubhāgyārogyasaṁpadaḥ* ।
śatruhāniḥ paro mokṣaḥ stūyate sā na kiṁ janaiḥ ॥*oṁ*॥

Resulting from its recitation, kingly status, great fortune, freedom from afflictions, wealth, loss of enemies and the final liberation are achieved by people as the Mother's blessings. Why then should they not recite it ?

इति देव्याः कीलकस्तोत्रं सम्पूर्णम्

iti devyāḥ kīlakastotraṁ sampūrṇam

Hymn of the Pin of the Goddess concluded.

अथ वेदोक्तं रात्रिसूक्तम्

6. *Atha Vedoktaṁ Rātrisūktam*

Vedic Hymn of the Night (Ṛgveda X.127.1–8)

ॐ रात्रीत्याद्यष्टर्चस्य सूक्तस्य कुशिकः सौभरो रात्रिर्वा भारद्वाजो ऋषिः, रात्रिर्देवता, गायत्री छन्दः, देवीमाहात्म्यपाठे विनियोगः ।

oṁ rātrītyādyaṣṭarcasya sūktasya kuśikaḥ saubharo rātrirvā bhārdvājo ṛṣiḥ, rātrirdevatā, gāyatrī chandaḥ, devīmāhātmya-pāṭhe viniyogaḥ ।

Oṁ. Of this Hymn of the Night comprising eight verses of the *Ṛgveda*, *Kuśika*, the descendant of *Sobhari*, or *Rātri* (Night) or *Bhārdvāja* is the seer, *Rātri* is the deity, *Gāyatrī* is the metre. It is here presented in the course of recitation of the Glory of the Goddess.

ॐ रात्री व्यख्यदायती पुरुत्रा देव्यक्षभिः ।
विश्वा अधि श्रियोऽधित ॥१॥

1. *oṁ. rātrī vyakhyadāyatī purutrā devyakṣabhiḥ* ।
viśvā adhi śriyo 'dhita ॥

Oṁ. The Goddess Night arriving, illumines all directions with her eyes. She has decked herself with all glories.

ओर्वप्रा अमर्त्यानिवतो देव्युद्वतः । ज्योतिषा बाधते तमः ॥२॥

2. *orvaprā amartyānivato devyudvataḥ* । *jyotiṣā bādhate tamaḥ* ॥

The immortal Goddess has filled the space, far and wide, the heights, the breadth and the depths. With her radiance, she drives away the darkness.

निरु स्वसारमस्कृतोषसं देव्यायती । अपेदु हासते तमः ॥३॥

3. *niru svasāramaskṛtoṣasaṁ devyāyatī* । *apedu hāsate tamaḥ* ॥

The Goddess comes expelling her sister (*Uṣas*) at whose arrival darkness disappears likewise.

सा नो अद्य यस्या वयं नि ते यामन्नविक्ष्महि ।
वृक्षे न वसतिं वयः ॥४॥

4. *sā no adya yasyā vayaṁ ni te yāmannavikṣmahi* ।
vṛkṣe na vasatiṁ vayaḥ ॥

May She, on whose arrival we rest in our homes as do the birds in their nests on trees, be pleased with us.

नि ग्रामासो अविक्षत नि पद्वन्तो नि पक्षिणः ।
नि श्येनासश्चिदर्थिनः ॥५॥

5. *ni grāmāso avikṣata ni padvanto ni pakṣiṇaḥ* ।
ni śyenāsaścidarthinaḥ ॥

The villagers have gone to rest, so too the walking animals, flying birds, even hawks who lust for prey.

यावया वृक्यं वृकं यवयस्तेनमूर्म्ये । अथा नः सुतरा भव ॥६॥

6. *yāvayā vṛkyaṁ vṛkaṁ yavayastenamūrmye* ।
athā naḥ sutarā bhava ॥

Ward off the she-wolf and the wolf and the thief. O Undulating Goddess! be exceedingly kind to us to let us pass through.

उप मा पेपिशत्तमः कृष्णं व्यक्तमस्थित । उष ऋणेव यातय ॥७॥

7. *upa mā pepiśattamaḥ kṛṣṇaṁ vyaktamasthita* ।
uṣa ṛṇeva yātaya ॥

The pervasive and palpable darkness has come near me. O *Uṣas* (Dawn), the Presiding Deity of Night! dispel it like my debts.

उप ते गा इवाकरं वृणीष्व दुहितर्दिवः । रात्रि स्तोमं न जिग्युषे ॥८॥

8. *upa te gā ivākaraṁ vṛṇīṣva duhitardivaḥ* ।
rātri stomaṁ na jigyuṣe ॥

O Daughter of Heaven! with the offer of this Hymn as a cow, I approach you. Accept it as a Victor does.

इति वेदोक्तं रात्रिसूक्तम् ।

iti vedoktaṁ rātrisūktam ।

The Hymn of the Night of the Veda concluded*.

---

* This Hymn has been interpreted by scholars in more than one ways. Some of the words are difficult in their meaning. We have endeavoured to remain closest to the letter even while interpreting the spirit.

अथ तन्त्रोक्तं रात्रिसूक्तम्

7. *Atha Tantroktaṁ Rātrisūktam*

Hymn of the Night from *Tantra*

Given below is the Sanskrit text in Devanāgarī and Roman scripts. For English translation, please see verses 70 (2nd line) to 87 (3rd line) of the First chapter of the Glory of the Goddess (Saptaśatī) [pages 117 to 122].

ॐ विश्वेश्वरीं जगद्धात्रीं स्थितिसंहारकारिणीम् ।
निद्रां भगवतीं विष्णोरतुलां तेजसः प्रभुः ।।१।।

1. *oṁ. viśveśvarīṁ jagaddhātrīṁ sthitisaṁhārakāriṇīm* ।
nidrāṁ bhagavatīṁ viṣṇoratulāṁ tejasaḥ prabhuḥ ।।

ब्रह्मोवाच

brahmovāca

त्वं स्वाहा त्वं स्वधा त्वं हि वषट्कारः स्वरात्मिका ।
सुधा त्वमक्षरे नित्ये त्रिधा मात्रात्मिका स्थिता ।।२।।

2. *tvaṁ svāhā tvaṁ svadhā tvaṁ hi vaṣaṭkāraḥ svarātmikā* ।
sudhā tvamakṣare nitye tridhā mātrātmikā sthitā ।।

अर्धमात्रास्थिता नित्या यानुच्चार्या विशेषतः ।
त्वमेव सन्ध्या सावित्री त्वं देवि जननी परा ।।३।।

3. *ardhamātrāsthitā nityā yānuccāryā viśeṣataḥ* ।
tvameva sandhyā sāvitrī tvaṁ devi jananī parā ।।

त्वयैतद्धार्यते विश्वं त्वयैतत्सृज्यते जगत् ।
त्वयैतत्पाल्यते देवि त्वमत्स्यन्ते च सर्वदा ।।४।।

4. *tvayaitaddhāryate viśvaṁ tvayaitatsṛjyate jagat* ।
tvayaitatpālyate devi tvamatsyante ca sarvadā ।।

विसृष्टौ सृष्टिरूपा त्वं स्थितिरूपा च पालने ।
तथा संहृतिरूपान्ते जगतोऽस्य जगन्मये ।।५।।

5. *visṛṣṭau sṛṣṭirūpā tvaṁ sthitirūpā ca pālane* ।
tathā saṁhṛti rūpānte jagato 'sya jaganmaye ।।

महाविद्या महामाया महामेधा महास्मृतिः ।
महामोहा च भवती महादेवी महासुरी ।।६।।

6. *mahāvidyā mahāmāyā mahāmedhā mahāsmṛtiḥ* ।
mahāmohā ca bhavatī mahādevī mahāsurī ।।

प्रकृतिस्त्वं च सर्वस्य गुणत्रयविभाविनी ।
कालरात्रिर्महारात्रिर्मोहरात्रिश्च दारुणा ।।७।।

7. *prakṛtistvaṁ ca sarvasya guṇatrayavibhāvinī* ।
kālarātrirmahārātrirmoharātriśca dāruṇā ।।

त्वं श्रीस्त्वमीश्वरी त्वं ह्रीस्त्वं बुद्धिर्बोधलक्षणा ।
लज्जा पुष्टिस्तथा तुष्टिस्त्वं शान्तिः क्षान्तिरेव च ।।८।।

8. *tvaṁ śrīstvamīśvarī tvaṁ hrīstvaṁ buddhirbodhalakṣaṇā* ।
lajjā puṣṭistathā tuṣṭistvaṁ śāntiḥ kṣāntireva ca ।।

खड्गिनी शूलिनी घोरा गदिनी चक्रिणी तथा ।
शङ्खिनी चापिनी बाणभुशुण्डीपरिघायुधा ।।९।।

9. *khaḍginī śūlinī ghorā gadinī cakriṇī tathā* ।
śaṅkhinī cāpinī bāṇabhuśuṇḍīparighāyudhā ।।

सौम्या सौम्यतराशेषसौम्येभ्यस्त्वतिसुन्दरी ।
परापराणां परमा त्वमेव परमेश्वरी ।।१०।।

10. *saumyā saumyatarāśeṣasaumyebhyastvatisundarī* ।
parāparāṇaṁ paramā tvameva parameśvarī ।।

यच्च किञ्चित् क्वचिद्वस्तु सदसद्वाखिलात्मके ।
तस्य सर्वस्य या शक्तिः सा त्वं किं स्तूयसे तदा ।।११।।

11. *yacca kiñcit kvacidvastu sadasadvākhilātmake* ।
tasya sarvasya yā śaktiḥ sā tvaṁ kiṁ stūyase tadā ।।

यया त्वया जगत्स्रष्टा जगत्पात्यत्ति यो जगत् ।
सोऽपि निद्रावशं नीतः कस्त्वां स्तोतुमिहेश्वरः ।।१२।।

12. *yayā tvayā jagatsraṣṭā jagatpātyatti yo jagat* ।
so 'pi nidrāvaśaṁ nītaḥ kastvāṁ stotumiheśvaraḥ ।।

विष्णुः शरीरग्रहणमहमीशान एव च ।
कारितास्ते यतोऽतस्त्वां कः स्तोतुं शक्तिमान् भवेत् ।।१३।।

13. *viṣṇuḥ śarīragrahaṇamahamīśāna eva ca* ।
kāritāste yato 'tastvāṁ kaḥ stotuṁ śaktimān bhavet ।।

सा त्वमित्थं प्रभावैः स्वैरुदारैर्देवि संस्तुता ।
मोहयैतौ दुराधर्षावसुरौ मधुकैटभौ ।।१४।।

14. *sā tvamitthaṁ prabhāvaiḥ svairudārairdevi saṁstutā* ।
mohayaitau durādharṣāvasurau madhukaiṭabhau ।।

प्रबोधं च जगत्स्वामी नीयतामच्युतो लघु ।
बोधश्च क्रियतामस्य हन्तुमेतौ महासुरौ ।।१५।।

15. *prabodhaṁ ca jagatsvāmī nīyatāmacyuto laghu* ।
bodhaśca kriyatāmasya hantumetau mahāsurau ।।

इति रात्रिसूक्तम्
iti rātrisūktam
The Hymn of the Night concluded.

श्रीदेव्यथर्वशीर्षम्

8. *Śrīdevyatharvaśīrṣaṁ*

The Highest Meaning of the Goddess according to the *Atharvaveda.*

[This Hymn has been highly rated in the *Atharvaveda.* Its recitation brings the grace of the Goddess very soon. Although it has not been mentioned anywhere as a limb of the Glory of the Goddess (*Saptaśatī*), it is very beneficial if recited before the commencement of the recital of the Glory of the Goddess.]

ॐ सर्वे वै देवा देवीमुपतस्थुः कासि त्वं महादेवीति ।।१।।

1. *oṁ. sarve vai devā devīmupatasthuḥ kāsi tvaṁ mahādevīti*।

Oṁ. All the gods approached the Goddess and enquired: O Great Goddess! who are you?

साब्रवीत् - अहं ब्रह्मस्वरूपिणी। मत्तः प्रकृतिपुरुषात्मकंजगत् ।
शून्यं चाशून्यं च ।।२।।

2. *sābravīt – ahaṁ brahmasvarūpiṇī* । *mattaḥ*
prakṛtipuruṣātmakaṁ jagat । *śūnyaṁ cāśūnyaṁ ca* ।।

She said: I am the Female Form of *Brahman.* From me is born this world of *Prakṛti* and *Puruṣa,* (also) the manifest and the unmanifest (or, of illusive appearance and true existence).

अहमानन्दानानन्दौ। अहं विज्ञानाविज्ञाने । अहं ब्रह्माब्रह्मणी वेदितव्ये ।
अहं पञ्चभूतान्यपञ्चभूतानि । अहमखिलं जगत् ।।३।।

3. *ahamānandānānandau* । *ahaṁ vijñānāvijñāne* ।
ahaṁ brahmābrahmaṇī veditavye । *ahaṁ*
pañcabhūtañyapañcabhūtāni । *ahamakhilaṁ jagat* ।।

I am the form of bliss and blisslessness. I am the spiritual knowledge as well as non-spiritual knowledge. I am *Brahman* as well as non-*Brahman,* which must be understood. I am five elements in their composite form as well as their disintegrated, individual parts. I am this entire universe.

वेदोऽहमवेदोऽहम् । विद्याहमविद्याहम्। अजाहमनजाहम् ।
अधश्चोर्ध्वं च तिर्यक्चाहम् ।।४।।

4. *vedo 'hamavedo 'haṁ । vidyāhamavidyāham । ajāhamanajāham । adhaścordhvaṁ ca tiryakcāham ।*

I am the *Veda*, as also the non-*Veda*. I am knowledge as well as nescience. I am unborn as well as not-unborn. I am below, I am above and I am transverse.

अहं रुद्रेभिर्वसुभिश्चरामि । अहमादित्यैरुत विश्वदेवैः ।
अहं मित्रावरुणावुभौ बिभर्मि । अहमिन्द्राग्नी अहमश्विनावुभौ ।।५।।

5. *ahaṁ rudrebhirvasubhiścarāmi । ahamādityairuta viśvadevaiḥ । ahaṁ mitrāvaruṇāvubhau bibharmi । ahamindrāgnī ahamaśvināvubhau ।।*

I move about as *Rudras* and *Vasus*. I wander as the *Ādityas* and the *Viśvadevas*. I nourish and nurture both *Mitra* and *Varuṇa*. I am *Indra* and *Agni*, I am two *Aśvinīkumāras*.

अहं सोमं त्वष्टारं पूषणं भगं दधामि ।
अहं विष्णुमुरुक्रमं ब्रह्माणमुत प्रजापतिं दधामि ।।६।।

6. *ahaṁ somaṁ tvaṣṭāraṁ pūṣaṇaṁ bhagaṁ dadhāmi । ahaṁ viṣṇumurukramaṁ brahmāṇamuta prajāpatiṁ dadhāmi ।।*

I hold *Soma, Tvaṣṭā, Pūṣā* and *Bhaga*. I hold *Viṣṇu* of wide strides, *Brahmā* and *Prajāpati*.

अहं दधामि द्रविणं हविष्मते सुप्राव्ये यजमानाय सुन्वते ।
अहं राष्ट्री सङ्गमनी वसूनां चिकितुषी प्रथमा यज्ञियानाम् ।
अहं सुवे पितरमस्य मूर्धन्मम योनिरप्स्वन्तः समुद्रे ।
य एवं वेद। स दैवीं सम्पदमाप्नोति ।।७।।

7. *ahaṁ dadhāmi draviṇaṁ haviṣmate suprāvye yajamānāya sunvate* । *ahaṁ rāṣṭrī saṅgamanī vasūnāṁ cikituṣī prathamā yajñiyānām* । *ahaṁ suve pitaramasya mūrdhanmama yonirapsvantaḥ samudre* । *ya evaṁ veda* । *sa daivīṁ sampadamāpnoti* ।।

I hold wealth for the sacrificer who is engaged in performing sacrifice for offering oblations to the gods. I am the ruler, the fellow traveller with *Vasus*, the Intelligence, and I am the foremost among the gods deserving sacrifice. I give birth to the Supreme Father of this all. Settled in the depth of the ocean, I am the cause of generating all. Whoever knows it, attains to the divine wealth.

ते देवा अब्रुवन्—
te devā abruvan—
नमो देव्यै महादेव्यै शिवायै सततं नमः ।
नमः प्रकृत्यै भद्रायै नियताः प्रणताः स्म ताम् ।।८।।

8. *namo devyai mahādevyai śivāyai satataṁ namaḥ* ।
namaḥ prakṛtyai bhadrāyai niyatāḥ praṇatāḥ sma tām ।।

Those gods then said:

Obeisance to the Goddess, the Supreme Goddess, obeisance forever to Śivā, the Goddess of Felicity. Obeisance to *Prakṛti*, the Primordial Nature and to *Bhadrā*, the Noble One. We bow in salutation to her unfailingly.

तामग्निवर्णां तपसा ज्वलन्तीं वैरोचनीं कर्मफलेषु जुष्टाम् ।
दुर्गां देवीं शरणं प्रपद्यामहेऽसुरान्नाशयित्र्यै ते नमः ।।६।।

9. *tāmagnivarṇāṁ tapasā jvalantīṁ*
vairocanīṁ karmaphaleṣu juṣṭām ।
durgā devīṁ śaraṇaṁ prapadyāmahe 'surān–
nāśayitryai te namaḥ ॥

We seek refuge in the Goddess *Durgā* of the hue of fire, resplendent with penance, lustrous and the bestower of the fruits of action. Obeisance to you, O Annihilator of the demons.

देवीं वाचमजनयन्त देवास्तां विश्वरूपाः पशवो वदन्ति ।
सा नो मन्द्रेषमूर्जं दुहाना धेनुर्वागस्मानुप सुष्टुतैतु ।।१०।।

10. *devīṁ vācamajanayanta devāstāṁ viśvarūpāḥ paśavo*
vadanti ।
sā no mandreṣamūrjaṁ duhānā dhenurvāgasmānupa
suṣṭutaitu ॥

Speech that was originated by the gods is used by different types of living beings for expression. May that Presiding Goddess of Speech who, like the wish fulfilling cow, gives food, strength and bliss, be pacified and come near us.

कालरात्रीं ब्रह्मस्तुतां वैष्णवीं स्कन्दमातरम् ।
सरस्वतीमदितिं दक्षदुहितरं नमामः पावनां शिवाम् ।।११।।

11. *kālarātrīṁ brahmastutāṁ vaiṣṇavīṁ skandamātaram* ।
sarasvatīmaditiṁ dakṣaduhitaraṁ namāmaḥ pāvanāṁ śivām ॥

We pay obeisance to the Night of Death (or the Destroyer of Death), Consort of *Viṣṇu* adored by the *Vedas*, the Mother of *Skanda; Sarasvatī*, the Mother of gods; the Daughter of *Dakṣa* and the Felicific Goddess who wipes out all sins.

महालक्ष्म्यै च विद्महे सर्वशक्त्यै च धीमहि।
तन्नो देवी प्रचोदयात् ।।१२।।

12. *mahālakṣmyai ca vidmahe sarvaśaktyai ca dhīmahi* ।
tanno devī pracodayāt ।।

We know the Supreme *Lakṣmī* and meditate upon that Omnipotent Power. May that Goddess inspire us with knowledge, devotion and prosperity.

अदितिर्ह्यजनिष्ट दक्ष या दुहिता तव ।
तां देवा अन्वजायन्त भद्रा अमृतबन्धवः ।।१३।।

13. *aditirhyajaniṣṭa dakṣa yā duhitā tava* ।
tāṁ devā anvajāyanta bhadrā amṛtabandhavaḥ ।।

O *Dakṣa*! that your daughter *Aditi* became the Mother and to her were born the gods, the brothers of Ambrosia.

कामो योनिः कमला वज्रपाणिर्गुहा हसा मातरिश्वाभ्रमिन्द्रः ।
पुनर्गुहा सकला मायया च पुरूच्यैषा विश्वमातादिविद्योम् ।।१४।।*

14*. *kāmo yoniḥ kamalā vajrapāṇir-*
guhā hasā mātariśvābhramindraḥ ।
punarguhā sakalā, māyayā ca
purūcyaiṣā viśvamātādividyom ।।

Kāma, Yoni, Kamalā, Vajrapāṇi, Guhā, Ha, Sa, Mātariśvā, Abhra, Indra, Punarguhā, Sa, Ka, La, and *Māyā*: This is the Mother of the Universe. She is the root of all knowledge and identical with *Brahman*.

Kāma is desire. It is the primal drive for creation:

कामस्तदग्रे समवर्तताधि मनसो रेतः प्रथमं यदासीत् ।**

kāmastadagre samavartatādhi manaso retaḥ prathamaṁ yadāsīt ।**

---

* This (14th) *mantra* is considered to be the crest jewel of all *mantras*.

** Ṛgveda, X.129.4

Desire is the first seed. It is the forerunner of all creation. *Kāma* in this (*Kāmo* yoniḥ, etc.) *mantra* is represented by क (*ka*); yoni is the womb of creation, it is represented by ए (*e*); *Kamalā* by ई (*ī*); *Vajrapāṇī-Indra* by ल (*la*); *guhā* by ह्रीं (*hrīṁ*); these are followed by the letters ह (*ha*) and स (*sa*); then *Mātariśvā*, Wind, is represented by क (*ka*); *Abhra*, Sky, by ह (*ha*); *Indra* by ल (*la*); *Punaḥ-guhā* by ह्रीं (*hrīṁ*); then again the letters स (*sa*), क (*ka*) and ल (*la*) and finally *Māyā*, represented by ह्रीं (*hrīṁ*).

This is the *mahāmantra*, the great mystic *mantra* of the '*pañcadaśī kādī mahāvidyā:* क (*ka*), ए (*e*), ई (*ī*), ल (*la*), ह्रीं (*hrīṁ*), ह (*ha*), स (*sa*), क (*ka*), ह (*ha*), ल (*la*), ह्रीं (*hrīṁ*), स (*sa*), क (*ka*), ल (*la*), ह्रीं (*hrīṁ*).

While the *kādividyā mahāmantra* begins with क (*ka*), the *hādividyā mahāmantra* begins with the seed-syllable ह (*ha*), and consists of the following seed syllables: ह (*ha*), स (*sa*), क (*ka*), ल (*la*), ह्रीं (*hrīṁ*), ह (*ha*), स (*sa*), क (*ka*), ल (*la*), ह्रीं (*hrīṁ*), ह (*ha*), स (*sa*), क (*ka*), ल (*la*), ह्रीं (*hrīṁ*). According to one interpretation, the first set of five syllables of *kādividyā*, i.e., क (*ka*), ए (*e*), ई (*ī*), ल (*la*) and ह्रीं (*hrīṁ*) represents the कारणशरीर – *kāraṇa śarīra* (the causal body), the next six syllables, ह (*ha*), स (*sa*), क (*ka*), ह (*ha*), ल (*la*) and ह्रीं (*hrīṁ*), the सूक्ष्म शरीर – *sūkṣma śarīra* (the subtle body) and the last four, स (*sa*), क (*ka*), ल (*la*) and ह्रीं (*hrīṁ*), स्थूल शरीर – *sthūla śarīra* (the gross body).

Following import has been ascribed to this *kādi mahāmantra:*

(i) The *Mahātripurasundarī*, the Mother Goddess, is both *Śiva* and *Śakti*. They are not separate or different.

(ii) She includes *Brahmā*, *Viṣṇu* and *Śiva*, the Creator, Sustainer and Annihilator respectively, of the Divine Trinity.

(iii) She is *Sarasvatī* (the Consort of *Brahmā*), *Lakṣmī* (the Consort of *Viṣṇu*) and *Gaurī* (the Consort of *Śiva*).

(iv) She is *Śiva* and *Śakti* in complete harmony and, as such, bestower of Transcendental Knowledge and the intrinsic Nature of *Brahman*.

(v) In her, she incorporates both pure and impure forms of meditation.

(vi) She is the essence of Truth, the Ultimate Reality].

एषाऽऽत्मशक्तिः । एषा विश्वमोहिनी । पाशाङ्कुशबाणधरा । एषा
श्रीमहाविद्या । य एवं वेद स शोकं तरति ॥१५॥

15. *eṣā ''tmaśaktiḥ* । *eṣā viśvamohinī* । *pāśāṅkuśabāṇadharā* ।
eṣā śrīmahāvidyā । *ya evaṁ veda sa śokaṁ tarati* ॥

She is the Energy of the Supreme Self. She is Enchantress of the Universe. She is the Wielder of the Snare, Hook and Arrow. She is *Śrīmahāvidyā.* He who knows this, sails across grief.

नमस्ते अस्तु भगवति मातरस्मान् पाहि सर्वतः ॥१६॥

16. *namaste astu bhagavati mātarasmān pāhi sarvataḥ* ।

Obeisance to you O Supreme Mother Goddess! protect us in all the ways.

सैषाष्टौ वसवः । सैषैकादश रुद्राः । सैषा द्वादशादित्याः ।
सैषा विश्वेदेवाः सोमपा असोमपाश्च । सैषा यातुधाना असुरा रक्षांसि
पिशाचा यक्षाः सिद्धाः । सैषा सत्त्वरजस्तमांसि ।
सैषा ब्रह्मविष्णुरुद्ररूपिणी । सैषा प्रजापतीन्द्रमनवः ।
सैषा ग्रहनक्षत्रज्योतींषि । कलाकाष्ठादिकालरूपिणी ।
तामहं प्रणौमि नित्यम् ॥

पापहारिणीं देवीं भुक्तिमुक्तिप्रदायिनीम् ।
अनन्तां विजयां शुद्धां शरण्यां शिवदां शिवाम् ॥१७॥

17. *saiṣāṣṭau vasvah* । *saiṣaikādaśa rudrāḥ* । *saiṣā*
dvādaśādityāḥ । *saiṣā viśvedevāḥ somapā asomapāśca* । *saiṣā*
yātudhānā asurā rakṣāṁsi piśācā yakṣāḥ siddhāḥ । *saiṣā*
sattvarajastamāṁsi । *saiṣā brahmaviṣṇurudrarūpiṇī* । *saiṣā*
prajāpatīndramanavaḥ । *saiṣā grahanakṣatrajyotīṁṣi* ।
kalākāṣṭhādikālarupiṇī । *tāmahaṁ praṇaumi nityam* ॥
pāpahāriṇīṁ devīṁ bhuktimuktipradāyinīm ।
anantāṁ vijayāṁ śuddhāṁ śaraṇyāṁ śivadāṁ śivām ।

She is eight *Vasus.* She is eleven *Rudras.* She is twelve *Ādityas.* She is *Viśvedevāḥ* who drink and do not drink *Soma.* She is *yātudhānas, asuras* and *rākṣasas* (different classes of demons), she is *piśācas* (goblins), she is the *yakṣas* (demigods or ghosts) and *siddhas* (the accomplished souls). She is goodness, passion and inertia. She is the true Nature of the Trinity of *Brahmā, Viṣṇu* and *Rudra.* She is *Prajāpati, Indra* and *Manu.* She is the planets, asterisms and the stars. She is the true nature of Time, its divisions and extremities. I pay obeisance to her always.

She is the allayer of sins, the Goddess who bestows the worldly prosperity and final beatitude. She is infinite. She is the bestower of victory. She is pure. She is the refuge. She is the bestower of felicity. She is Felicity herself. To her, our obeisance.

वियदीकारसंयुक्तं वीतिहोत्रसमन्वितम् ।
अर्धेन्दुलसितं देव्या बीजं सर्वार्थसाधकम् ।।१८।।

18. *viyadīkāra saṁyuktaṁ vītihotrasamanvitam ।*
ardhendulasitaṁ devyā bījaṁ sarvārthasādhakam ।।

एवमेकाक्षरं ब्रह्म यतयः शुद्धचेतसः ।
ध्यायन्ति परमानन्दमया ज्ञानाम्बुराशयः ।।१९।।*

19*. *evamekākṣaraṁ brahma yatayaḥ śuddhacetasaḥ ।*
dhyāyanti paramānandamayā jñānāmburāśayaḥ ।।

This seed of the Goddess is furnished with *viyat* (Sky, i.e., *ha*) and *īkāra* (the sound of *ī*), it is connected with *vītihotra* (Fire), i.e., the sound of *ra* and is adorned with

---

* This single syllable seed mantra (ह्रीं – *hrīṁ*) is considered to be the 'Devī-Praṇava' (Oṁ of the Goddess) and, like *Oṁ,* is full of extensive purport. In it are incorporated will, knowledge and action; existence, consciousness and bliss; non-dual, indivisible substratum of the universe and the pulsating harmony of Lord *Śiva* and his Energy.

the crescent moon (̐). In this way, this seed (*hrīṁ*) fulfils all aspirations. It is single-syllable *Brahman.* Ascetics whose minds are pure, who are oceans of spiritual knowledge and are immersed in the supreme bliss, meditate on it.

वाङ्माया ब्रह्मसूस्तस्मात् षष्ठं वक्त्रसमन्वितम् ।
सूर्योऽवामश्रोत्रबिन्दुसंयुक्तष्टात्तृतीयकः ।
नारायणेन सम्मिश्रो वायुश्चाधरयुक् ततः ।
विच्चे नवार्णकोऽर्णः स्यान्महदानन्ददायकः ॥२०॥

20. *vāṅmāyā brahmasūstasmāt ṣaṣṭhaṁ vaktrasamanvitam* ।
sūryo 'vāmaśrotrabindusaṁyuktaṣṭāttṛtīyakaḥ ।
nārāyaṇena sammiśro vāyuścādharayuk tataḥ ।
vicce navārṇako 'rṇaḥ syānmahadānandadāyakaḥ ॥

Incorporated in this *navārṇa mantra* which is the bestower of the highest bliss are: *vāṅ* – *vāṇī* (*aiṁ*) (Speech), *māyā* (the Deluding Power) (*hrīṁ*), *brahmasū-kāma (klīm)* (*Desire*), thereafter the sixth consonant – *c*, with *ā* (i.e., *cā*), *sūrya* (Sun) – *m, avāma śrotra* (the right ear) – *u* together with the *anusvāra,* a nasal dot (i.e., *muṅ*), the third consonant *ḍ*, of the '*ṭa*-cluster (*ṭavarga*) with *ā* (*ḍā*) (i.e., *Nārāyaṇa*), *vāyu* – *ya* (air), the same *adhara, y* with *ai* (*yai*) and *vicce.*

[Thus *hrīṁ klim cāmuṇḍāyai vicce*]

[In this *mantra,* the devotee prays to the Goddesses *Mahāsarasvatī, Mahālakṣmī* and *Mahākālī* seeking their blessings for the highest spiritual knowledge and freedom from the knots of ignorance.]

हृत्पुण्डरीकमध्यस्थां प्रातःसूर्यसमप्रभाम् ।
पाशाङ्कुशधरां सौम्यां वरदाभयहस्तकाम् ॥
त्रिनेत्रां रक्तवसनां भक्तकामदुघां भजे ॥२१॥

21. *hṛtpuṇḍarīkamadhyasthāṁ prātaḥ sūryasamaprabhām* ।
pāśāṅkuśadharāṁ saumyāṁ varadābhayahastakām ।
trinetrāṁ raktavasanāṁ bhaktakāmadughāṁ bhaje ॥

I worship her who resides in the centre of the lotus of heart, is lustrous like the rising sun, wields a snare and a goad, is charming and gentle, whose hands bear the signs of blessings and freedom from fear, who has three eyes, is dressed in red garments and, like the wish-fulfilling cow, grants the desires of the devotees.

नमामि त्वां महादेवीं महाभयविनाशिनीम् ।
महादुर्गप्रशमनीं महाकारुण्यरूपिणीम् ॥२२॥

22. *namāmi tvāṁ mahādevīṁ mahābhayavināśinīm* ।
mahādurgapraśamanīṁ mahākāruṇyarūpiṇīm ॥

O Great Goddess! I pay obeisance to you. You destroy the greatest fears and mitigate the worst obstacles. You are the embodiment of the highest compassion.

यस्याः स्वरूपं ब्रह्मादयो न जानन्ति तस्मादुच्यते अज्ञेया । यस्या अन्तो न लभ्यते तस्मादुच्यते अनन्ता । यस्या लक्ष्यं नोपलक्ष्यते तस्मादुच्यते अलक्ष्या । यस्या जननं नोपलभ्यते तस्मादुच्यते अजा । एकैव सर्वत्र वर्तते तस्मादुच्यते एका । एकैव विश्वरूपिणी तस्मादुच्यते नैका । अत एवोच्यते अज्ञेयानन्तालक्ष्याजैका नैकेति ॥२३॥

23. *yasyāḥ svarūpaṁ brahmādayo na jānanti tasmāducyate ajñeyā* । *yasyā anto na labhyate tasmāducyate anantā* । *yasyā lakṣyaṁ nopalakṣyate tasmāducyate alakṣyā* । *yasyā jananaṁ nopalabhyate tasmāducyate ajā* । *ekaiva sarvatra vartate tasmāducyate ekā* । *ekaiva viśvarūpiṇī tasmāducyate naikā* । *ata evocyate ajñeyānantālakṣyājaikā naiketi* ॥

Her true nature is not comprehended by *Brahmā* and others, therefore she is called Incomprehensible. Her end is not traceable, therefore she is called Infinite. She can neither be observed nor beheld, therefore she is called Unobservable. Her origin is Inconceivable, therefore she is called Unborn. She alone prevails everywhere, therefore she is called One and Only. She is the one who is the true nature of the entire universe, therefore she is called Not-One but Many. Hence, she is called Incomprehensible, Infinite, Unobservable, Unborn, One and Only; and (also) One but Many.

मन्त्राणां मातृका देवी शब्दानां ज्ञानरूपिणी ।
ज्ञानानां चिन्मयातीता* शून्यानां शून्यसाक्षिणी ।
यस्याः परतरं नास्ति सैषा दुर्गा प्रकीर्तिता ।।२४।।

24. *mantrāṇāṁ mātṛkā devī śabdānāṁ jñānarūpiṇī* ।
jñānānāṁ cinmayātītā * *śūnyānāṁ śūnyasākṣiṇī* ।
yasyāḥ paratarаṁ nāsti saiṣā durgā prakīrtitā ।।

Among *mantras,* the Goddess is the Mother Syllable. Among words, she is of the Nature of Knowledge. Among forms of knowledge, she is the Supreme Consciousness and among voids, she is the Witness of the Voids. She verily is known as *Durgā,* beyond whom there is none.

तां दुर्गां दुर्गमां देवीं दुराचारविघातिनीम् ।
नमामि भवभीतोऽहं संसारार्णवतारिणीम् ।।२५।।

25. *tāṁ durgāṁ durgamāṁ devīṁ durācāravighātinīm* ।
namāmi bhavabhīto 'haṁ saṁsārārṇavatāriṇīm ।।

I pay obeisance to that *Durgā,* the Impassable One, who destroys depravity and delivers from the ocean of birth and death, afraid as I am of metempsychosis.

इदमथर्वशीर्षं योऽधीते स पञ्चाथर्वशीर्षजपफलमाप्नोति । इदमथर्वशीर्षमज्ञात्वा योऽर्चां स्थापयति – शतलक्षं प्रजप्त्वापि सोऽर्चासिद्धिं न विन्दति । शतमष्टोत्तरं चास्य पुरश्चर्याविधिः स्मृतः ।

idamatharvaṣīrṣaṁ yo 'dhīte sa pañcātharvaśīrṣa-japaphalamāpnoti । *idamatharvaśīrṣamajñatvā yo 'rcāṁ sthāpayati – śatalakṣaṁ prajaptvāpi so 'rcāsiddhiṁ na vindati* । *śatamaṣṭottaraṁ cāsya purścaryāvidhiḥ smṛtaḥ* ।

---

* Another recension (hereafter AR) : चिन्मयानंदा cinmayānandā

दशवारं पठेद् यस्तु सद्यः पापैः प्रमुच्यते ।
महादुर्गाणि तरति महादेव्याः प्रसादतः ।।26।।

26. *daśavāraṁ paṭhed yastu sadyaḥ pāpaiḥ pramucyate* ।
mahādurgāṇi tarati mahādevyāḥ prasādataḥ ।।

He who studies this *Atharvaśīrṣa*, reaps the fruit of chanting the five *Atharvaśīrṣas.* He who, without knowing this *Atharvaśīrṣa* installs the deity for worship does not ever attain to accomplishment even if he recites millions of *mantras.* The rule for its initiatory rite is that it should be recited one hundred and eight times.

He who recites it ten times is instantly delivered from sins and by the grace of the Great Goddess, even the worst of his difficulties and obstructions are allayed.

सायमधीयानो दिवसकृतं पापं नाशयति । प्रातरधीयानो रात्रिकृतं पापं नाशयति । सायं प्रातः प्रयुञ्जानो अपापो भवति । निशीथे तुरीयसंध्यायां जप्त्वा वाक्सिद्धिर्भवति । नूतनायां प्रतिमायां जप्त्वा देवतासांनिध्यं भवति । प्राण-प्रतिष्ठायां जप्त्वा प्राणानां प्रतिष्ठा भवति । भौमाश्विन्यां महादेवीसंनिधौ जप्त्वा महामृत्युं तरति । स महामृत्युं तरति य एवं वेद । इत्युपनिषत् ।।

sāyamadhīyāno divasakṛtaṁ pāpaṁ nāśayati । *prātaradhīyāno rātrikṛtaṁ pāpaṁ nāśayati* । *sāyaṁ prātaḥ prayuñjāno apāpo bhavati* । *niśīthe turīyasandhyāyāṁ japtvā vāksiddhirbhavati* । *nūtanāyāṁ pratimayaṁ japtvā devatāsāṁnidhyaṁ bhavati* । *prāṇapratiṣṭhāyāṁ japtvā prāṇānāṁ pratiṣṭhā bhavati* । *bhaumāśvinyāṁ mahādevīsaṁnidhau japtvā mahāmṛtyuṁ tarati* । *sa mahāmṛtyuṁ tarati ya evam veda* । *ityupaniṣat* ।।

Read in the evening, it alleviates the sins committed during the day. Read in the morning, it alleviates the sins committed at night. He becomes sinless who reads it in the evening and morning. He who performs the fourth *sandhyā* at midnight* achieves speech-accomplishment. If *japa* is performed before the new image of the Goddess, proximity to the Goddess is attained. If *japa* is performed during the course of ceremonial consecration of the image, vital breath (life) is established. If *japa* is performed in the proximity of the Goddess in the *bhaumāśvin* (*amṛtasiddhi*) conjunction**, one is absolved of the Great Death. He who knows it is absolved of the Great Death. This is *upaniṣat*, the knowledge of *Brahman*, which destroys ignorance.

---

* Worshippers of *Śrividyā* must perform four *sandhyās*. *Turīya* means fourth. Fourth worship is performed at midnight.

** *Bhaumāśvin yoga* (conjunction): Conjunction of the Mars and *Aśvin*, the first of the 27 nakṣatras or lunar mansions (consisting of three stars). It is known as the *Amṛtasiddhi* (accomplishment of immortality) *yoga*.

अथ नवार्णविधिः

9. *Atha Navārṇavidhiḥ*

The System of Worship

After reciting the *rātrisūkta* and *devyatharvaśirṣa*; *viniyoga, nyāsa, dhyāna,* etc., may be performed with the *navārṇa mantra* as follows:

श्री गणपतिर्जयति। 'ॐ अस्य श्रीनवार्णमन्त्रस्य ब्रह्मविष्णुरुद्रा ऋषयः, गायत्र्युष्णिगनुष्टुभश्छन्दांसि, श्री महाकालीमहालक्ष्मीमहासरस्वत्यो देवताः, ऐं बीजम्, ह्रीं शक्तिः, क्लीं कीलकम्, श्रीमहाकालीमहालक्ष्मीमहासरस्वतीप्रीत्यर्थे जपे विनियोगः।'

śrī gaṇapatirjayati । *'oṁ asya śrīnavārṇamantrasya brahmaviṣṇurudrā ṛṣayaḥ, gāyatryuṣṇiganuṣṭubhaśchandāṁsi, śrīmahākālīmahālakṣmīmahāsarasvatyo devatāh, aiṁ bījaṁ, hrīṁ śaktiḥ, klīṁ kīlakaṁ, śrīmahākālīmahālakṣmī-mahāsarasvatīprītyarthe jape viniyogaḥ* ।'

May Lord Gaṇapāti be victorious.

Oṁ. Of this *navārṇamantra, Brahmā, Viṣṇu* and *Rudra* are the seers. *Gāyatrī, Uṣṇik* and *Anuṣṭup* are the metres. *Śri Mahākālī, Mahālakṣmī* and *Mahāsaraṣvatī* are the deities. *aiṁ* is the seed, *hrīṁ* is the energy, *klīṁ* is the pin. It is here presented for felicitating *Śrī Mahākālī Mahālakṣmī* and *Mahāsarasvatī,* in the process of quiet repetition (*japa*).

(After reciting this, drop the water.)

ऋष्यादिन्यासः

ṛṣyādinyāsaḥ

Assigning to the seers, etc.

ब्रह्मविष्णुरुद्रऋषिभ्यो नमः, शिरसि। गायत्र्युष्णिगनुष्टुप्छन्दोभ्यो नमः, मुखे । महाकालीमहालक्ष्मीमहासरस्वतीदेवताभ्यो नमः, हृदि । ऐं बीजाय नमः, गुह्ये । ह्रीं शक्तये नमः, पादयोः । क्लीं कीलकाय नमः, नाभौ ।

brahmaviṣṇurudrarṣibhyo namaḥ, śirasi ।
gāyatryuṣṇiganuṣṭupchandobhyo namaḥ, mukhe ।
mahākālīmahālakṣmīmahāsarasvatīdevatābhyo namaḥ,
hṛdi । aiṁ bījāya namaḥ, guhye । hrīṁ śaktaye namaḥ,
pādayoḥ । klīṁ kīlakāya namaḥ, nābhau ।

Obeisance to the seers *Brahmā, Viṣṇu, Rudra*: Head (touch the head with right hand fingers). (Likewise, touch mouth, heart, anus, feet and navel respectively pronouncing the following *mantras*):

Obeisance to *Gāyatrī, Uṣṇik* and *Anuṣṭup* metres: Mouth

Obeisance to the deities *Mahākālī*

Mahālakṣmī and *Mahāsarasvatī* : Heart

Obeisance to the Seed *aiṁ* : Anus

Obeisance to the Energy *hrīṁ* : Feet

Obeisance to the Pin *klīṁ* : Navel.

Following this, wash and purify hands with the following *bīja mantra* (seed *mantra*) :

ॐ ऐं ह्रीं क्लीं चामुण्डायै विच्चे ।

Oṁ aiṁ hrīṁ klīṁ cāmuṇḍāyai vicce ।

and assign the hands.

करन्यास:

karanyāsaḥ

Assigning the hands.

ॐ ऐं अङ्गुष्ठाभ्यां नमः ।

oṁ. aiṁ aṅguṣṭhābhyāṁ namaḥ ।

Oṁ. Obeisance to *aiṁ* through both thumbs. (Touch both the thumbs with the forefingers of each hand).

ॐ ह्रीं तर्जनीभ्यां नमः ।

oṁ hrīṁ tarjanībhyāṁ namaḥ ।

Oṁ. Obeisance to *hrīm* through forefingers. (Touch both the forefingers with thumbs.)

ॐ क्लीं मध्यमाभ्यां नमः ।

oṁ klīṁ madhyamābhyāṁ namaḥ ।

Oṁ. Obeisance to *klīṁ* through the middle fingers. (Touch both the middle fingers with thumbs)

ॐ चामुण्डायै अनामिकाभ्यां नमः ।

oṁ cāmuṇḍāyai anāmikābhyāṁ namaḥ ।

Oṁ. Obeisance to *Cāmuṇḍā* through the ring fingers. (Touch the ring fingers.)

ॐ विच्चे कनिष्ठिकाभ्यां नमः ।

oṁ vicce kaniṣṭhikabhyāṁ namaḥ ।

Oṁ. Obeisance to *vicce* through the little fingers. (Touch the little fingers.)

ॐ ऐं ह्रीं क्लीं चामुण्डायै विच्चे करतलकरपृष्ठाभ्यां नमः ।

oṁ aiṁ hrīṁ klīṁ cāmuṇḍāyai vicce karatalakarapṛṣṭhā-bhyāṁ namaḥ.

Oṁ. Obeisance to *aiṁ hrīṁ klīṁ cāmuṇḍā vicce* through the palms and back of both the hands. (Touch the palms and back of both the hands).

हृदयादिन्यासः

hṛdayādinyāsaḥ

Assigning the heart, etc.

[In this, heart and other organs as indicated are touched with all the five fingers of the right hand]:

ॐ ऐं हृदयाय नमः

oṁ aiṁ hṛdayāya namaḥ

Oṁ. Obeisance to *aiṁ* through the heart : (heart).

ॐ ह्रीं शिरसे स्वाहा

oṁ hrīṁ śirase svāhā

Oṁ. Offering for *hrīṁ* through the head : (head).

ॐ क्लीं शिखायै वषट्

oṁ klīṁ śikhāyai vaṣaṭ

Oṁ. Offering to *klīṁ* through the crown of the head : (crown (tuft) of the head).

ॐ चामुण्डायै कवचाय हुम्

oṁ cāmuṇḍāyai kavacāya huṁ

Oṁ. Salutation to *Cāmuṇḍā* through the armour : (left shoulder with right hand fingers and right shoulder with left hand fingers by crossing the arms).

ॐ विच्चे नेत्रत्रयाय वौषट्

oṁ vicce netratrayāya vauṣaṭ

Oṁ. Offering to *vicce* through the three eyes : (two eyes and middle of the forehead with the tips of the fingers of the right hand).

ॐ ऐं ह्रीं क्लीं चामुण्डायै विच्चे अस्त्राय फट्

oṁ aiṁ hrīṁ klīṁ cāmuṇḍāyai vicce astrāya phaṭ

(Reciting this, move the right hand in a circle above the head from the back, moving leftwards and bring it to the right side; then clap on the left palm with fore and middle fingers.)

अक्षरन्यास:

akṣaranyāsaḥ

Assigning the syllables

[Reading the following *mantras,* touch the indicated organs with the right hand fingers.]

ॐ ऐं नमः शिखायाम् ।

oṁ aiṁ namaḥ śikhāyām ।

Oṁ. Obeisance to *aiṁ* through the crown *(tuft)* of the head: (Crown (tuft) of the head)

ॐ ह्रीं नमः, दक्षिणनेत्रे ।

oṁ hrīṁ namaḥ dakṣiṇanetre ।

Oṁ. Obeisance to *hrīṁ* through the right eye : (right eye)

ॐ क्लीं नमः वामनेत्रे ।

oṁ klīṁ namaḥ, vāmanetre ।

Oṁ. Obeisance to *klīm* through the left eye : (left eye)

ॐ चां नमः, दक्षिणकर्णे ।

oṁ cāṁ namaḥ, dakṣiṇakarṇe ।

Oṁ. Obeisance to *cāṁ* through the right ear : (right ear)

ॐ मुं नमः, वामकर्णे ।

oṁ muṁ namaḥ vāmakarṇe ।

Oṁ. Obeisance to *muṁ* through the left ear : (left ear)

ॐ डां नमः, दक्षिणनासापुटे ।

oṁ ḍāṁ namaḥ dakṣiṇanāsāpuṭe ।

Oṁ. Obeisance to *ḍāṁ* through the right nostril : (right nostril)

ॐ यैं नमः, वामनासापुटे ।

oṁ yaiṁ namaḥ vāmanāsāpuṭe ।

Oṁ. Obeisance to *yaiṁ* through the left nostril : (left nostril)

ॐ विं नमः, मुखे ।

oṁ viṁ namaḥ, mukhe ।

Oṁ. Obeisance to *vim* through the mouth : (mouth)

ॐ च्चें नमः गुह्ये ।

oṁ cceṁ namaḥ guhye ।

Oṁ. Obeisance to cceṁ through the anus : (anus).

(After this, touch all the organs from top to toe with both the hands, reading the seed *mantra.* This should be followed by snapping the fingers in all directions for assigning the directions, with the following *mantras*):

दिङ्न्यासः

diṅnyāsaḥ

Assigning the directions.

ॐ ऐं प्राच्यै नमः ।

oṁ aiṁ prācyai namaḥ ।

Oṁ. Obeisance to *aiṁ* in the East.

ॐ ऐं आग्नेय्यै नमः ।

oṁ aiṁ āgneyyaī namaḥ ।

Oṁ. Obeisance to *aiṁ* in the South-East.

ॐ ह्रीं दक्षिणायै नमः ।

oṁ hrīṁ dakṣiṇāyai namaḥ ।

Oṁ. Obeisance to *hrīṁ* in the South.

ॐ ह्रीं नैर्ऋत्यै नमः ।

oṁ hrīṁ nairṛtyai namaḥ ।

Oṁ. Obeisance to *hrīṁ* in the South-West.

ॐ क्लीं प्रतीच्यै नमः ।

oṁ klīṁ pratīcyai namaḥ ।

Oṁ. Obeisance to *klīṁ* in the West.

ॐ क्लीं वायव्यै नमः ।

oṁ klīṁ vāyavyai namaḥ ।

Oṁ. Obeisance to *klīṁ* in the North-West.

ॐ चामुण्डायै उदीच्यै नमः ।

oṁ cāmuṇḍāyai udīcyai namaḥ ।

Oṁ. Obeisance to *Cāmuṇḍā* in the North.

ॐ चामुण्डायै ऐशान्यै नमः

oṁ cāmuṇḍāyai aiśānyai namaḥ ।

Oṁ. Obeisance to *Cāmuṇḍā* in the North East.

ॐ ऐं ह्रीं क्लीं चामुण्डायै विच्चे ऊर्ध्वायै नमः ।

oṁ aiṁ hrīṁ klīṁ cāmuṇḍāyai vicce ūrdhvāyai namaḥ ।

Oṁ. Obeisance to *hrīṁ klīṁ cāmuṇḍā vicce,* Upwards.

ॐ ऐं ह्रीं क्लीं चामुण्डायै विच्चे भूम्यै नमः ।

oṁ aiṁ hrīṁ klīṁ cāmuṇḍāyai vicce bhūmyai namaḥ ।

Obeisance to *hrīṁ klīṁ cāmuṇḍā vicce,* on Earth.

(Besides the foregoing system of *nyāsa* which has been given according to the prevailing tradition, there are, elsewhere available, *sārasvatanyāsa, mātṛkāgaṇanyāsa, ṣaḍdevīnyāsa, brahmādinyāsa, bījamantranyāsa, vilomabīja-nyāsa, mantra-vyāptinyāsa,* etc.).

ध्यानम्

dhyānaṁ

Meditation

खड्गं चक्रगदेषुचापपरिघाञ्छूलं भुशुण्डीं शिरः
शङ्खं संदधतीं करैस्त्रिनयनां सर्वाङ्गभूषावृताम् ।
नीलाश्मद्युतिमास्यपाददशकां सेवे महाकालिकां
यामस्तौत्स्वपिते हरौ कमलजो हन्तुं मधुं कैटभम् ॥१॥

1. *khaḍgaṁ cakragadeṣucāpaparighāñchūlaṁ bhuśuṇḍīṁ śiraḥ*
śaṅkhaṁ sandadhatīṁ karaistrinayanāṁ sarvāṅgabhūṣāvṛtām ।
nīlāśmadyutimāsyapādadaśakāṁ seve mahākālikāṁ
yāmastautsvapite harau kamalajo hantuṁ madhuṁ kaiṭabhaṁ ॥

I worship Goddess *Māhākālī,* the Supreme Controller of Time, who was invoked by the lotus-born *Brahmā* for slaying *Madhu* and *Kaiṭabha* when Lord *Viṣṇu* had gone to sleep. In her ten hands, she holds a sword, a discus, a mace, an arrow, a bow, a bar, a pike, a missile, a skull and a conch. She has three eyes and all the limbs of her body are adorned with ornaments. She is lustrous like sapphire. She has ten faces and ten feet.

अक्षस्त्रक्परशुं गदेषुकुलिशं पद्मं धनुः कुण्डिकां
दण्डं शक्तिमसिं च चर्म जलजं घण्टां सुराभाजनम्।
शूलं पाश सुदर्शने च दधतीं हस्तैः प्रसन्नाननां
सेवे सैरिभमर्दिनीमिह महालक्ष्मीं सरोजस्थिताम् ॥२॥

2. *akṣasrakparaśuṁ gadeṣukuliśaṁ padmaṁ dhanuḥ kuṇḍikāṁ*
daṇḍaṁ śaktimasiṁ ca carma jalajaṁ ghaṇṭāṁ surābhājanam ।
śūlaṁ pāśasudarśane ca dadhatīṁ hastaiḥ prasannānanāṁ
seve sairibhamardinīmiha mahālakṣmīṁ sarojasthitām ॥

I worship Goddess *Māhālakṣmī*, the Great Bestower of Fortune, of the Benign Disposition, the Destroyer of *Mahiṣāsura*. She is seated on the lotus. In her hands, she holds the rosary of beads, a battle axe, a mace, an arrow, a thunderbolt, a lotus, a bow, a pitcher, a sceptre, a spear, a sword, a shield, a conch, a bell, a wine glass, a pike, a snare and a discus.

घण्टाशूलहलानि शङ्खमुसले चक्रं धनुः सायकं
हस्ताब्जैर्दधतीं घनान्तविलसच्छीतांशुतुल्यप्रभाम्।
गौरीदेहसमुद्भवां त्रिजगतामाधारभूतां महा-
पूर्वामत्र सरस्वतीमनुभजे शुम्भादिदैत्यार्दिनीम् ॥३॥

ghaṇṭāśūlahalāni śaṅkhamusale cakraṁ dhanuḥ sāyakaṁ
hastābjairdadhatīṁ ghanāntavilasacchītāṁśutulyaprabhām।
gaurīdehasamudbhavāṁ trijagatāmādhārabhutāṁ mahā-
pūrvāmatra sarasvatīmanubhaje śuṁbhādidaityārdinīm॥

I unfailingly worship the foremost Goddess, *Māhāsarasvatī*, the Great Bestower of Supreme Knowledge, the Tormentor of Demons *Śuṁbha*, etc. She is manifested from the body of *Gaurī*, the White Complexioned Goddess. She holds in her lotus hands a bell, a pike, a plough, a conch, a pestle, a disc, a bow and an arrow. Her effulgence is like the glow of the autumnal moon. She is the substratum of the three worlds,

(After this, worship the rosary with the *mantra* : ऐं ह्रीं अक्षमालिकायै नमः। *aiṁ hrīṁ akṣamālikāyai namaḥ,* and pray:)

ॐ मां माले महामाये सर्वशक्तिस्वरूपिणि ।
चतुर्वर्गस्त्वयि न्यस्तस्तस्मान्मे सिद्धिदाभव ॥

oṁ māṁ māle mahāmāye sarvaśaktisvarūpiṇi ।
caturvargastvayi nyastastasmānme siddhidā bhava ॥

Oṁ. O My Rosary, the Illusive Great Power! you are of the nature of all Energy. All the four objectives of life are vested in you. Bestow, therefore, all accomplishments on me.

ॐ अविघ्नं कुरु माले त्वं गृह्णामि दक्षिणे करे ।
जपकाले च सिद्ध्यर्थं प्रसीद मम सिद्धये ॥

oṁ avighnaṁ kuru māle tvaṁ gṛhṇāmi dakṣiṇe kare ।
japakāle ca siddhyarthaṁ prasīda mama siddhaye ॥

Oṁ. O Rosary! I take you in my right hand. Remove all obstructions. Be compassionate to me so that I may attain to *siddhi,* accomplishment, and bless me with success.

ॐ अक्षमालाधिपतये सुसिद्धिं देहि देहि सर्वमन्त्रार्थसाधिनि साधय
साधय सर्वसिद्धिंपरिकल्पय परिकल्पय मे स्वाहा ।

oṁ akṣamālādhipataye susiddhiṁ dehi dehi sarva
mantrārthasādhini sādhaya sādhaya sarvasiddhiṁ
parikalpaya parikalpaya me svāhā ।

Oṁ. O Presiding Deity of the Rosary Beads! bless me, bless me with higher accomplishment. Lend me success, lend me success, you who bestow success in achievement of the purport of all *mantras.* Endow me, endow me with all accomplishments: I beseech you with the offering of this prayer.

(After this, quietly repeat (*japa*) 108 times, the *mantra*, ॐ ऐं ह्रीं क्लीं चामुण्डायै विच्चे । *oṁ aiṁ hrīṁ klīṁ cāmuṇḍāyai vicce*– and reading the following *mantra*, offer the *japa* to the Goddess into her left hand.)

गुह्यातिगुह्यगोप्त्री त्वं गृहाणास्मत्कृतं जपम् ।
सिद्धिर्भवतु मे देवि त्वत्प्रसादान्महेश्वरि ॥

guhyātiguhyagoptrī tvaṁ gṛhāṇāsmatkṛtaṁ japam ।
siddhirbhavatu me devi tvatprasādānmaheśvari ॥

O Goddess! you are the protector of the innermost secrets. Kindly accept my quiet recitation (*japa*) of the *mantra*. O Supreme Ruler! may I, with your grace, attain to the ultimate accomplishment.

सप्तशतीन्यासः
10. *Saptaśatīnyāsaḥ*

Assigning the *Saptaśatī*

प्रथममध्यमोत्तरचरित्राणां ब्रह्मविष्णुरुद्रा ऋषयः
श्रीमहाकालीमहालक्ष्मीमहासरस्वत्यो देवताः, गायत्र्युष्णिगनुष्टुभश्छन्दांसि,
नन्दाशाकम्भरीभीमाः शक्तयः, रक्तदन्तिकादुर्गाभ्रामर्यो बीजानि,
अग्निवायुसूर्यास्तत्त्वानि, ऋग्यजुःसामवेदा ध्यानानि, सकलकामनासिद्धये
श्रीमहाकालीमहालक्ष्मीमहासरस्वतीदेवताप्रीत्यर्थे जपे विनियोगः ।

*prathamamadhyamottarcaritrāṇāṁ brahmaviṣṇurudrā ṛṣyaḥ
śrīmahākālīmahālakṣmīmahāsarasvatyo devatāḥ,
gāyatryuṣṇiganuṣṭubhaśchandāṁsi, nandāśākam-
bharībhīmāḥ śaktayaḥ, raktadantikādurgābhrāmaryo bījāni,
agnivāyusūryāstattvāni, ṛgyajuḥsāmavedā dhyānāni,
sakalakāmanā siddhaye
śrīmahākālīmahālakṣmīmahāsarasvatī devatāprītyarthe
jape viniyogaḥ* ।

Of the first, middle and final acts, *Brahmā*, *Viṣṇu* and *Rudra* are the seers. *Śrīmahākālī*, *Mahālakṣmī* and *Mahāsarasvatī* are the deities. *Gāyatrī*, *Uṣṇik* and *Anuṣṭup* are the metres. Goddesses *Nandā*, *Śākambharī* and *Bhīmā* are the Energies. *Raktadantikā*, *Durgā* and *Bhrāmarī* are the seeds. Fire, Air and Sun are the essences. *Ṛg*, *Yajuḥ* and *Sāma* are the meditations. It is here presented, this recitation, for accomplishment of all intents and desires and for the felicity of *Śrī Mahākālī*, *Śrī Mahālakṣmī* and *Śrī Mahāsarasvatī*.

ॐ खड्गिनी शूलिनी घोरा गदिनी चक्रिणी तथा ।
शङ्खिनी चापिनी बाणभुशुण्डी परिघायुधा ।।१।।

अङ्गुष्ठाभ्यां नमः ।

1. *oṁ khaḍginī śūlinī ghorā gadinī cakriṇī tathā* ।
śaṅkhinī cāpinī bāṇabhuśuṇḍī parighāyudhā ।।

aṅguṣṭhābhyāṁ namaḥ ।

You are *Khaḍginī*, the Wielder of the Sword; *Śulinī*, the Wielder of the Pike; *Ghorā*, the Formidable One; *Gadinī*, the Wielder of the Mace and *Cakriṇī*, the Wielder of the Discus. You are *Śaṅkhinī*, Supporting the Conch; *Cāpinī*, Supporting a Bow and an Arrow; *Bhuśuṇḍī*, a Missile and *Parigha*, a Bar.

Obeisance through the thumbs.

ॐ शूलेन पाहि नो देवि पाहि खड्गेन चाम्बिके ।
घण्टास्वनेन नः पाहि चापज्यानिःस्वनेन च ॥२॥

तर्जनीभ्यां नमः ।

2. *oṁ śulena pāhi no devi pāhi khaḍgena cāmbike* ।
ghaṇṭāsvanena naḥ pāhi cāpajyāniḥsvanena ca ॥

tarjanībhyāṁ namaḥ ।

Protect us O Goddess! with your pike; O Mother! protect us with your sword. Protect us with the sound of your bell and with the twang of your bow.

Obeisance through the forefingers.

ॐ प्राच्यां रक्ष प्रतीच्यां च चण्डिके रक्ष दक्षिणे ।
भ्रामणेनात्मशूलस्य उत्तरस्यां तथेश्वरि ॥३॥

मध्यमाभ्यां नमः ॥

3. *oṁ prācyāṁ rakṣa pratīcyāṁ ca caṇḍike rakṣa dakṣiṇe* ।
bhrāmaṇenātmaśūlasya uttarasyāṁ tatheśvari ॥

madhyamābhyāṁ namaḥ ॥

Protect us O *Caṇḍikā*! in the East as well as in the West. Protect us in the South and, O Supreme Goddess! protect us in the North by revolving your pike.

Obeisance through the middle fingers.

ॐ सौम्यानि यानि रूपाणि त्रैलोक्ये विचरन्ति ते ।
यानि चात्यर्थघोराणि तै रक्षास्मांस्तथा भुवम् ।।४।।
अनामिकाभ्यां नमः ।।

4. *oṁ saumyāni yāni rūpāṇi trailokye vicaranti te* ।
yāni cātyarthaghorāṇitairakṣāsmāṁstathā bhuvam ।।
anāmikābhyāṁ namaḥ ।।

In whichever gentle or frightful forms, you wander in the three worlds, with them, please protect us as well as this earth.

Obeisance through the ring fingers.

ॐ खड्गशूलगदादीनि यानि चास्त्राणितेऽम्बिके ।
करपल्लवसङ्गीनि तैरस्मान् रक्ष सर्वतः ।।५।।
कनिष्ठिकाभ्यां नमः ।।

5. *oṁ khaḍgaśūlagadādīni yāni cāstrāṇite 'mbike* ।
karapallavasaṅgīni tairasmān rakṣa sarvataḥ ।।
kaniṣṭhikābhyāṁ namaḥ ।।

Sword, pike, mace and whichever other weapons are held in the palms of your hands, O Mother, protect us with them in all directions.

Obeisance through the little fingers.

ॐ सर्वस्वरूपे सर्वेशे सर्वशक्तिसमन्विते ।
भयेभ्यस्त्राहि नो देवि दुर्गे देवि नमोऽस्तु ते ।।६।।
करतलकरपृष्ठाभ्यां नमः ।।

6. *oṁ sarvasvarūpe sarveśe sarvaśaktisamanvite* ।
bhayebhyastrāhi no devi durge devi namo 'stu te ।।
karatalakarapṛṣṭhābhyāṁ namaḥ ।।

Obeisance to you O Goddess *Durgā*! you are the True Nature of all, you are the Supreme Authority of all. You are endowed with all powers. Protect us from all fears.

Obeisance through the palm and back of hands.

ॐ खड्गिनी शूलिनीघोरा॰ ..... हृदयाय नमः ।

oṁ khaḍginī śūlinī ghorā॰ ..... hṛdayāya namaḥ ।

Oṁ. The Wielder of the Sword and Pike, the Formidable One॰ ..... Obeisance to you through the heart.

ॐ शूलेन पाहि नो देवि॰ ..... शिरसे स्वाहा ।

oṁ śūlena pāhi no devi॰ ..... śirase svāhā ।

Oṁ. Protect us, O Goddess, with the pike॰.....

Obeisance through the head.

ॐ प्राच्यां रक्ष प्रतीच्यां च॰ ..... शिखायैवषट् ।

oṁ prācyāṁ rakṣa pratīcyāṁ ca॰ ..... śikhāyai vaṣaṭ ।

Oṁ. Protect us in the East and in the North ..... Offering through the crown (tuft) of the head.

ॐ सौम्यानि यानि रूपाणि॰ ..... कवचाय हुम् ।

oṁ saumyāni yāni rūpāṇi॰ ..... kavacāya huṁ ।

Oṁ. Whichever your gentle forms॰ ..... Offering through the armour. (By crossing arms, touching the left shoulder with the right hand and the right shoulder with the left hand.)

ॐ खड्गशूलगदादीनि॰ ..... नेत्रत्रयायवौषट्

oṁ khaḍgaśūlagadādīni॰ ..... netratrayāya vauṣaṭ

Oṁ. Sword, pike, mace, etc.॰ ......Offering through the three eyes.

ॐ सर्वस्वरूपे सर्वेशे॰ ..... अस्त्राय फट्

oṁ sarvasvarūpe sarveśe॰ ..... astrāya phaṭ

Oṁ. O the True Nature of All! the Ruler of All॰ .....

Reciting this, move the right hand in a circle above the head from the back moving leftwards and bring it to the right side; then clap on the left palm with fore and middle fingers.*

ध्यानम्

dhyānam

Meditation

विद्युद्दामसमप्रभां मृगपतिस्कन्धस्थितां भीषणां
कन्याभिः करवालखेटविलसद्धस्ताभिरासेविताम् ।
हस्तैश्चक्रगदासिखेटविशिखांश्चापं गुणं तर्जनीं
बिभ्राणमनलात्मिकां शशिधरां दुर्गां त्रिनेत्रां भजे ॥

vidyuddāmasamaprabhāṁ mṛgapatiskandhasthitāṁ bhīṣaṇāṁ
kanyābhiḥ karavālakheṭa vilasaddhastābhirāsevitām।
hastaiścakragadāsikheṭaviśikhāṅścāpaṁ guṇaṁ tarjanīṁ
bibhrāṇamanalātmikāṁ śaśidharāṁ durgāṁ trinetrāṁ bhaje ॥

I meditate upon the Three-Eyed *Durgā*, dazzling like the fire. She is effulgent like lightning, sits on the shoulder of the lion, the king of beasts, and bears formidable looks. Maidens holding scimitars and shields in their hands attend upon her. In her hands, she wields the discus, mace, sword, shield, arrow and bow and *tarjanī-mudrā*, the warning sign. The moon adorns her head.

---

* The text of the above *mantras*, which has been given earlier and repeated here in brief, should be chanted in full with actions as indicated.

श्रीदुर्गासप्तशती

11. *Śrīdurgāsaptaśatī*

Seven Hundred Verses to *Durgā*

प्रथम चरित

Prathama Carita

The First Act

(Chapter One)

श्रीमहाकालीमाहात्म्यम्

Śrī Mahākālīmāhātmyam

Glory of Śrīmahākālī

विनियोग:
Viniyogaḥ
Presentation

ॐ प्रथमचरित्रस्य ब्रह्मा ऋषिः, महाकाली देवता, गायत्री छन्दः, नन्दा शक्तिः, रक्तदन्तिका बीजम्, अग्निस्तत्त्वम्, ऋग्वेदः स्वरूपम्, श्रीमहाकालीप्रीत्यर्थे प्रथमचरित्रजपे विनियोगः ।

oṁ prathamacaritrasya brahmā ṛṣiḥ, mahākālī devatā, gāyatrī chandaḥ, nandā śaktiḥ, raktadantikā bījaṁ, agnistattvaṁ, ṛgvedaḥ svarūpaṁ, śrīmahākālī prītyarthe prathamacaritrajape viniyogaḥ ।

Oṁ. Of this First Act, *Brahmā* is the seer, *Mahākālī* is the deity, *Gāyatrī* is the metre, *Nandā* is the energy, *Raktadantikā* is the seed, *Agni* (Fire) is the essence, *Ṛgveda* is the true nature. Presented here is the recitation of the First Act for the felicity of *Śrī Mahākālī.*

प्रथमोऽध्यायः

prathamo 'dhyāyaḥ

Chapter One

[The Seer *Medhā* describes the glory of the Goddess to the king *Suratha* and the trader *Samādhi* in this episode of slaying of the demons *Madhu* and *Kaiṭabha* by the Goddess.]

ध्यानम्

dhyānam

Meditation

ॐ खड्गं चक्रगदेषुचापपरिघाञ्छूलं भुशुंडीं शिरः
शङ्खं संदधतीं करैस्त्रिनयनां सर्वाङ्गभूषावृताम् ।
नीलाश्मद्युतिमास्य पाददशकां सेवे महाकालिकां
यामस्तौत्स्वपिते हरौ कमलजो हन्तुं मधुं कैटभम् ॥

oṁ khaḍgaṁ cakragadeṣucāpaparighañcchūlaṁ bhuṣuṇḍīṁ śiraḥ
śaṅkhaṁ sandadhatīṁ karaistrinayanāṁ sarvāṅgabhūṣāvṛtām ।
nīlāśmadyutimāsyapādadaśakāṁ seve mahākālikāṁ
yāmastautsvapite harau kamalajo hantuṁ madhuṁ kaiṭabham ॥

I WORSHIP GODDESS *MAHĀKĀLĪ*, THE SUPREME CONTROLLER OF TIME, WHO WAS INVOKED BY THE LOTUS-BORN *BRAHMĀ* FOR SLAYING *MADHU* AND *KAIṬABHA*, WHEN LORD *VIṢṆU* HAD GONE TO SLEEP. IN HER TEN HANDS, SHE HOLDS A SWORD, A DISCUS, A MACE, AN ARROW, A BOW, A BAR, A PIKE, A MISSILE, A SKULL AND A CONCH. SHE HAS THREE EYES AND ALL THE LIMBS OF HER BODY ARE ADORNED WITH ORNAMENTS. SHE IS LUSTROUS LIKE SAPPHIRE. SHE HAS TEN FACES AND TEN FEET.

ॐ नमश्चण्डिकायै

oṁ namaścaṇḍikāyai

Oṁ. Obeisance to *Caṇḍikā*, the slayer of the demon *Caṇḍa*

ॐ ऐं मार्कण्डेय उवाच ।।१।।

1. *oṁ aiṁ mārkaṇḍeya uvāca*

सावर्णिः सूर्यतनयो यो मनुः कथ्यतेऽष्टमः ।
निशामय तदुत्पत्तिं विस्तराद् गदतो मम ।।२।।

2. *sāvarṇiḥ sūryatanayo yo manuḥ kathyate 'ṣṭamaḥ* ।
niśāmaya tadutpattiṁ vistarād gadato mama ।।

Oṁ. aiṁ Mārkaṇḍeya said

Sāvarṇi was the son of Sun and known as the eighth *Manu.* Now listen, I shall tell, in detail, the story of his birth.

महामायानुभावेन यथा मन्वन्तराधिपः ।
स बभूव महाभागः सावर्णिस्तनयो रवेः ।।३।।

3. *mahāmāyānubhāvena yathā manvantarādhipaḥ* ।
sa babhūva mahābhāgaḥ sāvarṇistanayo raveḥ ।।

(I shall narrate) how, by the grace of *Mahāmāyā,* the Great Illusive Power, the blessed *Sāvarṇi,* the son of Sun, became the Lord of one era of *Manu.*

स्वारोचिषेऽन्तरे पूर्वं चैत्रवंशसमुद्भवः ।
सुरथो नाम राजाभूत्समस्ते क्षितिमण्डले ।।४।।

4. *svārociṣe 'ntare pūrvaṁ caitravaṁśasamudbhavaḥ* ।
suratho nāma rājābhūtsamaste kṣitimaṇḍale ।।

In the ancient times, there was a king, *Suratha.* He was born in the *Caitra* dynasty, during the era of *Svārociṣa Manu.* He (*Suratha*) ruled over the entire earth.

तस्य पालयतः सम्यक् प्रजाः पुत्रानिवौरसान् ।
बभूवुः शत्रवो भूपाः कोलाविध्वंसिनस्तदा ॥५॥

5. *tasya pālayataḥ samyak prajāḥ putrānivaurasān* ।
babhūvuḥ śatravo bhūpāḥ kolāvidhvaṁsinastadā ॥

He looked after his subjects like his children. Still the *Kolāvidhvaṁsī* (destroyers of *Kolā*) clan of *kṣatriyas* became his enemies.

तस्य तैरभवद् युद्धमतिप्रबलदण्डिनः ।
न्यूनैरपि स तैर्युद्धे कोलाविध्वंसिभिर्जितः ॥६॥

6. *tasya tairabhavad yuddhamatiprabaladaṇḍinaḥ* ।
nyūnairapi sa tairyuddhe kolāvidhavaṁsibhirjitaḥ ॥

Although *Suratha* was a formidable ruler and the *Kolāvidhvaṁsī* were less in number (than the king's forces), the king was vanquished by them.

ततः स्वपुरमायातो निजदेशाधिपोऽभवत् ।
आक्रान्तः स महाभागस्तैस्तदा प्रबलारिभिः ॥७॥

7. *tataḥ svapuramāyāto nijadeśādhipo'bhavat* ।
ākrāntaḥ sa mahābhāgastaistadā prabalāribhiḥ ॥

अमात्यैर्बलिभिर्दुष्टैर्दुर्बलस्य दुरात्मभिः ।
कोशो बलं चापहृतं तत्रापि स्वपुरे ततः ॥८॥

8. *amātyairbalibhirduṣṭairdurbalasya durātmabhiḥ* ।
kośo balaṁ cāpahṛtaṁ tatrāpi svapure tataḥ ॥

Thereafter, he returned to his city and ruled over his own country (no longer remaining the emperor of the earth). There too, the powerful enemies invaded the blessed king. (Seeing him weak and powerless), the strong and treacherous ministers usurped his treasure and the armed forces.

ततो मृगयाव्याजेन हृतस्वाम्यः स भूपतिः ।
एकाकी हयमारुह्य जगाम गहनं वनम् ।।९।।

9. *tato mṛgayāvyājena hṛtasvāmyaḥ sa bhūpatiḥ* ।
ekākī hayamāruhya jagāma gahanaṁ vanam ।।

Then the king, having lost his lordship, left alone on a horse for a dense forest under the pretext of hunting.

स तत्राश्रममद्राक्षीद् द्विजवर्यस्य मेधसः ।
प्रशान्तश्वापदाकीर्णं मुनिशिष्योपशोभितम् ।।१०।।

10. *sa tatrāśramamadrākṣīd dvijavaryasya medhasaḥ* ।
praśāntaśvāpadākīrṇaṁ muniśiṣyopaśobhitam ।।

There he saw the hermitage of the noble sage *Medhā*. It was the sanctuary of many beasts living (together) peacefully and was adorned by the sage's disciples.

तस्थौ कंचित्स कालं च मुनिना तेन सत्कृतः ।
इतश्चेतश्चविचरंस्तस्मिन्मुनिवराश्रमे ।।११।।

11. *tasthau kañcitsakālaṁ ca muninā tena satkṛtaḥ* ।
itaścetaśca vicaraṁstasminmunivarāśrame ।।

Receiving the sage's hospitality, he stayed in the former's hermitage for sometime, wandering here and there.

सोऽचिन्तयत्तदा तत्र ममत्वाकृष्टचेतन[1]: ।
मत्पूर्वैः पालितं पूर्वं मयाहीनं पुरं हि तत् ।।१२।।

12. *so 'cintayattadā tatra mamatvākṛṣṭacetanaḥ*[1] ।
matpūrvaiḥ pālitaṁ pūrvaṁ mayā hīnaṁ puraṁ hi tat ।।

मद्भृत्यैस्तैरसद्वृत्तैर्धर्मतः पाल्यते न वा ।
न जाने स प्रधानो मे शूरहस्ती सदामदः ।।१३।।

13. *madbhṛtyaistairasadvṛttairdharmataḥ pālyate na vā* ।
na jāne sa pradhāno me śūrahastī sadāmadaḥ ।।

---

[1] Another reading (hereafter AR): ममत्वाकृष्टमानसः *mamatvākṛṣṭa-mānasaḥ*

मम वैरिवशं यातः कान् भोगानुपलप्स्यते ।
ये ममानुगता नित्यं प्रसादधनभोजनैः ।।१४।।

14. *mama vairivaśaṁ yātaḥ kān bhogānupalapsyate* ।
ye mamānugatā nityaṁ prasādadhanabhojanaiḥ ।।

अनुवृत्तिं ध्रुवं तेऽद्य कुर्वन्त्यन्यमहीभृताम् ।
असम्यग्व्ययशीलैस्तैः कुर्वद्भिः सततं व्ययम् ।।१५।।

15. *anuvṛttiṁ dhruvaṁ te 'dya kurvantyanyamahībhṛtām* ।
asamyagvyayaśīlaistaiḥ kurvadbhiḥ satataṁ vyayam ।।

संचितः सोऽतिदुःखेन क्षयं कोशो गमिष्यति ।
एतच्चान्यच्च सततं चिन्तयामास पार्थिवः ।।१६।।

16. *sañcitaḥ so 'tiduḥkhena kṣayaṁ kośo gamiṣyati* ।
etaccānyacca satataṁ cintayāmāsa parthivaḥ ।।

There, then, his mind led astray by a sense of attachment, he started worrying: 'The city which was once nurtured by my ancestors, is now without me.. Is it now being looked after by my unscrupulous servants or not; in accordance with the prescribed rules of law? I do not know what ordeal my brave elephant, who always used to be in high spirits, is going through at the hands of my enemies. Those who were pampered by me with condescension, food and fortune and followed me would, most certainly, be serving the other kings. The treasure which I had earned with great pain would now be in the hands of the indiscreet spendthrifts and, being recklessly spent and squandered by them, would by now be empty.' The king constantly brooded over these and other matters.

तत्र विप्राश्रमाभ्याशे वैश्यमेकं ददर्श सः ।
स पृष्टस्तेन कस्त्वं भो हेतुश्चागमनेऽत्र कः ।।१७।।

17. *tatra viprāśramābhyāśe vaiśyamekaṁ dadarśa saḥ* ।
sa pṛṣṭastena kastvaṁ bho hetuścāgamane 'tra kaḥ ।।

सशोक इव कस्मात्त्वं दुर्मना इव लक्ष्यसे ।
इत्याकर्ण्य वचस्तस्य भूपतेः प्रणयोदितम् ।।१८।।

18. *saśoka iva kasmāttvaṁ durmanā iva lakṣyase* ।
ityākarṇya vacastasya bhūpateḥ praṇayoditam ।।

प्रत्युवाच स तं वैश्यः प्रश्रयावनतो नृपम् ।।१९।।

19. *pratyuvāca sa taṁ vaiśyaḥ praśrayāvanato nṛpam* ।।

There, in the vicinity of the hermitage, he saw a *vaiśya* (trader) and asked him. 'Who are you and what is the purpose of your arrival here? Why, as if struck by grief, do you appear to be so upset ?' Hearing these words, spoken by the king out of concern, the trader bowed and humbly replied.

वैश्य उवाच ।।२०।।

20. *vaiśya uvāca*

समाधिर्नाम वैश्योऽहमुत्पन्नो धनिनां कुले ।।२१।।

21. *samādhirnāma vaiśyo 'hamutpanno dhaninām kule* ।।

The trader said

My name is *Samādhi*, I am a trader born in an affluent family.

पुत्रदारैर्निरस्तश्च धनलोभादसाधुभिः ।
विहीनश्च धनैदरैः पुत्रैरादाय मे धनम् ।।२२।।

22. *putradārairnirastaśca dhanalobhādasādhubhiḥ* ।
vihīnaśca dhanairdāraiḥ putrairādāya me dhanam ।।

वनमभ्यागतो दुःखी निरस्तश्चाप्तबन्धुभिः ।
सोऽहं न वेद्मि पुत्राणां कुशलाकुशलात्मिकाम् ।।२३।।

23. *vanamabhyāgato duḥkhī nirastaścāptabandhubhiḥ* ।
so 'haṁ na vedmi putrāṇāṁ kuśalākuśalātmikām ।।

प्रवृत्तिं स्वजनानां च दाराणां चात्र संस्थितः ।
किं नु तेषां गृहे क्षेममक्षेमं किं नु साम्प्रतम् ।।२४।।

24. *pravṛttiṁ svajanānāṁ ca dārāṇāṁ cātra saṁsthitaḥ* ।
kiṁ nu teṣāṁ gṛhe kṣemamakṣemaṁ kiṁ nu sāṁpratam ।।

कथं ते किं नु सद्वृत्ता दुर्वृत्ता किं नु मे सुताः ।।२५।।

25. *kathaṁ te kiṁ nu sadvṛttā durvṛttā kiṁ nu me sutāḥ* ।।

My wicked wives and sons, lusting for my wealth, have banished me. Deprived of wealth by my wives and sons who have usurped it, I have come to this forest, anguished and forsaken by my kith and kin. Staying here, I am not aware of the well-being or otherwise of my sons and wives, I do not know their intentions, whether, as of now, they are safe at home or not, whether my sons are observing righteous conduct or are vile.

राजोवाच ।।२६।।

26. *rājovāca*

यैर्निरस्तो भवांल्लुब्धैः पुत्रदारादिभिर्धनैः ।।२७।।

27. *yairnirasto bhavānllubdhaiḥ putradārādibhirdhanaiḥ* ।।

तेषु किं भवतः स्नेहमनुबध्नाति मानसम् ।।२८।।

28. *teṣu kiṁ bhavataḥ snehamanubadhnāti mānasam* ।।

The king said

Why does your mind nurture the ties of affection for those greedy wives and sons who have banished you for money?

वैश्य उवाच ।।२९।।

29. *vaiśya uvāca*

एवमेतद्यथा प्राह भवानस्मद्गतं वचः ।।३०।।

30. *evametadyathā prāha bhavānasmadgataṁ vacaḥ*

The trader said

What you speak of me is quite true.

किं करोमि न बध्नाति मम निष्ठुरतां मनः ।
यैः संत्यज्य पितृस्नेहं धनलुब्धैर्निराकृतः ॥३१॥

31. *kiṁ karomi na badhnāti mama niṣṭhuratāṁ manaḥ* ।
yaiḥ saṁtyajya pitṛsnehaṁ dhanalubdhairnirākṛtaḥ ॥

पतिस्वजनहार्दं च हार्दि तेष्वेव मे मनः ।
किमेतन्नाभिजानामि जानन्नपि महामते ॥३२॥

32. *patisvajanahārdaṁ ca hārdi teṣveva me manaḥ* ।
kimetannābhijānāmi jānannapi mahāmate ॥

यत्प्रेमप्रवणं चित्तं विगुणेष्वपि बन्धुषु ।
तेषां कृते मे निःश्वासो दौर्मनस्यं च जायते ॥३३॥

33. *yatpremapravaṇaṁ cittaṁ viguṇeṣvapi bandhuṣu* ।
teṣām kṛte me niḥśvāso daurmanasyaṁ ca jāyate ॥

What shall, O Noble One, I do? My heart refuses to be ruthless. It still yearns for love of those who, for their lust for money, have forsaken the love of their father, husband and nearest kin. Why is it, I know and yet know not, that this my heart should be so full of love for those worthless relatives, should breathe heavy for their sake and be so afflicted with sorrow ?

करोमि किं यन्न मनस्तेष्वप्रीतिषु निष्ठुरम् ॥३४॥

34. *karomi kiṁ yanna manasteṣvaprītiṣu niṣṭhuram* ॥

What must I do since my heart does not assume ruthlessness for those unloving persons?

मार्कण्डेय उवाच ॥३५॥

35. *mārkaṇḍeya uvāca* ॥

ततस्तौ सहितौ विप्र तं मुनिं समुपस्थितौ ॥३६॥

36. *tatastau sahitau vipra taṁ muniṁ samupasthitau* ॥

समाधिर्नाम वैश्योऽसौ स च पार्थिवसत्तमः ।
कृत्वा तु तौ यथान्यायं यथार्हं तेन संविदम् ।।३७।।

37. *samādhirnāma vaiśyo 'sau sa ca pārthivasattamaḥ* ।
kṛtvā tu tau yathānyāyaṁ yathārhaṁ tena saṁvidam ।।

उपविष्टौ कथाः काश्चिच्चक्रतुर्वैश्यपार्थिवौ ।।३८।।

38. *upaviṣṭau kathāḥ kāściccakraturvaiśyapārthivau* ।।

Mārkaṇḍeya said

Then, O Sage! both, the trader *Samādhi* and the noble king (*Suratha*) presented themselves before the sage (*Medhā*). After observing due courtesies and congenialities, the trader and the king sat down and initiated some conversation.

राजोवाच ।।३९।।

39. *rājovāca* ।।

भगवंस्त्वामहं प्रष्टुमिच्छाम्येकं वदस्व तत् ।।४०।।

40. *bhagavanstvāmahaṁ praṣṭumicchāmyekaṁ vadasva tat* ।।

The King said

O Revered Seer! I want to ask you a question. Please give me the answer.

दुःखाय यन्मे मनसः स्वचित्तायत्ततां विना ।
ममत्वं गतराज्यस्य राज्याङ्गेष्वखिलेष्वपि ।।४१।।

41. *duḥkhāya yanme manasaḥ svacittāyattatāṁ vinā* ।
mamatvaṁ gatarājyasya rājyāṅgeṣvakhileṣvapi ।।

Since my mind is not under my control, I suffer from agony. Although I have lost my kingdom as well as all its limbs, I yet cannot overcome attachment to them.

जानतोऽपि यथाज्ञस्य किमेतन्मुनिसत्तम ।
अयं च निकृतः[2] पुत्रैर्दारैर्भृत्यैस्तथोज्झितः ॥४२॥

42. *jānato 'pi yathājñasya kimetanmunisattama* ।
ayaṁ ca nikṛtaḥ[2] putrairdārairbhṛtyaistathojjhitaḥ ॥

O Noble Sage! what is it that despite knowing that it (the kingdom, etc.) is no longer mine, I suffer like an ignoramus fool. This (trader) too has been forsaken by his sons, wives and servitors.

स्वजनेन च संत्यक्तस्तेषु हार्दी तथाप्यति ।
एवमेष तथाहं च द्वावाप्यत्यन्तदुःखितौ ॥४३॥

43. *svajanena ca saṁtyaktasteṣu hārdī tathāpyati* ।
evameṣa tathāhaṁ ca dvāvāpyatyantaduḥkhitau ॥

Although forsaken by his kith and kin, he yet nurtures great attachment to them. (In this way), he and I are both in great anguish.

दृष्टदोषेऽपि विषये ममत्वाकृष्टमानसौ ।
तत्किमेत[3]न्महाभाग यन्मोहो ज्ञानिनोरपि ॥४४॥

44. *dṛṣṭadoṣe 'pi viṣaye mamatvākṛṣṭamānasau* ।
tatkimeta[3]nmahābhāga yanmoho jñāninorapi ॥

ममास्य च भवत्येषा विवेकान्धस्य मूढता ॥४५॥

45. *mamāsya ca bhavatyeṣā vivekāndhasya mūḍhatā* ॥

We see the evil inherent in it, yet due to attachment our minds are distracted. Why is it then, O Noble Sage, that even the intelligent ones get deluded? My sense of discrimination, as well as his, have been blinded by our imbecility.

---

[2] AR : निष्कृतः *niṣkṛtaḥ*

[3] AR : तत्केनैत *tatkenaita*

ऋषिरुवाच ।।४६।।

46. *ṛṣiruvāca* ।।

ज्ञानमस्ति समस्तस्य जन्तोर्विषयगोचरे ।।४७।।

47. *jñānamasti samastasya jantorviṣayagocare* ।।

The Seer said

All the beings have knowledge of the objects of the senses.

विषयश्च[4]महाभाग याति[5] चैवं पृथक् पृथक् ।
दिवान्धाः प्राणिनः केचिद्रात्रावन्धास्तथापरे ।।४८।।

48. *viṣayaśca[4] mahābhāga yāti[5] caivaṁ pṛthak pṛthak* ।
divāndhāḥ prāṇinaḥ kecidrātrāvandhāstathāpare ।।

But, O Noble One! in each case, the perception of objects by the senses follows a different route. Some beings suffer from day-blindness while the others from night-blindness.

केचिद्दिवा तथा रात्रौ प्राणिनस्तुल्यदृष्टयः ।
ज्ञानिनो मनुजाः सत्यं किं तु ते[6] न हि केवलम् ।।४९।।

49. *keciddivā tathā rātrau prāṇinastulyadṛṣṭayaḥ* ।
jñānino manujāḥ satyaṁ kiṁ tu te[6] na hi kevalam ।।

There are some who have the same vision during the day as well as night. It is true that humans have understanding but they are not the only ones who do,

यतो हि ज्ञानिनः सर्वे पशुपक्षिमृगादयः ।
ज्ञानं च तन्मनुष्याणां यत्तेषां मृगपक्षिणाम् ।।५०।।

50. *yato hi jñāninaḥ sarve paśupakṣimṛgādayaḥ* ।
jñānaṁ ca tanmanuṣyāṇāṁ yatteṣāṁ mṛgapakṣiṇām ।।

---

[4] AR : विषयाश्च *viṣayāśca*

[5] AR : यान्ति: *yānti*

[6] AR : किंनु ते *kiṁnu te*

for all – beasts, birds, animals, etc. – understand. Understanding in humans is as it is in those animals.

मनुष्याणां च यत्तेषां तुल्यमन्यत्तथोभयोः ।
ज्ञानेऽपि सति पश्यैतान् पतङ्गाञ्छावचञ्चुषु ॥५१॥

51. *manuṣyāṇāṁ ca yatteṣāṁ tulyamanyattathobhayoḥ* ।
jñāne 'pi sati paṣyaitān pataṅgāñchāvacañcuṣu ॥

कणमोक्षादृतान्मोहात्पीड्यमानानपि क्षुधा ।
मानुषा मनुजव्याघ्र साभिलाषा सुतान् प्रति ॥५२॥

52. *kaṇamokṣādṛtānmohātpīḍyamānānapi kṣudhā* ।
mānuṣā manujavyāghra sābhilāṣā sutān prati ॥

लोभात्प्रत्युपकाराय नन्वेतान्[7]किं न पश्यसि ।
तथापि ममतावर्त्ते मोहगर्ते निपातिताः ॥५३॥

53. *lobhātpratyupakārāya nanvetān*[7]*kiṁ na paśyasi* ।
tathāpi mamatāvartte mohagarte nipātitāḥ ॥

महामायाप्रभावेण संसारस्थितिकारिणा[8] ।
तन्नात्र विस्मयः कार्यो योगनिद्रा जगत्पतेः ॥५४॥

54. *mahāmāyā prabhāveṇa saṁsārasthitikāriṇā*[8] ।
tannātra vismayaḥ kāryo yoganidrā jagatpateḥ ॥

महामाया हरेश्चैषा[9] तया सम्मोह्यते जगत् ।
ज्ञानिनामपि चेतांसि देवी भगवती हि सा ॥५५॥

55. *mahāmāyā hareścaiṣā*[9] *tayā sammohyate jagat* ।
jñānināmapi cetāṁsi devī bhagavatī hi sā ॥

---

[7] AR: नन्वेते *nanvete*

[8] AR: कारिणः *kāriṇaḥ*

[9] AR: चैतत् *caitat*

बलादाकृष्य मोहाय महामाया प्रयच्छति ।
तया विसृज्यते विश्वं जगदेतच्चराचरम् ॥५६॥

56. *balādākṛṣya mohāya mahāmāyā prayacchati* ।
tayā visṛjyate viṣvaṁ jagadetaccarācaram ॥

सैषा प्रसन्ना वरदा नृणां भवति मुक्तये ।
सा विद्या परमा मुक्तेर्हेतुभूता सनातनी ॥५७॥

57. *saiṣā prasannā varadā nṛṇāṁ bhavati muktaye* ।
sā vidyā paramā mukterhetubhūtā sanātanī ॥

संसारबन्धहेतुश्च सैव सर्वेश्वरेश्वरी ॥५८॥

58. *saṁsārabandhahetuśca saiva sarveśvareśvarī* ॥

This capacity (of understanding) is identical in both humans and them (birds and animals). Look at those birds who, despite having understanding, are out of attachment, putting the grains of food into the beaks of their young ones although they are themselves troubled by hunger. O Valorous King! don't you see that men, despite their faculty of understanding, expect, out of covetousness, reciprocation from their children because fallen into the pit of delusion, they get caught in the whirl of attachment. This is due to the impact of *Mahāmāyā*, the Great Deluding Power, who is the cause of the sustenance of this world. One needs not be surprised about this. This *Mahāmāyā* of Lord *Viṣṇu*, the ruler of this world, is his *Yoganidrā*, the Divine Sleep. By it is the world deluded. That Sovereign Goddess forcefully draws away the consciousness even of the men of knowledge and deludes them. By her is created this entire universe of the animates and the inanimates. On being pleased, she grants the boon of final liberation to men. She is the Supreme Knowledge, the Cause of Salvation, the Eternal Existence; verily she, the Empress of all rulers, is also the cause of worldly bondage.

राजोवाच ॥५९॥

59. *rājovāca* ॥

भगवन् का हि सा देवी महामायेति यां भवान् ॥६०॥

60. *bhagavan kā hi sā devī mahāmāyeti yāṁ bhavān* ॥

ब्रवीति कथमुत्पन्ना सा कर्मास्याश्च[10] किं द्विज ।
यत्प्रभावा[11] च सा देवी यत्स्वरूपा यदुद्भवा ॥६१॥

61. *bravīti kathamutpannā sā karmāsyāśca[10] kiṁ dvija* ।
yatprabhāvā[11] ca sā devī yatsvarūpā yadudbhavā ॥

तत्सर्वं श्रोतुमिच्छामि त्वत्तो ब्रह्मविदां वर ॥६२॥

62. *tatsarvaṁ śrotumicchāmi tvatto brahmavidāṁ vara* ॥

The King said

O Revered Seer! who is that Goddess *Mahāmāyā* about whom you speak? How was she born? What are her actions? O Wise Seer! I want to hear all about her: what is her essential strength? What is her true nature? What is her origin? You are the best among those who are proficient in the Vedic knowledge.

ऋषिरुवाच ॥६३॥

63. *ṛṣiruvāca* ॥

नित्यैव सा जगन्मूर्तिस्तस्या सर्वमिदं ततम्॥६४॥

64. *nityaiva sā jaganmūrtistasyā sarvamidaṁ tatam*

The Seer said

In truth, she is eternal, this world is her form, all this is pervaded by her.

---

[10] AR : कर्म चास्याश्च *karma cāsyāśca*

[11] AR : यत्स्वभावा *yatsvabhāvā*

तथापि तत्समुत्पत्तिर्बहुधा श्रूयतां मम ।
देवानां कार्यसिद्ध्यर्थमाविर्भवति सा यदा ॥६५॥

65. *tathāpi tatsamutpattirbahudhā śrūyatāṁ mama* ।
devānāṁ kāryasiddhyarthamāvirbhavati sā yadā ॥

उत्पन्नेति तदा लोके सा नित्याप्यभिधीयते ।
योगनिद्रां यदा विष्णुर्जगत्येकार्णवीकृते ॥६६॥

66. *utpanneti tadāloke sā nityāpyabhidhīyate* ।
yoganidrāṁ yadā viṣṇurjagatyekārṇavīkṛte ॥

आस्तीर्यशेषमभजत्कल्पान्ते भगवान् प्रभुः ।
तदा द्वावसुरौ घोरौ विख्यातौ मधुकैटभौ ॥६७॥

67. *āstīryaśeṣamabhajatkalpānte bhagavān prabhuḥ* ।
tadā dvāvasurau ghorau vikhyātau madhukaiṭabhau ॥

विष्णुकर्णमलोद्भूतौ हन्तुं ब्रह्माणमुद्यतौ ।
स नाभिकमले विष्णोः स्थितो ब्रह्मा प्रजापतिः ॥६८॥

68. *viṣṇukarṇamalodbhūtau hantuṁ brahmāṇamudyatau* ।
sa nābhikamale viṣṇoḥ sthito brahmā prajāpatiḥ ॥

दृष्ट्वा तावसुरौ चोग्रौ प्रसुप्तं च जनार्दनम् ।
तुष्टाव योगनिद्रां तामेकाग्रहृदयस्थितः ॥६९॥

69. *dṛṣṭvā tāvasurau cograu prasuptaṁ ca janārdanam* ।
tuṣṭāva yoganidrāṁ tāmekāgrahṛdaysthitaḥ ॥

विबोधनार्थाय हरेर्हरिनेत्रकृतालयाम्[12] ।
विश्वेश्वरीं जगद्धात्रीं स्थितिसंहारकारिणीम् ॥७०॥

70. *vibodhanārthāya harerharinetrakṛtālayām*[12] ।
viśveśvarīṁ jagaddhātrīṁ sthitisaṁhārakāriṇīm ॥

---

[12] In some copies ब्रह्मोवाच – *brahmovāca* – follows this line itself and in place of निद्रां भगवतीं – *nidrāṁ bhagavatīṁ* – the next half śloka is स्तौमि निद्रां भगवतीं विष्णोरतुल तेजसः॥ – *staumi nidrāṁ bhagavatīṁ viṣṇoratula-tejasaḥ*॥ 'I eulogise the Revered Goddess, the Sleep of *Viṣṇu* of the incomparable lustre.'

निद्रां भगवतीं विष्णोरतुलां तेजसः प्रभुः ॥७१॥

71. *nidrāṁ bhagavatīṁ viṣṇoratulāṁ tejasaḥ prabhuḥ* ॥

Even so, in multifarious ways is she born. Listen to me. When for accomplishing the objectives of the gods, she manifests herself, she is said to be born in the world although she is eternal. When the whole world had become a single ocean and *Viṣṇu*, the Lord and Master of this universe, had retired to his Divine Sleep on the bed of *Śeṣa*, the Great Serpent of a Thousand Hoods, two frightful demons known as *Madhu* and *Kaiṭabha*, appeared from the dirt of the ears of Lord *Viṣṇu*, ready to kill *Brahmā*. *Brahmā*, the Lord of Progeny, was seated on the lotus of *Viṣṇu*'s navel. When he saw those ferocious demons approaching and Lord *Viṣṇu*, the Protector of his Devotees in deep sleep, Brahmā commenced, with full concentration, invoking that *Yoganidrā*, the Cosmic Divine Sleep, the Upholder, Sustainer and Destroyer of the Universe, the Supreme Sovereign of incomparable refulgence, in order to awaken *Hari* (*Viṣṇu*) in whose eyes she had made her dwelling.

ब्रह्मोवाच ॥७२॥

72. *brahmovāca* ॥

त्वं स्वाहा त्वं स्वधा त्वं हि वषट्कारः स्वरात्मिका ॥७३॥

73. *tvaṁ svāhā tvaṁ svadhā tvaṁ hi vaṣaṭkāraḥ svarātmikā* ॥

सुधा त्वमक्षरे नित्ये त्रिधा मात्रात्मिका स्थिता ।
अर्धमात्रास्थिता नित्या यानुच्चार्या विशेषतः ॥७४॥

74. *sudhā tvamakṣare nitye tridhā mātrātmikā sthitā* ।
ardhamātrā sthitā nityā yānuccāryā viśeṣataḥ ॥

Brahmā said

You are *Svāhā*, the Energy of Fire, you are *Svadhā*, the Will Power, you verily are *Vaṣaṭkāra*, the symbol of oblations. You verily are the life-giving ambrosia. In the eternal syllables of ॐ, you are settled as three syllabic instants (*a*, *u* and *m*) along with the eternal half syllable in the form of a dot(.) which cannot be specifically pronounced.

त्वमेव[13] संध्या सावित्री त्वं देवि जननी परा ।
त्वयैतद्धार्यते विश्वं त्वयैतत्सृज्यते जगत् ।।७५।।

75. *tvameva*[13] *sandhyā sāvitrī tvaṁ devi jananīparā* ।
tvayaitaddhāryate viśvaṁ tvayaitatsṛjyate jagat ।।

You are *Sandhyā*, the Twilight and the Transition between two *yugas* (eras). You are *Sāvitrī*, the Ray of Light and Bestower of Wisdom. You, O Goddess! are the Mother Supreme. This universe is upheld by you, this world is created by you.

त्वयैतत्पाल्यते देवि त्वमत्स्यन्ते च सर्वदा ।
विसृष्टौ सृष्टिरूपा त्वं स्थितिरूपा च पालने ।।७६।।

76. *tvayaitatpālyate devi tvamatsyante ca sarvadā* ।
visṛṣṭau sṛṣṭirūpā tvaṁ sthitirūpā ca pālane ।।

तथा संहृतिरूपान्ते जगतोऽस्य जगन्मये ।
महाविद्या महामाया महामेधा महास्मृतिः ।।७७।।

77. *tatha saṁhṛtirupante jagato 'sya jaganmaye* ।
mahāvidyā mahāmāyā mahāmedhā mahāsmṛtiḥ ।।

O Goddess! by you is this world nurtured and by you it is always brought to dissolution. You are the form of this creation when it is in the process of being created and you, the form of its sustenance when it is sustained. And since, O Pervasive Power of the Universe (*Jaganmayī*)! this world is composed of you, you are the form of

[13] AR : सा त्वं *sā tvaṁ*

annihilation at its end. You are *Mahāvidyā*, the Great Knowledge; *Mahāmāyā*, the Great Illusion; *Mahāmedhā*, the Great Intelligence and *Mahāsmṛti*, the Great Memory.

महामोहा च भवती महादेवी महासुरी[14] ।
प्रकृतिस्त्वं च सर्वस्य गुणत्रयविभाविनी ॥७८॥

78. *mahāmohā ca bhavatī mahādevī mahāsurī*[14] ।
prakṛtistvaṁ ca sarvasya guṇatrayavibhāvinī ॥

You, O Esteemed Lady, are *Mahāmohā*, the Great Delusion; *Mahādevī*, the Great Goddess and *Mahāsurī*, the Supreme Spirit. You are *Prakṛti*, the source of three modes (*sattva, rajas* and *tamas*) which you cause to be perceived in all things and beings.

कालरात्रिर्महारात्रिर्मोहरात्रिश्च दारुणा ।
त्वं श्रीस्त्वमीश्वरी त्वं ह्रीस्त्वं बुद्धिर्बोधलक्षणा ॥७९॥

79. *kālarātrirmahārātrirmoharātriśca dāruṇā* ।
tvaṁ śrīstvamīśvarī tvaṁ hrīstvaṁ buddhirbodhalakṣaṇā ॥

You are *Kālarātri*, the Night of Death; *Mahāratri*, the terrible Long Night (the night of great dissolution) and *Moharātri*, the Night of Delusion. You are *Śrī*, the Great Fortune; you are *Īśvarī*, the Great Empress. You are *Hrī*, Modesty and *Bodhalakṣaṇā* Buddhi, the Ultimate Wisdom symbolising highest intelligence.

लज्जा पुष्टिस्तथा तुष्टिस्त्वं शान्तिः क्षान्तिरेव च ।
खड्गिनी शूलिनी घोरा गदिनी चक्रिणी तथा ॥८०॥

80. *lajjā puṣṭistathā tuṣṭistvaṁ śāntiḥ kṣāntireva ca* ।
khaḍginī śūlinī ghorā gadinī cakriṇī tathā ॥

You are *Lajjā*, Bashfulness; *Puṣṭi*, Strength; *Tuṣṭi*, Satisfaction; *Śānti*, Peace; *Kṣānti*, Forgiveness. You are *Khaḍginī*, Wielder of the Sword; *Śūlinī*, Wielder of the Pike;

---

[14] AR : महेश्वरी *maheśvarī*

Ghorā, the Formidable One; *Gadinī*, Wielder of the Mace and *Cakriṇī*, Wielder of the Discus.

शङ्खिनी चापिनी बाणभुशुण्डीपरिघायुधा ।
सौम्या सौम्यतराशेषसौम्येभ्यस्त्वतिसुन्दरी ॥८१॥

81. *śaṇkhinī cāpinī bāṇabhuśuṇḍīparighāyudhā* ।
saumyā saumyatarāśeṣasaumyebhyastvatisundarī ॥

You are *Śaṅkhinī*, Supporting a Conch; *Cāpinī*, Supporting a Bow, and Wielder of *Bāṇa*, the Arrow, *Bhuśuṇḍī*, the Missile and *Parigha*, the Bar. You are Charming, More Charming, and even among the very charming and beautiful ones, you are the the Most Beautiful.

परापराणां परमा त्वमेव परमेश्वरी ।
यच्च किञ्चित्क्वचिद्वस्तु सदसद्वाखिलात्मिके ॥८२॥

82. *parāparāṇāṁ paramā tvameva parameśvarī* ।
yacca kiñcitkvacidvastu sadasadvākhilātmike ॥

तस्य सर्वस्य या शक्तिः सा त्वं किं स्तूयसे तदा[15]।
यया त्वया जगत्स्रष्टा जगत्पात्यत्ति[16] यो जगत् ॥८३॥

83. *tasya sarvasya yā śaktiḥ sā tvaṁ kiṁ stūyase tadā*[15] ।
yayā tvayā jagatsraṣṭa jagatpātyatti[16] *yo jagat* ॥

सोऽपि निद्रावशं नीतः कस्त्वां स्तोतुमिहेश्वरः ।
विष्णुः शरीरग्रहणमहमीशान एव च ॥८४ ॥

84. *so 'pi nidrāvaśaṁ nītaḥ kastvāṁ stotumiheśvaraḥ* ।
viṣṇuḥ śarīragrahaṇamahamīśāna eva ca ॥

कारितास्ते यतोऽतस्त्वां कः स्तोतुं शक्तिमान् भवेत् ।
सा त्वमित्थं प्रभावैः स्वैरुदारैर्देवि संस्तुता ॥८५॥

85. *kāritāste yato 'tastvāṁ kaḥ stotuṁ śaktimān bhavet* ।
sā tvamitthaṁ prabhāvaiḥ svairudārairdevi saṁstutā ॥

---

[15]AR: मया *mayā*

[16]AR: पातात्ति *pātātti*

मोहयैतौ दुराधर्षावसुरौ मधुकैटभौ ।
प्रबोधं च जगत्स्वामी नीयतामच्युतो लघु ॥८६॥

86. *mohayaītau durādharṣāvasurau madhukaiṭabhau* ॥
prabodhaṁ ca jagatsvāmī nīyatāmacyuto laghu ॥

बोधश्च क्रियतामस्य हन्तुमेतौ महासुरौ ॥८७॥

87. *bodhaśca kriyatāmasya hantumetau mahāsurau* ॥

Among the transcendental and the terrestrial, you are verily the highest. You, verily, are the Supreme Ruler. Whichever and whatever things, existent or inexistent in this universe, you are the Energy of them all. What praise, then, can be offered to you? By you has been put to sleep even that one Lord who is the creator of the world, who sustains the world and who devours the world. Who, then, including *Viṣṇu,* I and *Śiva* who have been embodied by you, is powerful enough to eulogise you? O Goddess! you are lauded by your own generous powers; using them now, delude these unassailable demons, *Madhu* and *Kaiṭabha*; awaken Lord *Viṣṇu,* the Master of the World, from his sleep without delay and endow him with the will to kill these great demons.

ऋषिरुवाच ॥८८॥

88. *ṛṣiruvāca.*

एवं स्तुता तदा देवी तामसी तत्र वेधसा ॥८९॥

89. *evaṁ stutā tadā devī tāmasī tatra vedhasā* ॥

विष्णोः प्रबोधनार्थाय निहन्तुं मधुकैटभौ ।
नेत्रास्यनासिकाबाहुहृदयेभ्यस्तथोरसः ॥९०॥

90. *viṣnoḥ prabodhanārthāya nihantuṁ madhukaiṭabhau* ।
netrāsyanāsikābāhuhṛdayebhyastathorasaḥ ॥

निर्गम्य दर्शने तस्थौ ब्रह्मणोऽव्यक्तजन्मनः ।
उत्तस्थौ च जगन्नाथस्तया मुक्तो जनार्दनः ॥९१॥

91. *nirgamya darśane tasthau brahmaṇo 'vyaktajanmanaḥ* ।
uttasthau ca jagannāthastayā mukto janārdanaḥ ॥

The Seer said

When in order to awaken Lord *Viṣṇu* for slaying *Madhu-Kaiṭabha, Brahmā* thus extolled the Goddess *Tāmasī*, the Deity of Darkness, she exited from his (*Viṣṇu*'s) eyes, mouth, nostrils, arms, heart and chest and stood before the eyes of *Brahmā*, of the Unmanifest Origin. Freed from her, arose (*Viṣṇu*) the Ruler of the World and the Protector of his Devotees,

एकार्णवेऽहि शयनात्ततः स ददृशे च तौ ।
मधुकैटभौ दुरात्मानावतिवीर्यपराक्रमौ ॥९२॥

92. *ekārṇave 'hi śayanāttataḥ sa dadṛeśe ca tau* ।
madhukaiṭabhau durātmānāvativīryaparākramau ॥

from his bed of the Great Serpent (*Śeṣa*) on the infinite expanse of the ocean. Then he saw *Madhu-Kaiṭabha*, the evil-natured and mighty untamable demons.

क्रोधरक्तेक्षणावत्तुं[17] ब्रह्माणं जनितोद्यमौ ।
समुत्थाय ततस्ताभ्यां युयुधे भगवान् हरिः ॥९३॥

93. *krodharakteksaṇāvattuṁ*[17] *brahmāṇaṁ janitodyamau* ।
samutthāya tatastābhyāṁ yuyudhe bhagavān hariḥ ॥

पञ्चवर्षसहस्राणि बाहुप्रहरणो विभुः ।
तावप्यति बलोन्मत्तौ महामायाविमोहितौ ॥९४॥

94. *pañcavarṣasahasrāṇi bāhupraharṇo vibhuḥ* ।
tāvapyati balonmattau mahāmāyā vimohitau ॥

---

[17]AR: क्रोधरक्तेक्षणौ हन्तुं *krodharakteksaṇau hantuṁ*

उक्तवन्तौ वरोऽस्मत्तो व्रियतामिति केशवम् ॥९५॥

95. *uktavantau varo 'smatto vriyatāmiti keśavam.*

Their eyes were bloodshot with anger and they were bent upon devouring *Brahmā.* Then Lord *Hari* (*Viṣṇu*) got up and engaged them in hand to hand combat for five thousand years. Intoxicated as they were with their might and deluded by *Mahāmāyā,* the Great Illusive Power, they offered *Keśava* (*Viṣṇu*) to ask from them the boon of his choice.

श्री भगवानुवाच ॥९६॥

96. *Śrī bhagavānuvāca*

भवतामद्य मे तुष्टौ मम वध्यावुभावपि ॥९७॥

97. *bhavatāmadya me tuṣṭau mama vadhyāvubhāvapi* ॥

किमन्येन वरेणात्र एतावद्धिवृतं मम[18] ॥९८॥

98. *kimanyena vareṇātra etāvaddhivṛtaṁ mama*[18] ॥

The Lord said

If you two are pleased with me, then accept death at my hands. This is all I ask for; what have I to do with any other boon?

ऋषिरुवाच ॥९९॥

99. *ṛṣiruvāca*

वञ्चिताभ्यामिति तदा सर्वमापोमयं जगत् ॥१००॥

100. *vañcitābhyāmiti tadā sarvamāpomayaṁ jagat* ॥

विलोक्य ताभ्यां गदितो भगवान् कमलेक्षणः[19] ।
आवां जहि न यत्रोर्वी सलिलेन परिप्लुता ॥१०१॥

101. *vilokya tābhyāṁ gadito bhagavān kamalekṣaṇaḥ*[19] ।
āvāṁ jahi na yatrorvī salilena pariplutā ॥

---

[18] AR: मया *mayā*

[19] In some copies of the *Mārkaṇḍeya Purāṇa,* the following is an

The Seer said

Thus tricked, when they found that the entire world consisted only of water, they asked the Lotus Eyed Lord : 'Kill us at a place where the earth is not inundated'.

ऋषिरुवाच ॥१०२॥

102. *ṛṣiruvāca*

तथेत्युक्त्वा भगवता शङ्खचक्रगदाभृता ।
कृत्वा चक्रेण वै च्छिन्ने जघने शिरसी तयोः ॥१०३॥

103. *tathetyuktvā bhagavatā śaṅkhacakragadābhṛtā* ।
kṛtvā cakreṇa vai cchinne jaghane śirasī tayoḥ ॥

The Seer said

'So be it,' said the Lord, the Wielder of the Conch, Discus and Mace, and placing the heads of the two, on his loins, chopped them off with the discus.

एवमेषा समुत्पन्ना ब्रह्मणा संस्तुता स्वयम् ।
प्रभावमस्या देव्यास्तु भूयःशृणु वदामि ते ॥ ऐं ॐ ॥१०४॥

104. *evameṣā samutpannā brahmaṇā saṁstutā svayam* ।
prabhāvamasyā devyāstu bhūyaḥ śṛṇu vadāmi te ॥*aiṁ oṁ*॥

This is how, when *Brahma* had extolled her, the Goddess had manifested herself. Now, listen, I shall tell you more about the glory of the Goddess. Aiṁ Oṁ.

इति श्रीमार्कण्डेयपुराणे सावर्णिके मन्वन्तरे देवीमाहात्म्ये

Additional line : प्रीतौ स्वस्तव युद्धेन श्लाघ्यस्त्वं मृत्युरावयोः। *prītau svastava yuddhena ślāghyastvaṁ mṛtyurāvayoḥ*। We two are pleased with your battle and appreciate your desire to kill us.

मधुकैटभवधो नाम प्रथमोऽध्यायः ॥१॥

iti śrīmārkaṇḍeyapurāṇe sāvarṇike manvantare devīmāhātmye madhukaiṭabhavadho nāma prathamo 'dhyāyaḥ ॥1॥

Thus ends the first chapter called Slaying of *Madhu-Kaiṭabhà* during the era of *Sāvarṇi Manu* in the Glory of the Goddess, (narrated) in the *Mārkaṇḍeya Purāṇa.*

उवाच १४, अर्धश्लोकाः २४, श्लोकाः ६६, एवमादितः १०४

uvāca 14, *ardhaślokāḥ* 24, *ślokaḥ* 66 , *evamāditaḥ* 104

uvāca 14, half ślokas 24, ślokas 66, total from the beginning 104.

श्रीदुर्गासप्तशती

Śrīdurgāsaptaśatī

Seven Hundred Verses to *Durgā*

मध्यमचरित

Madhyamacarita

The Middle Act

(Chapters Two-Four)

श्रीमहालक्ष्मीमाहात्म्यम्

Śrīmahālakṣmīmāhātmyam

Glory of *Śrīmahālakṣmī*

विनियोगः

Viniyogaḥ

Presentation

ॐ मध्यमचरित्रस्य विष्णुर्ऋषिः, महालक्ष्मीर्देवता,
उष्णिक्छन्दः, शाकम्भरी शक्तिः, दुर्गा बीजम्,
वायुस्तत्त्वम्, यजुर्वेदः स्वरूपम्,
श्रीमहालक्ष्मीप्रीत्यर्थं मध्यमचरित्रजपे विनियोगः।

oṁ madhyamacaritrasya viṣṇurṛṣiḥ, mahālakṣmīrdevatā,
uṣnikchandaḥ, śākambharī śaktiḥ, durgā bījam,
vāyustattvam, yajurvedaḥ svarūpam, śrīmahālakṣmī-
prityarthaṁ madhyamacaritrajape viniyogaḥ.

Oṁ. Of this Middle Act, *Viṣṇu* is the seer, *Mahālakṣmī* is the deity, *Uṣṇik* is the metre, *Śākambharī* is the energy, *Durgā* is the seed, *Vāyu* (Air) is the essence, *Yajurveda* is the true nature. Presented here is the recitation of the Middle Act for the felicity of *Śrīmahālakṣmī*.

द्वितीयोऽध्यायः

dvitīyo 'dhyāyaḥ

Chapter Two

The Goddess manifests from the lustre of the gods and kills the forces of *Mahiṣāsura*.

ध्यानम्

dhyānam

Meditation

ॐ अक्षस्रक्परशुं गदेषुकुलिशं पद्मं धनुष्कुण्डिकां
दण्डं शक्तिमसिं च चर्म जलजं घण्टां सुराभाजनम् ।
शूलं पाशसुदर्शने च दधतीं हस्तैः प्रसन्नाननां
सेवे सैरिभमर्दिनीमिह महालक्ष्मीं सरोजस्थिताम् ॥

oṁ. akṣasrakparaśuṁ gadeṣukuliśaṁ padmaṁ dhanuṣkuṇḍikāṁ
daṇḍaṁ śaktimasiṁ ca carma jalajaṁ ghaṇṭāṁ surābhājanam ।
śūlaṁ pāṣasudarśane ca dadhatīṁ hastaiḥ prasannānanāṁ
seve sairibhamardinīmiha mahālakṣmīṁ sarojasthitām ॥

OṀ. I WORSHIP GODDESS *MAHĀLAKṢMĪ*, THE GREAT BESTOWER OF FORTUNE, OF THE BENIGN DISPOSITION, THE DESTROYER OF *MAHIṢĀSURA*. SHE IS SEATED ON THE LOTUS. IN HER HANDS, SHE HOLDS THE ROSARY OF BEADS, A BATTLE AXE, A MACE, AN ARROW, A THUNDERBOLT, A LOTUS, A BOW, A PITCHER, A SCEPTRE, A SPEAR, A SWORD, A SHIELD, A CONCH, A BELL, A WINE GLASS, A PIKE, A SNARE AND A DISCUS.

ॐ ह्रीं ऋषिरुवाच ।।१।।

1. *oṁ. hrīṁ ṛṣiruvāca*

देवासुरमभूद्युद्धं पूर्णमब्दशतं पुरा ।
महिषेऽसुराणामधिपे देवानां च पुरन्दरे ।।२।।

2. *devāsuramabhūdyuddhaṁ pūrṇamabdaśataṁ purā* ।।'
mahiṣe 'surāṇāmadhipe devānāṁ ca purandare ।।

Oṁ. Hrīṁ. The Seer said

A war of hundred years raged between the gods and the demons in the ancient times. At that time, *Mahiṣāsura* was the commander of the demons' forces and *Indra*, of the gods.

तत्रासुरैर्महावीर्यैर्देवसैन्यं पराजितम् ।
जित्वा च सकलान् देवानिन्द्रोऽभून्महिषासुरः ।।३।।

3. *tatrāsurairmahāvīryairdevasainyaṁ parājitam* ।
jitvā ca sakalān devānindro 'bhūnmahiṣāsuraḥ ।।

There the mighty demons defeated the armies of the gods. Having vanquished all the gods, *Mahiṣāsura* became *Indra.*

ततः पराजिता देवाः पद्मयोनिं प्रजापतिम् ।
पुरस्कृत्य गतास्तत्र यत्रेशगरुडध्वजौ ।।४।।

4. *tataḥ parājitā devāḥ padmayoniṁ prajāpātim* ।
puraskṛtya gatāstatra yatreśagaruḍadhvajau ।।

Then the defeated gods, led by the lotus-born *Brahmā*, went where there were Lord *Śiva* and Lord *Viṣṇu* whose banner is *Garuḍa.*

यथावृत्तं तयोस्तद्वन्महिषासुरचेष्टितम् ।
त्रिदशाः कथयामासुर्देवाभिभव विस्तरम् ।।५।।

5. *yathāvṛttaṁ tayostadvanmahiṣāsuraceṣṭitam* ।।
tridaśāḥ kathayāmāsurdevābhibhava vistaram ।।

The gods narrated to both of them in factual detail the actions of *Mahiṣāsura* and their defeat.

सूर्येन्द्राग्न्यनिलेन्दूनां यमस्य वरुणस्य च ।
अन्येषां चाधिकारान् स स्वयमेवाधितिष्ठति ।।६।।

6. *sūryendrāgnyanilendūnāṁ yamasya varuṇasya ca* ।
anyeṣāṁ cādhikārān sa svayamevādhitiṣṭhati ।।

(They said): The demon has usurped the authority of Sun, *Indra*, Fire, Air, Moon, *Yama*, *Varuṇa* and the others and has taken over the functions of all.

स्वर्गान्निराकृताः सर्वे तेन देवगणा भुवि ।
विचरन्ति यथा मर्त्या महिषेण दुरात्मना ।।७।।

7. *svargānnirākṛtāḥ sarve tena devagaṇā bhuvi* ।
vicaranti yathā martyā mahiṣeṇa durātmanā ।।

Expelled from heaven by the wicked *Mahiṣa*, all the gods are now wandering on earth like the mortals.

एतद्वः कथितं सर्वममरारिविचेष्टितम् ।
शरणं वः प्रपन्नाः स्मो वधस्तस्य विचिन्त्यताम् ।।८।।

8. *etadvaḥ kathitaṁ sarvamamarāriviceṣṭitam* ।
śaraṇaṁ vaḥ prapannāḥ smo vadhastasya vicintyatām ।।

We have described to you all that the enemy of the gods has done and come in your refuge. Please think of a strategy to kill him.

इत्थं निशम्य देवानां वचांसि मधुसूदनः ।
चकार कोपं शम्भुश्च भ्रुकुटीकुटिलाननौ ।।९।।

9. *itthaṁ niśamya devānāṁ vacāṁsi madhusūdanaḥ* ।
cakāra kopaṁ śambhuśca bhrukuṭīkuṭilānanau ।।

Hearing these words of the gods, the anger of *Viṣṇu*, the Slayer of *Madhu*, and *Śiva* was roused, their brows were raised and visages curved with rage.

ततोऽतिकोपपूर्णस्य चक्रिणोवदनात्ततः ।
निश्चक्राम महत्तेजो ब्रह्मणः शंकरस्य च ।।१०।।

10. *tato 'tikopapūrṇasya cakriṇovadanāttataḥ* ।
niścakrāma mahattejo brahmaṇaḥ śaṅkarasya ca ।।

In that state of extreme anger, great light emanated from the faces of *Viṣṇu*, the Wielder of the Discus, *Brahmā* and *Śivā*.

अन्येषां चैव देवानां शक्रादीनां शरीरतः ।
निर्गतं सुमहत्तेजस्तच्चैक्यं समगच्छत ।।११।।

11. *anyeṣāṁ caiva devānāṁ śakrādīnāṁ śarīrataḥ* ।
nirgataṁ sumahattejastaccaikyaṁ samagacchata ।।

From the bodies of the other gods like *Indra* also, blazing effulgence was released. This effulgence got united and focused.

अतीव तेजसः कूटं ज्वलन्तमिव पर्वतम् ।
ददृशुस्ते सुरास्तत्र ज्वालाव्याप्यदिगन्तरम् ।।१२।।

12. *atīvā tejasaḥ kūṭaṁ jvalantamiva parvatam* ।
dadṛśuste surāstatra jvālāvyāpyadigantaram ।।

There the gods saw the blazing light which appeard like a mountain of fire, its flames spreading in all the directions.

अतुलं तत्र तत्तेजः सर्वदेवशरीरजम् ।
एकस्थं तदभून्नारी व्याप्तलोकत्रयं त्विषा ।।१३।।

13. *atulaṁ tatra tattejaḥ sarvadevaśarīrajam* ।
ekasthaṁ tadabhūnnārī vyāptalokatrayaṁ tviṣā ।।

When this unsurpassable light coming out of the bodies of all the gods got focused in one place, it assumed the form of a woman who permeated all the three worlds.

यदभूच्छाम्भवं तेजस्तेनाजायत तन्मुखम् ।
याम्येन चाभवन् केशा बाहवो विष्णुतेजसा ।।१४।।

14. *yadabhūcchāmbhavaṁ tejastenājāyata tanmukham* ।
yāmyena cābhavan keśā bāhavo viṣṇutejasā ।।

That light which got released from the face of *Śiva*, attained to the form of her face. From *Yama*, the god of Death, came her hair and from the lustre of *Viṣṇu*, her arms.

सौम्येन स्तनोर्युग्मं मध्यं चैन्द्रेण चाभवत् ।
वारुणेन च जङ्घोरू नितम्बस्तेजसा भुवः ।।१५।।

15. *saumyena stanoryugmaṁ madhyaṁ caindreṇa cābhavat* ।
vāruṇena ca jaṅghorū nitambastejasā bhuvaḥ ।।

From the lustre of the Moon, her two breasts were formed and from the lustre of *Indra*, her midriff. Her thighs and shanks came from *Varuṇa*'s light and buttocks from that of Earth.

ब्रह्मणस्तेजसा पादौ तदङ्गुल्योऽर्कतेजसा ।
वसूनां च कराङ्गुल्यः कौबेरेण च नासिका ।।१६।।

16. *brahmaṇastejasā pādau tadaṅgulyo 'rkatejasā* ।।
vasūnāṁ ca karāṅgulyaḥ kaubereṇa ca nāsikā ।।

Her feet appeared from the lustre of *Brahmā*, toes from Sun's, fingers of hands from *Vasus* and nose from *Kubera*'s lustre.

तस्यास्तु दन्ताः सम्भूताः प्राजापत्येन तेजसा ।
नयनत्रितयं जज्ञे तथा पावकतेजसा ।।१७।।

17. *tasyāstu dantāḥ sambhūtāḥ prājāpatyena tejasā* ।
nayanatritayaṁ jajñe tathā pāvakatejasā ।।

From *Prajāpati*'s light appeared her teeth and from that of Fire, her three eyes.

भ्रुवौ च संध्ययोस्तेजः श्रवणावनिलस्य च ।
अन्येषां चैव देवानां सम्भवस्तेजसां शिवा ॥१८॥

18. *bhruvau ca sandhyayostejaḥ śravaṇāvanilasya ca* ।
anyeṣāṁ caiva devānāṁ saṁbhavastejasāṁ śivā ॥

Her brows were produced from the sparkle of *Sandhyā* (transition-time) and ears from *Anila* (Wind). Effulgence of the other gods too contributed to the emergence of the Auspicious Goddess.

ततः समस्तदेवानां तेजोराशिसमुद्भवाम् ।
तां विलोक्य मुदं प्रापुरमरा महिषार्दिताः[1] ॥१९॥

19. *tataḥ samastadevānāṁ tejorāśisamudbhavām* ।
tāṁ vilokya mudaṁ prāpuramarā mahiṣārditāḥ[1] ॥

Tormented by *Mahiṣa*, the gods were delighted to see that Goddess emerging from their accumulated effulgence.

शूलं शूलाद्विनिष्कृष्य ददौ तस्यौ पिनाकधृक् ।
चक्रं च दत्तवान् कृष्णः समुत्पाद्य[2]स्वचक्रतः ॥२०॥

20. *śūlaṁ sūlādviniṣkṛṣya dadau tasyau pinākadhṛk* ।
cakraṁ ca dattavān kṛṣṇaḥ samutpādya[2]*svacakrataḥ* ॥

Śiva, the Wielder of the *Pināka* bow, drew a pike from his own pike and gave it to her and *Viṣṇu* produced a discus from his own discus and presented that to her.

---

[1]Additional reading in some copies after this: ततो देवा ददुस्तस्यै स्वानि स्वान्यायुधानि च। ऊचुर्जयजयेत्युच्चैर्जयन्तीं ते जयैषिणः ॥ *tato devā dadustasyai svāni svānyāyudhāni ca*। *ūcurajayajayetyuccairjayantīṁ te jayaiṣiṇaḥ*॥ Then the gods, aspiring for victory presented to her their weapons with the loud chants: victory, victory to *Jayantī*, the Ever Victorious Goddess.

[2]AR: समुत्पाट्य *samutpāṭya*

शङ्खं च वरुणः शक्तिं ददौ तस्यै हुताशनः ।
मारुतो दत्तवांश्चापं बाणपूर्णे तथेषुधी ।।२१।।

21. *śaṅkhaṁ ca varuṇaḥ śaktiṁ dadau tasyai hutāśanaḥ* ।
māruto dattavānścāpaṁ bāṇapūrṇe tatheṣudhī ॥

Varuṇa gave the conch; *Hutāśana* (Fire), missile and *Māruta* (Air), bow and two quivers full of arrows.

वज्रमिन्द्रः समुत्पाद्य[3] कुलिशादमराधिपः ।
ददौ तस्यै सहस्राक्षो घण्टामैरावताद् गजात् ।।२२।।

22. *vajramindraḥ samutpādya*[3] *kuliśādamarādhipaḥ* ।
dadau tasyai sahasrākṣo ghaṇṭāmairāvatād gajāt ॥

Indra, the Thousand-Eyed King of the gods, drew from his thunderbolt and gave her a thunderbolt, along with the bell (taken) from the elephant *Airāvata* (Indra's mount).

कालदण्डाद्यमो दण्डं पाशं चाम्बुपतिर्ददौ ।
प्रजापतिश्चाक्षमालां ददौ ब्रह्मा कमण्डलुम् ।।२३।।

23. *kāladaṇḍādyamo daṇḍaṁ pāśaṁ cāmbupātirdadau* ।
prajāpatiścākṣamālāṁ dadau brahmā kamaṇḍalum ॥

From the Sceptre of Death, *Yama* gave her the sceptre and *Varuṇa*, the Regent Lord of the Waters, gave her the snare. *Prajāpati* gave her a rosary of beads and *Brahmā*, the water pot.

समस्तरोमकूपेषु निजरश्मीन् दिवाकरः ।
कालश्च दत्तवान् खड्गं तस्याश्चर्म[4] च निर्मलम् ।।२४।।

24. *samastaromakūpeṣu nijaraśmīn divākaraḥ* ।
kālaśca dattavān khaḍgaṁ tasyāścarma[4] *ca nirmalam* ॥

With his rays, the Sun filled the pores of her skin. *Kāla*, the Eternal Time, gave her a sword and a shining shield.

[3]AR: समुत्पाट्य *samutpāṭya*

[4]AR: तस्यै चर्म *tasyai carma*

क्षीरोदश्चामलं हारमजरे च तथाम्बरे ।
चूडामणिं तथा दिव्यं कुण्डले कटकानि च ॥२५॥

25. *kṣīrodaścāmalaṁ hāramajare ca tathāmbare* ।
cūḍāmaṇiṁ tathā divyaṁ kuṇḍale kaṭakāni ca ॥

Kṣīrasāgara, the Ocean of Milk (Lord *Viṣṇu*'s abode), gave her a crystal necklace, two undecaying garments, a crest jewel, two earrings and a set of bangles,

अर्धचन्द्रं तथा शुभ्रं केयूरान् सर्वबाहुषु ।
नूपुरौ विमलौ तद्वद् ग्रैवेयकमनुत्तमम् ॥२६॥

26. *ardhacandraṁ tathā śubhraṁ keyūrān sarvabāhuṣu* ।
nūpurau vimalau tadvad graiveyakamanuttamam ॥

a shimmering crescent and spotless bracelets for all her arms, and equally spotless anklets and an excellent collar;

अङ्गुलीयकरत्नानि समस्तास्वाङ्गुलीषु च ।
विश्वकर्मा ददौ तस्यै परशुं चातिनिर्मलम् ॥२७॥

27. *aṅgulīyakaratnāni samastāsvāṅgulīṣu ca* ।
viśvakarmā dadau tasyai paraśuṁ cātinirmalam ॥

along with the bejewelled rings for all her fingers. *Viśvakarmā,* the architect of the gods, presented her a stainless battle axe;

अस्त्राण्यनेकरूपाणि तथाभेद्यं च दंशनम् ।
अम्लानपङ्कजां मालां शिरस्युरसि चापराम् ॥२८॥

28. *astrāṇyanekarūpāṇi tathābhedyaṁ ca daṁśanam* ।
amlānapaṅkajāṁ mālāṁ śirasyurasi cāparām ॥

(he also gave her) a large variety of weapons, an impenetrable armour and a garland of never withering lotuses each for her head and neck.

अददज्जलधिस्तस्यै पङ्कजं चातिशोभनम् ।
हिमवान् वाहनं सिहं रत्नानि विविधानि च ।।२६।।

29. *adadajjaladhistasyai paṅkajaṁ cātiśobhanam ।*
himavān vāhanaṁ siṁhaṁ ratnāni vividhāni ca ।।

The Ocean gave her an exceedingly beautiful lotus while *Himālaya*, the King of Mountains, presented her a Lion for riding and a variety of jewels.

ददावशून्यं सुरया पानपात्रं धनाधिपः ।
शेषश्च सर्वनागेशो महामणिविभूषितम् ।।३०।।

30. *dadāvaśunyaṁ surayā pānapātraṁ dhanādhipaḥ ।*
śeṣaśca sarvanāgeśo mahāmaṇivibhūṣitam ।।

नागहारं ददौ तस्यै धत्ते यः पृथिवीमिमाम् ।
अन्यैरपि सुरैर्देवी भूषणैरायुधैस्तथा ।।३१।।

31. *nāgahāraṁ dadau tasyai dhatte yaḥ pṛthivīmimām ।*
anyairapi surairdevī bhūṣaṇairāyudhaistathā ।।

सम्मानिता ननादोच्चैः साट्टहासं मुहुर्मुहुः ।
तस्या नादेन घोरेण कृत्स्नमापूरितं नभः ।।३२।।

32. *sammānitā nanādoccaiḥ sāṭṭahāsaṁ muhurmuhuḥ ।*
tasyā nādena ghoreṇa kṛtsnamāpūritaṁ nabhaḥ ।।

Kubera, the Lord of Treasure, gave her an ever-full vessel of spirit. *Śeṣa*, the Lord of all Serpents, who supports this earth, gave her a necklace studded with serpents' jewels. The other gods also honoured the Goddess with jewels and weapons. Thus honoured, the Goddess repeatedly roared and laughed aloud and rent the sky with her terrifying roar.

अमायितातिमहता प्रतिशब्दो महानभूत् ।
चुक्षुभुः सकला लोकाः समुद्राश्च चकम्पिरे ।।३३।।

33. *amāyitātimahatā pratiśabdo mahānabhūt ।*
cukṣubhuḥ sakalā lokāḥ samudrāśca cakampire ।।

Such was the resounding roar that it could not be contained anywhere. There was commotion in all the worlds and the oceans trembled.

चचाल वसुधा चेलुः सकलाश्च महीधराः ।
जयेति देवाश्च मुदा तामूचुः सिंहवाहिनीम्[5] ।।३४।।

34. *cacāla vasudhā celuḥ sakalāśca mahīdharāḥ* ।
jayeti devāśca mudā tāmūcuḥ siṁhavāhinīm[5] ।।

The earth quaked and all the mountains shivered. 'Victory to the Goddess Riding the Lion', said the delighted gods.

तुष्टुवुर्मुनयश्चैनां भक्तिनम्रात्ममूर्तयः ।
दृष्ट्वा समस्तं संक्षुब्धं त्रैलोक्यममरारयः ।।३५।।

35. *tuṣṭuvurmunayaścaināṁ bhaktinamrātmamūrtayaḥ* ।
dṛṣṭvā samastaṁ saṁkṣubdhaṁ trailokyamamararāyaḥ ।।

सन्नद्धाखिलसैन्यास्ते समुत्तस्थुरुदायुधाः ।
आः किमेतदिति क्रोधादाभाष्य महिषासुरः ।।३६।।

36. *sannaddhākhilasainyāste samuttasthurudāyudhāḥ* ।
āḥ kimetaditi krodhādābhāṣya mahiṣāsuraḥ ।।

Sages, who were the pictures of humility, paid obeisance with deep devotion and extolled her. Demons, the enemies of the gods, noticed that the entire universe was in ferment. Preparing their forces for battle, they stood up and picked up their weapons. Seething with anger, *Mahiṣāsura* exclaimed, 'Ah! what is it?'

अभ्यधावत तं शब्दमशेषैरसुरैर्वृतः ।
स ददर्श ततो देवीं व्याप्तलोकत्रयां त्विषा ।।३७।।

37. *abhyadhāvata taṁ śabdamaśeṣairasurairvṛtaḥ* ।
sa dadarśa tato devīṁ vyāpta lokatrayāṁ tviṣā ।।

---

[5]AR: सिंहवाहनाम् *siṁhavāhanām*

Surrounded by his force of demons, he charged towards that roar. Then he saw the Goddess who, with her lustre, was illuminating the three worlds.

पादाक्रान्त्या नतभुवं किरीटोल्लिखिताम्बराम् ।
क्षोभिताशेषपातालां धनुर्ज्यानिःस्वनेन ताम् ।।३८।।

38. *pādākrāntyā natabhuvaṁ kirīṭollikhitāmbarām* ।
kṣobhitāśeṣapātālāṁ dhanurjyāniḥśvanena tām ।।

The earth sank as she thumped her feet. Like lightning in the sky, shone her crown. All the nether regions quivered with the twang of her bow.

दिशो भुजसहस्त्रेण समन्ताद् व्याप्य संस्थिताम् ।
ततः प्रववृते युद्धं तया देव्या सुरद्विषाम् ।।३९।।

39. *diśo bhujasahasreṇa samantād vyāpya saṁsthitām* ।
tataḥ pravavṛte yuddhaṁ tayā devyā suradviṣām ।।

With her thousand arms she stood permeating all the directions. Presently, the war between the Goddess and the enemies of the gods commenced.

शस्त्रास्त्रैर्बहुधा मुक्तैरादीपितदिगन्तरम् ।
महिषासुरसेनानीश्चिक्षुराख्यो महासुरः ।।४०।।

40. *śastrāstrairbahudhā muktairādīpitadigantaram* ।
mahiṣāsurasenānīścikṣurākhyo mahāsuraḥ ।।

युयुधे चामरश्चान्यैश्चतुरङ्गबलान्वितः ।
रथानामयुतैः षड्भिरुदग्राख्यो महासुरः ।।४१।।

41. *yuyudhe cāmaraścānyaiścaturaṅgabalānvitaḥ* ।
rathānāmayutaiḥ ṣaḍbhirudagrākhyo mahāsuraḥ ।।

With a variety of arms and weapons let loose, directions began to dazzle. There was a demon *Cikṣu* by name; he was a commander of *Mahiṣāsura.* He fought with the Goddess. With the other army of four divisions, *Cāmara* also fought. *Udagra,* another great demon, fought with his sixty thousand charioteers.

अयुध्यतायुतानां च सहस्रेण महाहनुः ।
पञ्चाशद्भिश्च नियुतैरसिलोमा महासुरः ॥४२॥

42. *ayudhyatāyutānāṁ ca sahasreṇa mahāhanuḥ* ।
pañcāśadbhiśca niyutairasilomā mahāsuraḥ ॥

Mahāhanu, another great demon, with ten million charioteers and *Asilomā*, whose body-hairs were sharp as swords, fought with fifty million of them.

अयुतानां शतैः षड्भिर्बाष्कलो युयुधे रणे ।
गजवाजिसहस्रौघैरनेकैः परिवारितः[6] ॥४३॥

43. *ayutānāṁ śataiḥ ṣaḍbhirbāṣkalo yuyudhe raṇe* ।
gajavājisahasraughairanekaiḥ parivāritaḥ[6] ॥

वृतो रथानां कोट्या च युद्धे तस्मिन्नयुध्यत ।
बिडालाख्योऽयुतानां च पञ्चाशद्भिरथायुतैः ॥४४॥

44. *vṛto rathānāṁ koṭyā ca yuddhe tasminnayudhyata* ।
biḍālākhyo 'yutānāṁ ca pañcāśadbhirathāyutaiḥ ॥

युयुधे संयुगे तत्र रथानां परिवारितः[7] ।
अन्ये च तत्रायुतशो रथनागहयैर्वृताः ॥४५॥

45. *yuyudhe saṁyuge tatra rathānāṁ parivāritaḥ*[7] ॥
anye ca tatrāyutaśo rathanāgahayairvṛtāḥ ॥

युयुधुः संयुगे देव्या सह तत्र महासुराः ।
कोटिकोटिसहस्रैस्तु रथानां दन्तिनां तथा ॥४६॥

46. *yuyudhuḥ saṁyuge devyā saha tatra mahāsurāḥ* ।
koṭikoṭisahasraistu rathānāṁ dantīnāṁ tathā ॥

---

[6]Additional reading hereafter in some copies : गजवाजिसहस्रौघैरनेकैरुग्र-दर्शनः *gajavājisahasraughairanekairugradarśanaḥ: Ugradarśana* with thousands of cavaliers and demons mounted on elephants...

[7] Additional reading hereafter in some copies: कृतःकालो रथानां च रणे पञ्चाशतायुतैः। युयुधे संयुगे तत्र तावद्भिः परिवारितः॥ *kṛtah kālo rathānaṁ ca raṇe pañcāśatāyutaiḥ*। *yuyudhe saṁyuge tatra tāvadbhiḥ parivāritaḥ*॥ In that war, *Kṛtaḥ Kāla* fought with five million chariots, attacking from all sides.

हयानां च वृतो युद्धे तत्राभून्महिषासुरः ।
तोमरैर्भिन्दिपालैश्च शक्तिभिर्मुसलैस्तथा ॥४७॥

47. *hayānāṁ ca vṛto yuddhe tatrābhūnmahiṣāsuraḥ* ।
tomarairbhindipālaiśca śaktibhirmusalaistathā ॥

युयुधुः संयुगे देव्या खड्गैः परशुपट्टिशैः ।
केचिच्च चिक्षिपुः शक्तीः केचित्पाशांस्तथापरे ॥४८॥

48. *yuyudhuḥ saṁyuge devyā khaḍgaiḥ paraśupaṭṭiśaiḥ* ।
kecicca cikṣipuḥ śaktīḥ kecitpāśānstathāpare ॥

Bāṣkala, accompanied by six million charioteers also fought in the war. *Parivārita*[8], another demon, with several forces of cavaliers, troops on elephants, and ten million charioteers fought too. A demon, *Biḍāla* by name, had a force of five thousand million charioteers at his disposal. They together fought there in all directions. In addition, thousands of other mighty demons, mounted on chariots, elephants and horses arrived there and fought with the Goddess. *Mahiṣāsura* himself, surrounded by millions and millions of troops – charioteers, cavaliers and elephant-mounted – was present there. They attacked the Goddess with clubs, javelins, missiles, pestles, swords, battle–axes and spears. Some threw missiles while some others, snares.

देवीं खड्गप्रहारैस्तु ते तां हन्तुं प्रचक्रमुः ।
सापि देवी ततस्तानि शस्त्राण्यस्त्राणि चण्डिका ॥४९॥

49. *devīṁ khaḍgaprahāraistu te tāṁ hantuṁ pracakramuḥ* ।
sāpi devī tatastāni śastrāṇyastrāṇi caṇḍikā ॥

लीलयैव प्रचिच्छेद निजशस्त्रास्त्रवर्षिणी ।
अनायस्तानना देवी स्तूयमाना सुरर्षिभिः ॥५०॥

50. *līlayaiva praciccheda nijaśastrāstravarṣiṇī* ।
anāyastānanā devī stūyamānā surarṣibhiḥ ॥

[8] *Parivārita* literally means 'encircled from all directions'.

मुमोचासुरदेहेषु शस्त्राण्यस्त्राणि चेश्वरी ।
सोऽपि क्रुद्धो धुतसटो देव्या वाहनकेसरी ॥५१॥

51. *mumocāsuradeheṣu śastraṇyastrāṇi ceśvarī* ।
so 'pi kruddho dhutasaṭo devyā vāhanakesarī ॥

चचारासुरसैन्येषु वनेष्विव हुताशनः ।
निःश्वासान् मुमुचे यांश्च युध्यमाना रणेऽम्बिका ॥५२॥

52. *cacārāsurasainyeṣu vaneṣviva hutāśanaḥ* ।
niḥśvāsān mumuce yānśca yudhymānā raṇe 'mbikā ॥

त एव सद्यः सम्भूता गणाःशतसहस्त्रशः ।
युयुधुस्ते परशुभिर्भिन्दिपालासिपट्टिशैः ॥५३॥

53. *ta eva sadyaḥ saṁbhūtā gaṇāḥ śatasahasraśaḥ* ।
yuyudhuste paraśubhirbhindipālāsipaṭṭiśaiḥ ॥

Some moved ahead to kill the Goddess by striking her with their swords. The Goddess *Caṇḍikā*, too, playfully rained weapons on them and cut back all their weapons and arms without any indication of fatigue on her face, even as the gods and seers praised and complimented her. The Lion, the mount of the Goddess, too, was in rage, and shaking his mane, moved about in the army of the demons like wild fire in the forests. When the Mother let her breaths out, hundreds of thousands of her attendants immediately appeard from them. They, too, fought with battle axes, javelins, swords and spears.

नाशयन्तोऽसुरगणान् देवीशक्त्युपबृंहिताः ।
अवादयन्त पटहान् गणाः शङ्खांस्तथापरे ॥५४॥

54. *nāśayanto 'suragaṇān devīśaktyupabṛṁhitāḥ* ।
avādayanta paṭahān gaṇāḥ śaṅkhānstathāpare ॥

Supplemented with the energy of the Goddess, the attendants, even as they killed the hosts of demons, went about beating the drums while the others sounded the conches.

मृदङ्गांश्च तथैवान्ये तस्मिन् युद्धमहोत्सवे ।
ततो देवी त्रिशूलेन गदया शक्तिवृष्टिभिः[9] ।।५५।।

55. *mṛdaṅgaṅśca tathaivānye tasmin yuddhamahotsave* ।
tato devī triśūlena gadayā śaktivṛṣṭibhiḥ[9] ।।

खड्गादिभिश्च शतशो निजघान महासुरान् ।
पातयामास चैवान्यान् घण्टास्वनविमोहितान् ।।५६।।

56. *khaḍgādibhiśca śataśo nijaghāna mahāsurān* ।
pātayāmāsa caivānyān ghaṇṭāsvanavimohitān ।।

Still others beat tabors in that great festival of war. Then the Goddess, with her trident and mace and by raining missiles and using swords, slayed hundreds of the mighty demons along with many others who were bewildered by the noise of her bell.

असुरान् भुवि पाशेन बद्ध्वा चान्यानकर्षयत् ।
केचिद् द्विधा कृतास्तीक्ष्णैः खड्गपातैस्तथापरे ।।५७।।

57. *asurān bhuvi pāśena baddhvā cānyānakarṣayat* ।
kecid dvidhā kṛtāstīkṣṇaiḥ khaḍgapātaistathāpare ।।

Many of them, trapped in the net were dragged on earth while the others were sliced into two pieces each with the strikes of the sharp sword.

विपोथिता निपातेन गदया भुवि शेरते ।
वेमुश्च केचिद्रुधिरं मुसलेन भृशं हताः ।।५८।।

58. *vipothitā nipātena gadayā bhuvi śerate* ।
vemuśca kecidrudhiraṁ musalena bhṛśaṁ hatāḥ ।।

Many slept on earth forever as the mace struck them. Some, fatally injured by the pestle, emitted blood.

---

[9] AR: शरवृष्टिभिः *śaravṛṣṭibhiḥ*

केचिन्निपतिता भूमौ भिन्नाः शूलेन वक्षसि ।
निरन्तराः शरौघेण कृताः केचिद्रणाजिरे ।।५९।।

59. *kecinnipatitā bhūmau bhinnāḥ śūlena vakṣasi* ।
nirantarāḥ śaraugheṇa kṛtāḥ kecidraṇājire ।।

With the pike tearing their chests, some fell on earth. Several went down as arrows unremittingly rained on them in the theatre of war.

श्येनानुकारिणः[10] प्राणान् मुमुचुस्त्रिदशार्दनाः ।
केषांचिद् बाहवश्छिन्नाश्छिन्नग्रीवास्तथापरे ।।६०।।

60. *śyenānukāriṇaḥ*[10] *prāṇān mumucustridaśārdanāḥ* ।
keṣāñcid bāhavaśchinnāśchinnagrīvāstathāpare ।।

शिरांसि पेतुरन्येषामन्ये मध्ये विदारिताः ।
विच्छिन्नजङ्घास्त्वपरे पेतुरुर्व्यां महासुराः ।।६१।।

61. *śirāṁsi peturanyeṣāmanye madhye vidāritāḥ* ।
vicchinnajaṅghāstvapare peturuvyāṁ mahāsurāḥ ।।

Demons, who tormented the gods and pounced upon them like eagles, lost their lives. Arms of some were axed and of some, necks. There were others whose heads rolled while there were those who were sliced through the middle. Other mighty demons, with their thighs chopped off, fell on the earth.

एकबाह्वक्षिचरणाः केचिद्देव्या द्विधा कृताः ।
छिन्नेऽपि चान्ये शिरसि पतिताः पुनरुत्थिताः ।।६२।।

62. *ekabāhvakṣicaraṇāḥ keciddevyā dvidhā kṛtāḥ* ।
chinne 'pi cānye śirasi patitāḥ punarutthitāḥ ।।

कबन्धा युयुधुर्देव्या गृहीतपरमायुधाः ।
ननृतुश्चापरे तत्र युद्धे तूर्यलयाश्रिताः ।।६३।।

63. *kabandhā yuyudhurdevyā gṛhītaparamāyudhāḥ* ।
nanṛtuścāpare tatra yuddhe tūryalayāśritāḥ ।।63।।

---

[10]AR: सेनानुकारिणः *senānukāriṇaḥ*

The Gooddess first left some of them with one arm, one leg and one eye and then ripped apart each of them into two. Some who, though rendered headless, rose again as torsoes and, armed with fierce weapons, started fighting with the Goddess. The other torsoes danced to the beat of battle-drums.

कबन्धाश्छिन्नशिरसः खड्गशक्त्यृष्टिपाणयः ।
तिष्ठ तिष्ठेति भाषन्तो देवीमन्ये महासुराः[11] ।।६४।।

64. *kabandhāśchinnaśirasaḥ khaḍgaśaktyṛṣṭipāṇayaḥ* ।
tiṣṭha tiṣṭheti bhāṣanto devīmanye mahāsurāḥ[11] ।।

Many headless torsoes of the demons charged with their swords, missiles and double-edged spears while the other great demons shouted 'stop', 'stop,' at the Goddess.

पतितै रथनागाश्वैरसुरैश्च वसुन्धरा ।
अगम्या साभवत्तत्र यत्राभूत्स महारणः ।।६५।।

65. *patitai rathanāgāśvairasuraiśca vasundharā* ।
agamyā sābhavattatra yatrābhūtsa mahāraṇaḥ ।।

The battleground where this great war was fought was filled so much with chariots and bodies of elephants, horses and demons that passage through it became impossible.

शोणितौघा महानद्यः सद्यस्तत्र प्रसुस्रुवुः ।
मध्ये चासुरसैन्यस्य वारणासुरवाजिनाम् ।।६६।।

66. *śoṇitaughā mahānadyaḥ sadystatra prasusruvuḥ* ।
madhye cāsurasainyasya vāraṇāsuravājinām ।।

So much blood poured from the bodies of the army of demons, that great streams of blood of elephants, horses and demons at once started flowing.

[11]Additional reading in some copies hereafter: रुधिरौघविलुप्ताङ्गाः संग्रामे लोमहर्षणे। *rudhiraughaviluptāṅgāḥ saṅgrāme lomaharṣaṇe* (In that hair-raising war, limbs of many were lost in the stream of blood).

क्षणेन तन्महासैन्यमसुराणां तथाम्बिका ।
निन्ये क्षयं यथा वह्निस्तृणदारुमहाचयम् ।।६७।।

67. *kṣaṇena tanmahāsainyamasurāṇāṁ tathāmbikā ।*
ninye kṣyaṁ yathā vahnistṛṇadārumahācayam ।।

The Mother destroyed the great army of demons in a moment, just as a large heap of wood and straws is consumed by fire in no time.

स च सिंहो महानादमुत्सृजन्धुतकेसरः ।
शरीरेभ्योऽमरारीणामसूनिव विचिन्वति ।।६८।।

68. *sa ca sīṁho mahānādamutsṛjandhutakesaraḥ ।*
śarīrebhyo 'marārīṇāmasūniva vicinvati ।।

The Lion also roared aloud shaking its mane and wrenched, as it were, the lives out of the bodies of the demons.

देव्या गणैश्च तैस्तत्र कृतं युद्धं महासुरैः ।
यथैषां[12] तुतुषुर्देवाः[13] पुष्पवृष्टिमुचो दिवि ।।ॐ।।६९।।

69. *devyā gaṇaiśca taistatra kṛtaṁ yuddhaṁ mahāsuraiḥ ।*
yathaiṣām[12] tutuṣurdevāḥ[13] puṣpavṛṣṭimuco divi ।।oṁ ।।

Attendants of the Goddess also gave such a fight to the mighty demons that the gods in heaven showered flowers on them. Oṁ

इति श्रीमार्कण्डेयपुराणे सावर्णिके मन्वन्तरे देवीमाहात्म्ये—

---

[12] AR: यथैनां *yathaināṁ*

[13] AR: तुष्टुवुर्देवाः *tuṣṭuvurdevāḥ*

महिषासुरसैन्यवधो नाम द्वितीयोऽध्यायः ॥२॥

iti śrīmārkaṇḍeyapurāṇe sāvarṇike manvantare devīmāhātmye mahiṣāsurasainyavadho nāma dvitīyo 'dhyāyaḥ ॥2॥

Thus ends the second chapter called 'Slaying of the Forces of *Mahiṣāsura*' during the era of *Sāvarṇi Manu*, in the 'Glory of the Goddess' (narrated) in the *Mārkaṇḍeya Purāṇa.*

उवाच १, श्लोकाः ६८, एवम् ६९, एवमादितः १७३

uvāca 1, *ślokāḥ* 68, *evaṁ* 69, *evamāditaḥ* 173

uvāca1, ślokas 68, total 69, from beginning upto here 173.

तृतीयोऽध्याय:

tṛtīyo 'dhyāyaḥ

Chapter Three

Slaying of *Mahiṣāsura* and his Commanders.

ध्यानम्

dhyānam

Meditation

ॐ उद्यद्भानुसहस्त्रकान्तिमरुणक्षौमां शिरोमालिकां
रक्तालिप्तपयोधरां जपवटीं विद्यामभीतिंवरम् ।
हस्ताब्जैर्दधतीं त्रिनेत्रविलसद्वक्त्रारविन्दश्रियं
देवीं बद्धहिमांशुरत्नमुकुटां वन्देऽरविन्दस्थिताम् ॥

oṁ. udyadbhānusahasrakāntimaruṇakṣaumāṁ śiromālikāṁ
raktāliptapayodharāṁ japavaṭīm vidyāmabhītiṁvaram ।
hastābjairdadhatīṁ trinetravilasadvaktrāravindaśriyaṁ
devīṁ baddhahimāṁśuratnamukuṭāṁ vande 'ravindasthitām ॥

OṀ. LIKE A THOUSAND RISING SUNS IS THE EFFULGENCE OF THE GODDESS. SHE IS DRESSED IN A RED SILK CLOTH AND WEARS A GARLAND OF SKULLS. HER BREASTS ARE ANOINTED WITH BLOOD. IN HER LOTUS LIKE HANDS, SHE HAS A ROSARY AND DISPLAYS SIGNS OF KNOWLEDGE, BLESSINGS, FEARLESSNESS AND BOONS. THREE EYES LEND GREAT CHARM TO HER LOTUS-LIKE VISAGE. TO HER, SEATED ON A LOTUS, WITH HER HEAD ADORNED WITH THE MOON AND A CROWN STUDDED WITH GEMS, I PAY OBEISANCE.

ॐ ऋषिरुवाच ।।१।।

1. *oṁ. ṛṣiruvāca* ॥

निहन्यमानं तत्सैन्यमवलोक्य महासुरः ।
सेनानीश्चिक्षुरः कोपाद्ययौ योद्धुमथाम्बिकाम् ।।२।।

2. *nihanyamānaṁ tatsainyamavalokya mahāsuraḥ* ।
senānīścikṣuraḥ kopādyayau yoddhumathāmbikām ॥

Oṁ. The Seer said

Seeing total devastation of the demonaic forces, *Cikṣura,* their commander, seething with anger, advanced to fight with the Mother.

स देवीं शरवर्षेण ववर्ष समरेऽसुरः ।
यथा मेरुगिरेः शृङ्गं तोयवर्षेण तोयदः ।।३।।

3. *sa devīṁ śaravarṣeṇa vavarṣa samare 'suraḥ* ।
yathā merugireḥ sṛṅgaṁ toyavarṣeṇa toyadaḥ ॥

He hurled arrows at the Goddess as a cloud showers rain on the peak of the *Meru* mountain.

तस्यच्छित्त्वा ततो देवी लीलयैव शरोत्करान् ।
जघान तुरगान् बाणैर्यन्तारं चैव वाजिनाम् ।।४।।

4. *tasyacchittvā tato devī līlayaiva śarōtkarān* ।
jaghāna turagān bāṇairyantāraṁ caiva vājinām ॥

Thereupon, the Goddess playfully cut asunder his bunch of arrows, killed the horses and slayed the charioteer with her arrows.

चिच्छेद च धनुः सद्यो ध्वजं चाति समुच्छ्रितम् ।
विव्याध चैव गात्रेषु छिन्नधन्वानमाशुगैः ।।५।।

5. *ciccheda ca dhanuḥ sadyo dhvajaṁ cāti samucchritam* ।
vivyādha caīva gātreṣu chinnadhanvānamāśugaiḥ ॥

She promptly cut apart his bow and high-flying banner. His bow having been destroyed, she pierced his limbs with her fast-moving arrows.

सच्छिन्नधन्वा विरथो हताश्वो हतसारथिः ।
अभ्यधावत तां देवीं खड्गचर्मधरोऽसुरः ॥६॥

6. *sacchinnadhanvā viratho hatāśvo hatasārathiḥ* ।
abhyadhāvata tāṁ devīṁ khaḍgacarmadharo 'suraḥ ॥

His bow was broken, he was rendered without a chariot, his horse and charioteer were killed. Now the demon, carrying a sword and a shield, ran towards the Goddess.

सिंहमाहत्य खड्गेन तीक्ष्णधारेण मूर्धनि ।
आजघान भुजे सव्ये देवीमप्यतिवेगवान् ॥७॥

7. *siṁhamāhatya khaḍgena tīkṣṇadhāreṇa mūrdhani* ।
ājaghāna bhuje savye devīmapyativegavān ॥

With his sharp-edged sword, he hit the Lion on his head and struck with great force at the left arm of the Goddess.

तस्याः खड्गो भुजं प्राप्य पफाल नृपनन्दन ।
ततो जग्राह शूलं स कोपादरुणलोचनः ॥८॥

8. *tasyāḥ khaḍgo bhujaṁ prāpya paphāla nṛpanandana* ।
tato jagrāha śūlaṁ sa kopādaruṇalocanaḥ ॥

चिक्षेप च ततस्तत्तु भद्रकाल्यां महासुरः ।
जाज्वल्यमानं तेजोभी रविबिम्बमिवाम्बरात् ॥९॥

9. *cikṣepa ca tatastattu bhadrakālyāṁ mahāsuraḥ* ।
jājvalyamānaṁ tejobhī ravibimbamivāmbarāt ॥

As soon as, O Prince, his sword struck the arm of the Goddess, it (the sword) was broken into pieces. His eyes redshot with anger, he then picked up a pike and hurled it at *Bhadrakālī*, the Gentle *Kālī*. It dazzled like the orb of sun falling from heaven.

दृष्ट्वा तदापतच्छूलं देवी शूलममुञ्चत ।
तच्छूलं शतधा तेन नीतं[1] स च महासुरः ॥१०॥

10. *dṛṣṭvā tadāpatacchūlaṁ devī śūlamamuñcata* ।
tacchūlaṁ śatadhā tena nītaṁ[1] *sa ca mahāsuraḥ* ॥

Seeing the pike approaching her, the Goddess, too, threw a pike which split the mighty demon's pike into a hundred pieces and also shred him into several parts.

हते तस्मिन्महावीर्ये महिषस्य चमूपतौ ।
आजगाम गजारूढश्चामरस्त्रिदशार्दनः ॥११॥

11. *hate tasmin mahāvīrye mahiṣasya camūpatau* ।
ājagāma gajārūḍhaścāmarastridaśārdanaḥ ॥

When that mighty commander of *Mahiṣa* was slayed, *Cāmara*, the tormentor of the gods, came riding on an elephant.

सोऽपि शक्तिं मुमोचाथ देव्यास्तामम्बिका द्रुतम् ।
हुंकाराभिहतां भूमौ पातयामास निष्प्रभाम् ॥१२॥

12. *so 'pi śaktiṁ mumocātha devyāstāmambikā drutam* ।
huṅkārābhihatāṁ bhūmau pātayāmāsa niṣprabhām ॥

He also hurled a missile at the Goddess but she struck back at it, made it infructuous and fell it down on the earth with a resounding roar.

भग्नां शक्तिं निपतितां दृष्ट्वा क्रोधसमन्वितः ।
चिक्षेप चामरः शूलं बाणैस्तदपि साच्छिनत् ॥१३॥

13. *bhagnāṁ śaktiṁ nipatitāṁ dṛṣṭvā krodhasamanvitaḥ* ।
cikṣepa cāmaraḥ śūlaṁ bāṇaistadapi sācchinat ॥

As he saw his missile broken and fallen, *Cāmara*, full of anger, threw a pike which, too, was broken by her with arrows.

---

[1]AR: तेन तच्छतधा नीतं *tena tacchatadhā nītaṁ*

ततः सिंहः समुत्पत्य गजकुम्भान्तरे स्थितः ।
बाहुयुद्धेन युयुधे तेनोच्चैस्त्रिदशारिणा ॥१४॥

14. *tataḥ siṁhaḥ samutpatya gajakuṁbhāntare sthitaḥ* ।
bāhuyuddhena yuyudhe tenoccaistridaśāriṇā ॥

Then the Lion jumped on the elephant's head and engaged that enemy of the gods in a fierce hand to hand fight.

युद्ध्यमानौ ततस्तौ तु तस्मान्नागान्महीं गतौ ।
युयुधातेऽतिसंरब्धौ प्रहारैरतिदारुणैः ॥१५॥

15. *yuddhyamānau tatastau tu tasmānnāgānmahīṁ gatau* ।
yuyudhāte 'ti saṁrabdhau prahārairatidāruṇaiḥ ॥

Fighting with each other, both of them climbed down from the elephant and came on earth. Both were in terrible rage and began hitting each other severely.

ततो वेगात्खमुत्पत्य निपत्य च मृगारिणा ।
करप्रहारेण शिरश्चामरस्य पृथक्कृतम् ॥१६॥

16. *tato vegātkhamutpatya nipatya ca mṛgāriṇā* ।
karaprahāreṇa śirṣcāmarasya pṛthakkṛtam ॥

Then, the Lion jumped high into the sky and swiftly coming down, hit *Cāmara* with hands and chopped his head off his body.

उदग्रश्च रणे देव्या शिलावृक्षादिभिर्हतः ।
दन्तमुष्टितलैश्चैव करालश्च निपातितः ॥१७॥

17. *udagraśca raṇe devyā śilāvṛkṣādibhirhataḥ* ।
dantamuṣṭitalaiścaiva karālaśca nipātitaḥ ॥

Udagra, too, was killed by the Goddess with rocks and trees. *Karāla* also met with the same fate with the blows of teeth, fists and slaps.

देवी क्रुद्धा गदापातैश्चूर्णयामास चोद्धतम् ।
वाष्कलं भिन्दिपालेन बाणैस्ताम्रं तथान्धकम् ।।१८।।

18. *devī kruddhā gadāpataiścūrṇayāmāsa coddhatam* ।
vāṣkalaṁ bhindipālena bāṇaistāmraṁ tathāndhakam ।।

The angry Goddess made mincemeat of *Uddhata* with the blows of her mace. While *Vāṣkala* was killed with javeline, *Tāmra* and *Andhaka* were slayed with arrows.

उग्रास्यमुग्रवीर्यं च तथैव च महाहनुम् ।
त्रिनेत्रा च त्रिशूलेन जघान परमेश्वरी ।।१९।।

19. *ugrāsyamugravīryaṁ ca tathaiva ca mahāhanum* ।
trinetrā ca triśūlena jaghāna parameśvarī ।।

The Three-Eyed Sovereign Goddess slayed *Ugrāsya*, one with the frightful face; *Ugravīrya*, the one of the fierce prowess and also *Mahāhanu*, the one of the conspicuous chin, with her trident.

बिडालस्यासिना कायात्पातयामास वै शिरः ।
दुर्धरं दुर्मुखं चोभौ शरैर्निन्ये यमक्षयम्[2] ।।२०।।

20. *biḍalasyāsinā kāyātpātayāmāsa vai śiraḥ* ।
durdharaṁ durmukhaṁ cobhau śarairninye yamakṣayam[2] ।।

She felled the head of *Biḍāla*, one of cat's face, from his body with the sword and dispatched *Durdhara*, the

---

[2] Two additional ślokas hereafter in some copies:
कालं च कालदण्डेन कालरात्रिरपातयत् । उग्रदर्शनमत्युग्रैः खड्गपातैरताडयत् ।।
असिनैवासिलोमानमच्छिदत्सा रणोत्सवे । गणैः सिंहेन देव्या च जयक्ष्वेडाकृतोत्सवैः ।।
kālaṁ ca kāladaṇḍena kālarātrirapātayat । *ugradarśanamatyugraiḥ khaḍgapātairatāḍayat* ।। *asinaivāsilomānamacchidatsā raṇotsve* । *gaṇaiḥ siṁhena devyā ca jayakṣveḍākṛtotsavaiḥ* ।। The deadly demon *Kāla* was felled by that Night of Dissolution with the Sceptre of Death and the fierce-looking *Ugradarśana*, with the razor-sharp sword. In that festival of war, she pierced *Asilomā* of sword-like hair with the sword. Thus did attendants and the Lion of the Goddess celebrate the victory.

unstoppable and *Durmukha*, of hideous face, to the house of Death with her arrows.

एवं संक्षीयमाणे तु स्वसैन्ये महिषासुरः ।
माहिषेण स्वरूपेण त्रासयामास तान् गणान् ।।२१।।

21. *evaṁ saṁkṣīyamāṇe tu svasainye mahiṣāsuraḥ* ।
māhiṣena svarūpeṇa trāsayāmāsa tān gaṇān ।।

When *Mahiṣāsura* saw his forces being thus decimated, he assumed the form of a buffalo and started terrorising the attendants of the Goddess.

कांश्चित्तुण्डप्रहारेण क्षुरक्षेपैस्तथापरान् ।
लाङ्गूलताडितांश्चान्याञ्छृङ्गांगाभ्यां च विदारितान् ।।२२।।

22. *kāñścittuṇḍaprahāreṇa kṣurakṣepaistathāparān* ।
lāṅgūlatāḍitāṁścānyāñchṛṅgābhyāṁ ca vidāritān ।।

वेगेन कांश्चिदपरान्नादेन भ्रमणेन च ।
निःश्वासपवनेनान्यान् पातयमास भूतले ।।२३।।

23. *vegena kāñścidaparānnādena bhramaṇena ca* ।
niḥśvāsapavanenānyān pātayāmāsa bhūtale ।।

He killed some of them by striking with his snout, some with hoofs; some he beat with his tail and the others he tore apart with his horns. He felled some of them with the sheer velocity of his movement, others with his roar and some by twirling them around. Some he felled merely with his heavy breath.

निपात्य प्रमथानीकमभ्यधावत सोऽसुरः ।
सिंहं हन्तुं महादेव्याः कोपं चक्रे ततोऽम्बिका ।।२४।।

24. *nipātya pramathānīkamabhyadhāvata so 'suraḥ* ।
siṁhaṁ hantuṁ mahādevyāḥ kopaṁ cakre tato 'mbikā ।।

After thus felling down the attendants of the Goddess, he charged to kill the Lion of the Great Goddess. Now the Mother was enraged.

सोऽपि कोपान्महावीर्यः खुरक्षुण्णमहीतलः ।
शृङ्गाभ्यां पर्वतानुच्चांश्चिक्षेप ननाद च ॥२५॥

25. *so 'pi kopānmahāvīryaḥ khurakṣunnamahītalaḥ* ।
śṛṅgābhyāṁ parvatānuccāṁścikṣepa nanāda ca ॥

The mighty demon, equally angry, started digging the earth with his hoofs, lifting and throwing the peaks of mountains with his horns and began roaring.

वेगभ्रमणविक्षुण्णा मही तस्य व्यशीर्यत ।
लाङ्गूलेनाहतश्चाब्धिः प्लावयामास सर्वतः ॥२६॥

26. *vegabhramaṇavikṣuṇṇā mahī tasya vyaśīryata* ।
lāṅgūlenāhataścābdhiḥ plāvayāmāsa sarvataḥ ॥

By the force of his movement, the earth shook and was shattered. By the lashes of his tail, the ocean was inundated in all directions.

धुतशृङ्गविभिन्नाश्च खण्डं खण्डं[3] ययुर्घनाः ।
श्वासानिलास्ताः शतशो निपेतुर्नभसोऽचलाः ॥२७॥

27. *dhutaśṛṅgavibhinnāśca khaṇḍaṁ khaṇḍaṁ*[3] *yayurghanāḥ* ।
śvāsānilāstāḥ śataśo nipeturnabhaso 'calāḥ ॥

Clouds were torn into patches by his hard-hitting horns. Mountains, in hundreds, fell from heaven, as it were, by the force of his breath.

इति क्रोधसमाध्मातमापतन्तं महासुरम् ।
दृष्ट्वा सा चण्डिका कोपं तद्वधाय तदाकरोत् ॥२८॥

28. *iti krodhasamādhmātamāpatantaṁ mahāsuram* ।
dṛṣṭvā sā caṇḍikā kopaṁ tadvadhāya tadākarot ॥

When *Caṇḍikā*, that Goddess in rage, saw the great demon charging towards her in anger, she let lose her temper to kill him.

---

[3]AR: खण्डखण्डं *khaṇḍakhaṇḍaṁ*

सा क्षिप्त्वा तस्य वै पाशं तं बबन्ध महासुरम् ।
तत्याज माहिषं रूपं सोऽपि बद्धो महामृधे ॥२९॥

29. *sā kṣiptvā tasya vai pāśaṁ taṁ babandha mahāsuram* ।
tatyāja māhiṣaṁ rūpaṁ so 'pi baddho mahāmṛdhe ॥

She threw the snare on him and bound him tight in it. Thus bound, in that great battle, he abandoned the form of a buffalo.

ततः सिंहोऽभवत्सद्यो यावत्तस्याम्बिका शिरः ।
छिनत्ति तावत्पुरुषः खड्गपाणिरदृश्यत ॥३०॥

30. *tataḥ siṁho 'bhavatsadyo yāvattasyāmbikā śiraḥ* ।
chinatti tāvatpuruṣaḥ khaḍgapāṇiradṛśyata ॥

Promptly then he became a lion. Just when the Mother was about to chop his head, he appeared as a man with a sword in hand.

तत एवाशु पुरुषं देवी चिच्छेद सायकैः ।
तं खड्गचर्मणा सार्धं ततः सोऽभून्महागजः ॥३१॥

31. *tata evāśu puruṣaṁ devī ciccheda sāyakaiḥ* ।
taṁ khadgacarmaṇā sārdhaṁ tataḥ so 'bhūnmahāgajaḥ ॥

Immediately the Goddess pierced that man, raining arrows at him and with the help of the sword and shield. Now, then, he became a giant elephant.

करेण च महासिंहं तं चकर्ष जगर्ज च ।
कर्षतस्तु करं देवी खड्गेन निरकृन्तत ॥३२॥

32. *kareṇa ca mahāsiṁhaṁ taṁ cakarṣa jagarja ca* ।
karṣtastu karaṁ devī khaḍgena nirakṛntata ॥

He roared and attempted to pull the great lion with his trunk. Even as he pulled it, the Goddess cut his trunk with her sword.

ततो महासुरो भूयो माहिषं वपुरास्थितः ।
तथैव क्षोभयामास त्रैलोक्यं सचराचरम् ।।३३।।

33. *tato mahāsuro bhūyo māhiṣaṁ vapurāsthitaḥ* ।
tathaiva kṣobhayāmāsa trailokyaṁ sacarācaram ॥

Then the great demon returned to the buffalo's body and snorted, tormenting all the moving and stationary entites of the three worlds.

ततः क्रुद्धा जगन्माता चण्डिका पानमुत्तमम् ।
पपौ पुनः पुनश्चैव जहासारुणलोचना ।।३४।।

34. *tataḥ kruddhā jaganmātā caṇḍikā pānamuttamam* ।
papau punaḥ punaścaiva jahāsāruṇalocanā ॥

The enraged Mother of the Universe, then, started drinking the excellent spirit and, her eyes redshot, laughing again and again.

ननर्द चासुरः सोऽपि बलवीर्यमदोद्धतः ।
विषाणाभ्यां च चिक्षेप चण्डिकां प्रति भूधरान् ।।३५।।

35. *nanarda cāsuraḥ so 'pi balavīryamadoddhataḥ* ।
viṣāṇābhyāṁ ca cikṣepa caṇḍikāṁ prati bhūdharān ॥

Intoxicated with power, the boorish demon roared and began throwing mountains at *Caṇḍikā*, the Formidable Goddess.

सा च तान् प्रहितांस्तेन चूर्णयन्ती शरोत्करैः ।
उवाच तं मदोद्धूतमुखरागाकुलाक्षरम् ।।३६।।

36. *sā ca tān prahitāṁstena cūrṇayantī śarotkaraiḥ* ।
uvāca taṁ madoddhūtamukharāgākulākṣaram ॥

She repulsed those mountains with a heap of arrows. Even as she began to speak, her mouth became red and speech faltered due to the impact of the drink.

देव्युवाच ॥३७॥

37. *devyuvāca* ॥

गर्ज गर्ज क्षणं मूढ मधु यावत्पिबाम्यहम्।
मया त्वयि हतेऽत्रैव गर्जिष्यन्त्याशु देवता: ॥३८॥

38. *garja garja kṣaṇaṁ mūḍha madhu yāvatpibāmyaham* ।
mayā tvayi hate 'traiva garjiṣyantyāśu devatāḥ ॥

The Goddess said

Roar, roar for a while, you fool, till I consume the spirit. Soon, when I have killed you, the gods will start roaring.

ऋषिरुवाच ॥३९॥

39. *ṛṣiruvāca* ॥

एवमुक्त्वा समुत्पत्य साऽऽरूढां तं महासुरम्।
पादेनाक्रम्य कण्ठे च शूलेनैनमताडयत् ॥४०॥

40. *evamuktvā samutpatya sā ''rūḍhāṁ taṁ mahāsuram* ।
pādenākramya kaṇṭhe ca śūlenainamatāḍayat ॥

The Seer said

Saying thus, she jumped in a swift motion and mounted that great demon. Nabbing him with her foot, she struck him with her pike.

तत: सोऽपि पदाऽऽक्रान्तस्तया निजमुखात्तत:।
अर्धनिष्क्रान्त एवासीद्[4] देव्या वीर्येण संवृत: ॥४१॥

41. *tataḥ so 'pi padā ''krāntastayā nijamukhāttataḥ* ।
ardhaniṣkrānta evāsīd[4] *devyā vīryeṇa saṁvṛtaḥ* ॥

Even as he was nabbed down with her foot, he started to come out in another form through his mouth. When he was still half way out, he was restrained by the Goddess with her strength.

---

[4]AR: एवाति *evāti*

अर्धनिष्क्रान्त एवासौ युध्यमानो महासुरः ।
तया महासिना देव्या शिरश्छित्त्वा निपातितः[5] ॥४२॥

42. *ardhaniṣkrānta evāsau yudhyamāno mahāsuraḥ* ।
tayā mahāsinā devyā śirśchittvā nipātitaḥ[5] ॥

Although only half-out, the great demon started fighting. Then the Goddess chopped off his head with a large sword and felled it.

ततो हाहाकृतं सर्वं दैत्यसैन्यं ननाश तत् ।
प्रहर्षं च परं जग्मुः सकला देवतागणाः ॥४३॥

43. *tato hāhākṛtaṁ sarvaṁ daityasainyaṁ nanāśa tat* ।
praharṣaṁ ca paraṁ jagmuh sakalā devatāgaṇāḥ ॥

Then the entire army of the demons, lamenting aloud, took to their heels and the whole lot of the gods became extremely delighted.

तुष्टुवुस्तां सुरा देवीं सह दिव्यैर्महर्षिभिः ।
जगुर्गन्धर्वपतयो ननृतुश्चाप्सरोगणाः ॥ॐ॥४४॥

44. *tuṣṭuvustāṁ surā devīṁ saha divyairmahṛṣibhiḥ* ।
jagurgandharvapatayo nanṛtuścāpsaroganāḥ ॥*oṁ*॥

The gods, accompained by the divine seers, eulogised the Goddess. Chiefs of the *Gandharvas* sang and *Apsarās* danced. Oṁ

इति श्रीमार्कण्डेयपुराणे सावर्णिके मन्वन्तरे

---

[5]In a few copies, these additional ślokas hereafter: एवं स महिषो नाम ससैन्यः ससुहृद्गणः। त्रैलोक्यं मोहयित्वा तु तया देव्या विनाशितः॥ त्रैलोक्यस्थैस्तदा भूतैर्महिषे विनिपातिते। जयेत्युक्तं ततः सर्वैः सदेवासुरमानवैः॥ *evaṁ sa mahiṣo nāma sasainyaḥ sasuhṛdgaṇaḥ। trailokyaṁ mohayitvā tu tayā devyā vināśitaḥ*॥ *trailokyasthaistadā bhūtairmahiṣe vinipātite। jayetyuktuṁ tataḥ sarvaiḥ sadevāsuramānavaiḥ*॥ In this way, by that Goddess was *Mahiṣa*, along with his army and friends, slayed, deluding the three worlds. After the fall of *Mahiṣa*, all the beings of the three worlds, including the gods, demons and humans, chanted 'Victory' (to the Goddess).

देवीमाहात्म्ये महिषासुरवधोनाम तृतीयोऽध्याय: ॥३॥

iti śrī mārkaṇḍeyapurāṇe sāvarṇike manvantare devīmāhātmye mahiṣāsuravadhonāma tṛtīyo 'dhyāyaḥ ॥3॥

Thus ends the third chapter called 'Slaying of *Mahiṣāsura*' during the era of *Sāvarṇi Manu,* in the 'Glory of the Goddess,' (narrated) in the *Mārkaṇḍeya Purāṇa.*

उवाच ३, श्लोका: ४१, एवम् ४४, एवमादित: २१७

uvāca 3, *ślokāḥ* 41, *evam* 44, *evamāditaḥ* 217

uvāca 3, ślokas 41, total 44, from the beginning up to here 217.

चतुर्थोऽध्यायः

caturtho 'dhyāyaḥ

Chapter Four

Praise of the Goddess by *Indra* and the other gods

ध्यानम्

dhyānam

Meditation

ॐ कालाभ्राभां कटाक्षैररिकुलभयदां मौलिबद्धेन्दुरेखां
शङ्खं चक्रं कृपाणं त्रिशिखमपि करैरुद्वहन्तीं त्रिनेत्राम् ।
सिंहस्कन्धाधिरूढां त्रिभुवनमखिलं तेजसा पूरयन्तीं
ध्यायेद् दुर्गां जयाख्यां त्रिदशपरिवृतां सेवितां सिद्धिकामैः ॥

oṁ. kālābhrābhāṁ kaṭākṣairarikulabhayadāṁ
maulibaddhendurekhāṁ
śaṅkhaṁ cakraṁ kṛpāṇaṁ triśikhamapi karair-
udvahantīṁ trinetrām ।
siṁhaskandhādhirūḍhāṁ tribhuvanamakhilaṁ
tejasā pūrayantīṁ
dhyāyed durgāṁ jayākhyāṁ tridaśaparivṛtāṁ
sevitāṁ siddhikāmaiḥ ॥

OṀ. MEDITATE UPON *DURGĀ*, THE IMPASSABLE, KNOWN AS *JAYĀ*, VICTORY. HER GLOWING BODY IS OF THE HUE OF THE DARK CLOUDS. WITH HER SIDE GLANCES, SHE INSTILLS FEAR AMONG THE HOSTS OF ENEMIES. ON HER HEAD A STREAK OF MOON SHINES. IN HER HANDS, SHE WIELDS A CONCH, A DISCUS, A SCIMITAR AND A TRIDENT. SHE HAS THREE EYES AND IS SADDLED ON THE SHOULDER OF THE LION. WITH HER EFFULGENCE SHE FILLS ALL THE THREE WORLDS. SHE IS SURROUNDED BY THE GODS. THOSE WHO DESIRE THE ULTIMATE ACCOMPLISHMENT, ATTEND ON HER.

ॐ ऋषिरुवाच[1] ॥१॥

1. *oṁ. ṛṣiruvāca*[1]

शक्रादयः सुरगणा निहतेऽतिवीर्ये
तस्मिन्दुरात्मनि सुरारिबले च देव्या।
तां तुष्टुवुः प्रणतिनम्रशिरोधरांसा
वाग्भिः प्रहर्षपुलकोद्गमचारुदेहाः ॥२॥

2. *śakrādayaḥ suragaṇā nihate 'tivīrye*
tasminduratmani surāribale ca devyā ।
tāṁ tuṣṭuvuḥ praṇatinamraśirodharāṁsā
vāgbhiḥ praharṣapulakodgamacārudehāḥ ॥

Oṁ. The Seer said

The wicked and the mighty demon having been killed along with his army by the Goddess, *Indra* and the other gods bowed their heads with their shoulders in obeisance to her and started eulogising her. Due to extreme joy, their bodies had horripilation.

देव्या यया ततमिदं जगदात्मशक्त्या।
निश्शेषदेवगणशक्तिसमूहमूर्त्या।
तामम्बिकामखिलदेवमहर्षिपूज्यां
भक्त्या नताः स्म विदधातु शुभानि सा नः ॥३॥

3. *devyā yayā tatamidaṁ jagadātmaśaktyā*
niḥśeṣadevagaṇaśaktisamūhamūrtyā ।
tāmambikāmakhiladevamaharṣipūjyām
bhaktyā natāḥ sma vidadhātu śubhāni sā naḥ ॥

---

[1]Additional reading after this in some copies: ततः सुरगणाः सर्वे देव्या इन्द्रपुरोगमाः। स्तुतिमारेभिरेकर्तुं निहते महिषासुरे॥ *tataḥ suragaṇāḥ sarve devyā indrapurogamāḥ* । *stutimārebhirekartuṁ nihate mahiṣāsure* ॥ Then, following *Mahiṣāsura*'s death at the hands of the Goddess, all the gods led by *Indra* began singing her eulogy.

(They said:) She is the Goddess by whose intrinsic energy the whole world is pervaded. Of the cumulated energy of all the gods is she the embodiment. By all the gods and seers is she worshipped. We bow to that Mother with loving devotion. May she bring us auspiciousness.

यस्याः प्रभावमतुलं भगवाननन्तो
ब्रह्मा हरश्च न हि वक्तुमलं बलं च ।
सा चण्डिकाखिलजगत्परिपालनाय
नाशाय चाशुभभयस्य मतिं करोतु ।।४।।

4. *yasyāḥ prabhāvamatulaṁ bhagavānananto*
brahmā haraśca na hi vaktumalaṁ balaṁ ca ।
sā caṇḍikākhilajagatparipālanāya
nāśāya cāśubhabhayasya matiṁ karotu ।।

Lord *Śeṣa*, the Great Serpent; Lord *Brahmā*, the Creator and Lord *Śiva*, the Destroyer; are not competent to express her incomparable majesty. May that *Caṇḍikā*, the Annihilator of Evil, contemplate protection of the world and destruction of inauspicious fear.

या श्रीः स्वयं सुकृतिनां भवनेष्वलक्ष्मीः
पापात्मनां कृतधियां हृदयेषु बुद्धिः।
श्रद्धा सतां कुलजनप्रभवस्य लज्जा
तां त्वां नताः स्म परिपालय देवि विश्वम् ।।५।।

5. *yā śrīḥ svayaṁ sukṛtināṁ bhavaneṣvalakṣmīḥ*
pāpātmanāṁ kṛtadhiyāṁ hṛdayeṣu buddhiḥ ।
śraddhā satāṁ kulajanaprabhavasya lajjā
tāṁ tvāṁ natāḥ sma paripālaya devi viśvam ।।

We bow before you who are Wealth and Fortune in the homes of the virtuous, Adversity for sinners, Intelligence in the minds of the wise, Reverential Faith in saintly persons and Modesty in noble people. Please, O Goddess! protect this universe.

किं वर्णयाम तव रूपमचिन्त्यमेतत्
किं चातिवीर्यमसुरक्षयकारि भूरि ।
किं चाहवेषु चरितानि तवाद्भुतानि
सर्वेषु देव्यसुरदेवगणादिकेषु ॥६॥

6. *kiṁ varṇayāma tava rūpamacintyametat*
kiṁ cātivīryamasurakṣayakāri bhūri ।
kiṁ cāhaveṣu caritāni tavādbhutāni
sarveṣu devyasuradevagaṇādikeṣu ॥

How, O Goddess, can we describe your inconceivable form? How can we narrate your immense and abundant valour with which you annihilate the demons? How can we expound your prodigious actions which were witnessed by all the demons and the gods?

हेतुः समस्तजगतां त्रिगुणापि दोषै-
र्न ज्ञायसे हरिहरादिभिरप्यपारा ।
सर्वाश्रयाखिलमिदं जगदंशभूत-
मव्याकृता हि परमा प्रकृतिस्त्वमाद्या ॥७॥

7. *hetuḥ samastajagatāṁ triguṇāpi doṣair-*
na jñāyase hariharādibhirapyapārā ।
sarvāśrayākhilamidaṁ jagdaṁśabhūtam-
avyākṛtā hi paramā prakṛtistvamādyā ॥

You are the cause of this entire creation. Even though all the three modes – *sattva* (goodness or lightness), *rajas* (activity or passion) and *tamas* (darkness or stupor) – are present in you, you are not seen to be affected by them. You are unfathomable even for Lord *Viṣṇu* and Lord *Śiva*. You are the substratum of the universe which is only a fraction of you. You are the elemental, supreme and primordial nature of all this.

यस्याः समस्तसुरता समुदीरणेन
तृप्तिं प्रयाति सकलेषु मखेषु देवि।
स्वाहासि वै पितृगणस्य च तृप्तिहेतु-
रुच्चार्यसे त्वमत एव जनैः स्वधा च ॥८॥

8. *yasyāḥ samastasuratā samudīraṇena*
tṛptiṁ prayāti sakaleṣu makheṣu devi ।
svāhāsi vai pitṛgaṇasya ca tṛptihetur-
uccāryase tvamata eva janaiḥ svadhā ca ॥

O Goddess! You are *Svāhā* (oblation), which when pronounced during the sacrifices, satiates the gods. You are also pronounced as *Svadhā* (oblation for the manes) by people for the satisfaction of the manes.

या मुक्तिहेतुरविचिन्त्यमहाव्रता त्व[2]-
मभ्यस्यसे सुनियतेन्द्रियतत्त्वसारैः।
मोक्षार्थिभिर्मुनिभिरस्तसमस्तदोषैर्-
विद्यासि सा भगवती परमा हि देवि ॥९॥

9. *yā muktiheturavicintyamahāvratā tva*[2]*-*
mabhyasyase suniyatendriyatattvasāraiḥ ।
mokṣārthibhirmunibhirastasamastadoṣair-
vidyāsi sā bhagavatī paramā hi devi ॥

You O Goddess! are the Knowledge Supreme and Sovereign Supreme for those seeking to attain to the final beatitude. The unblemished ascetics, desiring liberation, devoted to you as the Ultimate Reality, practise strict control over their senses, perform inconceivable penances and worship you.

---

[2]AR: च अभ्य *ca abhya*

शब्दात्मिका सुविमलर्ग्यजुषां निधान-
मुद्गीथरम्यपदपाठवतां च साम्नाम् ।
देवी त्रयी भगवती भवभावनाय
वार्ता च सर्वजगतां परमार्तिहन्त्री ॥१०॥

10. *śabdātmikā suvimalrgyajuṣāṁ nidhānam-*
udgītharamyapadapāṭhavatāṁ ca sāmnām ।
devī trayī bhagvatī bhavabhāvanāya
vārtā ca sarvajagatāṁ paramārtihantrī ॥

You are the very spirit of the Word. You are the home of the holy *Ṛg* and *Yajur Vedas.* You are the substratum of the *Sāmaveda* consisting of beautiful hymns (*padapāṭha*) of *Udgītha* (*Oṁkāra*). O Goddess! you are *Trayī* (*Ṛgveda, Sāmaveda* and *Yajurveda*) and *Bhagavatī* (endowed with six majesties*). For creation and sustenance of life, you manifest yourself as *Vārtā* (agriculture and other means of sustenance). You are the great destroyer of the afflictions of this world.

मेधासि देवि विदिताखिलशास्त्रसारा
दुर्गासि दुर्गभवसागरनौरसङ्गा ।
श्रीः कैटभारि हृदयैककृताधिवासा
गौरी त्वमेव शशिमौलिकृतप्रतिष्ठा ॥११॥

11. *medhāsi devi viditākhilaśastrasārā*
durgāsi durgabhavasāgaranaurasaṅgā ।
śrī kaiṭabhārihṛdayaikakṛtādhivāsā
gaurī tvameva śaśimaulikṛtapratiṣṭhā ॥

O Goddess! as *Medhā,* you are the facilitator of knowledge of the essence of all scriptures. As *Durgā,* you are the boat that takes persons across the sea of metempsychosis, yet you are devoid of all attachment.

---

* These are: *Jñāna* (knowledge), *bala* (power), *aiśvarya* (supreme authority), *Vīrya* (prowess), *Śakti* (energy) and *teja* (lustre).

As *Lakṣmī,* you alone are the occupier of the heart of Lord *Viṣṇu,* the enemy of *Kaiṭabha* and as *Gaurī,* you are highly regarded by Lord *Śiva* who wears the crown of the moon.

ईषत्सहासममलं परिपूर्णचन्द्र-
बिम्बानुकारि कनकोत्तमकान्तिकान्तम् ।
अत्यद्भुतं प्रहतमात्तरुषा तथापि
वक्त्रं विलोक्य सहसा महिषासुरेण ।।१२।।

12. *īṣatsahāsamamalaṁ paripūrṇacandra-*
bimbānukāri kanakottamakāntikāntam ।
atyadbhutaṁ prahatamāttaruṣā tathāpi
vaktraṁ vilokya sahasā mahiṣāsureṇa ।।

Your pellucid visage, with a soft smile on it, resembles the orb of the full moon and its splendour, the lustre of the purest gold. It is strange that even then *Mahiṣāsura,* on seeing it, suddenly flew into rage.

दृष्ट्वा तु देवि कुपितं भ्रुकुटीकराल-
मुद्यच्छशाङ्क सदृशच्छवि यन्न सद्यः ।
प्राणान्मुमोच महिषस्तदतीव चित्रं
कैर्जीव्यते हि कुपितान्तकदर्शनेन ।।१३।।

13. *dṛṣṭvā tu devi kupitaṁ bhrukuṭī karālam-*
udyacchaśāṅka sadṛśacchavi yanna sadyaḥ ।
prāṇānmumoca mahiṣastadatīva citraṁ
kairjīvyate hi kupitāntakadarśanena ।।

Greater (than this) is the surprise that *Mahiṣa* did not quit breathing in the instant of seeing you angry, your brow being terribly raised and your face becoming red with rage like the rising red moon, for who can survive after looking at Death in anger?

देवि प्रसीद परमा भवती भवाय
सद्यो विनाशयसि कोपवती कुलानि ।
विज्ञातमेतदधुनैव यदस्तमेत-
न्नीतं बलं सुविपुलं महिषासुरस्य ।।१४।।

14. *devi prasīda paramā bhavatī bhavāya*
sadyo vināśayasi kopavatī kulāni ।
vijñātametadadhunaiva yadastametan-
nītaṁ balaṁ suvipulaṁ mahiṣāsurasya ।।

O Goddess! be gracious to us, you are the intrinsic nature of Ultimate Reality. Pleased, you bring ascendance to the world and enraged, you destroy whole clans instantly. This we have realized just now when the entire capacious army of *Mahiṣāsura* has been annihilated by you in a matter of minutes.

ते सम्मता जनपदेषु धनानि तेषां
तेषां यशांसि न च सीदति धर्मवर्गः ।
धन्यास्त एव निभृतात्मज भृत्यदारा
येषां सदाभ्युदयदा भवती प्रसन्ना ।।१५।।

15. *te sammatā janapadeṣu dhanāni teṣāṁ*
teṣāṁ yaśāṁsi na ca sīdati dharmavargaḥ ।
dhanyāsta eva nibhṛtātmaja bhṛtyadārā
yeṣāṁ sadābhyudayadā bhavatī prasannā ।।

Those, O Venerable Bestower of Ascendance! who are blessed with your pellucid grace, are honoured in the country, theirs is the wealth and glory, their pursuit of righteousness never does suffer, they alone along with their children, servants and wives are fortunate.

धर्म्याणि देवि सकलानि सदैव कर्मा-
ण्यत्यादृत: प्रतिदिनं सुकृती करोति।
स्वर्गं प्रयाति च ततो भवती प्रसादा-
ल्लोकत्रयेऽपि फलदा ननु देवि तेन ॥१६॥

16. *dharmyāṇi devi sakalāni sadaiva karmā-*
ṇyatyādṛtaḥ prātidinaṁ sukṛtī karoti ।
svargaṁ prayāti ca tato bhavatī prasādāl-
lokatraye 'pi phaladā nanu devi tena ॥

O Blessed Goddess! it is with your grace that a noble person is enabled to perform righteous acts faithfully everyday. Thereafter he goes to heaven. Certainly, therefore, you are the dispenser of the desired fruit to the people in the three worlds.

दुर्गे स्मृता हरसि भीतिमशेषजन्तो:
स्वस्थै: स्मृता मतिमतीव शुभां ददासि।
दारिद्र्यदु:खभयहारिणि का त्वदन्या
सर्वोपकारकरणाय सदाऽऽर्द्रचित्ता ॥१७॥

17. *durge smṛtā harasi bhītimaśeṣajantoḥ*
svasthaiḥ smṛtā matimatīva śubhāṁ dadāsi ।
dāridryaduḥkhbhayahāriṇi kā tvadanyā
sarvopakārakaraṇāya sadā ''rdracittā ॥

O *Durgā*, the Allayer of Obstructions! on being remembered, you alleviate the fears of all beings. Those who are established in the self are blessed with pious intellect when they remember you. Who else but you are the dispeller of indigence, pain and fear? Always full of compassion, you are engaged in the welfare of all.

एभिर्हतैर्जगदुपैति सुखं तथैते
कुर्वन्तु नाम नरकाय चिराय पापम् ।
संग्राममृत्युमधिगम्य दिवं प्रयातु
मत्वेति नूनमहितान् विनिहंसि देवि ।।१८।।

18. *ebhirhatairjagadupaiti sukhaṁ tathaite*
kurvantu nāma narakāya cirāya pāpam ।
saṅgrāmamṛtyumadhigamya divaṁ prayātu
matveti nūnamahitān vinihaṁsi devi ।।

O Goddess! you slay these demons so that the world attains to happiness and, even though they have been committing sins to deserve hell for a long duration, these wrong doers are slayed by you certainly to help them go to celestial abodes.

दृष्ट्वैव किं न भवती प्रकरोति भस्म
सर्वासुरानरिषु यत्प्रहिणोषि शस्त्रम् ।
लोकान् प्रयान्तु रिपवोऽपि हि शस्त्रपूता
इत्थं मतिर्भवति तेष्वपि तेऽतिसाध्वी ।।१९।।

19. *dṛṣṭvaiva kiṁ na bhavatī prakaroti bhasma*
sarvāsurānariṣu yatprahiṇoṣi śastram ।
lokān prayāntu ripavo 'pi hi śastrapūtā
itthaṁ matirbhavati teṣvapi te 'tisādhvī ।।

Why, O Blessed Lady! you do not reduce these enemies of the gods to ashes with just an adverse glance? Why have you to kill them with weapons? Your intention indeed is that they be purified with the touch of your weapons and attain to the higher worlds; such is your benevolence even towards your enemies.

खड्गप्रभानिकरविस्फुरणैस्तथोग्रैः
शूलाग्रकान्तिनिवहेन दृशोऽसुराणाम् ।
यन्नागता विलयमंशुमदिन्दुखण्ड-
योग्याननं तव विलोकयतां तदेतत् ॥२०॥

20. *khaḍgaprabhānikaravisphuraṇaistathograiḥ*
śūlāgrakāntinivahena dṛśo 'surāṇām ।
yannāgatā vilayamaṁśumadindukhaṇḍa-
yogyānanaṁ tava vilokayatāṁ tadetat ॥

That even with the frightful dazzle of your sword and the fire-spewing tip of your pike, the demons were not deprived of their eyesight was because they were looking at your beautiful face which is like the delightful glow of the rays of the moon.

दुर्वृत्तवृत्तशमनं तव देवि शीलं
रूपं तथैतदविचिन्त्यमतुल्यमन्यैः ।
वीर्यं च हन्तृ हृतदेवपराक्रमाणां
वैरिष्वपि प्रकटितैव दया त्वयेत्थम् ॥२१॥

21. *durvṛttavṛttaśamanaṁ tava devi śīlaṁ*
rūpaṁ tathaitadavicintyamatulyamanyaiḥ ।
vīryaṁ ca hantṛ hṛtadevaparākramāṇāṁ
vairiṣvapi prakaṭitaiva dayā tvayettham ॥

O Goddess! your disposition quells thc foul behaviour of the wicked. Your form is inconceivable and incomparable with any one. Your valour is so fierce that it kills even those who, with their might, had crushed the might of the gods. In this way, you have only demonstrated your compassion even to the enemies.

केनोपमा भवतु तेऽस्य पराक्रमस्य
रूपं च शत्रु भयकार्यतिहारि कुत्र ।
चित्ते कृपा समरनिष्ठुरता च दृष्टा
त्वय्येव देवि वरदे भुवनत्रयेऽपि ॥२२॥

22. *kenopamā bhavatu te 'sya parākramasya*
rūpaṁ ca śatru bhayakāryatihāri kutra ।
citte kṛpā samaraniṣṭhuratā ca dṛṣṭā
tvayyeva devi varade bhuvanatraye 'pi ॥

O Goddess, Dispenser of Boons! with whom can your valour be compared? Where else is the charming form which, at the same time, rouses fear and distress among the enemies? In the three worlds, only in you is seen compassion in heart and ruthlessness in battle.

त्रैलोक्यमेतदखिलं रिपुनाशनेन
त्रातं त्वया समरमूर्धनि तेऽपि हत्वा ।
नीता दिवं रिपुगणा भयमप्यपास्त-
मस्माकमुन्मदसुरारिभवं नमस्ते ॥२३॥

23. *trailokyametadakhilaṁ ripunāśanena*
trātaṁ tvayā samaramūrdhani te 'pi hatvā ।
nītā divaṁ ripugaṇā bhayamapyapāstam-
asmākamunmadasurāribhavaṁ namaste ॥

Our obeisance to you, O Mother. By annihilating the enemies, you have saved the three worlds and even by killing them, you have sent them to celestial regions. In so doing, you have allayed our fears of those foolish foes of the gods.

शूलेन पाहि नो देवि पाहि खड्गेन चाम्बिके।
घण्टास्वनेन नः पाहि चापज्यानिःस्वनेन च ॥२४॥

24. *śūlena pāhi no devi pāhi khaḍgena cāmbike* ।
ghaṇṭāsvanena naḥ pāhi cāpajyāniḥsvanena ca ॥

Protect us, O Goddess! with your pike. O Mother! protect us with your sword. Protect us with the sound of your bell and with the twang of your bow.

प्राच्यां रक्ष प्रतीच्यां च चण्डिके रक्ष दक्षिणे।
भ्रामणेनात्मशूलस्य उत्तरस्यां तथेश्वरि ॥२५॥

25. *prācyāṁ rakṣa pratīcyāṁ ca caṇḍike rakṣa dakṣiṇe* ।
bhrāmaṇenātmaśūlasya uttarasyāṁ tatheśvari ॥

Protect us, O *Caṇḍikā*, in the East as well as in the West. Protect us in the South and, O Supreme Goddess! protect us in the North by revolving your pike.

सौम्यानि यानि रूपाणि त्रैलोक्ये विचरन्ति ते।
यानि चात्यर्थघोराणि तै रक्षास्मांस्तथा भुवम् ॥२६॥

26. *saumyāni yāni rūpāṇi trailokye vicaranti te* ।
yāni cātyarthaghorāṇi tai rakṣāsmāṁstathā bhuvam ॥

In whichever gentle or frightful forms you wander in the three worlds, with them please protect us as well as the earth.

खड्गशूलगदादीनि यानि चास्त्राणि तेऽम्बिके।
करपल्लवसङ्गीनि तैरस्मान् रक्ष सर्वतः ॥२७॥

27. *khaḍgaśūlagadādīni yāni cāstrāṇi te 'mbike* ।
karapallavasaṅgīni tairasmān rakṣa sarvataḥ ॥

Sword, pike, mace and whichever other weapons are held in your palms, with them, O Mother, protect us in all directions.

ऋषिरुवाच ॥२८॥

28. *ṛṣiruvāca*

एवं स्तुता सुरैर्दिव्यैः कुसुमैर्नन्दनोद्भवैः।
अर्चिता जगतां धात्री तथा गन्धानुलेपनैः ॥२९॥

29. *evaṁ stutā surairdivyaiḥ kusumairnandanodbhavaiḥ* ।
arcitā jagatāṁ dhātrī tathā gandhānulepanaiḥ ॥

भक्त्या समस्तैस्त्रिदशैर्दिव्यैर्धूपैस्तु[3] धूपिता ।
प्राह प्रसादसुमुखी समस्तान् प्रणतान् सुरान् ॥३०॥

30. *bhaktyā samastaistridaśairdivyairdhūpaistu*[3] *dhūpitā* ।
prāha prasādasumukhī samastān praṇatān surān ॥

The seer said

Thus worshipped by all the gods with panegyrics, celestial flowers of the *Nandana* garden, unguents and heavenly incenses, the Mother of the pellucid disposition spoke to them whose heads were bowed down in obeisance and loving devotion.

देव्युवाच ॥३१॥

31. *devyuvāca*

व्रियतां त्रिदशाः सर्वे यदस्मत्तोऽभिवाञ्छितम्[4] ॥३२॥

32. *vriyatāṁ tridaśāḥ sarve yadasmatto 'bhivāñchitaṁ*[4] ॥

The Goddess said

Tell me O gods! what boons do all of you seek from me.

---

[3]AR: धूपैः सुधूपिता *dhūpaih sudhūpitā*

[4]In some later editions of the *Mārkaṇḍeya Purāṇa* following is the additional half śloka: ददाम्यहमतिप्रीत्या स्तवैरेभिः सुपूजिता। *dadāmyahamati-prītyā stvairebhiḥ supūjitā*। – "Worshipped most appropriately with these hymns, I shall grant (the boons) with great pleasure."

In a few editions the following is the addition : कर्तव्यमपरं यच्च दुष्करं तन्नविद्महे। इत्याकर्ण्य वचो देव्याः प्रत्यूचुस्ते दिवौकसः॥ *kartavyamaparaṁ yacca duṣkaraṁ tannavidmahe*। *ityākarṇya vaco devyāḥ pratyūcuste divaukasaḥ*॥ "I do not know of any other arduous act to be accomplished by me." Hearing these words of the Goddess, those dwellers of heaven (gods) replied.

देवा ऊचुः ॥३३॥

33. *devā ūcuḥ*

भगवत्या कृतं सर्वं न किंचिदवशिष्यते ॥३४॥

34. *bhagavatyā kṛtaṁ sarvaṁ na kiñcidavaśiṣyate* ॥

यदयं निहतः शत्रुरस्माकं महिषासुरः ।
यदि चापि वरो देयस्त्वयास्माकं महेश्वरि ॥३५॥

35. *yadayaṁ nihataḥ śatrurasmākaṁ mahiṣāsuraḥ* ।
yadi cāpi varo deyastvayāsmākaṁ maheśvari ॥

संस्मृता संस्मृता त्वं नो हिंसेथाः परमापदः ।
यश्च मर्त्यः स्तवैरेभिस्त्वां स्तोष्यत्यमलानने ॥३६॥

36. *saṁsmṛtā saṁsmṛtā tvaṁ no hiṁsethāḥ paramāpadaḥ* ।
yaśca martyaḥ stavairebhistvāṁ stoṣyatyamalānane ॥

तस्य वित्तर्द्धिविभवैर्धनदारादिसम्पदाम् ।
वृद्धयेऽस्मत्प्रसन्ना त्वं भवेथाः सर्वदाम्बिके ॥३७॥

37. *tasya vittarddhivibhavairdhanadārādisaṁpadām* ।
vṛddhaye 'smatprasannā tvaṁ bhavethāḥ sarvadāmbike ॥

The gods said

The Supreme Goddess has done everything, nothing remains now that our enemy *Mahiṣāsura* has been slain. Even then, O Supreme Sovereign, if a boon is to be granted by you to us, then please deliver us from great calamity (if and when there is any), everytime we remember you. Moreover, O Mother of Pellucid Countenance! any mortal who, with these hymns, eulogises you, may be blessed with ever increasing wealth, prosperity, power, wife, and other fortunes.

ऋषिरुवाच ॥३८॥

38. *ṛṣiruvāca*

इति प्रसादिता देवैर्जगतोऽर्थे तथाऽऽत्मनः ।
तथेत्युक्त्वा भद्रकाली बभूवान्तर्हिता नृप ॥३९॥

39. *iti prasāditā devairjagato 'rthe tathā ''tmanaḥ* ।
tathetyuktvā bhadrakālī babhūvāntarhitā nṛpa ॥

The Seer said

O king! thus felicitated by the gods, *Bhadrakālī,* the Gentle Goddess of Dark Complexion, said, for their welfare and that of the world, 'so be it' and became invisible.

इत्येतत्कथितं भूप सम्भूता सा यथा पुरा ।
देवी देवशरीरेभ्यो जगत्त्रयहितैषिणी ॥४०॥

40. *ityetatkathitaṁ bhūpa saṁbhūtā sā yathā purā* ।
devī devaśarīrebhyo jagattrayahitaiṣiṇī ॥

I have, o king, fully narrated how, in the ancient times, the Goddess, the Benefactor of the Three Worlds, had manifested herself from the bodies of the gods.

पुनश्च गौरी देहात्सा[5] समुद्भूता यथाभवत् ।
वधाय दुष्टदैत्यानां तथा शुम्भनिशुम्भयोः ॥४१॥

41. *punaśca gaurī dehātsā*[5] *samudbhūtā yathābhavat* ।
vadhāya duṣṭadaityānāṁ tathā śumbhaniśumbhayoḥ ॥

रक्षणाय च लोकानां देवानामुपकारिणी ।
तच्छृणुष्व मयाऽऽख्यातं यथावत्कथयामि ते ॥ह्रीं ॥ॐ॥४२॥

42. *rakṣaṇāya ca lokānāṁ devānāmupakāriṇī* ।
tacchṛṇuṣva mayā ''khyātaṁ yathāvatkathayāmi te
॥ hrīṁ ॥ oṁ ॥

---

[5]AR: गौरीदेहा सा अथवा गौरी देहा सा *gaurīdehā sā* or *gaurī dehā sā*

Now listen. I shall describe, as it happened, the origin of the Goddess, the Benefactor of the gods, from the body of *Gaurī*, the White Complexioned Consort of Lord *Śiva*, for slaying the wicked demons and *Śumbha-Niśumbha* for the protection of the worlds. Oṁ

इति श्रीमार्कण्डेयपुराणे सावर्णिके मन्वन्तरे देवीमाहात्म्ये
शक्रादिस्तुतिर्नाम चतुर्थोऽध्यायः ॥४॥

īti śrī mārkaṇḍeyapurāṇe sāvarṇike manvantare
devīmāhātmye śakrādistutirnāma caturtho 'dhyāyaḥ ॥4॥

Thus ends the fourth chapter called 'Praise by *Indra* and the Other Gods' during the era of *Sāvarṇi Manu*, (narrated) in the *Mārkanḍeya Purāṇa*.

उवाच ५, अर्धश्लोकौ २, श्लोकाः ३५, एवम् ४२, एवमादितः २५६
uvāca 5, *ardhaślokau* 2, *ślokāḥ* 35, *evam* 42, *evamāditaḥ* 259

uvāca 5, half ślokas 2, ślokas 35, total 42,
from beginning up to here 259.

श्रीदुर्गासप्तशती
Śrīdurgāsaptaśatī
Seven Hundred Verses to *Durgā*

उत्तर / उत्तमचरित
Uttara / UttamaÇarita

The Final Act

(Chapters Five-Thirteen)

श्री महासरस्वतीमाहात्म्यग्
Śrī Mahāsarasvatīmāhātmyam

Glory of *Śrīmahāsarasvatī*

विनियोगः

viniyogaḥ

Presentation

ॐ अस्य श्रीउत्तरचरित्रस्य रुद्र ऋषिः, महासरस्वती देवता, अनुष्टुप् छन्दः, भीमा शक्तिः, भ्रामरी बीजम्, सूर्यस्तत्त्वम्, सामवेदः स्वरूपम्, महासरस्वतीप्रीत्यर्थे उत्तरचरित्रपाठे विनियोगः ।

oṁ. asya śrīuttarcaritrasya rudra ṛṣiḥ, mahāsarasvatī devatā, anuṣṭup chandaḥ, bhīmā śaktiḥ, bhrāmarī bījam, sūryastattvam, sāmavedaḥ svarūpam, mahāsarasvatīprītyarthe uttaracaritra pāṭhe viniyogaḥ

Oṁ. Of this Final Act, *Rudra* is the seer, *Mahāsarasvatī* is the deity, *anuṣṭup* is the metre, *Bhīmā* is the energy, *Bhrāmarī* is the seed, Sun is the true essence, *Sāmaveda* is the true nature.

Presented here is the recitation of the Final Act for the felicity of *Mahāsarasvatī*.

पञ्चमोऽध्यायः॥

pañcamo 'dhyāyaḥ॥

Chapter Five

Eulogy of the Goddess by the gods and conversation between the Goddess and the messenger of *Śumbha*

ध्यानम्

dhyānam

Meditation

ॐ घण्टाशूलहलानि शङ्खमुसले चक्रं धनुः सायकं
हस्ताब्जैर्दधतीं घनान्तविलसच्छीतांशुतुल्यप्रभाम्।
गौरीदेहसमुद्भवां त्रिजगतामाधारभूतां महा-
पूर्वामत्र सरस्वतीमनुभजे शुम्भादिदैत्यार्दिनीम्॥

oṁ. ghaṇṭāśūlahalāni śaṅkhamusale cakraṁ dhanuḥ sāyakaṁ
hastābjairdadhatīṁ ghanāntavilasacchītāṁśutulyaprabhām ।
gaurīdehasamudbhavāṁ trijagatāmādhārabhūtāṁ mahā-
pūrvāmatra sarasvatīmanubhaje śumbhādidaityārdinīm ॥

OṀ. I UNFAILINGLY WORSHIP THE FOREMOST GODDESS, *MAHĀSARASVATĪ*, THE GREAT BESTOWER OF SUPREME KNOWLEDGE, THE TORMENTOR OF DEMONS *ŚUMBHA*, ETC. SHE IS MANIFESTED FROM THE BODY OF *GAURĪ*, THE WHITE COMPLEXIONED GODDESS. SHE HOLDS IN HER LOTUS HANDS, A BELL, A PIKE, A PLOUGH, A CONCH, A PESTLE, A DISC, A BOW AND AN ARROW. HER EFFULGENCE IS LIKE THE GLOW OF THE AUTUMNAL MOON. SHE IS THE SUBSTRATUM OF THE THREE WORLDS.

ॐ क्लीं ऋषिरुवाच ।।१।।

1. *oṁ klīṁ. ṛṣiruvāca*

पुरा शुम्भनिशुम्भाभ्यामसुराभ्यां शचीपतेः ।
त्रैलोक्यं यज्ञभागाश्च हृता मदबलाश्रयात् ।।२।।

2. *purā śumbhaniśumbhābhyāmasurābhyāṁ śacīpateḥ* ।
trailokyaṁ yajñabhāgāśca hṛtā madabalāśrayāt ।।

Oṁ Klīṁ. The Seer said

In the ancient times, *Śumbha* and *Niśumbha*, intoxicated with power, had snatched from *Indra*, the consort of *Śacī*, the empire of the three worlds and the share of oblations in the sacrifices.

तावेव सूर्यतां तद्वदधिकारं तथैन्दवम् ।
कौबेरमथ याम्यं च चक्राते वरुणस्य च ।।३।।

3. *tāveva sūryatāṁ tadvadadhikāraṁ tathaindavam* ।
kauberamatha yāmyaṁ ca cakrāte varuṇasya ca ।।

तावेव पवनर्द्धिं च चक्रतुर्वह्निकर्म च[1] ।
ततो देवा विनिर्धूता भ्रष्टराज्या पराजिताः ।।४।।

4. *tāveva pavanarddhiṁ ca cakraturvahnikarma ca*[1] ।
tato devā vinirdhūtā bhraṣṭarājyā parājitāḥ ।।

हृताधिकारास्त्रिदशास्ताभ्यां सर्वे निराकृताः ।
महासुराभ्यां तां देवीं संस्मरन्त्यपराजिताम् ।।5।।

5. *hṛtādhikārāstridaśāstābhyāṁ sarve nirākṛtāḥ* ।
mahāsurābhyāṁ tāṁ devīṁ saṁsmarantyaparājitām ।।

---

[1] Additional reading in some copies: अन्येषां चाधिकारान् स स्वयमेवाधितिष्ठति *anyeṣāṁ cādhikārān sa svayamevādhitiṣṭhati*. He also seized the authority of the others and vested it in himself.

तयास्माकं वरो दत्तो यथाऽऽपत्सु स्मृताखिलाः ।
भवतां नाशयिष्यामि तत्क्षणात्परमापदः ॥६॥

6. *tayāsmākaṁ varo datto yātha ''patsu smṛtākhilāḥ* ।
bhavatāṁ nāśayiṣyāmi tatkṣaṇātparamāpadaḥ ॥

In the same way, they started exercising the authority of the Sun; the Moon; *Kubera,* the Treasurer of the Gods and Regent of the Northern Quarter; *Yama* (Death); and *Varuṇa,* the Regent of the Ocean and of the Western Quarter. They also usurped the functions of *Pavana* (Air) and *Agni* (Fire). Thus were all the gods slighted and their dominions taken away. They were defeated and exiled by those mighty demons. When they were, thus, deprived, the gods remembered the invincible Goddess and recalled: She had given us the boon, 'whenever any great calamity befalls you and you remember me, I shall instantly drive away the calamity'.

इति कृत्वा मतिं देवा हिमवन्तं नगेश्वरम् ।
जग्मुस्तत्र ततो देवीं विष्णुमायां प्रतुष्टुवुः ॥७॥

7. *iti kṛtvā matiṁ devā himavantaṁ nageśvaram* ।
jagmustatra tato devīṁ viṣṇumāyāṁ pratuṣṭuvuḥ ॥

Thinking thus, the gods went to *Himālaya,* the King of the Mountains and there they began to extol the Goddess, the Illusive Power of *Viṣṇu.*

देवा ऊचुः ॥८॥

8. *devā ūcuḥ*
The gods said

नमो देव्यै महादेव्यै शिवायै सततं नमः ।
नमः प्रकृत्यै भद्रायै नियताः प्रणताः स्म ताम् ॥९॥

9. *namo devyai mahādevyai śivāyai satataṁ namaḥ* ।
namaḥ prakṛtyai bhadrāyai niyatāḥ praṇatāḥ sma tām ॥

Obeisance to the Goddess, the Supreme Goddess. Obeisance forever to *Śivā*, the Goddess of Felicity. Obeisance to *Prakṛti*, the Primordial Nature. Obeisance to *Bhadrā*, the Laudable. We bow in salutation to her and unfailingly.

रौद्रायै नमो नित्यायै गौर्यै धात्र्यै नमो नमः ।
ज्योत्स्नायै चेन्दुरूपिण्यै सुखायै सततं नमः ॥१०॥

10. *raudrāyai namo nityāyai gauryai dhātryai namo namaḥ* ।
jyotsnāyai cendurūpiṇyai sukhāyai satataṁ namaḥ ॥

Obeisance to *Raudrā*, the Formidable. Obeisance to *Nityā*, the Eternal. Obeisance to *Gaurī*, the Fair Complexioned. Obeisance to *Dhātrī*, the Nurturer. Obeisance to *Jyotsnā*, the Effulgence and Intrinsic Nature of the Moon. Obeisance always to *Sukhā*, the Felicity.

कल्याण्यै प्रणतां वृद्ध्यै सिद्ध्यै कुर्मो नमो नमः ।
नैर्ऋत्यै भूभृतां लक्ष्म्यै शर्वाण्यै ते नमो नमः ॥११॥

11. *kalyānyai praṇatāṁ vṛdhyai siddhyai kurmo namo namaḥ* ।
nairṛtyai bhūbhṛtāṁ lakṣmyai śarvāṇyai te namo namaḥ ॥

Obeisance again and again to *Vṛddhi*, the Augmentation and *Siddhi*, the Accomplishment, engaged in the welfare of those who seek refuge in her. Obeisance, Obeisance to *Nairṛti*, the Fortune of the Demons; *Lakṣmī*, the Prosperity of the Kings and *Śarvāṇī*, the consort of Lord *Śiva*.

दुर्गायै दुर्गपारायै सारायै सर्वकारिण्यै ।
ख्यात्यै तथैव कृष्णायै धूम्रायै सततं नमः ॥१२॥

12. *durgāyai durgapārāyai sārāyai sarvakāriṇyai* ।
khyātyai tathaiva kṛṣnāyai dhūmrāyai satataṁ namaḥ ॥

Obeisance again and again to *Durgā*, the Impassable, *Durgapārā*, the Deliverer from Calamity; *Sārā*, the Quintessence of All; *Sarvakāriṇī*, the Cause of All; *Khyāti*, the Fame; *Kṛṣṇā*, the Dark–Complexioned (or the

Consort of *Viṣṇu*) and *Dhūmrā*, the One Risen from the Smoke of the Sacrificial Fire.

अतिसौम्यातिरौद्रायै नतास्तस्यै नमो नमः ।
नमो जगत्प्रतिष्ठायै देव्यै कृत्यै नमो नमः ॥१३॥

13. *atisaumyātiraudrāyai natāstasyai namo namaḥ* ।
namo jagatpratiṣṭhāyai devyai kṛtyai namo namaḥ ॥

We bow before and pay obeisance to *Atisaumyā*, Extremely Gentle and Charming and *Atiraudrā*, Extremely Wrathful. Obeisance again and again to the Goddess *Kṛti*, the Substratum of the World.

या देवी सर्वभूतेषु विष्णुमायेतिशब्दिता ।
नमस्तस्यै ॥१४॥ नमस्तस्यै ॥१५॥ नमस्तस्यै नमो नमः ॥१६॥

yā devī sarvabhūteṣu viṣṇumāyeti śabditā ।
14 *namastasyai* ॥ 15 *namastasyai* ॥ 16 *namastasyai namo namaḥ* ॥

To the Goddess who is known among all beings as *Viṣṇumāyā*, the Illusive Power of Lord *Viṣṇu*: obeisance, obeisance, obeisance again and again.

या देवी सर्वभूतेषु चेतनेत्यभिधीयते ।
नमस्तस्यै ॥१७॥ नमस्तस्यै ॥१८॥ नमस्तस्यै नमो नमः ॥१९॥

yā devī sarvabhūteṣu cetanetyabhidhīyate ।
17 *namastasyai* ॥ 18 *namastasyai* ॥ 19 *namastasyai namo namaḥ*॥

To the Goddess who is known as *Cetanā*, the Consciousness, in all beings: obeisance, obeisance, obeisance again and again.

या देवी सर्वभूतेषु बुद्धिरूपेण संस्थिता ।
नमस्तस्यै ॥२०॥ नमस्तस्यै ॥२१॥ नमस्तस्यै नमो नमः ॥२२॥

yā devī sarvabhūteṣu buddhirūpeṇa saṁsthitā ।
20 *namastasyai* ॥ 21 *namastasyai* ॥ 22 *namastasyai namo namaḥ* ॥

To the Goddess who abides in all beings as *Buddhi*, the Intellect: obeisance, obeisance, obeisance again and again.

या देवी सर्वभूतेषु निद्रारूपेण संस्थिता।
नमस्तस्यै ॥२३॥ नमस्तस्यै ॥२४॥ नमस्तस्यै नमो नमः ॥२५॥

yā devī sarvabhūteṣu nidrārūpeṇa saṁsthitā ।
23 *namastasyai* ॥ 24 *namastasyai* ॥ 25 *namastasyai namo namaḥ* ॥

To the Goddess who abides in all beings as *Nidrā*, Sleep: obeisance, obeisance, obeisance again and again.

या देवी सर्वभूतेषु क्षुधारूपेण संस्थिता।
नमस्तस्यै ॥२६॥ नमस्तस्यै ॥२७॥ नमस्तस्यै नमो नमः ॥२८॥

yā devī sarvabhūteṣu kṣudhārūpeṇa saṁsthitā ।
26 *namastasyai* ॥ 27 *namastasyai* ॥ 28 *namastasyai namo namaḥ* ॥

To the Goddess who abides in all beings as *Kṣudhā*, Hunger: obeisance, obeisance, obeisance again and again.

या देवी सर्वभूतेषुच्छायारूपेण संस्थिता।
नमस्तस्यै ॥२९॥ नमस्तस्यै ॥३०॥ नमस्तस्यै नमो नमः ॥३१॥

yā devī sarvabhūteṣucchāyārūpeṇa saṁsthitā ।
29 *namastasyai* ॥ 30 *namastasyai* ॥ 31 *namastasyai namo namaḥ* ॥

To the Goddess who abides in all beings as *Chāyā*, Reflection: obeisance, obeisance, obeisance again and again.

या देवी सर्वभूतेषु शक्तिरूपेण संस्थिता।
नमस्तस्यै ॥३२॥ नमस्तस्यै ॥३३॥ नमस्तस्यै नमो नमः ॥३४॥

yā devī sarvabhūteṣū śaktirupeṇa saṁsthitā ।
32 *namastasyai* ॥ 33 *namastasyai* ॥ 34 *namastasyai namo namaḥ* ॥

To the Goddess who abides in all beings as *Śaktī*, Energy: obeisance, obeisance, obeisance again and again.

या देवी सर्वभूतेषु तृष्णारूपेण संस्थिता ।
नमस्तस्यै ॥३५॥ नमस्तस्यै ॥३६॥ नमस्तस्यै नमो नमः ॥३७॥

yā devī sarvabhūteṣu tṛṣṇānrūpeṇa saṁsthitā ।
35 *namastasyai* ॥ 36 *namastasyai* ॥ 37 *namastasyai namo namaḥ* ॥

To the Goddess who abides in all beings as *Tṛṣṇā*, Desire: obeisance, obeisance, obeisance again and again.

या देवी सर्वभूतेषु क्षान्तिरूपेण संस्थिता ।
नमस्तस्यै ॥३८॥ नमस्तस्यै ॥३९॥ नमस्तस्यै नमो नमः ॥४०॥

yā devī sarvabhūteṣu kṣāntirūpeṇa saṁsthitā ।
38 *namastasyai* ॥ 39 *namastasyai* ॥ 40 *namastasyai namo namaḥ* ॥

To the Goddess who abides in all beings as *Kṣānti*, Forgiveness: obeisance, obeisance, obeisance again and again.

या देवी सर्वभूतेषु जातिरूपेण संस्थिता ।
नमस्तस्यै ॥४१॥ नमस्तस्यै ॥४२॥ नमस्तस्यै नमो नमः ॥४३॥

yā devī sarvabhūteṣu jātirūpeṇa saṁsthitā ।
41 *namastasyai* ॥ 42 *namastasyai* ॥ 43 *namastasyai namo namaḥ* ॥

To the Goddess who abides in all beings as *Jāti*, Lineage: obeisance, obeisance, obeisance again and again.

या देवी सर्वभूतेषु लज्जारूपेण संस्थिता ।
नमस्तस्यै ॥४४॥ नमस्तस्यै ॥४५॥ नमस्तस्यै नमो नमः ॥४६॥

yā devī sarvabhūteṣu lajjārūpeṇa saṁsthitā ।
44 *namastasyai* ॥ 45 *namastasyai* ॥ 46 *namastasyai namo namaḥ* ॥

To the Goddess who abides in all beings as *Lajjā*, Modesty: obeisance, obeisance, obeisance again and again.

या देवी सर्वभूतेषु शान्तिरूपेण संस्थिता ।
नमस्तस्यै ॥४७॥ नमस्तस्यै ॥४८॥ नमस्तस्यै नमो नमः ॥४९॥

yā devī sarvabhūteṣu śāntirūpeṇa saṁsthitā ।
47 *namastasyai* ॥ 48 *namastasyai* ॥ 49 *namastasyai namo namaḥ* ॥

To the Goddess who abides in all beings as *Śānti*, Tranquility : obeisance, obeisance, obeisance again and again.

या देवी सर्वभूतेषु श्रद्धारूपेण संस्थिता ।
नमस्तस्यै ॥५०॥ नमस्तस्यै ॥५१॥ नमस्तस्यै नमो नमः ॥५२॥

yā devī sarvabhūteṣu śraddhārūpeṇa saṁsthitā ।
50 *namastasyai* ॥ 51 *namastasyai* ॥ 52 *namastasyai namo namaḥ* ॥

To the Goddess who abides in all beings as *Śraddhā*, Reverential Faith : obeisance, obeisance, obeisance again and again.

या देवी सर्वभूतेषु कान्तिरूपेण संस्थिता ।
नमस्तस्यै ॥५३॥ नमस्तस्यै ॥५४॥ नमस्तस्यै नमो नमः ॥५५॥

yā devī sarvabhūteṣu kāntirūpeṇa saṁsthitā ।
53 *namastasyai* ॥ 54 *namastasyai* ॥ 55 *namastasyai namo namaḥ* ॥

To the Goddess who abides in all beings as *Kānti*, Brilliance : obeisance, obeisance, obeisance again and again.

या देवी सर्वभूतेषु लक्ष्मीरूपेण संस्थिता।
नमस्तस्यै ।।५६।। नमस्तस्यै ।।५७।। नमस्तस्यै नमो नमः ।।५८।।

yā devī sarvabhūteṣu laksmīrūpeṇa saṁsthitā ।
56 *namastasyai* ॥ 57 *namastasyai* ॥ 58 *namastasyai namo namaḥ* ॥

To the Goddess who abides in all beings as *Lakṣmī*, Prosperity and Fortune: obeisance, obeisance, obeisance again and again.

या देवी सर्वभूतेषु वृत्तिरूपेण संस्थिता ।
नमस्तस्यै ।।५९।। नमस्तस्यै ।।६०।। नमस्तस्यै नमो नमः ।।६१।।

yā devī sarvabhūteṣu vṛttirūpeṇa saṁsthitā ।
59 *namastasyai* ॥ 60 *namastasyai* ॥ 61 *namastasyai namo namaḥ* ॥

To the Goddess who abides in all beings as *Vṛtti*, Occupation : obeisance, obeisance, obeisance again and again.

या देवी सर्वभूतेषु स्मृतिरूपेण संस्थिता ।
नमस्तस्यै ।।६२।। नमस्तस्यै ।।६३।। नमस्तस्यै नमो नमः ।।६४।।

yā devī sarvabhūteṣu smṛtirūpeṇa saṁsthitā ।
62 *namastasyai* ॥ 63 *namastasyai* ॥ 64 *namastasyai namo namaḥ* ॥

To the Goddess who abides in all beings as *Smṛti*, Recollection: obeisance, obeisance, obeisance again and again.

या देवी सर्वभूतेषु दयारूपेण संस्थिता ।
नमस्तस्यै ।।६५।। नमस्तस्यै ।।६६।। नमस्तस्यै नमो नमः ।।६७।।

yā devī sarvabhūteṣu dayārūpeṇa saṁsthitā ।
65 *namastasyai* ॥ 66 *namastasyai* ॥ 67 *namastasyai namo namaḥ* ॥

To the Goddess who abides in all beings as *Dayā*, Compassion : obeisance, obeisance, obeisance again and again.

या देवी सर्वभूतेषु तुष्टिरूपेण संस्थिता ।
नमस्तस्यै ॥६८॥ नमस्तस्यै ॥६९॥ नमस्तस्यै नमो नमः ॥७०॥

yā devī sarvabhūteṣu tuṣṭirūpeṇa saṁsthitā ।
68 *namastasyai* ॥ 69 *namastasyai* ॥ 70 *namastasyai namo namaḥ* ॥

To the Goddess who abides in all beings as *Tuṣṭi, Gratification* : obeisance, obeisance, obeisance again and again.

या देवी सर्वभूतेषु मातृरूपेण संस्थिता ।
नमस्तस्यै ॥७१॥ नमस्तस्यै ॥७२॥ नमस्तस्यै नमो नमः ॥७३॥

yā devī sarvabhūteṣu matṛrūpeṇa saṁsthitā ।
71 *namastasyai* ॥ 72 *namastasyai* ॥ 73 *namastasyai namo namaḥ* ॥

To the Goddess who abides in all beings as *Mātā*, the Mother : obeisance, obeisance, obeisançe again and again.

या देवी सर्वभूतेषु भ्रान्तिरूपेण संस्थिता ।
नमस्तस्यै ॥७४॥ नमस्तस्यै ॥७५॥ नमस्तस्यै नमो नमः ॥७६॥

yā devī sarvabhūteṣu bhrāntirūpeṇa saṁsthitā ।
74 *namastasyai* ॥ 75 *namastasyai* ॥ 76 *namastasyai namo namaḥ* ॥

To the Goddess who abides in all beings as *Bhrānti*, Confusion : obeisance, obeisance, obeisance again and again.

इन्द्रियाणामधिष्ठात्री भूतानां चाखिलेषु या ।
भूतेषु सततं तस्यै व्याप्तिदेव्यै नमो नमः ॥७७॥

77. *indriyāṇāmadhiṣṭhatrī bhūtānāṁ cākhileṣu yā* ।
bhūteṣu satataṁ tasyai vyāptidevyai namo namaḥ ॥

We pay obeisance again and again and continually to the Goddess *Vyāpti*, the Permeating Spirit, who, as the Substratum of the Senses, abides in all beings and elements.

चितिरूपेण या कृत्स्नमेतद्व्याप्य स्थिता जगत् ।
नमस्तस्यै ॥७८॥ नमस्तस्यै ॥७९॥ नमस्तस्यै नमो नमः ॥८०॥

citirūpeṇa yā kṛtsnametadvyāpya sthitā jagat ।
78 *namastasyai* ॥ 79 *namastasyai* ॥ 80 *namastasyai namo namaḥ* ॥

To the Goddess who as *Citi*, Wisdom, pervades as the Abiding Spirit in the entire world: obeisance, obeisance, obeisance again and again.

स्तुता सुरैः पूर्वमभीष्टसंश्रया-
त्तथा सुरेन्द्रेण दिनेषु सेविता ।
करोतु सा नः शुभहेतुरीश्वरी
शुभानि भद्राण्यभिहन्तु चापदः ॥८१॥

81. *stutā suraiḥ pūrvamabhīṣṭasaṁśrayāt-*
tathā surendreṇa dineṣu sevitā ।
karotu sā naḥ śubhaheturīśvarī
śubhāni bhadrāṇyabhihantu cāpadaḥ ॥

May the Supreme Goddess, the Sovereign Empress, the Instrument of Fortune, whom the gods, led by *Indra*, eulogised and served for many days in the olden times, bestow auspiciousness and blessings upon us and obliterate all calamities.

या साम्प्रतं चोद्धतदैत्यतापितै-
रस्माभिरीशा च सुरैर्नमस्यते ।
या च स्मृता तत्क्षणमेव हन्ति नः
सर्वापदो भक्ति विनम्रमूर्तिभिः ।।८२।।

82. *yā sāmpratam̐ coddhatadaityatāpitair-*
asmābhirīśā ca surairnamasyate ।
yā ca smṛta tatkṣaṇameva hanti naḥ
sarvāpado bhakti vinamramūrtibhiḥ ।।

We, the gods, now tormented by the impudent demons, pay obeisance to that Supreme Empress who, on being remembered by the persons with bowed heads and with devotion, humility and reverence, instantly destroys all calamities.

ऋषिरुवाच ।।८३।।

83. *ṛṣiruvāca*

एवं स्तवादियुक्तानां देवानां तत्र पार्वती ।
स्नातुमभ्याययौ तोये जाह्नव्या नृपनन्दन ।।८४।।

84. *evam̐ stavādiyuktānām̐ devānām̐ tatra pārvatī* ।
snātumabhyāyayau toye jāhnavyā nṛpanandana ।।

The Seer Said

When, O Prince! the gods were thus eulogising with hymns, *Pārvatī*, the Daughter of *Himālaya*, came there to take a bath in the water of *Gaṅgā*, the Daughter of the seer *Jāhnu*.

साब्रवीत्तान् सुरान् सुभ्रूर्भवद्भिः स्तूयतेऽत्र का ।
शरीरकोशतश्चास्याः समुद्भूताब्रवीच्छिवा ।।८५।।

85. *sābravīttān surān subhrūrbhavadbhiḥ stuyate 'tra kā* ।
śarīrakośataścāsyāḥ samudbhūtābravīcchivā ।।

स्तोत्रं ममैतत्क्रियते शुम्भदैत्यनिराकृतैः ।
देवैः समस्तैः[2] समरे निशुम्भेन पराजितैः ॥८६॥

86. *stotraṁ mamaitatkriyate śumbhadaityanirākṛtaiḥ* ।
devaiḥ samastaiḥ[2] *samare niśuṁbhena parājitaiḥ* ॥

She, of the beautiful brow, asked those gods who they were eulogising there. Then from within her body appeared *Śivā*, the Felicity, and said: humiliated by the demon *Śumbha* and defeated by *Niśumbha* in the battle, these gods who have gathered here are chanting hymns in my praise.

शरीरकोशाद्य[3]त्तस्याः पार्वत्या निःसृताम्बिका ।
कौशिकीति[4] समस्तेषु ततो लोकेषु गीयते ॥८७॥

87. *sarīrakośādya*[3]*ttasyāḥ pārvatyā niḥsṛitāmbikā* ।
kauśikīti[4] *samasteṣu tato lokeṣu gīyate* ॥

Since *Ambikā*, the Mother, had appeared from the *kośa*, the vesture, of *Pārvatī*, she is celebrated as *Kauśikī* in all the worlds.

तस्यां विनिर्गतायां तु कृष्णाभूत्सापि पार्वती ।
कालिकेति समाख्याता हिमाचलकृताश्रया ॥८८॥

88. *tasyā vinirgatāyāṁ tu kṛṣṇābhūtsāpi pārvatī* ।
kāliketi samākhyātā himācalakṛtāśrayā ॥

Following her (*Kauśikī's*) exit from *Pārvatī's* body, *Pārvatī* too became dark-complexioned and came to be known as *Kālikā*, the Black, and took shelter in the *Himālaya*.

ततोऽम्बिकां परं रूपं बिभ्राणां सुमनोहरम् ।
ददर्श चण्डो मुण्डश्च भृत्यौ शुम्भनिशुम्भयोः ॥८९॥

89. *tato'mbikāṁ paraṁ rūpaṁ bibhrāṇāṁ sumanoharam* ।
dadarśa caṇḍo muṇḍaśca bhṛtyau śumbhaniśumbhayoḥ ॥

---

[2]AR: समस्तैः *samastaiḥ*

[3]AR: कोषात् *koṣāt*

[4]AR: कौषिकीति *kauṣikīti*

Then *Caṇḍa* and *Muṇḍa*, the two ministers of *Śumbha* and *Niśumbha* came there and happened to see *Ambikā* donning an exquisitely charming form.

ताभ्यां शुम्भाय चाख्याता अतीव सुमनोहरा ।
काप्यास्ते स्त्री महाराज भासयन्ती हिमाचलम् ॥९०॥

90. *tābhyāṁ śumbhāya cākhyātā atīva sumanoharā* ।
kāpyāste strī mahārāja bhāsayantī himācalam ॥

Śumbha was told by them about her beauty saying that some extremely attractive woman was illuminating *Himālaya.*

नैव तादृक् क्वचिद्रूपं दृष्टं केनचिदुत्तमम् ।
ज्ञायतां काप्यसौ देवी गृह्यतां चासुरेश्वर ॥९१॥

91. *naiva tādṛk kvacidrūpaṁ dṛṣṭaṁ kenaciduttamam* ।
jñāyatāṁ kāpyasau devī gṛhyatāṁ cāsureśvara ॥

O Demon King! nobody would have seen such an exquisitely beautiful form anywhere. Find out who that Goddess is and take her.

स्त्रीरत्नमतिचार्वङ्गी द्योतयन्ती दिशस्त्विषा ।
सा तु तिष्ठति दैत्येन्द्र तां भवान् द्रष्टुमर्हति ॥९२॥

92. *strīratnamaticārvaṅgī dyotayantī diśastviṣā* ।
sā tu tiṣṭhati daityendra tāṁ bhavān draṣṭumarhati ॥

O Ruler of Demons! you ought to see her. She is a jewel among women. She has lovely limbs and, sitting there, is spreading lustre in all the directions.

यानि रत्नानि मणयो गजाश्वादीनि वै प्रभो ।
त्रैलोक्ये तु समस्तानि साम्प्रतं भान्ति ते गृहे ॥९३॥

93. *yāni ratnāni maṇayo gajāśvādīni vai prabho* ।
trailokye tu samastāni sāmpratam bhānti te gṛhe ॥

Your house, O Lord! is adorned with all the gems, jewels, elephants and horses, that are there in the three worlds.

ऐरावतः समानीतो गजरत्नं पुरन्दरात् ।
पारिजाततरुश्चायं तथैवोच्चैःश्रवा हयः ॥९४॥

94. *airāvataḥ samānīto gajaratnaṁ purandarāt* ।
pārijātataruścāyaṁ tathaivoccaiḥśravā hayaḥ ॥

You have taken *Airāvata,* that gem of an elephant; *Pārijāta,* the wish-fulfilling tree and *Uccaiḥśravā,* the horse from *Purandara* (*Indra*).

विमानं हंससंयुक्तमेतत्तिष्ठति तेऽङ्गणे ।
रत्नभूतमिहानीतं यदासीद्वेधसोऽद्भुतम् ॥९५॥

95. *vimānaṁ haṁsasaṁyuktametattiṣṭhati te 'ṅgaṇe* ।
ratnabhūtamihānītaṁ yadāsīdvedhaso 'dbhutam ॥

From *Brahmā,* the Creator, you have taken this wonderful heavenly car which, piloted by the celestial swan, is a gem too. It is there in your courtyard.

निधिरेष महापद्मः समानीतो धनेश्वरात् ।
किंजल्किनीं ददौ चाब्धिर्मालामम्लानपङ्कजाम् ॥९६॥

96. *nidhireṣa mahāpadmaḥ samānīto dhaneśvarāt* ।
kiñjalkinīṁ dadau cābdhirmālāmamlānapaṅkajām ॥

You have brought *Mahāpadma,* the celestial treasure from *Kubera,* the treasurer of the gods. The ocean has gifted you *Kiñjalkinī,* the garland of unwithering lotuses.

छत्रं ते वारुणं गेहे काञ्चनस्त्रावितिष्ठति ।
तथायं स्यन्दनवरो यः पुरासीत् प्रजापतेः ॥९७॥

97. *chatraṁ te vāruṇaṁ gehe kāñcanasrāvitiṣṭhati* ।
tathāyaṁ syandanavaro yaḥ purāsīt prajāpateḥ ॥

The gold-dripping royal umbrella of *Varuṇa,* the Regent of Oceans, is there in your house and so is this excellent chariot which earlier belonged to *Prajāpati,* the Patriarch of the Progeny.

मृत्योरुत्क्रान्तिदा नाम शक्तिरीश त्वया हृता ।
पाशः सलिलराजस्य भ्रातुस्तव परिग्रहे ॥९८॥

98. *mṛtyorutkrāntidā nāma śaktirīśa tvayā hṛtā* ।
pāśaḥ salilarājasya bhrātustava parigrahe ॥

निशुम्भस्याब्धिजाताश्च समस्ता रत्नजातयः ।
वह्निरपि[5] ददौ तुभ्यमग्निशौचे च वाससी ॥९९॥

99. *niśuṁbhasyābdhijātāśca samastā ratnajātayaḥ* ।
vahnirapi[5] *dadau tubhayamagniśauce ca vāsasī* ॥

You have, O Master, snatched from *Mṛtyu*, Death, the *Utkrāntidā Śakti*, the missile with which he wrings life out from creatures while your brother, *Niśumbha*, has taken possession of the snare and all the varieties of gems of *Varuṇa*, the Regent of Waters. *Vahni*, Fire, has also presented two perennially sanctified garments to you.

एवं दैत्येन्द्र रत्नानि समस्तान्याहृतानि ते ।
स्त्रीरत्नमेषा कल्याणी त्वया कस्मान्न गृह्यते ॥१००॥

100. *evaṁ daityendra ratnāni samastānyāhṛtāni te* ।
striratnameṣā kalyaṇī tvayā kasmānna gṛhyate ॥

In this way, o demon king! all the gems have been taken by you. Why don't you also take this auspicious gem of a woman?

ऋषिरुवाच ॥१०१॥

101. *ṛsiruvāca*

The Seer said

निशम्येति वचः शुम्भः स तदा चण्डमुण्डयोः ।
प्रेषयामास सुग्रीवं दूतं देव्या महासुरम्[6] ॥१०२॥

102. *niśamyeti vacaḥ śuṁbhaḥ sa tadā caṇḍamuṇḍayoḥ* ।
preṣayāmāsa sugrīvaṁ dūtaṁ devyā mahāsuram[6] ॥

---

[5]AR: वह्निश्चापि *vahniścāpi*

[6]Additional reading in some copies hereafter : शुम्भ उवाच *śumbha uvāca, Śumbha* said.

After hearing these words of *Caṇḍa-Muṇḍa*, *Śumbha* sent a giant-demon, *Sugrīva*, to the Goddess, as his messenger.

इति चेति च वक्तव्या सा गत्वा वचनान्मम ।
यथा चाभ्येति सम्प्रीत्या तथा कार्यं त्वया लघु ।।१०३।।

103. *iti ceti ca vaktavyā sā gatvā vacanānmama* ।
yathā cābhyeti samprītyā tathā kāryaṁ tvayā laghu ।।

Tell her, on my behalf, these words, speaking in such a manner that she is pleased and comes to me immediately.

स तत्र गत्वा यत्रास्ते शैलोद्देशेऽतिशोभने ।
सा देवी तां ततः[7] प्राह श्लक्ष्णं मधुरया गिरा ।।१०४।।

104. *sa tatra gatvā yatrāste śailoddeśe 'tiśobhane* ।
sā devī tāṁ tataḥ[7] *prāha ślakṣṇaṁ madhurayā girā* ।।

On reaching that beautiful mountainous region where she was staying, he spoke to her gently in sweet words.

दूत उवाच ।।१०५।।

105. *dūta uvāca*

देवि दैत्येश्वरः शुम्भस्त्रैलोक्ये परमेश्वरः ।
दूतोऽहं प्रेषितस्तेन त्वत्सकाशमिहागतः ।।१०६।।

106. *devi daityeśvaraḥ śumbhastrailokye parameśvaraḥ* ।
dūto 'haṁ preṣitastena tvatsakāśamihāgataḥ ।।

The Messenger said

O Venerable Lady! I am the messenger of *Śumbha*, the Sovereign Supreme of the three worlds. I am his messenger; sent by him, I have come here to you.

---

[7]AR: तां च देवीं ततः *tāṁ ca devīṁ tataḥ*

अव्याहताज्ञः सर्वासु यः सदा देवयोनिषु ।
निर्जिताखिलदैत्यारिः स यदाह श्रृणुष्व तत् ।।१०७।।

107. *avyāhatājñaḥ sarvāsu yaḥ sadā devayoniṣu* ।
nirjitākhiladaityāriḥ sa yadāha śṛṇuṣva tat ।।

His command is inviolable among the gods of all origins. He has vanquished all the gods. Now listen to what he has said.

मम त्रैलोक्यमखिलं मम देवा वशानुगाः ।
यज्ञभागानहं सर्वानुपाश्नामि पृथक् पृथक् ।।१०८।।

108. *mama trailokyamakhilaṁ mama devā vaśānugāḥ* ।
yajñabhāgānahaṁ sarvānupāśnāmi pṛthak pṛthak ।।

All these three worlds are mine. The gods are my subjects and follow my command. Of each of them I receive the share in the sacrifices separately.

त्रैलोक्ये वररत्नानि मम वश्यान्यशेषतः ।
तथैव गजरत्नं[8] च हत्वा[9] देवेन्द्रवाहनम् ।।१०९।।

109. *trailokye vararatnāni mama vaśyānyaśeṣtaḥ* ।
tathaiva gajaratnaṁ[8] *ca hṛtvā*[9] *devendravāhanam* ।।

All the precious jewels of the three worlds are mine, so is that jewel of an elephant, the mount of *Indra* which I have captured from him.

क्षीरोदमथनोद्भूतमश्वरत्नं ममामरैः ।
उच्चैःश्रवससंज्ञं तत्प्रणिपत्य समर्पितम् ।।११०।।

110. *kṣīrodamathanodbhūtamaśvaratnaṁ mamāmaraiḥ* ।
uccaiḥsravasasaṁjñaṁ tatpraṇipatya samarpitam ।।

Uccaiḥśravas, the gem of a horse, which had emerged following the churning of the *Kṣīrasāgara*, the Ocean of Milk, has been presented reverentially to me by the gods.

---

[8]AR: गजरत्नानि *gajaratnāni*

[9]AR: हृतं *hṛtaṁ*

यानि चान्यानि देवेषु गन्धर्वेषूरगेषु च ।
रत्नभूतानि भूतानि तानि मय्येव शोभने ।।१११।।

111. *yāni cānyāni deveṣu gandharveṣūrageṣu ca* ।
ratnabhūtani bhūtāni tāni mayyeva śobhane ।।

O Beautiful Lady! even the other gem-like (precious and attractive) treasures which were in the possession of the gods, *gandharvas* and serpents, are now mine.

स्त्रीरत्नभूतां त्वां देवि लोके मन्यामहे वयम् ।
सा त्वमस्मानुपागच्छ यतो रत्नभुजो वयम् ।।११२।।

112. *strīratnabhūtāṁ tvāṁ devi loke manyāmahe vayam* ।
sā tvamasmānupāgaccha yato ratnabhujo vayam ।।

We consider you to be a gem among women of the world and since we are the connoisseurs of the gems, you too must come to us.

मां वा ममानुजं वापि निशुम्भमुरुविक्रमम् ।
भज त्वं चञ्चलापाङ्गि रत्नभूतासि वै यतः ।।११३।।

113. *māṁ vā mamānujaṁ vāpi niśumbhamuruvikramam* ।
bhaja tvaṁ cañcalāpaṅgi ratnabhūtāsi vai yataḥ ।।

O Beauteous Maiden of Tremulous Glances! sincc you are a veritable gem too, come in my service or of the mighty *Niśumbha*, my younger brother.

परमैश्वर्यमतुलं प्राप्स्यसे मत्परिग्रहात् ।
एतद् बुद्ध्या समालोच्य मत्परिग्रहतां व्रज ।।११४।।

114. *paramaiśvaryamatulaṁ prāpsyase matparigrahāt* ।
etad buddhyā samālocya matparigrahatāṁ vraja ।।

If you marry me, you will get incomparable and unsurpassable fortune. Consider this carefully and come, marry me.

ऋषिरुवाच ।।११५।।

115. *ṛṣiruvāca*

इत्युक्ता सा तदा देवी गम्भीरान्तःस्मिता जगौ ।
दुर्गा भगवती भद्रा ययेदं धार्यते जगत् ।।११६।।

116. *ityuktā sā tadā devī gaṁbhīrāntaḥsmitā jagau* ।
durgā bhagavatī bhadrā yayedaṁ dhāryate jagat ।।

The Seer said

Being thus told, the Goddess *Durgā*, the Noble Sovereign by whom this world is upheld, smiled to herself and said in a contemplative tone.

देव्युवाच ।।११७।।

117. *devyuvāca*

सत्यमुक्तं त्वया नात्र मिथ्या किंचित्त्वयोदितम् ।
त्रैलोक्याधिपतिः शुम्भो निशुम्भश्चापि तादृशः ।।११८।।

118. *satymuktaṁ tvayā nātra mithyā kiñcittvayoditam* ।
trailokyādhipatiḥ śumbho niśumbhaścāpi tādṛśaḥ ।।

The Goddess said

There is no untruth in whatever has been mentioned by you; it is all true. *Śumbha* is the sovereign of the three worlds and so is *Niśumbha.*

किं त्वत्र यत्प्रतिज्ञातं मिथ्या तत्क्रियते कथम् ।
श्रूयतामल्पबुद्धित्वात्प्रतिज्ञा या कृता पुरा ।।११९।।

119. *kiṁ tvatra yatprātijñātaṁ mithyā tatkriyate katham* ।
śrūyatāmalpabuddhitvātpratijña yā kṛtā purā।।

But how can I render untrue the vow I have foolishly undertaken? Now hear this vow which I took much earlier.

यो मां जयति संग्रामे यो मे दर्पं व्यपोहति ।
यो मे प्रतिबलो लोके स मे भर्ता भविष्यति ।।१२०।।

120. *yo māṁ jayati saṅgrāme yo me darpaṁ vyapohati* ।
yo me pratibalo loke sa me bhartā bhaviṣyati ॥

He who conquers me in battle, he who extinguishes my pride, he who in this world matches me in valour, shall be my husband.

तदागच्छतु शुम्भोऽत्र निशुम्भो वा महासुरः ।
मां जित्वा किं चिरेणात्र पाणिं गृह्णातु मे लघु ।।१२१।।

121. *tādāgacchatu śumbho 'tra niśumbho vā mahāsuraḥ* ।
māṁ jitvā kim cireṇātra pāṇiṁ gṛhṇātu me laghu ॥

So, let *Śumbha* or the great demon *Niśumbha* himself come here and take my hand in marriage without loss of time. Why should there be any delay?

दूत उवाच ।।१२२।।

122. *dūta uvāca*

अवलिप्तासि मैवं त्वं देवि ब्रूहि ममाग्रतः ।
त्रैलोक्ये कः पुमांस्तिष्ठेदग्रे शुम्भनिशुम्भयोः ।।१२३।।

123. *avaliptāsi maivaṁ tvaṁ devi brūhi mamāgrataḥ* ।
trailokye kaḥ pumānstiṣṭhedagre śumbhaniśumbhayoḥ ॥

The Messenger said

Full of arrogance, O Revered Lady, you must be. You must not speak to me like this. Who in these three worlds is the man who can stand before *Śumbha* and *Niśumbha*?

अन्येषामपि दैत्यानां सर्वे देवा न वै युधि ।
तिष्ठन्ति सम्मुखे देवि किं पुनः स्त्री त्वमेकिका ।।१२४।।

124. *anyeṣāmapi daityānāṁ sarve devā na vai yudhi* ।
tiṣṭhanti sammukhe devi kiṁ punaḥ strī tvamekikā ॥

O Lady! even before the other demons, all the gods together cannot stand in the battle; then how can you, a mere woman, that too alone?

इन्द्राद्याः सकला देवास्तस्थुर्येषां न संयुगे ।
शुम्भादीनां कथं तेषां स्त्री प्रयास्यसि सम्मुखम् ।।१२५।।

125. *indrādyāḥ sakalā devāstasthuryeṣāṁ na saṁyuge* ।
śuṁbhādīnāṁ kathaṁ teṣāṁ strī prayāsyasi saṃmukham ।।

All the gods, including *Indra,* could not stand before *Śumbha* and the other demons in the battle. How will you, a woman, face them?

सा त्वं गच्छ मयैवोक्ता पार्श्वं शुम्भनिशुम्भयोः ।
केशाकर्षणनिर्धूतगौरवा मा गमिष्यसि ।।१२६।।

126. *sā tvaṁ gaccha mayaivoktā pārśvaṁ śumbhaniśumbhayoḥ* ।
keśākarsaṇanirdhūtagauravā mā gamiṣyasi ।।

So go, as I say, to *Śumbha* and *Niśumbha,* else, pulled by hair and dragged, you will have to go losing your dignity.

देव्युवाच ।।१२७।।

127. *devyuvāca*

एवमेतद् बली शुम्भो निशुम्भश्चातिवीर्यवान् ।
किं करोमि प्रतिज्ञा मे यदनालोचिता पुरा ।।१२८।।

128. *evametad balī śumbho niśumbhaścātivīryavān* ।
kiṁ karomi pratijñā me yadanālocitā purā ।।

The Goddess said

What you say is true. *Śumbha* is valorous, equally so is *Niśumbha.* But what shall I do now that I have earlier taken a vow without giving it a thought?

स त्वं गच्छ मयोक्तं ते यदेतत्सर्वमादृतः ।
तदाचक्ष्वासुरेन्द्राय स च युक्तं करोतु तत्[10] ।।ॐ।।१२६।।

129. *sa tvaṁ gaccha mayoktaṁ te yadetatsarvamādṛtaḥ* ।
tadācakṣvāsurendrāya sa ca yuktaṁ karotu tat[10] ।।oṁ।।

So, go and respectfully convey to the demon-king what I have told you. Let him consider it and then do what he deems appropriate. Oṁ

इति श्री मार्कण्डेयपुराणे सावर्णिके मन्वन्तरे देवीमाहात्म्ये
देव्या दूतसंवादो नाम पंचमोऽध्यायः ।।५।।

iti śrī mārkaṇḍeyapurāṇe sāvarṇike manvantare devīmāhātmye devyā dūtasaṁvādo nāma pañcamo 'dhyāyaḥ ।। 5 ।।

Thus ends the fifth chapter called 'Conversation between the Goddess and the Messenger' during the era of *Sāvarṇi Manu*, in the 'Glory of the Goddess' (narrated) in the *Mārkaṇḍeya Purāṇa.*

उवाच ९, त्रिपान्मत्राः ६६, श्लोकाः ५४, एवम् १२९, एवमादितः ३८८
uvāca 9, *tripānmantrāḥ* 66, *ślokāḥ* 54, *evam* 129, *evamāditaḥ* 388

uvāca 9, mantras of three quarters 66, ślokas 54, total 129, from beginning up to here 388.

---

[10] AR: यत् *yat*

षष्ठोऽध्यायः॥

ṣaṣṭho 'dhyāyaḥ॥

Chapter Six

Slaying of *Dhūmralocana*

ध्यानम्

dhyānam

Meditation

ॐ नागाधीश्वरविष्टरां फणिफणोत्तंसोरुरत्नावली-
भास्वद्देहलतां दिवाकरनिभां नेत्रत्रयोद्भासिताम्।
मालाकुम्भकपालनीरजकरां चन्द्रार्धचूडां परां
सर्वज्ञेश्वरभैरवाङ्कनिलयां पद्मावतीं चिन्तये॥

*oṁ. nāgādhīśvaraviṣṭarāṁ phaṇiphaṇottaṁsoruratnāvalī-
bhāsvaddehalatāṁ divākaranibhāṁ netratrayodbhāsitām*।
*mālākumbhakapālanīrajakarāṁ candrārdhacūḍāṁ parāṁ
sarvajñeśvarabhairavāṅkanilayāṁ padmāvatīṁ cintaye*॥

OṀ. I MEDITATE UPON THE SUPREME GODDESS *PADMĀVATĪ* WHO ABIDES IN THE LAP OF THE OMNISCIENT LORD *BHAIRAVA*. THE BODY OF THE KING OF SERPENTS IS HER SEAT AND HER BODY GLOWS WITH THE BRILLIANCE OF THE JEWELS OF THE HOODS OF THE SERPENT. HER LUSTRE MATCHES THE EFFULGENCE OF THE SUN. THREE SHINING EYES ADD TO THE BEAUTY OF HER FACE. A ROSARY, A PITCHER, A SKULL AND A LOTUS ARE HELD IN HER HANDS AND A CRESCENT MOON CROWNS HER HEAD.

ॐ ऋषिरुवाच ॥१॥

1. *oṁ ṛṣiruvāca*

इत्याकर्ण्य वचो देव्याः स दूतोऽमर्षपूरितः ।
समाचष्ट समागम्य दैत्यराजाय विस्तरात् ॥२॥

2. *ityākarṇya vaco devyāḥ sa dūto 'marṣapūritaḥ ।*
samācaṣṭa samāgamya daityarājāya vistarāt ॥

Oṁ. The Seer said

Hearing these words of the Goddess, the messenger, filled with anger, went to the demon-king and narrated the matter in detail.

तस्य दूतस्य तद्वाक्यमाकर्ण्यासुरराट् ततः ।
सक्रोधः प्राह दैत्यानामधिपं धूम्रलोचनम् ॥३॥

3. *tasya dūtasya tadvākyamākārṇyāsurarāṭ tataḥ ।*
sakrodhaḥ prāha daityānāmadhipaṁ dhūmralocanam ॥

The demon king, on hearing the words of his messenger, angrily ordered *Dhūmralocana*, the chief of the demons' army:

हे धूम्रलोचनाशु त्वं स्वसैन्यपरिवारितः ।
तामानय बलाद् दुष्टां केशाकर्षणविह्वलाम् ॥४॥

4. *he dhūmralocanāśu tvaṁ svasainyaparivāritaḥ ।*
tāmānaya balād duṣṭāṁ keśākarṣaṇavihvalām ॥

O *Dhūmralocana*! go immediately with your army and bring the shrew forcibly, dragging her by hair in a state of utter disquiet.

तत्परित्राणदः कश्चिद्यदि वोत्तिष्ठतेऽपरः ।
स हन्तव्योऽमरो वापि यक्षो गन्धर्व एव वा ॥५॥

5. *tatparitrāṇadaḥ kaścidyadi vottiṣṭhate 'paraḥ ।*
sa hantavyo 'maro vāpi yakṣo gandharva eva vā ॥

If anyone, a god, a *yakṣa* or a *gandharva*, is present there and comes to her rescue, kill him.

ऋषिरुवाच ॥६॥

6. *ṛṣiruvāca*

तेनाज्ञाप्तस्ततः शीघ्रं स दैत्यो धूम्रलोचनः ।
वृतः षष्ट्या सहस्राणामसुराणां द्रुतं ययौ ॥7॥

7. *tenājñāptastataḥ śīghraṁ sa daityo dhūmralocanaḥ* ।
vṛtaḥ ṣaṣṭyā sahasrāṇāmasurāṇāṁ drutaṁ yayau ॥

The Seer said

On being thus ordered by him, that demon *Dhūmralocana*, accompanied by a demon-army of sixty thousand, proceeded forthwith.

स दृष्ट्वा तां ततो देवीं तुहिनाचलसंस्थिताम् ।
जगादोच्चैः प्रयाहीति मूलं शुम्भनिशुम्भयोः ॥८॥

8. *sa dṛṣṭvā tāṁ tato devīṁ tuhinācalasaṁsthitām* ।
jagādoccaiḥ prayāhīti mūlaṁ śumbhaniśumbhayoḥ ॥

न चेत्प्रीत्याद्य भवती मद्भर्तारमुपैष्यति ।
ततो बलान्नयाम्येष केशाकर्षणविह्वलाम् ॥९॥

9. *na cetprītyādya bhavatī madbhartāramupaiṣyati* ।
tato balānnayāmyeṣa keśākarṣaṇavihvalām ॥

When he saw that Goddess sojourning in the *Himālaya*, he shouted, 'Go you now to *Śumbha-Niśumbha* on your own. If you do not of your own accord, then I shall drag you by your hair and take you to my master.'

देव्युवाच ॥१०॥

10. *devyuvāca*

दैत्येश्वरेण प्रहितो बलवान् बलसंवृतः ।
बलान्नयसि मामेवं ततः किं ते करोम्यहम् ॥११॥

11. *daityeśvreṇa prahito balavān balasaṁvṛtaḥ* ।
balānnayasi māmevaṁ tataḥ kiṁ te karomyaham ॥

The Goddess said

You have been deputed by the demon-king and are powerful. You are also accompanied by a large army. What can I do to you if you carry me by force?

ऋषिरुवाच ॥१२॥

12. *ṛṣiruvāca*

इत्युक्तः सोऽभ्यधावत्तामसुरो धूम्रलोचनः ।
हुंकारेणैव तं भस्म सा चकाराम्बिका ततः ॥13॥

13. *ityuktaḥ so 'bhyadhāvattāmasuro dhūmralocanaḥ* ।
huṁkāreṇaiva taṁ bhasma sā cakārāmbikā tataḥ ॥

The Seer said

Thus told, that demon *Dhūmralocana* charged towards her. Then the Mother reduced him to ashes with just a heave of hers.

अथ क्रुद्धं महासैन्यमसुराणां तथाम्बिका[1] ।
ववर्ष सायकैस्तीक्ष्णैस्तथा शक्तिपरश्वधैः ॥१४॥

14. *atha kruddhaṁ mahāsainyamasurāṇāṁ tathāmbikā*[1] ।
vavarṣa sāyakaistīkṣṇaistathā śaktiparaśvadhaiḥ ॥

Then the Mother and that large army of angry demons hailed sharp arrows, missiles and battle-axes at others.

ततो धुतसटः कोपात्कृत्वा नादं सुभैरवम् ।
पपातासुरसेनायां सिंहो देव्याः स्ववाहनः ॥१५॥

15. *tato dhutasaṭaḥ kopātkṛtvā nādaṁ subhairavam* ।
papātāsurasenāyāṁ siṁho devyāḥ svavāhanaḥ ॥

Meanwhile, the Lion, the mount of the Goddess, shaking his mane in anger, pounced on the demons' army with a terrifying roar.

---

[1]AR: तथाम्बिकाम् *tathāmbikām*

कांश्चित्करप्रहारेण दैत्यानास्येन चापरान् ।
आक्रम्य[2] चाधरेणान्यान्[3] स जघान[4] महासुरान् ।१६।।

16. *kāñścitkaraprahāreṇa daityānāsyena cāparān* ।
ākramya[2] *cādhareṇānyān*[3] *sa jaghāna*[4] *mahāsurān* ।।

He killed some of the fierce demons with the assault of his forearms, others with his jaws and some by attacking with his hind legs.

केषांचित्पाटयामास नखैः कोष्ठानि केसरी[5] ।
तथा तलप्रहारेण शिरांसि कृतवान् पृथक् ।।१७।।

17. *keśāñcitpāṭayāmāsa nakhaiḥ koṣṭhāni kesarī*[5] ।
tathā talaprahāreṇa śirāṁsi kṛtavān pṛthak ।।

The Lion tore apart the bellies of many with his claws and, with the blow of his paws, severed the heads of many from their bodies.

विच्छिन्नबाहुशिरसः कृतास्तेन तथापरे ।
पपौ च रुधिरं कोष्ठादन्येषां धुतकेसरः ।।१८।।

18. *vicchinabāhuśirasaḥ kṛtāstena tathāpare* ।
papau ca rudhiraṁ koṣṭhādanyeṣāṁ dhutakesaraḥ ।।

He rendered several others without arms and hands. Swaying his mane, he drank the blood from the bellies of the others.

क्षणेन तद्बलं सर्वं क्षयं नीतं महात्मना ।
तेन केसरिणा देव्या वाहनेनाति कोपिना ।।१९।।

19. *kṣaṇena tadbalaṁ sarvaṁ kṣayaṁ nītaṁ mahātmanā* ।
tena kesariṇā devyā vāhanenāti kopinā ।।

---

[2]AR: आक्रान्त्या *ākrāntyā*

[3]AR: चरणेनान्यान् *caraṇenānyān*

[4]AR: सञ्जघान/निजघान/जघान सुमहासुरान् *sañjaghāna/ nijaghāna/ jaghāna sumahāsurān.*

[5]AR: केशरी *keśarī* (In the Bengalī edition it is invariably *śa* and not *sa* for *kesarī*)

The mighty lion, that enraged mount of the Goddess, destroyed the entire force of demons in a moment.

श्रुत्वा तमसुरं देव्या निहतं धूम्रलोचनम् ।
बलं च क्षयितं कृत्स्नं देवी केसरिणा ततः ॥२०॥

20. *śrutvā tamasuraṁ devyā nihataṁ dhūmralocanam ।*
balaṁ ca kṣayitaṁ kṛtsnaṁ devī kesariṇā tataḥ ॥

चुकोप दैत्याधिपतिः शुम्भः प्रस्फुरिताधरः ।
आज्ञापयामास च तौ चण्डमुण्डौ महासुरौ ॥२१॥

21. *cukopa daityādhipatiḥ śumbhaḥ prasphuritādharaḥ ।*
ājñāpayāmāsa ca tau caṇḍamuṇḍau mahāsurau ॥

When *Śumbha*, the demon-king, heard that the demon *Dhūmralocana* had been slayed by the Goddess and the entire army by her lion, he was beside himself with anger and, his lips quivering, ordered the mighty demons, *Caṇḍa* and *Muṇḍa*:

हे चण्ड हे मुण्ड बलैर्बहुभिः[6] परिवारितौ ।
तत्र गच्छत गत्वा च सा समानीयतां लघु ॥२२॥

22. *he caṇḍa he muṇḍa balairbahubhiḥ*[6] *parivāritau ।*
tatra gacchata gatvā ca sā samānīyatāṁ laghu ॥

केशेष्वाकृष्य बद्ध्वा वा यदि वः संशयो युधि ।
तदाशेषायुधैः सर्वैरसुरैर्विनिहन्यताम् ॥२३॥

23. *keśeṣvākṛsya baddhvā vā yadi vaḥ saṁśayo yudhi ।*
tadāśeṣāyudhaiḥ sarvairasurairvinihanyatām ॥

O *Caṇḍa*! O *Muṇḍa*! go you there accompanied by a large army, bring her here dragging by hair or by binding her. If you have any doubt about bringing her in this manner, then kill her using all the weapons and the entire force of demons.

---

[6]AR: बहुलैः *bahulaiḥ*

तस्य हतायां दुष्टायां सिंहे च विनिपातिते ।
शीघ्रमागम्यतां बद्ध्वा गृहीत्वा तामथाम्बिकाम्॥ ॐ॥ २४॥

24. *tasya hatāyāṁ duṣṭāyāṁ siṁhe ca vīnipātite* ।
śīghramāgamyatāṁ baddhvā gṛhītvā tāmathāmbikām ॥oṁ॥

When she, the wicked one, is killed and the lion too has fallen, come back fast, bringing that *Ambikā* by binding her. oṁ

इति श्री मार्कण्डेयपुराणे सावर्णिके मन्वन्तरे देवीमाहात्म्ये
शुम्भनिशुम्भसेनानीधूम्रलोचनवधोनाम

षष्ठोऽध्यायः ॥६॥

iti śrīmārkaṇḍeyapurāne sāvarṇike manvantare
devīmāhātmye śumbhaniśumbhasenānīdhūmralocana-
vadhonāma ṣaṣṭho 'dhyāyaḥ ॥6॥

Thus ends the sixth chapter called 'Slaying of *Dhūmralocana*' during the era of *Sāvarṇi Manu*, in the 'Glory of the Goddess,' (narrated) in the *Mārkaṇḍeya Purāṇa.*

उवाच ४, श्लोकाः २०, एवम् २४, एवमादितः ४१२

uvāca 4, *ślokāḥ* 20, *evaṁ* 24, *evamāditaḥ* 412

uvāca 4, ślokas 20, total 24, from beginning up to here 412.

सप्तमोऽध्यायः

saptamo 'dhyāyaḥ

Chapter Seven

Slaying of *Caṇḍa* and *Muṇḍa*

ध्यानम्।

dhyānam

Meditation

ॐ ध्यायेयं रत्नपीठे शुककलपठितं शृण्वतीं श्यामलाङ्गीं
न्यस्तैकाङ्घ्रिंसरोजे शशिशकलधरां वल्लकीं वादयन्तीम्।
कह्लाराबद्धमालां नियमितविलसच्चोलिकां रक्तवस्त्रां
मातङ्गीं शङ्खपात्रां मधुरमधुमदां चित्रकोद्भासिभालाम्॥

oṁ. dhyāyeyaṁ ratnapīṭhe śukakalapaṭhitaṁ śṛṇvatīṁ śyāmalāṅgīṁ
nyastaikāṅghriṁsaroje śaśiśakaladharāṁ vallakīṁ vādayantīm ।
kalhārābaddhamālāṁ niyamitavilasaccolikāṁ raktavastrāṁ
mātangīṁ śaṅkhapātrāṁ madhuramadhumadāṁ citrakodbhāsibhālām ॥

OṀ. I MEDITATE UPON *MĀTAṄGĪ,* THE GODDESS WITH ELEPHANT-LIKE GAIT WHO, SITTING ON A BEJEWELLED THRONE, IS LISTENING TO THE SONOROUS RECITAL OF A PARROT. SHE IS DARK-COMPLEXIONED AND HAS PLACED ONE OF HER FEET ON A LOTUS. A DIGIT OF THE MOON ADORNS HER HEAD. SHE IS PLAYING THE STRINGS OF A LUTE AND WEARING A GARLAND OF WHITE LILIES. A BLOUSE AND A SAREE OF RED COLOUR COVER HER BODY. A VESSEL OF A CONCH SHELL IS HELD IN HER HAND. A FAINT INEBRIATION OF SWEET SPIRIT IS DISCERNIBLE ON HER FACE AND A SPOT OF VERMILLION SHINES ON HER FORHEAD.

ॐ ऋषिरुवाच ।।१।।

1. *oṁ. ṛṣiruvāca*

आज्ञप्तास्ते ततो दैत्याश्चण्डमुण्डपुरोगमाः ।
चतुरङ्गबलोपेता ययुरभ्युद्यतायुधाः ।।२।।

2. *ājñaptāste tato daityāścaṇḍamuṇḍapurogamāḥ* ।
caturaṅgabalopetā yayurabhyudyatāyudhāḥ ।।

Oṁ. The Seer said

At his (*śumbha's*) command advanced the demons' forces comprising all the four parts, i.e., elephants, chariots, cavalry and infantry, led by *Caṇḍa* and *Muṇḍa* and fully equipped with weapons.

ददृशुस्ते ततो देवीमीषद्धासां व्यवस्थिताम् ।
सिंहस्योपरि शैलेन्द्रशृङ्गे महति काञ्चने ।।३।।

3. *dadṛśuste tato devīmīṣaddhāsāṁ vyavasthitām* ।
siṁhasyopari śailendraśṛṅge mahati kāñcane ।।

Arriving at the golden peak of *Himālaya*, they saw the Goddess, slightly smiling, seated on the lion.

ते दृष्ट्वा तां समादातुमुद्यमं चक्रुरुद्यताः ।
आकृष्टचापासिधरास्तथान्ये तत्समीपगाः ।।४।।

4. *te dṛṣṭvā tāṁ samādātumudyamaṁ cakrurudyatāḥ* ।
ākṛṣṭacāpāsidharāstathānye tatsamīpagāḥ ।।

On seeing her, they proceeded to capture her. Some bent their bows, some drew their swords while the others went and stood close to her.

ततः कोपं चकारोच्चैरम्बिका तानरीन् प्रति ।
कोपेन चास्या वदनं मषी[1]वर्णमभूत्तदा ।।५।।

5. *tataḥ kopaṁ cakāroccairambikā tānarīn prati* ।
kopena cāsyā vadanaṁ maṣī[1] *varṇamabhūttadā* ।।

---

[1]AR: मसी masī

Then the Mother became very angry with those enemies and due to that anger her face turned jet-black.

भ्रुकुटीकुटिलात्तस्या ललाटफलकाद्द्रुतम् ।
काली करालवदना विनिष्क्रान्तासिपाशिनी ।।६।।

6. *bhrukuṭīkuṭilāttasyā lalāṭaphalakāddrutam* ।
kālī karālavadanā viniṣkrāntāsipāśinī ।।

From the crooked brow of her forehead instantly appeared *Kālī* of the Ferocious Face, wielding a sword and a snare.

विचित्रखट्वाङ्गधरा नरमालाविभूषणा ।
द्वीपिचर्मपरीधाना शुष्कमांसातिभैरवा ।।७।।

7. *vicitrakhaṭvāṅgadharā naramālāvibhūṣaṇā* ।
dvīpicarmaparīdhānā śuṣkamāṁsātibhairavā ।।

A speckled skull-topped club she held and a garland of human skulls was her ornament. She was covered with the skin of a leopard, her flesh was emaciated and she looked frightful.

अतिविस्तारवदना जिह्वाललनभीषणा ।
निमग्नारक्तनयना नादापूरितदिङ्मुखा ।।८।।

8. *ativistāravadanā jihvālalanabhīṣaṇā* ।
nimagnāraktanayanā nādāpūritadiṅmukhā ।।

Her mouth was enormous and tongue lolled out dreadfully. Her eyes were red and sunk deep. Directions reverberated with her loud roar.

सा वेगेनाभिपतिता घातयन्ती महासुरान् ।
सैन्ये तत्र सुरारीणामभक्षयत तद्बलम् ।।९।।

9. *sā vegenābhipatitā ghātayantī mahāsurān* ।
sainye tatra surārīṇāmabhakṣayata tadbalam ।।

Killing big demons, she pounced upon the enemies of the gods with tremendous speed and devoured their forces.

पार्ष्णिग्राहाङ्कुशग्राहियोधघण्टा समन्वितान् ।
समादायैकहस्तेन मुखे चिक्षेप वारणान् ॥१०॥

10. *pārṣnigrāhāṅkuśagrāhiyodhaghaṇṭā samanvitān* ।
samādāyaikahastena mukhe cikṣepa vāraṇān ॥

With just one hand she caught and swallowed the soldiers maintaining the rear of the army, the elephant-drivers holding hooks in their hands, the warriors and the elephants along with the bells around their necks.

तथैव योधं तुरगै रथं सारथिना सह ।
निक्षिप्य वक्त्रे दशनैश्चर्वयन्त्यति[2]भैरवम् ॥११॥

11. *tathaiva yodhaṁ turagai rathaṁ sārathinā saha* ।
nikṣipya vaktre daśanaiścarvayantyati[2] *bhairavam* ॥

Similarly, she gorged down horses and chariots along with charioteers and soldiers and chewed them with her fangs most frightfully.

एकं जग्राह केशेषु ग्रीवायामथ चापरम् ।
पादेनाक्रम्य चैवान्यमुरसान्यमपोथयत् ॥१२॥

12. *ekaṁ jagrāha keṣeṣu grīvāyāmatha cāparam* ।
pādenākramya caivānyamurasānyamapothayat ॥

One she grabbed by the hair and another by the neck; yet another she trampled under her feet and still another she annihilated by striking at his chest.

तैर्मुक्तानि च शस्त्राणि महास्त्राणि तथासुरैः ।
मुखेन जग्राह रुषा दशनैर्मथितान्यपि ॥१३॥

13. *tairmuktāni ca śastrāṇi mahāstrāṇi tathāsuraiḥ* ।
mukhena jagrāha ruṣā daśanairmathitānyapi ॥

---

[2]AR: चर्वयत्यति carvayatyati

She picked up with her mouth the great missiles and weapons shot by the demons and wrathfully crushed them with her fangs.

बलिनां तद् बलं सर्वमसुराणां दुरात्मनाम् ।
ममर्दाभक्षयच्चान्यानन्यांश्चाताडयत्तथा ।।१४।।

14. *balinām tadbalam sarvamasurāṇām durātmanām* ।
mamardābhakṣayaccānyānanyānścātāḍayattathā ।।

असिना निहताः केचित्केचित्खट्वाङ्ग ताडिताः[3] ।
जग्मुर्विनाशमसुरा दन्ताग्राभिहतास्तथा ।।१५।।

15. *asinā nihatāḥ kecitkecitkhaṭvāṅga tāḍitāḥ*[3] ।
jagmurvināśamasurā dantāgrābhihatāstathā ।।

She pounded and ground some, devoured and thrashed others fiercely, killed some with her sword, beat others with her skull-topped club and chewed many with the edges of her teeth. In this way, she decimated the entire force of those mighty and wicked demons.

क्षणेन तद्बलं सर्वमसुराणां निपातितम् ।
दृष्ट्वा चण्डोऽभिदुद्राव तां कालीमतिभीषणाम् ।।१६।।

16. *kṣaṇena tadbalam sarvamasurāṇām nipātitam* ।
dṛṣṭvā caṇḍo 'bhidudrāva tām kālimatibhīṣanām ।।

In a moment, the entire force of demons thus fell. Seeing this, *Caṇḍa* rushed towards that most fearful *Kālī*, the Goddess of Death.

शरवर्षैर्महाभीमैर्भीमाक्षीं तां महासुरः ।
छादयामास चक्रैश्च मुण्डः क्षिप्तैः सहस्रशः ।।१७।।

17. *śaravarṣairmahābhīmairbhīmākṣīm tām mahāsuraḥ* ।
chādayāmāsa cakraiśca muṇḍah kṣiptaiḥ sahasraśaḥ ।।

That mighty demon *Muṇḍa* covered the frightful-eyed Goddess by showering huge arrows and throwing thousands of discs at her.

[3]AR: ता रणे *tā raṇe*

तानि चक्राण्यनेकानि विशमानानि तन्मुखम् ।
बभुर्यथार्कबिम्बानि सुबहूनि घनोदरम् ॥१८॥

18. *tāni cakrāṇyanekāni viśamānāni tanmukham* ।
babhuryathārkabiṁbāni subahūni ghanodaram ॥

Those numerous discs, as they entered her mouth, looked like several shining orbs of the sun merging into the belly of a cloud.

ततो जहासातिरुषा भीमं भैरवनादिनी ।
कालीकरालवक्त्रान्तर्दुर्दर्शदशनोज्ज्वला ॥१९॥

19. *tato jahāsātiruṣā bhīmaṁ bhairavanādinī* ।
kālīkarālavaktrāntardurdarśadaśanojjvalā ॥

Then that *Kālī* of the Radiant Teeth, Shining in her dreadful mouth let out a frightening laughter in great fury.

उत्थाय च महासिं हं देवी चण्डमधावत ।
गृहीत्वा चास्य केशेषु शिरस्तेनासिनाच्छिनत्[1] ॥२०॥

20. *utthāya ca mahāsiṁ haṁ devī caṇḍamadhāvata* ।
gṛhītvā cāsya keśeṣu śirastenāsinācchinat[1] ॥

And raising then her great sword, the Goddess charged towards *Caṇḍa* with the sound of *haṁ* and, seizing him by his hair, severed his head with the sword.

अथ मुण्डोऽभ्यधावत्तां दृष्ट्वा चण्डं निपातितम् ।
तमप्यपातयद्भूमौ सा खड्गाभिहतं रुषा ॥२१॥

21. *atha muṇḍo 'bhyadhāvattāṁ dṛṣṭvā caṇḍaṁ nipātitam* ।
tamapyapātayadbhūmau sā khaḍgābhihataṁ ruṣā ॥

---

[1]Additional reading in some copies: छिन्ने शिरसिदैत्येन्द्रश्चक्रे नादं सुभैरवम्। तेन नादेन महता त्रासितं भुवनत्रयम्॥ *chinne śirasi daityendraścakre nādaṁ subhairavam*। *tena nādena mahatā trāsitaṁ bhuvanatrayam*॥ His head chopped off, the demon-king let out a frightful roar. With that loud roar he frightened the three worlds.

When *Muṇḍa* saw *Caṇḍa* slayed, he ran towards her. Angrily she razed him to the ground and killed him also with her sword.

हतशेषं ततः सैन्यं दृष्ट्वा चण्डं निपातितम् ।
मुण्डं च सुमहावीर्यं दिशो भेजे भयातुरम् ।।२२।।

22. *hataśeṣaṁ tataḥ sainyaṁ dṛṣṭvā caṇḍaṁ nipātitam* ।
muṇḍaṁ ca sumahāvīryaṁ diśo bheje bhayāturam ।।

On seeing *Caṇḍa* and the mighty *Muṇḍa* slayed, the residual army panicked and ran helter skelter.

शिरश्चण्डस्य काली च गृहीत्वा मुण्डमेव च ।
प्राह प्रचण्डाट्टहासमिश्रमभ्येत्य चण्डिकाम् ।।२३।।

23. *śiraścaṇḍasya kālī ca gṛhītvā muṇḍameva ca* ।
prāha pracaṇḍāṭṭahāsamiśramabhyetya caṇḍikām ।।

Then *Kālī* picked up the heads of *Caṇḍa* as well as *Muṇḍa*, went to *Caṇḍikā* letting out a roar of laughter, and said:

मया तवात्रोपहृतौ चण्डमुण्डौ महापशू ।
युद्धयज्ञे स्वयं शुम्भं निशुम्भं च हनिष्यसि ।।२४।।

24. *mayā tavātropahṛtau caṇḍamuṇḍau mahāpaśū* ।
yuddhayajñe svayaṁ śumbhaṁ niśumbhaṁ ca haniṣyasi ।।

Here I have presented to you *Caṇḍa* and *Muṇḍa*, two mighty animals, killed by me. Now, in the sacrifice of battle, you would yourself slay *Śumbha* and *Niśumbha*.

ऋषिरुवाच ।।२५।।

25. *ṛṣiruvāca*

तावानीतौ ततो दृष्ट्वा चण्डमुण्डौ महासुरौ ।
उवाच कालीं कल्याणीं ललितं चण्डिका वचः ।।२६।।

26. *tāvānītau tato dṛṣṭvā caṇḍamuṇḍau mahāsurau* ।
uvāca kālīṁ kalyāṇīṁ lalitaṁ caṇḍikā vacaḥ ।।

The Seer said.

Seeing those (skulls of the) mighty *Caṇḍa* and *Muṇḍa*, brought to her by the auspicious *Kālī*, *Caṇḍikā* spoke to her in graceful words:

यस्माच्चण्डं च मुण्डं च गृहीत्वा त्वमुपागता ।
चामुण्डेति ततो लोके ख्याता देवि भविष्यसि ॥ॐ॥२७॥

27. *yasmācaṇḍaṁ ca muṇḍaṁ ca gṛhītvā tvamupāgatā* ।
cāmuṇḍeti tato loke khyātā devi bhaviṣyasi ॥oṁ॥

Since you have come bringing *Caṇḍa* and *Muṇḍa*, you will, O Goddess, be known in the world as *Cāmuṇḍā*. oṁ

इति श्रीमार्कण्डेयपुराणे सावर्णिके मन्वन्तरे देवीमाहात्म्ये
चण्डमुण्डवधोनाम सप्तमोऽध्याय: ॥७॥

iti śrīmārkaṇḍeyapurāṇe sāvarṇike manvantare devīmāhātmye caṇḍamuṇḍavadhonāma saptamo 'dhyāyaḥ ॥7॥

Thus ends the seventh chapter called 'Slaying of *Caṇḍa* and *Muṇḍa*' during the era of *Sāvarṇi Manu*, in the 'Glory of the Goddess,' (narrated) in the *Mārkaṇḍeya Purāṇa*.

उवाच २, श्लोका: २५, एवम् २७, एवमादित: ४३९
uvāca 2, *ślokaḥ* 25, *evaṁ* 27, *evamāditaḥ* 439

uvāca 2, ślokas 25, total 27, from the beginning up to here 439.

अष्टमोऽध्यायः॥

aṣṭamo 'dhyāyaḥ॥

Chapter Eight

Slaying of *Raktabīja*

ध्यानम्

dhyānam

Meditation

ॐ अरुणां करुणातरङ्गिताक्षीं धृतपाशाङ्कुशबाणचापहस्ताम्।
अणिमादिभिरावृतां मयूखैरहमित्येव विभावये भवानीम्॥

oṁ. aruṇāṁ karuṇātaraṅgitākṣīṁ
dhṛtapāśāṅkuśabāṇacāpahastām ।
aṇimādibhirāvṛtāṁ mayūkhair-
ahamityeva vibhāvaye bhavānīm ॥

I MEDITATE UPON *BHAVĀNĪ*, THE SOURCE OF ALL EXISTENCE. SHE IS OF RUDDY HUE AND HER EYES ARE RIPPLING WITH COMPASSION. SHE IS HOLDING A SNARE, A HOOK, AN ARROW AND A BOW IN HER HANDS. *AṆIMĀ*, THE POWER OF BECOMING SMALL AS AN ATOM, AND THE OTHER *SIDDHIS* (DIVINE ACCOMPLISHMENTS) ATTEND UPON HER.

ॐ ऋषिरुवाच ॥१॥

1. oṁ ṛṣiruvāca

चण्डे च निहते दैत्ये मुण्डे च विनिपातिते ।
बहुलेषु च सैन्येषु क्षयितेष्वसुरेश्वरः ॥2॥

2. *caṇḍe ca nihate daitye muṇḍe ca vinipātite ।*
bahuleṣu ca sainyeṣu kṣayiteṣvasureśvaraḥ ॥

ततः कोपपराधीनचेताः शुम्भः प्रतापवान् ।
उद्योगं सर्वसैन्यानां दैत्यानामादिदेश ह ॥3॥

3. *tataḥ kopaparādhīnacetāḥ śumbhaḥ pratāpavān ।*
udyogaṁ sarvasainyānāṁ daityānāmādideśa ha ॥

Oṁ. The Seer Said

Caṇḍa and *Muṇḍa* having been slayed and a large chunk of army decimated, *Śumbha*, the mighty lord of demons was beside himself with anger. He commanded the entire army of demons to march for war.

अद्य सर्वबलैर्दैत्याः षडशीतिरुदायुधाः ।
कम्बूनां चतुरशीतिर्निर्यान्तु स्वबलैर्वृताः ॥४॥

4. *adya sarvabalairdaityāḥ ṣaḍaśītirudāyudhāḥ ।*
kambūnāṁ caturaśītirniryāntu svabalairvṛtāḥ ॥

Let eighty-six *Udāyudha* Chiefs of Demons, march along with their troops today. Eightyfour demons of the *Kambu* clan should go forth with their armies.

कोटिवीर्याणि पञ्चाशदसुराणां कुलानि वै ।
शतं कुलानि धौम्राणां निर्गच्छन्तु ममाज्ञया ॥५॥

5. *koṭivīryāṇi pañcāśadasurāṇāṁ kulāni vai ।*
śataṁ kulāni dhaumrāṇāṁ nirgacchantu mamājñayā ॥

Under my orders, let fifty chiefs of *Koṭivīrya* clan and a hundred of *Dhaumra* clan go with their armies.

कालका दौर्हृदा मौर्या कालकेयास्तथासुराः ।
युद्धाय सज्जा निर्यान्तु आज्ञया त्वरिता मम ॥६॥

6. *kālakā daurhṛdā mauryā kālakeyāstathāsurāḥ* ।
yuddhāya sajjā niryāntu ājñayā tvaritā mama ॥

I order the demons *Kālakas, Daurhṛdas, Mauryas* and *Kālakeyas*, ready for battle, to immediately proceed.

इत्याज्ञाप्यासुरपतिः शुम्भो भैरवशासनः ।
निर्जगाम महासैन्यसहस्रैर्बहुभिर्वृतः ॥७॥

7. *ityājñāpyāsurapatiḥ śumbho bhairavaśāsanaḥ* ।
nirjagāma mahāsainyasahasrairbahubhirvṛtaḥ ॥

After issuing these orders, *Śumbha*, the ferocious ruler of the demons, started himself along with thousands of troops armed with a variety of weapons.

आयान्तं चण्डिका दृष्ट्वा तत्सैन्यमतिभीषणम् ।
ज्यास्वनैः पूरयामास धरणीगगनान्तरम् ॥८॥

8. *āyāntaṁ caṇḍikā dṛṣṭvā tatsainyamatibhīṣaṇam* ।
jyāsvanaiḥ pūrayāmāsa dharaṇīgaganāntaram ॥

When *Caṇḍikā* saw that horriffic army approaching, she filled the space between the earth and heaven with the twang of her bow-string.

ततः[1] सिंहो महानादमतीव कृतवान् नृप ।
घण्टास्वनेन तन्नादमम्बिका[2] चोपबृंहयत् ॥९॥

9. *tataḥ*[1] *siṁho mahānādamatīva kṛtavān nṛpa* ।
ghaṇṭāsvanena tannādamambikā[2] *copabṛṁhayat* ॥

Then O king! the Lion made a loud roar which was augmented by the Mother by clanging the bell.

---

[1]AR: स च *sa ca*

[2]AR: तन्नादानम्बिका *tānnādānambikā*

धनुर्ज्यासिंहघण्टानां नादापूरितदिङ्मुखा ।
निनादैर्भीषणैः काली जिग्ये विस्तारितानना ॥१०॥

10. *dhanurjyāsiṁhaghaṇṭānāṁ nādāpūritadiṅmukhā ।*
ninādairbhīṣaṇaiḥ kāli jigye vistāritānanā ॥

Quarters resounded with the twang of the bow-string, roar of the Lion and clang of the bell. With the dreadful echoes of these sounds, *Kālī* extended her mouth further and, thus, became the Victor.

तं निनादमुपश्रुत्य दैत्यसैन्यैश्चतुर्दिशम् ।
देवी सिंहस्तथा काली सरोषैः परिवारिताः ॥११॥

11. *taṁ ninādamupaśrutya daityasainyaiścaturdiśam ।*
devī siṁhastathā kālī saroṣaiḥ parivāritāḥ ॥

When the demon-armies heard that tumultuous uproar, they angrily surrounded the Goddess (*Caṇḍikā*), the Lion and *Kālī* in the four directions.

एतस्मिन्नन्तरे भूप विनाशाय सुरद्विषाम् ।
भवायामरसिंहानामतिवीर्यबलान्विताः ॥१२॥

12. *etasminnantare bhūpa vināśāya suradviṣāṁ ।*
bhavāyāmarasiṁhānāmativīryabalānvitāḥ ॥

ब्रह्मेशगुहविष्णूनां तथेन्द्रस्य च शक्तयः ।
शरीरेभ्यो विनिष्क्रम्य तद्रूपैश्चण्डिकां ययुः ॥१३॥

13. *brahmeśaguhaviṣṇūnāṁ tathendrasya ca śaktayaḥ ।*
śarīrebhyo viniṣkramya tadrūpaiścaṇḍikāṁ yayuḥ ॥

Meanwhile, O king, the Energies of *Brahmā*, *Śiva*, *Guha* (*Kārtikeya*), *Viṣṇu* and *Indra*, came out of their bodies, assuming their respective forms. They were endowed with great valour and prowess and appeared in order to annihilate the enemies of the gods and to establish their superiority. They went to *Caṇḍikā*.

यस्य देवस्य यद्रूपं यथाभूषणवाहनम् ।
तद्वदेव हि तच्छक्तिरसुरान् योद्धुमाययौ ।।१४।।

14. *yasya devasya yadrūpaṁ yathābhūṣaṇavāhanam* ।
tadvadeva hi tacchaktirasurān yoddhumāyayau ।।

Each of these Energies was exactly of her consort's form, wore identical ornaments and had the identical mount. They had come to fight with the demons.

हंसयुक्तविमानाग्रे साक्षसूत्रकमण्डलुः ।
आयाता ब्रह्मणः शक्तिर्ब्रह्माणी साभिधीयते ।।१५।।

15. *haṁsayuktavimānāgre sākṣasūtrakamaṇḍaluḥ* ।
āyātā brahmaṇaḥ śaktirbrahmāṇī sābhidhīyate ।।

First of all came the Energy of *Brahmā*, known as *Brahmāṇī*, on a Swan-driven car. She had a Rosary of Beads and a Pot of Consecrated Water.

माहेश्वरी वृषारूढा त्रिशूलवरधारिणी ।
महाहिवलया प्राप्ता चन्द्ररेखाविभूषणा ।।१६।।

16. *māheśvarī vṛṣārūḍhā triśūlavaradhāriṇī* ।
mahāhivalayā prāptā candrarekhāvibhūṣaṇā ।।

Came *Māheśvarī*, the Energy of *Maheśa*, the Great Lord (*Śiva*), Saddled on a Bull, Supporting an Excellent Trident. She wore a Bracelet of the Great Serpent and a Digit of Moon was her ornament.

कौमारी शक्तिहस्ता च मयूरवरवाहना ।
योद्धुमभ्याययौ दैत्यानम्बिका गुहरूपिणी ।।१७।।

17. *kaumārī śaktihastā ca mayūravaravāhanā* ।
yoddhumabhyāyayau daityānambikā guharūpiṇī ।।

The Mother *Kaumārī*, of the form of *Guha*, Mounted on a Magnificent Peacock and Carrying a Missile in Hand, arrived to fight with the demons.

तथैव वैष्णवी शक्तिर्गरुडोपरि संस्थिता ।
शङ्खचक्रगदाशार्ङ्गखड्गहस्ताभ्युपाययौ ॥१८॥

18. *tathaiva vaiṣṇavī śaktirgaruḍopari saṁsthitā* ।
śaṅkhacakragadāśārṅgakhaḍgahastābhyupāyayau ॥

Likewise came the Energy of *Viṣṇu* seated on *Garuḍa*, the Chief of the Feathered Race. She had a Conch Shell, a Discus, a Mace, the *Śārṅga* bow and a Sword.

यज्ञ[3]वाराहमतुलं रूपं या बिभ्रतो[4] हरेः ।
शक्तिः साप्याययौ तत्र वाराहीं बिभ्रती तनुम् ॥१९॥

19. *yajña[3] vārāhamatulaṁ rūpaṁ yā bibhrato[4] hareḥ* ।
śāktih sāpyāyayau tatra vārāhīṁ bibhratī tanum ॥

The Energy of Lord *Hari* (*Viṣṇu*), who assumed the incomparable incarnation of *Yajña-Vārāha*, the Sacrificial Boar, also came embodying herself as *Vārāhī*, the Female Boar.

नारसिंही नृसिंहस्य बिभ्रती सदृशं वपुः ।
प्राप्ता तत्र सटाक्षेपक्षिप्तनक्षत्र संहतिः ॥२०॥

20. *nārasiṁhī nṛsiṁhasya bibhratī sadṛśaṁ vapuḥ* ।
prāptā tatra saṭākṣepakṣiptanakṣatra saṁhatiḥ ॥

Nārasiṁhī, taking the form similar to *Nṛsiṁha* (Man-Lion, the fourth incarnation of *Viṣṇu*) reached there. Stars in heaven went helter-skelter as she tossed her mane.

वज्रहस्ता तथैवैन्द्री गजराजोपरि स्थिता ।
प्राप्ता सहस्रनयना यथा शक्रस्तथैव सा ॥२१॥

21. *vajrahastā tathaivaindrī gajarājopari sthitā* ।
prāptā sahasranayanā yathā śakrastathaiva sā ॥

---

[3]AR: जज्ञे वाराह॰ *jajñe vārāha*॰

[4]AR: बिभ्रती *bibhratī*

Likewise, mounted on the Chief of Elephants, arrived *Aindrī* (the Energy of *Indra*); like *Śakra* (*Indra*), she too had a Thousand Eyes.

ततः परिवृतस्ताभिरीशानो देवशक्तिभिः ।
हन्यन्तामसुराः शीघ्रं मम प्रीत्याऽऽहचण्डिकाम् ।।२२।।

22. *tataḥ parivṛtastābhirīśāno devaśaktibhiḥ* ।
hanyantāmasurāḥ śīghraṁ mama prītyā "hacaṇḍikām ।।

Then Lord *Śiva*, surrounded by the Energies of the gods, told *Caṇḍikā:* kill the demons forthwith to please me.

ततो देवीशरीरात्तु विनिष्क्रान्तातिभीषणा ।
चण्डिकाशक्तिरत्युग्रा शिवाशतनिनादिनी ।।२३।।

23. *tato devīśarīrāttu viniṣkrāntātibhīṣaṇā* ।
caṇḍikāśaktiratyugrā śivāśataninādinī ।।

Then issued forth from the body of the Goddess the frightening and ferocious Energy *Caṇḍikā,* who yelled like a Hundred Jackals.

सा चाह धूम्रजटिलमीशानमपराजिता ।
दूत त्वं गच्छ भगवन् पार्श्वं शुम्भनिशुम्भयोः ।।२४।।

24. *sā cāha dhūmrajaṭilamīśānamaparājitā* ।
dūta tvaṁ gaccha bhagavan pārśvaṁ śumbhaniśumbhayoḥ ।।

She, The Invincible One, said to *Śiva* of the Dark, Matted Hair: 'O Lord! go to *Śumbha* and *Niśumbha* as ambassador.'

ब्रूहि शुम्भं निशुम्भं च दानवावतिगर्वितौ ।
ये चान्ये दानवास्तत्र युद्धाय समुपस्थिताः ।।२५।।

25. *brūhi śumbhaṁ niśumbhaṁ ca dānavāvatigarvitau* ।
ye cānye dānavāstatra yuddhāya samupasthitāḥ ।।

त्रैलोक्यमिन्द्रो लभतां देवाः सन्तु हविर्भुजः।
यूयं प्रयात पातालं यदि जीवितुमिच्छत ॥२६॥

26. *trailokyamindro labhatāṁ devāḥ santu havirbhujaḥ* ।
yūyaṁ prayāta pātālaṁ yadi jivītumicchata ॥

'Tell those two highly conceited demons, *Śumbha* and *Niśumbha,* and the other demons present there for combat: let *Indra* get (the empire of) the three worlds and the gods enjoy their share of oblations; return to *Pātāla,* the nethermost region, if you want to survive.'

बलावलेपादथ चेद्भवन्तो युद्धकाङ्क्षिणः।
तदागच्छत तृप्यन्तु मच्छिवाः पिशितेन वः ॥२७॥

27. *balāvalepādatha cedbhavanto yuddhakāṅkṣiṇah* ।
tadāgacchata tṛpyantu macchivāḥ piśitena vaḥ ॥

'If, however, the arrogance of strength goads you to battle, then come and let my jackals satiate themselves with your flesh.'

ययो नियुक्तो दौत्येन तया देव्या शिवः स्वयम्।
शिवदूतीति लोकेऽस्मिंस्ततः सा ख्यातिमागता ॥२८॥

28. *yayo niyukto dautyena tayā devyā śivaḥ svayam* ।
śivadūtīti loke 'sminstataḥ sā khyātimāgatā ॥

Since that Goddess had deputed Lord *Śiva* himself as ambassador, she came to be known in the world as *Śivadūtī,* the One for Whom (at whose request) *Śiva* went as ambassador.

तेऽपि श्रुत्वा वचो देव्या शर्वाख्यातं महासुराः।
अमर्षापूरिता जग्मुर्यत्र[5] कात्यायनी स्थिता ॥२९॥

29. *te 'pi śrutvā vaco devyā śarvākhyātaṁ mahāsurāḥ* ।
amarṣāpūritā jagmuryatra[5] *kātyāyanī sthitā* ॥

---

[5]AR: जग्मुर्यतः *jagmuryataḥ*

Those mighty demons too, on hearing the message of the Goddess from Lord *Śiva,* were filled with rage and went where *Kātyāyanī,* [the (adopted) daughter of the sage *Kātyāyana*] was present.

ततः प्रथममेवाग्रे शरशक्त्यृष्टिवृष्टिभिः ।
ववर्षरुद्धतामर्षास्तां देवीममरारयः ।।३०।।

30. *tataḥ prathamamevāgre śaraśaktyrṣṭivṛṣṭibhiḥ* ।
vavarṣaruddhatāmarṣāstāṁ devīmamarārayaḥ ।।

Then the angry enemies of the gods launched the offensive on the Goddess by hailing arrows, missiles and double-edged swords on her.

सा च तान् प्रहितान् बाणाञ्छूलशक्तिपरश्वधान् ।
चिच्छेद लीलयाऽऽध्मातधनुर्मुक्तैर्महेषुभिः ।।३१।।

31. *sā ca tān prahitān bāṇāñchūlaśaktiparśvadhān* ।
ciccheda līlayā ''dhmātadhanurmuktairmaheṣubhiḥ ।।

She, too, playfully cut those arrows, pikes, missiles and battle-axes aimed at her, into pieces, with great arrows shot from her bow following the twang of her bow.

तस्याग्रतस्तथा काली शूलपातविदारितान् ।
खट्वाङ्गपोथितांश्चारीन् कुर्वती व्यचरस्तदा ।।३२।।

32. *tasyāgratastathā kālī śūlapātavidāritān* ।
khaṭvāṅgapothitāṁścārīn kurvatī vyacarastadā ।।

Then *Kālī,* in the vanguard, started tearing the enemies apart with her pike as she moved ahead making mincemeat of them with her skull-topped club.

कमण्डलुजलाक्षेपहतवीर्यान् हतौजसः ।
ब्रह्माणी चाकरोच्छत्रून् येन येन स्म धावति ।।३३।।

33. *kamaṇḍalujalākṣepahatavīryān hataujasaḥ* ।
brahmāṇī cākarocchatrūn yena yena sma dhāvati ।।

Brahmāṇī, too, running in whichever direction, sprinkled the consecrated water from her pot on the enemies and destroyed their prowess and vitality.

माहेश्वरी त्रिशूलेन तथा चक्रेण वैष्णवी ।
दैत्याञ्जघान कौमारी तथा शक्त्यातिकोपना ।।३४।।

34. *māheśvarī triśūlena tathā cakreṇa vaiṣṇavī* ।
daityañjaghāna kaumārī tathā śaktyātikopanā ।।

Māheśvarī with her trident, *Vaiṣṇavī* with her disc and the enraged *Kaumārī* with her missile killed the demons.

ऐन्द्रीकुलिशपातेन शतशो दैत्यदानवाः ।
पेतुर्विदारिताः पृथ्व्यां रुधिरौघप्रवर्षिणः ।।३५।।

35. *aindrīkuliśapātena śataśo daityadānavāḥ* ।
peturvidāritāh pṛthvyāṁ rudhiraughapravarṣiṇaḥ ।।

Hundreds of demon offsprings of *Diti* (*Daityas*) and *Danu* (*Danavas*), were rent apart by *Aindrī* when she struck her thunderbolt; they fell on the earth, streams of blood flowing from their bodies.

तुण्डप्रहारविध्वस्ता दंष्ट्राग्रक्षतवक्षसः ।
वाराहमूर्त्या न्यपतंश्चक्रेण च विदारिताः ।।३६।।

36. *tuṇḍaprahāravidhvastā daṁṣṭrāgrakṣatavakṣasaḥ* ।
vārāhamūrtyā nyapataṁścakreṇa ca vidāritāḥ ।।

The embodied Energy of *Vārāha,* the Great Boar, destroyed many with the blow of her snout, many with the strike of the tips of her fangs into their chests and, with her disc, split many of them apart.

नखैर्विदारितांश्चान्यान् भक्षयन्ती महासुरान् ।
नारसिंही चचाराजौ नादापूर्णदिगम्बरा ।।३७।।

37. *nakhairvidāritāṁścānyān bhakṣayantī mahāsurān* ।
nārasiṁhī cacārājau nādāpurṇadigambarā ।।

Nārasiṁhī (the Energy of *Nṛsiṁha*), moved around filling the quarters with her roars and tore the other giant demons apart with her claws even as she swallowed them.

चण्डाट्टहासैरसुराः शिवदूत्यभिदूषिताः ।
पेतुः पृथिव्यां पतितांस्तांश्चखादाथ सा तदा ॥३८॥

38. *caṇḍāṭṭahāsairasurāḥ śivadūtyabhidūṣitāḥ* ।
petuḥ pṛthivyāṁ patitāṁstāṁścakhādātha sā tadā ॥

Many demons, mortified by the boisterous laughter of *Śivadūtī* fell on the earth and were then eaten by her.

इति मातृगणं क्रुद्धं मर्दयन्तं महासुरान् ।
दृष्ट्वाभ्युपायैर्विविधैर्नेशुर्देवारिसैनिकाः ॥३९॥

39. *iti mātṛgaṇaṁ kruddhaṁ mardayantaṁ mahāsurān* ।
dṛṣṭvābhyupāyairvividhairneśurdevārisainikāḥ ॥

On seeing the enraged host of the Mothers trampling the mighty demons in a variety of ways, soldiers of the demons' army took to their heels.

पलायनपरान् दृष्ट्वा दैत्यान् मातृगणार्दितान् ।
योद्धुमभ्याययौ क्रुद्धौ रक्तबीजो महासुरः ॥४०॥

40. *palāyanaparān dṛṣṭvā daityān mātṛgaṇārditān* ।
yoddhumabhyāyayau kruddhau raktabījo mahāsuraḥ ॥

Seeing that the demons, tormented by the cluster of Mothers, were running away, *Raktabīja*, the mighty demon came to fight.

रक्तबिन्दुर्यदा भूमौ पतत्यस्य शरीरतः ।
समुत्पतति मेदिन्यां[6] तत्प्रमाणस्तदासुरः ॥४१॥

41. *raktabinduryadā bhūmau patatyasya śarīrataḥ* ।
samutpatati medinyāṁ[6] *tatpramāṇastadāsuraḥ* ॥

---

[6]AR: न्यास्त॰ nyāsta॰

With each drop of blood dripping on earth from his body, a demon of equal magnitude would arise.

युयुधे स गदापाणिरिन्द्रशक्त्या महासुरः ।
ततश्चैन्द्रीस्ववज्रेण रक्तबीजमताडयत् ॥४२॥

42. *yuyudhe sa gadāpāṇirindraśaktyā mahāsuraḥ* ।
tataścaindrī svavajreṇa raktabījamatāḍayat ॥

That mighty demon, *Raktabīja*, wielding the mace in his hand, fought with *Aindrī*, who struck him with her Thunderbolt.

कुलिशेनाहतस्याशु बहु[7] सुस्राव शोणितम् ।
समुत्तस्थुस्ततो योधास्तद्रूपास्तत्पराक्रमाः ॥४३॥

43. *kuliśenāhatasyāśu bahu*[7] *susrāva śoṇitam* ।
samuttasthustato yodhāstadrūpāstatparākramāḥ ॥

He being wounded with the blow of the thunderbolt, blood started oozing immediately and profusely from him and from that blood arose the warriors of identical figures and equal valour.

यावन्तः पतितास्तस्य शरीराद्रक्तबिन्दवः ।
तावन्तः पुरुषा जातास्तद्वीर्यबलविक्रमाः ॥४४॥

44. *yāvantaḥ patitāstasya śarīrādraktabindavaḥ* ।
tāvantaḥ puruṣā jātāstadvīryabalavikramāḥ ॥

Equal in the number of drops of blood that fell from his body were the persons who came into being. In valour, strength and power, they were equal to him.

ते चापि युयुधुस्तत्र पुरुषा रक्तसम्भवाः ।
समं मातृभिरत्युग्रशस्त्रपातातिभीषणम् ॥४५॥

45. *te cāpi yuyudhustatra puruṣā raktasambhavāḥ* ।
samaṁ mātṛbhiratyugraśastrapātātibhīṣaṇam ॥

---

[7]AR: तस्य *tasya*

Those blood-born persons also fought firecely with the Mothers by hurling their dreadful weapons.

पुनश्च वज्रपातेन क्षतमस्य शिरो यदा ।
ववाह रक्तं पुरुषास्ततो जाताः सहस्रशः ।।४६।।

46. *punaśca vajrapātena kṣatamasya śiro yadā* ।
vavāha raktaṁ puruṣāstato jātāḥ sahasraśaḥ ।।

Again, when with the strike of the thunderbolt, his head was injured, blood streamed. From that, men in thouands were born.

वैष्णवी समरे चैनं चक्रेणाभिजघान ह ।
गदया ताडयामास ऐन्द्री तमसुरेश्वरम् ।।४७।।

47. *vaiṣnavī samare cainaṁ cakreṇābhijaghāna ha* ।
gadayā tāḍayāmāsa aindrī tamasureśvaram ।।

In the combat, *Vaiṣṇavī* struck that chief of demons with the discus while *Aindrī* beat him with the mace.

वैष्णवी चक्रभिन्नस्य रुधिरस्रावसम्भवैः ।
सहस्रशो जगद्व्याप्तं तत्प्रमाणैर्महासुरैः ।।४८।।

48. *vaiṣṇavī cakrabhinnasya rudhirasrāvasambhavaiḥ* ।
sahasraśo jagadvyāptaṁ tatpramāṇairmahāsuraiḥ ।।

Wounded by the discus of *Vaiṣṇavī*, as blood started flowing from him (*Raktabīja*), thousands of demons of equal might stood up therefrom and pervaded the entire world.

शक्त्या जघान कौमारी वाराही च तथासिना ।
माहेश्वरी त्रिशूलेन रक्तबीजं महासुरम् ।।४९।।

49. *śaktyā jaghāna kaumārī vārāhī ca tathāsinā* ।
māheśvarī triśūlena raktabījaṁ mahāsuram ।।

Kaumarī struck with a missle and *Vārāhī* with a sword. With her trident *Māheśvarī* struck *Raktabīja*, the mighty demon.

स चापि गदया दैत्यः सर्वा एवाहनत् पृथक् ।
मातृः कोपसमाविष्टो रक्तबीजो महासुरः ।।५०।।

50. *sa cāpi gadayā daityaḥ sarvā evāhanat pṛthak* ।
mātṝḥ kopa samāviṣṭo raktabījo mahāsuraḥ ।।

That great demon *Raktabīja*, too, in terrible anger, struck each of the Mothers separately with his mace.

तस्याहतस्य बहुधा शक्तिशूलादिभिर्भुवि ।
पपात यो वै रक्तौघस्तेनासञ्छतशोऽसुराः ।।५१।।

51. *tasyāhatasya bahudhā śaktiśūlādibhirbhuvi* ।
papāta yo vai raktaughastenāsañchataśo 'surāḥ ।।

Everytime – again and again – he was struck and wounded with missiles and pikes, etc., hundreds of demons sprung up from the stream of his blood that fell on earth.

तैश्चासुरासृक्सम्भूतैरसुरैः सकलं जगत् ।
व्याप्तमासीत्ततो देवा भयमाजग्मुरुत्तमम् ।।५२।।

52. *taiścāsurāsṛksambhūtairasuraiḥ sakalaṁ jagat* ।
vyāptamāsīttato devā bhayamājagmuruttamam ।।

The whole world was, thus, pervaded by the demons born of the blood of that demon (*Raktabīja*). Then the gods got very frightened.

तान् विषण्णान् सुरान् दृष्ट्वा चण्डिका प्राह सत्वरा ।
उवाच कालीं चामुण्डे विस्तीर्णं[8] वदनं कुरु ।।५३।।

53. *tān viṣaṇṇān surān dṛṣṭvā caṇḍikā prāha satvarā* ।
uvāca kālīṁ cāmuṇḍe vistīrṇaṁ[8] *vadanaṁ kuru* ।।

When *Caṇḍikā* saw the gods depressed, she immediately asked *Kālī: O Cāmuṇḍā!* expand your mouth further,

---

[8]AR: विस्तरं *vistaraṁ*

मच्छस्त्रपातसम्भूतान् रक्तबिन्दून्महासुरान् ।
रक्तबिन्दोः प्रतीच्छ त्वं वक्त्रेणानेन वेगिना[9] ।।५४।।

54. *macchastrapātasambhūtān raktabindūnmahāsurān* ।
raktabindoḥ pratīccha tvaṁ vaktreṇānena veginā[9] ।।

(and) instantly suck and swallow with that mouth the blood-drops and the terrible demons arising therefrom consequent upon the assault of my weapons.

भक्षयन्ती चर रणे तदुत्पन्नान्महासुरान् ।
एवमेष क्षयं दैत्यः क्षीणरक्तो भविष्यति ।।५५।।

55. *bhakṣayantī cara raṇe tadutpannānmahāsurān* ।
evameṣa kṣayaṁ daityaḥ kṣīṇarakto bhaviṣyati ।।

Keep moving in the battle while swallowing the mighty demons thus born. In this way the demon (*Raktabīja*) would be emptied of his blood and destroyed.

भक्ष्यमाणास्त्वया चोग्रा न चोत्पत्स्यन्ति चापरे[10] ।
इत्युक्त्वा तां ततो देवी शूलेनाभिजघान तम् ।।५६।।

56. *bhakṣyamāṇāstvayā cogrā na cotpatsyanti cāpare*[10] ।
ityuktvā tāṁ tato devī śūlenābhijaghāna tam ।।

When you swallow these frightful demons, more will not emerge. Telling her this, the Goddess struck him with the pike.

मुखेन काली जगृहे रक्तबीजस्य शोणितम् ।
ततोऽसावाजघानाथ गदया तत्र चण्डिकाम् ।।५७।।

57. *mukhena kālī jagṛhe raktabījasya śoṇitam* ।
tato 'sāvājaghānātha gadayā tatra caṇḍikām ।।

Kālī sucked the blood of *Raktabīja* into her mouth. Thereupon, he hit *Caṇḍikā* with his mace.

---

[9]AR: वेगिता *vegitā*.

[10]Additional reading after this in some copies: ऋषिरुवाच *ṛṣiruvāca*

न चास्या वेदनां चक्रे गदापातोऽल्पिकामपि ।
तस्याहतस्य देहात्तु बहु सुस्राव शोणितम् ॥५८॥

58. *na cāsyā vedanāṁ cakre gadāpāto 'lpikāmapi* ।
tasyāhatasya dehāttu bahu susrāva śoṇitam ॥

The strike of that mace did not, however, cause her even an iota of pain; from his body, blood flowed profusely.

यतस्ततस्तद्वक्त्रेण चामुण्डा सम्प्रतीच्छति ।
मुखे समुद्‌गता येऽस्या रक्तपातान्महासुराः ॥५९॥

59. *yatastatastadvaktreṇa cāmuṇḍā sampratīcchati* ।
mukhe samudgatā ye 'syā raktapātānmahāsurāḥ ॥

तांश्चखादाथ चामुण्डा पपौ तस्य च शोणितम् ।
देवी शूलेन वज्रेण[11] बाणैरसिभिर्ऋष्टिभिः ॥६०॥

60. *tāṁścakhādātha cāmuṇḍā papau tasya ca śoṇitam* ।
devī śūlena vajreṇa[11] *bāṇairasibhirṛṣṭibhiḥ* ॥

जघान रक्तबीजं तं चामुण्डापीतशोणितम् ।
स पपात महीपृष्ठे शस्त्रसङ्घसमाहतः[12] ॥६१॥

61. *jaghāna raktabījaṁ taṁ cāmuṇḍāpītaśoṇitam* ।
sa papāta mahīpṛṣṭhe śastrasaṅghasamāhataḥ[12] ॥

As soon as it (*Raktabīja's blood*) dropped, *Cāmuṇḍa* cupped it in her mouth. The big demons who sprang in her mouth from that blood, were eaten by her. She also drank the blood of *Raktabīja*. With pike, thunderbolt, arrows and spears, the Goddess slayed him, his blood having already been consumed by *Cāmuṇḍā*. Thus injured by a host of weapons, he fell on the ground.

---

[11]AR: चक्रेण *cakreṇa*

[12]AR: शस्त्रसंहतितो ततः *śastrasaṁhatito tataḥ*

नीरक्तश्च महीपाल रक्तबीजो महासुरः ।
ततस्ते हर्षमतुलमवापुस्त्रिदशा नृप ॥६२॥

62. *nīraktaśca mahīpāla raktabījo mahāsuraḥ* ।
tataste harṣamatulamavāpustridaśā nṛpa ॥

(Seeing) the mighty demon *Raktabīja* emptied of blood, o king! the gods then became immensely delighted.

तेषां मातृगणो जातो ननर्तासृङ्मदोद्धतः ॥ॐ॥६३॥

63. *teśāṁ mātṛgaṇo jāto nanartāsṛṅmadoddhataḥ* ॥*oṁ*॥

And the group of the Mothers, euphoric by drinking his blood, danced crazily. Oṁ

इति श्रीमार्कण्डेयपुराणे सावर्णिके मन्वन्तरे देवी माहात्म्ये
रक्तबीजवधो नामाष्टमोऽध्यायः ॥८॥

iti śrīmārkaṇḍeyapurāṇe sāvarṇike manvantare
devīmāhātmaye raktabījavadho nāmāṣṭamo 'dhyāyaḥ ॥8॥

Thus ends the eighth chapter called 'Slaying of *Raktabīja*' during the era of *Sāvarṇi Manu,* in the 'Glory of the Goddess,' (narrated) in the *Mārkaṇḍeya Purāṇa.*

उवाच १, अर्धश्लोकः १, श्लोकाः ६१, एवम् ६३, एवमादितः ५०२
uvāca 1, *ardhaślokaḥ* 1, *ślokāḥ* 61, *evaṁ* 63, *evamāditaḥ* 502

uvāca 1, half śloka 1, ślokas 61, total 63,
from beginning up to here 502.

नवमोऽध्यायः

navamo 'dhyāyaḥ

Chapter Nine

Slaying of *Niśumbha*

ध्यानम्

dhyānam

Meditation

ॐ बन्धूककाञ्चननिभं रुचिराक्षमालां
पाशाङ्कुशौ च वरदां निजबाहुदण्डैः ।
बिभ्राणमिन्दुशकलाभरणं त्रिनेत्र-
मर्धाम्बिकेशमनिशं वपुराश्रयामि ॥

oṁ. bandhūkakāñcananibhaṁ rucirākṣamālāṁ
pāśāṅkuśau ca varadāṁ nijabāhudaṇḍaiḥ ।
bibhrāṇaminduśakalābharaṇaṁ trinetram-
ardhāmbikeśamaniśaṁ vapurāśrayāmi ॥

OṀ. I SEEK REFUGE INCESSANTLY IN THE FORM OF *ARDHĀMBIKEŚA*, HALF *AMBIKĀ* AND HALF *ŚIVA* (THE *ARDHANĀRĪŚVARA*), RESEMBLING *BANDHŪKA*[1] FLOWER AND PURE GOLD, THUS BEARING THE LUSTRE OF THE MIXED HUES OF RED AND GOLD. SHE HAS A BEAUTIFUL ROSARY OF BEADS, A SNARE AND A HOOK IN HER (THREE) ARMS, (THE FOURTH) SIGNALLING BLESSING. SHE SHINES WITH THE HALF-MOON AS HER ORNAMENT AND HAS THREE EYES.

[1]pentapetes phoenicea (flower/plant)

ॐ राजोवाच ।।१।।

1. *oṁ. rajovāca*

विचित्रमिदमाख्यातं भगवन् भवता मम ।
देव्याश्चरितमाहात्म्यं रक्तबीजवधाश्रितम् ।।२।।

2. *vicitramidamākhyātaṁ bhagavan bhavatā mama* ।
devyāścaritamāhātmyaṁ raktabījavadhāśritam ।।

Oṁ. The King said

O Revered One! You have narrated to me this wonderous glory of the acts of the Goddess based on the slaying of *Raktabīja.*

भूयश्चेच्छाम्यहं श्रोतुं रक्तबीजे निपातिते ।
चकार शुम्भो यत्कर्म निशुम्भश्चातिकोपनः ।।३।।

3. *bhūyaścechāmyahaṁ śrotuṁ raktabīje nipātite* ।
cakāra śumbho yatkarma niśumbhaścātikopanaḥ ।।

I want to hear further about the action taken by the terribly enraged *Śumbha* and *Niśumbha* following the death of *Raktabīja.*

ऋषिरुवाच ।।४।।

4. *ṛṣiruvāca*

चकार कोपमतुलं रक्तबीजे निपातिते ।
शुम्भासुरो निशुम्भश्च हतेष्वन्येषु चाहवे ।।५।।

5. *cakāra kopamatulaṁ raktabīje nipātite* ।
śumbhāsuro niśumbhaśca hateṣvanyeṣu cāhave ।।

The Seer said

Following the death of *Raktabīja* and the others in the battle, the demons *Śumbha* and *Niśumbha* flew into boundless anger.

हन्यमानं महासैन्यं विलोक्यामर्षमुद्वहन् ।
अभ्यधावन्निशुम्भोऽथ मुख्ययासुरसेनया ।।६।।

6. *hanyamānaṁ mahāsainyaṁ vilokyāmarṣamudvahan* ।
abhyadhāvanniśumbho 'tha mukhyayāsurasenayā ।।

When *Niśumbha* saw his large army annihilated, he advanced, seething in anger, along with his major battalion.

तस्याग्रतस्तथा पृष्ठे पार्श्वयोश्चमहासुराः ।
संदष्टौष्ठपुटाः क्रुद्धा हन्तुं देवीमुपाययुः ।।७।।

7. *tasyāgratastathā pṛṣṭhe pārṣvayoścamahāsurāḥ* ।
saṁdaṣṭauṣṭhapuṭāh kruddhā hantuṁ devīmupāyayuḥ ।।

In front and rear, to his left and right, *Niśumbha* was covered by the mighty demons; they were biting their lips in anger even as they advanced to kill the Goddess.

आजगाम महावीर्यः शुम्भोऽपि स्वबलैर्वृतः ।
निहन्तुं चण्डिकां कोपात्कृत्वा युद्धं तु मातृभिः ।।८।।

8. *ājagāma mahāvīryaḥ śumbho 'pi svabalairvṛtaḥ* ।
nihantuṁ caṇḍikāṁ kopātkṛtvā yuddhaṁ tu mātṛbhiḥ ।।

The formidable *Śumbha,* too, surrounded by his army, arrived in anger, to kill *Caṇḍikā* after waging war with the Mothers.

ततो युद्धमतीवासीद्देव्या शुम्भनिशुम्भयोः ।
शरवर्षमतीवोग्रं मेघयोरिव वर्षतोः ।।९।।

9. *tato yuddhamatīvāsīddevyā śumbhaniśumbhayoḥ* ।
śaravarṣamatīvogram meghayoriva varṣatoḥ ।।

A fierce battle then ensued between the Goddess and *Śumbha-Niṣumbha* both of whom were like clouds raining dreadful arrows.

चिच्छेदास्ताञ्छरांस्ताभ्यां चण्डिका स्व[1]शरोत्करैः ।
ताडयामास चाङ्गेषु शस्त्रौघैरसुरेश्वरौ ॥१०॥

10. *cicchedāstañcharāṁstābhyāṁ caṇḍikā sva*[1]*śarotkaraiḥ* ।
tāḍayāmāsa cāṅgeṣu śastraughairasureśvarau ॥

With the cluster of her arrows, *Caṇḍikā* cut the arrows hurled by the two of them and also beat the limbs of those demon-chiefs with a multitude of arrows.

निशुम्भो निशितं खड्गं चर्म चादाय सुप्रभम् ।
आताडयन्मूर्ध्नि सिंहं देव्या वाहनमुत्तमम् ॥११॥

11. *niśumbho niśitaṁ khaḍgaṁ carma cādāya suprabham* ।
ātāḍayanmūrdhni siṁhaṁ devyā vāhanamuttamam ॥

Niśumbha picked up a sword and a shining shield and, with it, struck the head of the Lion, the excellent mount of the Goddess.

ताडिते वाहने देवी क्षुरप्रेणासिमुत्तमम् ।
निशुम्भस्याशु चिच्छेद चर्म चाप्यष्टचन्द्रकम् ॥१२॥

12. *tāḍite vāhane devī kṣurapreṇāsimuttamam* ।
niśuṁbhasyāśu ciccheda carma cāpyaṣṭacandrakam ॥

Her mount having been hurt, the Goddess cut *Niśumbha*'s sharp sword and shield studded with eight moons, with her razor-sharp arrow.

छिन्ने चर्मणि खड्गे च शक्तिं चिक्षेप सोऽसुरः ।
तामप्यस्य द्विधा चक्रे चक्रेणाभिमुखागताम् ॥१३॥

13. *chinne carmaṇi khaḍge ca śaktiṁ cikṣepa so 'suraḥ* ।
tāmapyasya dvidhā cakre cakreṇābhimukhāgatām ॥

When his shield and the sword were cut, that demon hurled a missile. That, too was, cut into two pieces with her discus when the Goddess saw it coming.

---

[1]AR: चण्डिकाऽऽशु। *caṇḍikā ''śu*

कोपाध्मातो निशुम्भोऽथ शूलं जग्राह दानवः ।
आयातं[2] मुष्टिपातेन देवी तच्चाप्यचूर्णयत् ।।१४।।

14. *kopādhmāto niśumbho 'tha śūlaṁ jagrāha dānavaḥ* ।
āyātaṁ[2] *muṣṭipātena devī taccāpyacūrṇayat* ।।

Inflamed with anger, that demon *Niśumbha* picked up a pike. When the Goddess saw it coming, she powdered it with the blow of her fist.

आविध्याथ[3] गदां सोऽपि चिक्षेप चण्डिकां प्रति ।
सापि देव्या त्रिशूलेन भिन्ना भस्मत्वमागता ।।१५।।

15. *āvidhyātha*[3] *gadāṁ so 'pi cikṣepa caṇḍikāṁ prati* ।
sāpi devyā triśūlena bhinnā bhasmatvamāgatā ।।

He, then, hurled a mace at *Caṇḍikā* which was also cut and reduced to ashes by the Goddess with her trident.

ततः परशुहस्तं तमायान्तं दैत्यपुङ्गवम् ।
आहत्य देवी बाणौघैरपातयत भूतले ।।१६।।

16. *tataḥ paraśuhastaṁ tamāyāntaṁ daityapuṅgavam* ।
āhatya devī bāṇaughairapātayata bhūtale ।।

As she saw that chief of demons charging towards her with a battle-axe in his hand, the Goddess wounded him with a torrent of her arrows and laid him on the ground.

तस्मिन्निपतिते भूमौ निशुम्भे भीमविक्रमे ।
भ्रातर्यतीव संक्रुद्धः प्रययौ हन्तुमम्बिकाम् ।।१७।।

17. *tasminnipatite bhūmau niśumbhe bhīmavikrame* ।
bhrātaryatīva saṁkruddhaḥ prayayau hantumambikām ।।

When *Niśumbha*, the fierce-fighter, was seen lying on the ground by his brother *Śumbha*, he, beside himself with anger, charged towards the Mother to kill her.

---

[2]AR: आयान्तं *āyāntaṁ*

[3]AR: अथादाय *athādāya*

स रथस्थस्तथात्युच्चैर्गृहीतपरमायुधैः ।
भुजैरष्टाभिरतुलैर्व्याप्याशेषं बभौ नभः ॥१८॥

18. *sa rathasthastathātyuccairgṛhītaparamāyudhaiḥ* ।
bhujairaṣṭābhiratulairvyāpyāśeṣaṁ babhau nabhaḥ ॥

Sitting in his chariot, holding excellent weapons in his eight matchless hands, he filled the entire firmament with his brilliance.

तमायान्तं समालोक्य देवी शङ्खमवादयत् ।
ज्याशब्दं चापि धनुषश्चकारातीव दुःसहम् ॥१९॥

19. *tamāyāntaṁ samālokya devī śaṅkhamavādayat* ।
jyāśabdaṁ cāpi dhanuṣaścakārātīva duḥsaham ॥

When the Goddess saw him coming, she sounded her conch and also made an extremely unbearable sound with the twang of her bow-string.

पूरयामास ककुभो निजघण्टास्वनेन च ।
समस्तदैत्यसैन्यानां तेजोवधविधायिना ॥२०॥

20. *pūrayāmāsa kakubho nijaghaṇṭāsvanena ca* ।
samastadaityasainyānāṁ tejovadhavidhāyinā ॥

Simultaneously, she filled the quarters with the sound of her bell. This killed the morale of all the demon troops.

ततः सिंहो महानादैस्त्याजितेभमहामदैः ।
पूरयामास गगनं गां तथैवदिशो[4] दश ॥२१॥

21. *tataḥ siṁho mahānādaistyājitebhamahāmadaiḥ* ।
pūrayāmāsa gaganaṁ gāṁ tathaivadiśo[4] *daśa* ॥

Then with his violent roars, hearing which the mighty elephants forsook their arrogance, the Lion rent the sky and filled the earth and all the ten directions.

---

[4]AR: तथोपदिशो *tathopadiśo*

ततः काली समुत्पत्य गगनं क्ष्मामताडयत् ।
कराभ्यां तन्निनादेन प्राक्स्वनास्ते तिरोहिताः ॥२२॥

22. *tataḥ kālī samutpatya gaganaṁ kṣmāmatāḍayat* ।
karābhyāṁ tanninādena prāksvanāste tirohitāḥ ॥

Then *Kālī* leapt into the sky and (coming down) thrashed the earth with her two hands. Such was the noise raised thereby that all the preceding sounds were drowned in it.

अट्टाट्टहासमशिवं शिवदूती चकार ह ।
तैः शब्दैरसुरास्त्रेसुः शुम्भः कोपं परं ययौ ॥२३॥

23. *aṭṭāṭṭahāsamaśivaṁ śivadūtī cakāra ha* ।
taiḥ śabdairasurāstresuḥ śumbhaḥ kopaṁ paraṁ yayau ॥

Śivadūtī laughed aloud ominously. With those sounds the demons were terror-stricken and *Śumbha* got extremely angry.

दुरात्मंस्तिष्ठ तिष्ठेति व्याजहाराम्बिका यदा ।
तदा जयेत्यभिहितं देवैराकाशसंस्थितैः ॥२४॥

24. *durātmaṁstiṣṭha tiṣṭheti vyājahārāmbikā yadā* ।
tadā jayetyabhihitiṁ devairākāśasaṁsthitaiḥ ॥

'Stop, stop you rascal', then said the Mother and the gods in heaven hailed her, saying, 'Victory to you, Victory'.

शुम्भेनागत्य या शक्तिर्मुक्ता ज्वालातिभीषणा ।
आयान्ती वह्निकूटाभा सा निरस्ता महोल्कया ॥२५॥

25. *śumbhenāgatya yā śaktirmuktā jvālātibhīṣaṇā* ।
āyāntī vahnikūṭābhā sā nirastā maholkayā ॥

The flaming missile that *Śumbha* hurled on coming there, shone like a mass of fire. It was, even as it was approaching, rendered infructuous by her with a giant firebrand.

सिंहनादेन शुम्भस्य व्याप्तं लोकत्रयान्तरम् ।
निर्घातनिःस्वनो घोरो जितवानवनीपते ।।२६।।

26. *siṁhanādena śumbhasya vyāptaṁ lokatrayāntaram* ।
nirghātaniḥsvano ghoro jitavānavanīpate ।।

The space between the three worlds resounded with the leonine roar of *Śumbha*. But, o king! louder was its violent echo which defeated all the other sounds.

शुम्भमुक्ताञ्छरान्देवी शुम्भस्तत्प्रहिताञ्छरान् ।
चिच्छेद स्वशरैरुग्रैः शतशोऽथ सहस्रशः ।।२७।।

27. *śumbhamuktāñcharāndevī śumbhastatprahitāñcharān* ।
ciccheda svaśarairugraiḥ śataśo 'tha sahasraśaḥ ।।

Arrows shot by *Śumbha* at the Goddess and those by the Goddess at *Śumbha* were cut into hundreds of thousands of pieces.

ततः सा चण्डिका क्रुद्धा शूलेनाभिजघान तम् ।
स तदाभिहतो भूमौ मूर्च्छितो निपपात ह ।।२८।।

28. *tataḥ sā caṇḍikā kruddhā śūlenābhijaghāna tam* ।
sa tadābhihato bhūmau mūrcchito nipapāta ha ।।

Then thc angry *Caṇḍikā* struck him with her pike. With that he swooned and fell on the earth.

ततो निशुम्भः सम्प्राप्य चेतनामात्तकार्मुकः ।
आजघान शरैर्देवीं कालीं केसरिणं तथा ।।२९।।

29. *tato niśumbhaḥ samprāpya cetanāmāttakārmukaḥ* ।
ājaghāna śarairdevīṁ kālīṁ kesariṇaṁ tathā ।।

Meanwhile, *Niśumbha*, on gaining consciousness, picked up his bow and hurt the Goddess *Kālī* and the Lion.

पुनश्च कृत्वा बाहूनामयुतं दनुजेश्वरः ।
चक्रायुधेन दितिजश्छादयमास चण्डिकाम् ।।३०।।

30. *punaśca kṛtvā bāhūnāmayutaṁ danujeśvaraḥ* ।
cakrāyudhena ditijaśchādayāmāsa caṇḍikām ।।

Then the lord of demons, that son of *Diti,* multiplied his arms into ten thousand and surrounded *Caṇḍikā* from all sides with the discs.

ततो भगवती क्रुद्धा दुर्गा दुर्गार्तिनाशिनी ।
चिच्छेद तानि चक्राणि स्वशरैः सायकांश्च तान् ॥३१॥

31. *tato bhagavatī kruddhā durgā durgārtināśinī* ।
ciccheda tāni cakrāṇi svaśaraiḥ sāyakāṁśca tān ॥

Then the venerable *Durgā,* Annihilator of Severe Miseries, cut in anger those discs and arrows with her arrows.

ततो निशुम्भो वेगेन गदामादाय चण्डिकाम् ।
अभ्यधावत वै हन्तुं दैत्यसेनासमावृतः ॥३२॥

32. *tato niśumbho vegena gadāmādāya caṇḍikām* ।
abhyadhāvata vai hantuṁ daityasenāsamāvṛtaḥ ॥

Niśumbha, surrounded by his army, then charged towards *Caṇḍikā* to kill her with his mace.

तस्यापतत एवाशु गदां चिच्छेद चण्डिका ।
खड्गेन शितधारेण स च शूलं समाददे ॥३३॥

33. *tasyāpatata evāśu gadāṁ ciccheda caṇḍikā* ।
khaḍgena śitadhāreṇa sa ca śūlaṁ samādade ॥

शूलहस्तं समायान्तं निशुम्भममरार्दनम् ।
हृदि विव्याध शूलेन वेगाविद्धेन चण्डिका ॥३४॥

34. *śūlahastaṁ samāyāntaṁ niśumbhamamarārdanam* ।
hṛdi vivyādha śūlena vegāviddhena caṇḍikā ॥

As soon as he came like this, *Caṇḍikā* cut his mace with her sharp-edged sword. Then he picked up a pike in his hand. Seeing *Niśumbha,* the tormentor of the gods, coming with a pike in hand, *Caṇḍikā* pierced his heart with a swiftly-hurled pike.

भिन्नस्य तस्य शूलेन हृदयान्निसृतोऽपरः ।
महाबलो महावीर्यस्तिष्ठेति पुरुषो वदन् ।।३५।।

35. *bhinnasya tasya śūlena hṛdayānnisṛto 'paraḥ* ।
mahābalo mahāvīryastiṣṭheti puruṣo vadan ।।

When his heart was torn with that pike, out of it came another extremely strong man saying, 'stop'.

तस्य निष्क्रामतो देवी प्रहस्य स्वनवत्ततः ।
शिरश्चिच्छेद खड्गेन ततोऽसावपतद्भुवि ।।३६।।

36. *tasya niṣkrāmato devī prahasya svanavattataḥ* ।
śiraścicheda khaḍgena tato 'sāvapatadbhuvi ।।

Even as he was coming out, the Goddess laughed aloud at his words and severed his head with her sword. Then he fell on the ground.

ततः सिंहश्चखादोग्रं[5]दंष्ट्राक्षुण्णशिरोधरान् ।
असुरांस्तांस्तथाकाली शिवदूती तथापरान् ।।३७।।

37. *tataḥ siṁhaścakhādograṁ*[5]*daṁṣṭrākṣuṇṇaśirodharān* ।
asurāṁstāṁstathākālī śivadūtītathāparān ।।

Now the Lion ate those demons after crushing their necks with his jaw-teeth even as *Kāli* and *Śivadūtī* consumed the others.

कौमारीशक्तिनिर्भिन्नाः केचिन्नेशुर्महासुराः ।
ब्रह्माणी मन्त्रपूतेन तोयेनान्ये निराकृताः ।।३८।।

38. *kaumārīśaktinirbhinnāḥ kecinneśurmahāsurāḥ* ।
brahmāṇī mantrapūtena toyenānye nirākṛtāḥ ।।

Being pierced with *Kaumārī's* missile, many of those mighty demons perished while *Brahmāṇī* slayed many others by sprinkling on them the water sanctified with the *mantras*.

---

[5]AR: दोग्रदंष्ट्रा *dogradaṁṣṭrā*.

माहेश्वरी त्रिशूलेन भिन्नाः पेतुस्तथापरे ।
वाराही तुण्डघातेन केचिच्चूर्णीकृता भुवि ॥३६॥

39. *māheśvarī triśūlena bhinnāḥ petustathāpare* ।
vārāhī tuṇḍaghātena keciccūrṇīkṛtā bhuvi ॥

Several others, torn apart by *Māheśvarī* with her trident, licked the dust while *Vārāhi* powdered many of them with the blows of her snout.

खण्डं खण्डं[6] च चक्रेण वैष्णव्या दानवाः कृताः ।
वज्रेण चैन्द्रीहस्ताग्रविमुक्तेन तथापरे ॥४०॥

40. *khaṇḍaṁ khaṇḍaṁ*[6] *ca cakreṇa vaiṣṇavyā dānavāḥ kṛtāḥ* ।
vajreṇa caindrīhastāgravimuktena tathāpare ॥

Vaiṣṇavī, with her discus, cut the demons into several pieces and many others lost their lives with the thunderbolt shot from *Aindrī's* hand.

केचिद्विनेशुरसुराः केचिन्नष्टा महाहवात् ।
भक्षिताश्चापरे कालीशिवदूतीमृगाधिपैः ॥ॐ॥४१॥

41. *kecidvineśurasurāḥ kecinnaṣṭā mahāhavāt* ।
bhakṣitāścāpare kālīśivadūtīmṛgādhipaiḥ ॥ oṁ ॥

Some demons were annihilated, some fled from the great war and the others were devoured by *Kālī, Śivadūtī* and the king of beasts (Lion). oṁ

इति श्रीमार्कण्डेयपुराणे सावर्णिके मन्वन्तरे देवीमाहात्म्ये निशुम्भवधो नाम नवमोऽध्यायः ॥६॥

iti śrīmārkaṇḍeyapurāṇe sāvarṇike manvantare—

---

[6]AR: खण्डखण्डं *khaṇḍakhaṇḍaṁ*

devīmāhātmye niśumbhavadho nāma navamo 'dhyāyaḥ ॥9॥

Thus ends the ninth chapter called 'Slaying of *Niśumbha*' during the era of *Sāvarṇi Manu*, in the 'Glory of the Goddess', (narrated) in the *Mārkaṇḍeya Purāṇa*.

उवाच २, श्लोकाः ३९, एवम् ४१, एवमादितः ५४३

uvāca 2, *ślokāḥ* 39, *evam* 41, *evamāditaḥ* 543

uvāca 2, ślokas 39, total 41; from the beginning up to here 543.

दशमोऽध्यायः

daśamo 'dhyāyaḥ

Chapter Ten

Slaying of *Śumbha*

ध्यानम्

dhyānam

Meditation

ॐ उत्तप्तहेमरुचिरां रविचन्द्रवह्नि-
नेत्रां धनुश्शरयुताङ्कुशपाशशूलम् ।
रम्यैर्भुजैश्च दधतीं शिवशक्तिरूपां
कामेश्वरीं हृदि भजामि धृतेन्दुलेखाम् ॥

oṁ. uttaptahemarucirāṁ ravicandravahni-
netrāṁ dhanuśśarayutāṅkuśapāśaśūlam ।
ramyairbhujaiśca dadhatīṁ śivaśaktirūpāṁ
kāmeśvarīṁ hṛdi bhajāmi dhṛtendulekhām ॥

I MEDITATE IN MY HEART UPON *KĀMEŚVARĪ*, THE CONTROLLER OF DESIRE AND *ŚIVAŚAKTI-RŪPĀ*, THE ENERGY INCARNATE OF LORD *ŚIVA*. HER COMPLEXION IS LIKE THE RED-HOT GOLD. SUN, MOON AND FIRE ARE HER THREE EYES. SHE HAS A BOW, AN ARROW, A HOOK, A SNARE AND A PIKE IN HER BEAUTIFUL HANDS AND A DIGIT OF MOON ADORNS HER FOREHEAD.

ॐ ऋषिरुवाच ॥१॥

1. *oṁ. ṛṣiruvāca*

निशुम्भं निहतं दृष्ट्वा भ्रातरं प्राणसम्मितम् ।
हन्यमानं बलं चैव शुम्भः क्रुद्धोऽब्रवीद्वचः ॥२॥

2. *niśumbhaṁ nihataṁ dṛṣtvā bhrātaraṁ prāṇasammitam ।*
hanyamānaṁ balaṁ caiva śumbhaḥ kruddho 'bravīdvacaḥ ॥

Oṁ. The seer said

When *Śumbha* saw his brother *Niśumbha*, who was dear to him as his own life, dead and also found that his army was being killed, he angrily said:

बलावलेपा[1]दुष्टे त्वं मा दुर्गे गर्वमावह ।
अन्यासां बलमाश्रित्य युद्ध्यसे यातिमानिनी ॥३॥

3. *balāvalepā[1] dduṣṭe tvaṁ mā durge garvamāvaha ।*
anyāsāṁ balamāśritya yudhyase yātimāninī ॥

Do not, O Wicked *Durgā*! be proud of your valour. You are arrogating power to yourself even though you are fighting with the assistance of the other female forces.

देव्युवाच॥४॥

4. *devyuvāca*

एकैवाहं जगत्यत्र द्वितीया का ममापरा ।
पश्यैता दुष्ट मय्येव विशन्त्यो मद्विभूतयः[2] ॥५॥

5. *ekaivāhaṁ jagatyatra dvitīyā kā mamāparā ।*
paśyaitā duṣṭa mayyeva viśantyo madvibhūtayaḥ[2] ॥

The Goddess said

You wicked one! I am the one and only in this world. Who else is there other than me? See these opulent manifestations of mine entering me.

---

[1]AR: पदु *padu*

[2]Additional reading hereafter in some copies : ऋषिरुवाच ṛṣiruvāca.

ततः समस्तास्ता देव्यो ब्रह्माणीप्रमुखा लयम् ।
तस्या देव्यास्तनौ जग्मुरेकैवासीत्तदाम्बिका ॥६॥

6. *tataḥ samastāstā devyo brahmāṇīpramukhā layam* ।
tasyā devyāstanau jagmurekaivāsīttadāmbikā ॥

Then all the goddesses, led by *Brahmāṇī*, entered the body of that Goddess whereupon the Mother alone remained there.

देव्युवाच ॥७॥

7. *devyuvāca* ॥

अहं विभूत्या बहुभिरिह रूपैर्यदास्थिता ।
तत्संहृतं मयैकैव तिष्ठाम्याजौ स्थिरो भव ॥8॥

8. *ahaṁ vibhūtyā bahubhiriha rūpairyadāsthitā* ।
tatsaṁhṛtaṁ mayaikaiva tiṣṭhāmyājau sthiro bhava ॥

The Goddess said

I had been standing here with many an opulent manifestation of mine. I, by myself, have withdrawn them and stand here alone. You, too, be steady now.

ऋषिरुवाच ॥९॥

9. *ṛṣiruvāca* ॥

ततः प्रववृते युद्धं देव्याः शुम्भस्य चोभयोः ।
पश्यतां सर्वदेवानामसुराणां च दारुणम् ॥10॥

10. *tataḥ pravavṛte yuddhaṁ devyāḥ śumbhasya cobhayoḥ* ।
paśyatāṁ sarvadevānāmasurāṇāṁ ca dāruṇam ॥

The Seer said

Then, even as the gods and the demons witnessed, a ruthless duel commenced between the Goddess and *Śumbha*.

शरवर्षैः शितैः शस्त्रैस्तथास्त्रैश्चैव दारुणैः ।
तयोर्युद्धमभूद्भूयः सर्वलोकभयङ्करम् ॥११॥

11. *śaravarṣaiḥ śitaiḥ śastraistathāstraiścaiva dāruṇaiḥ* ।
tayoryuddhamabhūdbhūyaḥ sarvalokabhayaṅkaram ॥

The cruel combat of arms and missiles that ensued between those two caused terror in all the worlds.

दिव्यान्यस्त्राणि शतशो मुमुचे यान्यथाम्बिका ।
बभञ्ज तानि दैत्येन्द्रस्तत्प्रतीघातकर्तृभिः ॥१२॥

12. *divyānyastrāṇi śataśo mumuce yānyathāmbikā* ।
babhañja tāni daityendrastatpratīghātakartṛbhiḥ ॥

Hundreds of celestial weapons hurled by the Mother were severed by the lord of demons who repulsed them with his weapons.

मुक्तानि तेन चास्त्राणि दिव्यानि परमेश्वरी ।
बभञ्ज लीलयैवोग्रहु[3]ङ्कारोच्चारणादिभिः ॥१३॥

13. *muktāni tena cāstrāṇi divyāni parameśvarī* ।
babhañja līlayaivograhu[3]*ṅkāroccāraṇādibhiḥ* ॥

Playfully the Mother, the Sovereign Supreme, cut the celestial weapons discharged by him, just by uttering *huṅ*, etc.

ततः शरशतैर्देवीमाच्छादयत सोऽसुरः ।
सापि[4]तत्कुपिता देवी धनुश्चिच्छेद चेषुभिः ॥१४॥

14. *tataḥ śaraśatairdevīmācchādayata so'suraḥ*।
sāpi[4] *tatkupitā devī dhanuściccheda ceṣubhiḥ*॥

Then that demon covered the Goddess with hundreds of arrows. The enraged Goddess cut his bow with her arrows.

---

[3]AR: हू hū

[4]AR: सा च sā ca

छिन्ने धनुषि दैत्येन्द्रस्तथा शक्तिमथाददे ।
चिच्छेद देवी चक्रेण तामप्यस्य करे स्थिताम् ।।१५।।

15. *chinne dhanuṣi daityendrastathā śaktimathādade* ।
ciccheda devī cakreṇa tāmapyasya kare sthitām ।।

His bow having been broken, the demon-king picked up a missile. While it was still in his hand, the Goddess smashed it too with her discus.

ततः खड्गमुपादाय शतचन्द्रं च भानुमत् ।
अभ्यधावत्तदा देवीं[5] दैत्यानामधिपेश्वरः ।।१६।।

16. *tataḥ khaḍgamupādāya śatacandraṁ ca bhānumat* ।
abhyadhāvattadā devīṁ[5] *daityānāmadhipeśvaraḥ* ।।

Then the sovereign of demons charged towards the Goddess with a sword and a shield which dazzled with one hundred moons (engraved on it).

तस्यापतत एवाशु खड्गं चिच्छेद चण्डिका ।
धनुर्मुक्तैः शितैर्बाणैश्चर्म चार्ककरामलम्[6] ।।१७।।

17. *tasyāpatata evāśu khaḍgaṁ ciccheda caṇḍikā* ।
dhanurmuktaiḥ śitairbāṇaiścarma cārkakarāmalam[6] ।।

Immediately as he came forword, *Caṇḍikā* cut his sword and shield which were as bright as the sun, with the sharp arrows delivered from her bow.

हताश्वः स तदा दैत्यश्छिन्नधन्वा विसारथिः ।
जग्राह मुद्गरं घोरमम्बिकानिधनोद्यतः ।।१८।।

18. *hatāśvaḥ sa tadā daityaśchinnadhanvā visārathiḥ* ।
jagrāha mudgaraṁ ghoramambikānidhanodyataḥ ।।

---

[5]AR: अभ्यधावत तां हन्तुं abhyadhāvata tāṁ hantuṁ

[6]Additional reading in some editions : अश्वांश्च पातयामास रथं सारथिना सह। *aśvāṁśca pātayāmāsa rathaṁ sārathinā saha*'. She felled his horses and the chariot along with the charioteer.

His horses slain, bow broken, charioteer no more, that demon picked up an awful mallet to kill the Mother.

चिच्छेदापततस्तस्य मुद्गरं निशितैः शरैः ।
तथापि सोऽभ्यधावत्तां मुष्टिमुद्यम्य वेगवान् ।।१९।।

19. *cicchedāpatatastasya mudgaraṁ niśitaiḥ śaraiḥ* ।
tathāpi so 'bhyadhāvattāṁ muṣṭimudyamya vegavān ।।

Even as he was advancing, the Goddess broke his mallet with sharp arrows. He then rushed towards her raising his fist.

स मुष्टिं पातयामास हृदये दैत्यपुङ्गवः ।
देव्यास्तं चापि सा देवी तलेनोरस्यताडयत् ।।२०।।

20. *sa muṣṭiṁ pātayāmāsa hṛdaye daityapuṅgavaḥ* ।
devyāstaṁ cāpi sā devi talenorasyatāḍayat ।।

That mighty demon hit the Goddess in her chest with his fist. Then the Goddess hit him back on his chest with the palm of her hand.

तलप्रहाराभिहतो निपपात महीतले ।
स दैत्यराजः सहसा पुनरेव तथोत्थितः ।।२१।।

21. *talaprahārābhihato nipapāta mahītale* ।
sa daityarājaḥ sahasā punareva tathotthitaḥ ।।

Struck with the blow of her palm, that demon king fell on the ground but immediately got up again.

उत्पत्य च प्रगृह्योच्चैर्देवीं गगनमास्थितः ।
तत्रापि सा निराधारा युयुधे तेन चण्डिका ।।२२।।

22. *utpatya ca pragṛhyoccairdevīm gaganamāsthitaḥ* ।
tatrāpi sā nirādhārā yuyudhe tena caṇḍikā ।।

Then he leapt and, seizing the Goddess, whizzed into the sky. There also, *Caṇḍikā* fought with him without any support.

नियुद्धं खे तदा दैत्यश्चण्डिका च परस्परम् ।
चक्रतुः प्रथमं सिद्धमुनिविस्मयकारकम् ॥२३॥

23. *niyuddhaṁ khe tadā daityaścaṇḍikā ca parasparam* ।
cakratuḥ prathamaṁ siddhamunivismayakārakam ॥

In the sky, the demon and *Caṇḍikā* then engaged in an internecine battle. This unprecedented battle stunned the *siddhas* (liberated beings) and the ascetics.

ततो नियुद्धं सुचिरं कृत्वा तेनाम्बिका सह ।
उत्पात्य भ्रामयामास चिक्षेप धरणीतले ॥२४॥

24. *tato niyuddhaṁ suciraṁ kṛtvā tenāmbikā saha* ।
utpātya bhrāmayāmāsa cikṣepa dharaṇītale ॥

Then, following a prolonged encounter with him, the Mother lifted and spun him around and threw him on the ground.

स क्षिप्तो धरणीं प्राप्य मुष्टिमुद्यम्य वेगितः ।
अभ्यधावत दुष्टात्मा चण्डिकानिधनेच्छया ॥२५॥

25. *sa kṣipto dharaṇīṁ prāpya muṣṭimudyamya vegitaḥ* ।
abhyadhāvata duṣṭātmā caṇḍikānidhanecchayā ॥

Fallen on earth, that evil–minded demon instantly got up and, raising his fist, charged at *Caṇḍikā* with the intention of killing her.

तमायान्तं ततो देवी सर्वदैत्यजनेश्वरम् ।
जगत्यां पातयामास भित्त्वा शूलेन वक्षसि ॥२६॥

26. *tamāyāntaṁ tato devī sarvadaityajaneśvaram* ।
jagatyāṁ pātayāmāsa bhittvā śūlena vakṣasi ॥

When the Goddess saw that lord of all the demons coming towards her, she pierced his chest with her pike and again threw him on the ground.

स गतासुः पपातोर्व्यां देवीशूलाग्रविक्षतः ।
चालयन् सकलां पृथ्वीं साब्धिद्वीपाम् सपर्वताम् ।।२७।।

27. *sa gatāsuḥ papātorvyāṁ devīśulāgravikṣataḥ* ।
cālayan sakalāṁ pṛthvīṁ sābdhidvīpāṁ saparvatām ।।

Now battered by the pike of the Goddess, he lost his life and fell on the ground shaking the entire earth, along with the oceans, continents and mountains.

ततः प्रसन्नमखिलं हते तस्मिन् दुरात्मनि ।
जगत्स्वास्थ्यमतीवाप निर्मलं चाभवन्नभः ।।२८।।

28. *tataḥ prasannamakhilaṁ hate tasmin durātmani* ।
jagatsvāsthyamatīvāpa nirmalaṁ cābhavannabhaḥ ।।

That rascal having been slayed, the whole world was immensely pleased and the sky became clear.

उत्पातमेघाः सोल्का ये प्रागासंस्ते शमं ययुः ।
सरितो मार्गवाहिन्यस्तथासंस्तत्र पातिते ।।२९।।

29. *utpātameghāḥ solkā ye prāgāsaṁste śamaṁ yayuḥ* ।
sarito mārgavāhinyastathāsaṁstatra pātite ।।

Ominous clouds and meteors which were witnessed as falling earlier, now subsided. With the demon fallen, rivers began flowing within their course.

ततो देवगणाः सर्वे हर्षनिर्भरमानसाः ।
बभूवुर्निहते तस्मिन् गन्धर्वा ललितं जगुः ।।३०।।

30. *tato devagaṇāḥ sarve harṣanirbharamānasāḥ* ।
babhūvurnihate tasmin gandharvāḥ lalitaṁ jaguḥ ।।

Then all the gods were filled with joy at his death and the *gandharvas* sang sweet songs.

अवादयंस्तथैवान्ये ननृतुश्चाप्सरोगणाः ।
ववुः पुण्यास्तथा वाताः सुप्रभोऽभूद्दिवाकरः ।।३१।।

31. *avādayaṁstathaivānye nanṛtuścāpsarogaṇāḥ* ।
vavuḥ puṇyāstathā vātāḥ suprabho 'bhūddivākaraḥ ।।

जज्वलुश्चाग्नयः शान्ताः शान्ता दिग्जनितस्वनाः ।।ॐ।।३२।।

32. *jajvaluścāgnayaḥ śāntāḥ śāntā digjanitasvanāḥ* ।।*oṁ*।।

Others played their musical instruments even as the celestial damsels danced. Gentle breeze started blowing, the sun regained its effulgence, sacred (sacrificial) fires burned in peace and the noise arising in the quarters subsided. Oṁ

इति श्रीमार्कण्डेयपुराणे सावर्णिके मन्वन्तरे देवीमाहात्म्ये शुम्भवधो नाम दशमोऽध्यायः ।।१०।।

iti śrīmārkaṇḍeyapurāṇe sāvarṇike manvantare devīmāhātmye śumbhavadho nāma daśamo 'dhyāyaḥ।।10।।

Thus ends the tenth chapter called 'Slaying of *Śumbha*' in the 'Glory of the Goddess', during the era of *Sāvarṇi Manu,* (narrated) in the *Mārkaṇḍeya Purāṇa.*

उवाच ४, अर्धश्लोकः १, श्लोकाः २७, एवम् ३२, एवमादितः ५७५

uvāca 4, ardhaślokaḥ 1, ślokāḥ 27, evaṁ 32, evamāditaḥ 575

uvāca 4, half śloka 1, ślokas 27, total 32,
total from beginning 575

एकादशोऽध्यायः

ekādaśo 'dhyāyaḥ

Chapter Eleven

The gods eulogise the Goddess and she grants them a boon

ध्यानम्

dhyānam

Meditation

ॐ बालरविद्युतिमिन्दुकिरीटां तुङ्गकुचां नयनत्रययुक्ताम् ।
स्मेरमुखीं वरदाङ्कुशपाशाभीतिकरां प्रभजे भुवनेशीम् ॥

oṁ. bālaraviduytimindukirīṭāṁ tuṅgakucāṁ nayanatrayayuktām ।।
smeramukhīṁ varadāṅkuśāpāśābhītikarāṁ prabhaje bhuvaneśīm ।।

OṀ. I EARNESTLY MEDITATE UPON *BHUVANEŚVARĪ*, THE EMPRESS OF THE WORLD, WHO IS EFFULGENT LIKE THE RISING SUN. SHE WEARS THE CROWN OF MOON, HAS ELEVATED BREASTS AND THREE EYES. HER FACE BLOOMS WITH A SMILE. HER HANDS SHOW THE SIGNS OF GRANTING BOONS AND FEARLESSNESS AND SHE HOLDS A HOOK AND A SNARE.

ॐ ऋषिरुवाच ॥१॥

1. *oṁ. ṛṣiruvāca*

देव्या हते तत्र महासुरेन्द्रे
सेन्द्राः सुरा वह्निपुरागमास्ताम् ।
कात्यायनीं तुष्टुवुरिष्टलाभाद्[1]
विकाशिवक्त्राब्ज[2] विकाशिताशाः ॥२॥

2. *devyā hate tatra mahāsurendre*
sendrāḥ surā vahnipurāgamāstām ।
kātyāyanīṁ tuṣṭuvuriṣṭalābhād[1]
vikāśivaktrābja[2] *vikāśitāśāḥ* ॥

Oṁ. The Seer said

When the mighty demon king *Śumbha* was slayed by the Goddess, *Indra* and the other gods led by Fire, commenced eulogising the Goddess *Kātyāyanī.* Their desired objective achieved, their faces were cheerful and illumined the quarters.

देवि प्रपन्नार्तिहरे प्रसीद
प्रसीद मातर्जगतोऽखिलस्य ।
प्रसीद विश्वेश्वरि पाहि विश्वं
त्वमीश्वरी देवि चराचरस्य ॥३॥

3. *devi prapannārtihare prasīda*
prasīda mātarjagato 'khilasya ।
prasīda viśveśvari pāhi viśvaṁ
tvamīśvarī devi carācarasya ॥

O Goddess! you are the Alleviator of the Distress of those who seek refuge in you. Be pleased with us. Be pleased, O Mother of the entire World. Be pleased, O

[1]AR: लम्भाद् lambhād

[2]AR: वक्त्रास्तु vaktrāstu

Empress of the Universe and protect the universe. Of animates and inanimates, you are the Supreme Ruler.

आधारभूता जगतस्त्वमेका महीस्वरूपेण यतः स्थितासि ।
अपां स्वरूपस्थितया त्वयैतदाप्यायते कृत्स्नमलङ्घ्यवीर्ये ।।४।।

4. *ādhārabhūtā jagatastvamekā*
mahīsvarūpeṇa yataḥ sthitāsi ।
apāṁ svarūpasthitayā tvayaitad-
āpyāyate kṛtsnamalaṅghyavīrye ।।

O Goddess of Inviolable Valour! Established in the form of Earth, you are the only Substratum of the World. Established in the form of Water, you satiate this world.

त्वं वैष्णवी शक्तिरनन्तवीर्या विश्वस्य बीजम् परमासि माया ।
सम्मोहितं देवि समस्तमेतत् त्वं वै प्रसन्ना भुवि मुक्तिहेतुः ।।५।।

5. *tvaṁ vaiṣṇavī śaktiranantavīryā*
viśvasya bījam paramāsi māyā ।
sammohitaṁ devi samastametat
tvaṁ vai prasannā bhuvi muktihetuḥ ।।

You, O *Vaiṣṇavī* of Infnite Power! are the Seed of the Universe and the Supreme Illusive Power. O Goddess! this world is deluded by you. If you are pleased, you are the source of final beatitude on this earth.

विद्याः समस्तास्तव देवि भेदाः स्त्रियः समस्ताः सकला जगत्सु ।
त्वयैकया पूरितमम्बयैतत् का ते स्तुतिः स्तव्यपरा परोक्तिः ।।६।।

6. *vidyāḥ samastāstava devi bhedāḥ*
striyaḥ samastāḥ sakalā jagatsu ।
tvayaikayā pūritamambayaitat
kā te stutiḥ stavyaparā paroktiḥ ।।

All types of knowledge, O Goddess! are your aspects, all the women in this world, your images. O Mother! by you alone is this world pervaded. What can be said in your praise? You are beyond eulogy and Ultimate Speech.

सर्वभूता यदा देवी स्वर्गमुक्ति प्रदायिनी[3]।
त्वं स्तुता स्तुतये का वा भवन्तु परमोक्तय: ।।७।।

7. *sarvabhūtā yadā devī svargamukti pradāyinī*[3] ।
tvaṁ stutā stutaye kā vā bhavantu paramoktayaḥ ॥

This itself is your eulogy that you embody all beings and are the Bestower of Heaven and Final Beatitude. What more in your praise may be said than this?

सर्वस्य बुद्धिरूपेण जनस्य हृदिसंस्थिते ।
स्वर्गापवर्गदे देवि नारायणि नमोऽस्तु ते ।।८।।

8. *sarvasya buddhirūpeṇa janasya hṛdi saṁsthite* ।
svargāpavargade devi nārāyaṇi namo 'stu te ।

You abide in everyone's mind as Intellect. You, O Goddess *Nārāyaṇī*, are the Energy of *Nārāyaṇa*. You are the Granter of Heaven and Liberation. Obeisance to you.

कलाकाष्ठादिरूपेण परिणामप्रदायिनि ।
विश्वस्योपरतौ शक्ते नारायणि नमोऽस्तु ते ।।६।।

9. *kalā kāṣṭhādirūpeṇa pariṇāmapradāyini* ।
viśvasyoparatau śakte nārāyaṇi namo 'stu te ॥

Obeisance to you O *Nārāyaṇī*! you, as ***kalā, kāṣṭhā,*** etc., represent various instruments of time (and, as such) of existence and change from one stage to another, eventually leading to dissolution.

सर्वमङ्गलमङ्गल्ये[4] शिवे सर्वार्थसाधिके ।
शरण्ये त्र्यम्बके गौरि नारायणि नमोऽस्तु ते ।।१०।।

10. *sarvamaṅgalamaṅgalye*[4] *śive sarvārthasādhike* ।
śaraṇye tryambake gauri nārāyaṇi namo 'stu te ॥

---

[3]AR: भुक्तिमुक्तिप्रदायिनी *bhuktimuktipradāyinī*

[4]AR: माङ्गल्ये *māṅgalye*

O Goddess *Nārāyaṇī*! Obeisance to you. You are the Home of Auspiciousness and Felicity. You Facilitate Accomplishment of all Objectives and Intents. O Three-eyed-Fair-complexioned Goddess! you are the Refuge of All.

सृष्टिस्थितिविनाशानां शक्तिभूते सनातनि ।
गुणाश्रये गुणमये नारायणि नमोऽस्तु ते ।।११।।

11. *sṛṣṭisthitivināśānāṁ śaktibhūte sanātani* ।
guṇāśraye guṇamaye nārāyaṇi namo 'stu te ॥

Obeisance to you O *Nārāyaṇī* ! you are the Veritable Power of Creation, Sustenance and Dissolution (but) you yourself are Eternity. You are the Substratum of the Three Modes and also Embody Them.

शरणागतदीनार्तपरित्राणपरायणे ।
सर्वस्यार्तिहरे देवि नारायणि नमोऽस्तु ते ।।१२।।

12. *śaraṇāgatadīnārtaparitrāṇaparāyaṇe* ।
sarvasyārtihare devi nārāyaṇi namo 'stu te ॥

Obeisance to you Goddess *Nārāyaṇī*! you are Ever Engaged in Deliverance of the Dejected and the Distressed Seeking Refuge in you. You are the Obliterator of Miseries of All.

हंसयुक्तविमानस्थे ब्रह्माणीरूपधारिणि ।
कौशाम्भःक्षरिके देवि नारायणि नमोऽस्तु ते ।।१३।।

13. *haṁsayuktavimānasthe brahmāṇīrūpadhāriṇi* ।
kauśāmbhaḥ kṣarike devi nārāyaṇi namo 'stu te ॥

Obeisance to you Goddess *Nārāyaṇi* ! In the form of *Brahmāṇī*, the Consort of *Brahmā*, you are seated in the celestial car yoked by a swan and sprinkle waters sanctified with the *kuśa* grass*.

* A kind of grass (Doa cynosuroides) considered holy: पवित्रार्थे इमे कुशाः; *pavitrārthe ime kuśāḥ* (these *kuśas* are for sanctifying)

त्रिशूलचन्द्राहिधरे महावृषभवाहिनि ।
माहेश्वरीस्वरूपेण नारायणि नमोऽस्तु ते ॥१४॥

14. *triśūlacandrāhidhare mahāvṛṣabhavāhini* ।
māheśvarīsvarūpeṇa nārāyaṇi namo 'stu te ॥

Obeisance to you *Nārāyaṇī*, in the form of *Māheśvarī*, the Energy of *Maheśvara Śiva*, Supporting a Trident, a Moon and a Serpent and Mounted on the Mighty Bull.

मयूरकुक्कुटवृते महाशक्तिधरेऽनघे ।
कौमारीरूपसंस्थाने नारायणि नमोऽस्तु ते ॥१५॥

15. *mayūrakukkuṭavṛte mahāśaktidhare 'naghe* ।
kaumārīrūpasaṁsthāne nārāyaṇi namo 'stu te ॥

Obeisance to you O Sinless *Nārāyaṇī*, in the form of *Kaumārī*, the Energy of *Kārtikeya*, surrounded by Peacocks and Cocks and Wielding the Great Missile.

शङ्खचक्रगदाशार्ङ्गगृहीतपरमायुधे ।
प्रसीद वैष्णवीरूपे नारायणि नमोऽस्तु ते ॥१६॥

16. *śaṅkhacakragadāśārṅgagṛhītaparamāyudhe* ।
prasīda vaiṣṇavīrūpe nārāyaṇi namo 'stu te ॥

Obeisance to you O *Nārāyaṇī* in the form of *Vaiṣṇavī*, the Consort of *Viṣṇu*, Wielding Excellent Weapons: a Conch, a Discus, a Mace and the *Śārṅga* Bow.

गृहीतोग्रमहाचक्रे दंष्ट्रोद्धृतवसुंधरे ।
वराहरूपिणि शिवे नारायणि नमोऽस्तु ते ॥१७॥

17. *gṛhītogramahācakre daṁṣṭroddhatavasundhare* ।
varāharūpiṇi śive nārāyaṇi namo 'stu te ॥

Obeisance to you Felicific *Nārāyaṇī* in the form of *Vārāhī*, the Female Boar, wielding the Powerful Discus and raising the Earth on your Tusks.

नृसिंहरूपेणोग्रेण हन्तुं दैत्यान् कृतोद्यमे ।
त्रैलोक्यत्राणसहिते नारायणि नमोऽस्तु ते ॥१८॥

18. *nṛsiṁharūpeṇogreṇa hantuṁ daityān kṛtodyame* ।
trailokyatrāṇasahite nārāyaṇi namo 'stu te ॥

Obeisance to you *Nārāyaṇī*, taking the Belligerent Form of *Nṛsiṁha*, the Man-Lion, in order to slay the demons and protect the three worlds.

किरीटिनि महावज्रे सहस्रनयनोज्ज्वले ।
वृत्रप्राणहरे चैन्द्रि नारायणि नमोऽस्तु ते ॥१९॥

19. *kirīṭini mahāvajre sahasranayanojjvale* ।
vṛtraprāṇahare caindri nārāyaṇi namo 'stu te ।

Obeisance to you *Nārāyaṇī*, who in the form of *Aindrī*, the Energy of *Indra*, Wearing the Crown, Wielding the Mighty Thunderbolt and having a Thousand Radiant Eyes, scraped life out of the demon *Vṛtra*.*

शिवदूती स्वरूपेण हतदैत्यमहाबले ।
घोररूपे महारावे नारायणि नमोऽस्तु ते ॥२०॥

20. *śivadūtī svarūpeṇa hatadaityamahābale* ।
ghorarūpe mahārāve nārāyaṇi namo 'stu te ।

Obeisance to you *Nārāyaṇī*, who in the Frightful Form as *Śivadūtī* of Formidable Valour, slayed the mighty force of demons with a frightening roar.

दंष्ट्राकरालवदने शिरोमालाविभूषणे ।
चामुण्डे मुण्डमथने नारायणि नमोऽस्तु ते ॥२१॥

21. *daṁṣṭrākarālavadane śiromālāvibhūṣaṇe* ।
cāmuṇḍe muṇḍamathane nārāyaṇi namo 'stu te ॥

Obeisance to you *Nārāyaṇī*, who as *Cāmuṇḍā*, slayed the demon *Muṇḍa*; Wearing a Garland of Skulls, your Face with its fangs is terrfying.

* A personification of darkness. In *purāṇas*, a demon killed by *Indra*

लक्ष्मिलज्जे महाविद्ये श्रद्धे पुष्टि[5]स्वधे ध्रुवे ।
महारात्रि[6] महाऽविद्ये[7] नारायणि नमोऽस्तु ते ।।२२।।

22. *lakṣmilajje mahāvidye śraddhe puṣṭi*[5] *svadhe dhruve* ।
mahārātri[6] *mahā 'vidye*[7] *nārāyaṇi namo 'stu te* ।

Obeisance O *Nārāyaṇī* ! you are *Lakṣmī*, the Good Fortune; *Lajjā*, Modesty; *Mahāvidyā*, the Transcendental Knowledge; *Śraddhā*, Reverential Faith; *Puṣti*, Nurturance; *Svadhā*, Will; *Dhruvā*, Constancy; *Mahārātri*, the Night of Dissolution; *Mahā Avidyā*, Great Nescience.

मेधे सरस्वति वरे भूति बाभ्रवि तामसि ।
नियते त्वं प्रसीदेशे नारायणि नमोऽस्तु ते[8] ।।२३।।

23. *medhe sarasvati vare bhūti bābhravi tāmasi* ।
niyate tvaṁ prasīdeśe nārāyaṇi namo 'stu te[8] ।।

Obeisance to you *Nārāyaṇī*! you are *Medhā*, Intelligence; *Sarasvatī*, Choicest Speech; *Bhūti*, Glory, *Bābhravī*, of Ruddy Hue; *Tāmasī*, of Dark Complexion; *Niyatā*, Self Possessed; *Īśā*, Supreme Ruler. Be pleased with us.

सर्वस्वरूपे सर्वेशे सर्वशक्तिसमन्विते ।
भयेभ्यस्त्राहि नो देवि दुर्गे देवि नमोऽस्तु ते ।।२४।।

24. *sarvasvarūpe sarveśe sarvaśaktisamanvite* ।
bhayebhyastrāhi no devi durge devi namo 'stu te ।।

---

[5]AR: पुष्टे *puṣṭe*

[6]AR: रात्रे *rātre*

[7]AR: महामाये *mahāmāye*

[8]Additional śloka after this in *Śāntanavī text*: सर्वतः पाणिपादान्ते सर्वतोऽक्षिशिरोमुखे। सर्वतः श्रवणघ्राणे नारायणि नमोऽस्तु ते। *sarvataḥ pāṇipādānte sarvato'kṣiśiromukhe* । *sarvataḥ śravaṇaghrāṇe nārāyaṇi namo'stu te*।। Obeisance to you *Nārāyaṇī*! your hands and feet are extended on all sides; your eyes, heads and faces are in all directions, your ears and noses are everywhere.

Obeisance to you O Goddess *Durgā*! you are the True Nature of all, you are the Supreme Authority of all, you are Endowed with all Powers. Protect us from all fears.

एतत्ते वदनं सौम्यं लोचनत्रयभूषितम् ।
पातु नः सर्वभीतिभ्यः कात्यायनि नमोऽस्तु ते ॥२५॥

25. *etatte vadanaṁ saumyaṁ locanatrayabhūṣitam*।
pātu naḥ sarvabhītibhyaḥ kātyāyani namo 'stu te ॥

Obeisance to you O *Kātyāyanī*! this your benevolent countenance shines with the three eyes. Protect us from all dangers.

ज्वालाकरालमत्युग्रमशेषासुरसूदनम् ।
त्रिशूलं पातु नो भीतेर्भद्रकालि नमोऽस्तु ते ॥२६॥

26. *jvālākarālamatyugramaśeṣāsurasūdanam* ।
triśūlaṁ pātu no bhīterbhadrakāli namo 'stu te ॥

Obeisance to you O *Bhadrakālī*! may your Frightful Trident, blazing with fierce flames, which annihilates all the demons, protect us.

हिनस्ति दैत्यतेजांसि स्वनेनापूर्य या जगत् ।
सा घण्टा पातु नो देवि पापेभ्योऽनः सुतानिव ॥२७॥

27. *hinasti daityatejāṁsi svanenāpūrya yā jagat* ।
sā ghaṇṭā pātu no devi pāpebhyo 'naḥ sutāniva ॥

O Goddess! may your Bell which, with its resonance, reverberates the worlds, and extinguishes the vitality of demons, protect us from evils like a mother protects her sons.

असुरासृग्वसापङ्कचर्चितस्ते करोज्ज्वलः ।
शुभाय खड्गो भवतु चण्डिके त्वां नता वयम् ॥२८॥

28. *asurāsṛgvasāpaṅkacarcitaste karojjvalaḥ* ।
śubhāya khaḍgo bhavatu caṇḍike tvāṁ natā vayam ॥

O *Caṇḍikā*! we bow down to you. May the bright sword, which is smeared with blood and fat of the demons, and is held in your hand, be felicitous to us.

रोगानशेषानपहंसि तुष्टा रुष्टा तु कामान्[9] सकलानभीष्टान् ।
त्वामाश्रितानां न विपन्नराणां त्वामाश्रिता ह्याश्रयतां प्रयान्ति ।।२६।।

29. *rogānaśeṣānapahaṁsi tuṣṭā*
ruṣṭā tu kāmān[9] *sakalānabhīṣṭān* ।
tvāmāśritānāṁ na vipannarāṇāṁ
tvāmāśritā hyāśrayatāṁ prayānti ।।

Pleased, you destroy all afflictions. Annoyed, you kill all the cherished desires. Those who seek refuge in you suffer no calamity. Those who have found refuge in you, grant refuge to others.

एतत्कृतं यत्कदनं त्वयाद्य धर्मद्विषां देवि महासुराणाम् ।
रूपैरनेकैर्बहुधाऽऽत्ममूर्तिं कृत्वाम्बिके तत्प्रकरोति कान्या ।।३०।।

30. *etatkṛtaṁ yatkadanaṁ tvayādya*
dharmadviṣāṁ devi mahāsurāṇām ।
rūpairanekairbahudhā ''tmamūrti
kṛtvāmbike tatprakaroti kānyā ।।

O Mother Goddess! who else but you could have wrought the havoc that you did today on these great demons, the enemies of righteousness, by multiplying yourself in many forms?

विद्यासु शास्त्रेषु विवेकदीपेष्वाद्येषु वाक्येषु च का त्वदन्या ।
ममत्वगर्तेऽतिमहान्धकारे विभ्रामयत्येतदतीव विश्वम् ।।३१।।

31. *vidyāsu śāstreṣu vivekadīpeṣ-*
vādyeṣu vākyeṣu ca kā tvadanyā ।
mamatvagarte 'ti mahāndhakāre
vibhrāmayatyetadatīva viśvam ।।

---

[9]AR: ददासि कामान् *dadāsi kāmān*

Who else but you abide in the sciences, scriptures and the *Vedas*, the primordial words, which enkindle the lamp of discrimination? Who else but you cause bewilderment in the world by confouding it in the abyss of darkness of attachment?

रक्षांसि यत्रोग्रविषाश्च नागा यत्रारयो दस्युबलानि यत्र ।।
दावानलो यत्र तथाब्धिमध्ये तत्र स्थिता त्वं परिपासि विश्वम् ।।३२।।

32. *rakṣāṁsi yatrogravişāśca nāgā*
yatrārayo dasyubalāni yatra ।
dāvānalo yatra tathābdhimadhye
tatra sthitā tvaṁ paripāsi viśvam ।।

You stand guarding the universe at places where there are demons, fiercely venomous snakes, the enemies and the forces of robbers; where forest-fire conflagrates and also in the midst of the deep seas.

विश्वेश्वरि त्वं परिपासि विश्वं विश्वात्मिका धारयसीति विश्वम् ।
विश्वेशवन्द्या भवती भवन्ति विश्वाश्रया ये त्वयि भक्तिनम्राः ।।३३।।

33. *viśveśvari tvaṁ paripāsi viśvaṁ*
viśvātmikā dhārayasīti viśvam ।
viśveśavandyā bhavatī bhavanti
viśvāśrayā ye tvayi bhaktinamrāḥ ।।

O Sovereign of the Universe! you nurture this universe. You are the soul and the substratum of this universe. You are reverenced by Lord *Siva*, the Ruler of this Universe. Those who beseech you with devotion become the refuge of the universe.

देवि प्रसीद पालय नोऽरिभीतेर्नित्यं यथासुरवधादधुनैव सद्यः ।
पापानि सर्वजगतां प्रशमं[10]नयाशु उत्पातपाकजनितांश्च महोपसर्गान् ।।३४।।

34. *devi prasīda pālaya no 'ribhīter-*
nityaṁ yathāsuravadhādadhunaiva sadyaḥ ।
pāpāni sarvajagatāṁ praśamaṁ[10] *nayāśu*
utpāta pākajanitāṁśca mahopasargān ॥

Be pleased O Goddess! just as you have protected us without delay from the demons, protect us always likewise. Quickly eradicate all evils and the resultant portents of the entire universe.

प्रणतानां प्रसीद त्वं देवि विश्वार्तिहारिणि ।
त्रैलोक्यवासिनामीड्ये लोकानां वरदा भव ।।३५।।

35. *praṇatānāṁ prasīda tvaṁ devi viśvārtihāriṇi* ।
trailokyavāsināmīḍye lokānāṁ varadā bhava ॥

Be pleased, O Goddess! with us who have sought refuge in you. You Allay the Suffering of the World. You are Worshipped by the Dwellers of the Three Worlds. Bless all the worlds with boons.

देव्युवाच ।।३६।।

36. *devyuvāca* ॥

वरदाहं सुरगणा वरं यन्मनसेच्छथ ।
तं वृणुध्वं प्रयच्छामि जगतामुपकारकम् ।।37।।

37. *varadāhaṁ suragaṇā varaṁ yanmanasecchatha* ।
taṁ vṛṇudhvaṁ prayacchāmi jagatāmupakārakam ॥

The Goddess said

I am the Bestower of Boons, O gods! Ask for the boon of your hearts' desire. I shall certainly grant it for the welfare of this world.

---

[10]AR: च शमं *ca śamaṁ*

देवा ऊचुः ॥३८॥

38. *devā ūcuḥ*

सर्वबाधाप्रशमनं त्रैलोक्यस्याखिलेश्वरि ।
एवमेव त्वया कार्यमस्मद्वैरिविनाशनम् ॥३९॥

39. *sarvabādhāpraśamanaṁ trailokyasyākhileśvari* ।
evameva tvayā kāryamasmadvairivināśanam ॥

The gods said

O Sovereign of all the Three Worlds! allay all the sufferings of the world and like now, keep destroying our enemies.

देव्युवाच॥४०॥

40. *devyuvāca*

वैवस्वतेऽन्तरे प्राप्ते अष्टाविंशतिमे युगे ।
शुम्भो निशुम्भश्चैवान्यावुत्पत्स्येते महासुरौ ॥४१॥

41. *vaivasvate 'ntare prāpte aṣṭāviṁśatime yuge* ।
śumbho niśumbhaścaivānyāvutpatsyete mahāsurau ॥

The Goddess said

In the era of *Vaivasvata Manu*, in the twenty-cighth *yuga*, two other mighty demons, *Śumbha* and *Niśumbha*, will be born.

नन्दगोपगृहे[11]जाता यशोदागर्भसम्भवा ।
ततस्तौ नाशयिष्यामि विन्ध्याचलनिवासिनी ॥४२॥

42. *nandagopagṛhe*[11] *jātā yaśodāgarbhasambhavā* ।
tatastau nāśayiṣyāmi vindhyācalanivāsinī ॥

Then I, born in the house of the cowherd *Nanda* from the womb of *Yaśodā*, shall reside in the *Vindhya* mountain and slay both of them.

---

[11]AR: कुले kule

पुनरप्यतिरौद्रेण रूपेण पृथिवीतले ।
अवतीर्य हनिष्यामि वैप्रचित्तांस्तु दानवान् ।।४३।।

43. *punarapyatiraudreṇa rūpeṇa pṛthivītale* ।
avatīrya haniṣyāmi vaipracittāṁstu dānavān ।।

Again I shall incarnate myself on the earth in the most formidable form and slay *vaipracitta* demons.

भक्षयन्त्याश्च तानुग्रान् वैप्रचित्तान्महासुरान् ।
रक्ता दन्ता भविष्यन्ति दाडिमीकुसुमोपमाः ।।४४।।

44. *bhakṣayantyāśca tānugrān vaipracittānmahāsurān* ।
raktā dantā bhaviṣyanti dāḍimīkusumopamāḥ ।।

ततो मां देवताः स्वर्गे मर्त्यलोके च मानवाः ।
स्तुवन्तो व्याहरिष्यन्ति सततं रक्तदन्तिकाम् ।।४५।।

45. *tato māṁ devatāḥ svarge martyaloke ca mānavāḥ* ।
stuvanto vyāhariṣyanti satataṁ raktadantikām ।।

While eating those mighty *vaipracitta* demons, my teeth will become red like the pomegranate flowers. Then the gods in heaven and men on earth shall eulogise me always, calling me *Raktadantikā*, the One with Red Teeth.

भूयश्च शतवार्षिक्यामनावृष्ट्यामनम्भसि ।
मुनिभिः संस्तुता भूमौ सम्भविष्याम्ययोनिजा ।।४६।।

46. *bhūyaśca śatavārṣikyāmanāvṛṣṭyāmanambhasi* ।
munibhiḥ saṁstutā bhūmau sambhaviṣyāmyayonijā ।।

ततः शतेन नेत्राणां निरीक्षिष्यामि यन्मुनीन् ।
कीर्तयिष्यन्ति मनुजाः शताक्षीमिति मां ततः ।।४७।।

47. *tataḥ śatena netrāṇāṁ nirīkṣiṣyāmi yanmunīn* ।
kīrtayiṣyanti manujāḥ śatākṣīmiti māṁ tataḥ ।।

Then again, when hundred years' long drought will be upon the earth and people will be without water, ascetics will eulogise me. I shall be born on the Earth but not from a Womb at that time. As I shall see those asceties with a hundred eyes, men shall extol me as *Śatākṣī,* One of a Hundred Eyes.

ततोऽहमखिलं लोकमात्मदेहसमुद्भवैः ।
भरिष्यामि सुराः शाकैरावृष्टेः प्राणधारकैः ।।४८।।

48. *tato 'hamakhilaṁ lokamātmadehasamudbhavaiḥ* ।
bhariṣyāmi surāḥ śākairāvṛṣṭeḥ prāṇadhārakaiḥ ।।

शाकम्भरीति विख्यातिं तदा यास्याम्यहं भुवि ।
तत्रैव च वधिष्यामि दुर्गमाख्यं महासुरम् ।।४९।।

49. *śākambharīti vikhyātiṁ tadā yāsyāmyahaṁ bhuvi* ।
tatraiva ca vadhiṣyāmi durgamākhyaṁ mahāsuram ।।

दुर्गा देवीति विख्यातं तन्मे नाम भविष्यति ।
पुनश्चाहं यदा भीमं रूपं कृत्वा हिमाचले ।।५०।।

50. *durgā devīti vikhyātaṁ tanme nāma bhaviṣyati* ।
punaścāhaṁ yadā bhīmaṁ rūpaṁ kṛtvā himācale ।।

रक्षांसि भक्षयिष्यामि[12]मुनीनां त्राणकारणात् ।
तदा मां मुनयः सर्वे स्तोष्यन्त्यानम्रमूर्तयः ।।५१।।

51. *rakṣāṁsi bhakṣyiṣyāmi*[12] *munīnāṁ trāṇakāraṇāt* ।
tadā māṁ munayaḥ sarve stoṣyantyānamramūrtayaḥ ।।

भीमा देवीति विख्यातं तन्मे नाम भविष्यति ।
यदारुणाख्यस्त्रैलोक्ये महाबाधां करिष्यति ।।५२।।

52. *bhīmā devīti vikhyātaṁ tanme nāma bhaviṣyati* ।
yadāruṇākhyastrailokye mahābādhāṁ kariṣyati ।।

तदाहं भ्रामरं रूपं कृत्वाऽसंख्येयषट्पदम् ।
त्रैलोक्यस्य हितार्थाय वधिष्यामि महासुरम् ।।५३।।

53. *tadāhaṁ bhrāmaraṁ rūpaṁ kṛtvā 'saṅkhyeyaṣaṭpadam* ।
trailokyasya hitārthāya vadhiṣyāmi mahāsuram ।।

---

[12]AR: क्षयिष्यामि kṣayīṣyāmi

At that time, I shall sustain the entire world with the life-saving vegetation produced from my body until rain comes. Then I shall attain fame on the earth as *Śākambharī*, the One who Nurtures with Vegetables. At that very time, I shall slay the mighty demon *Durga*. My name will then become famous as the Goddess *Durgā*. Once again, when donning a formidable form I shall be born and devour the demons sojourning in *Himācala* to save the sages, then all the sages shall, with great humility, propitiate me. Then I shall become famous by the name *Bhīmā devī*, the Formidable Goddess. When the demon *Aruṇa* will cause great havoc in the three worlds, I shall appear as countless Whirling Black Bees, each with six legs and for the welfare of the three worlds, kill that giant of a demon.

भ्रामरीति च मां लोकास्तदा स्तोष्यन्ति सर्वतः ।
इत्थं यदा यदा बाधा दानवोत्था भविष्यति ।।५४।।

54. *bhrāmarīti ca mām lokāstadā stoṣyanti sarvataḥ* ।
ittham̐ yadā yadā bādhā dānavotthā bhaviṣyati ।।

तदा तदावतीर्याहं करिष्याम्यरिसंक्षयम् ।।ॐ।।५५।।

55. *tadā tadāvatīryāham̐ kariṣyāmyarisam̐kṣayam* ।। om̐ ।।

People all over shall then propititate me as *Bhrāmarī*, the Whirling Black Bee. In this way, as and when there arises danger caused by demons, I shall incarnate myself and slay the enemies. om̐

इति श्रीमार्कण्डेयपुराणे सावर्णिके मन्वन्तरे देवीमाहात्म्ये देव्याः
स्तुतिर्नामैकादशोऽध्यायः ।।११।।

iti śrīmārkaṇḍeyapurāṇe sāvarṇike manvantare

devīmāhātmye devyāḥ stutirnāmaikādaśo 'dhyāyaḥ ॥11॥

Thus ends the eleventh chapter called 'Eulogy of the Goddess by the gods' during the era of *Sāvarṇi Manu,* in the 'Glory of the Goddess', (narrated) in the *Mārkaṇḍeya Purāṇa.*

उवाच ४, अर्धश्लोकः १, श्लोकाः ५०, एवम् ५५, एवमादितः ६३०

uvāca 4, *ardhaślokaḥ* 1, *ślokāḥ* 50, *evam* 55, *evamāditaḥ.* 630

uvāca 4, half śloka 1, ślokās 50, total 55,

from beginning up to here 630.

द्वादशोऽध्यायः

dvādaśo 'dhyāyaḥ

Chapter Twelve

Merits of Reciting the Eulogies of the Goddess

ध्यानम्

dhyānam

Meditation

ॐ विद्युद्दामसमप्रभां मृगपतिस्कन्धस्थितां भीषणां
कन्याभिः करवालखेटविलसद्धस्ताभिरासेविताम् ।
हस्तैश्चक्रगदासिखेटविशिखांश्चापं गुणं तर्जनीं ।
बिभ्राणमनलात्मिकां शशिधरां दुर्गां त्रिनेत्रां भजे ।।

Oṁ. Vidyuddāmasamaprabhāṁ mṛgapatiskandhasthitāṁ bhīṣaṇāṁ
kanyābhiḥ karavālakheṭavilasaddhastābhirāsevitām ।
hastaiścakragadāsikheṭaviśikhāṁścāpaṁ guṇaṁ tarjanīṁ
bibhrāṇamanalātmikāṁ śaśidharāṁ durgāṁ trinetrāṁ bhaje ।।

I MEDITATE UPON THE THREE-EYED *DURGĀ*, DAZZLING LIKE FIRE. SHE IS EFFULGENT LIKE LIGHTNING, SITS ON THE SHOULDER OF THE LION, THE KING OF BEASTS, AND BEARS FORMIDABLE LOOKS. MAIDENS HOLDING SCIMITARS AND SHIELDS IN THEIR HANDS ATTEND UPON HER. IN HER HANDS, SHE WIELDS THE DISCUS, MACE, SWORD, SHIELD, ARROW AND BOW AND *TARJANĪ-MUDRĀ*, THE WARNING SIGN. THE MOON ADORNS HER HEAD.

ॐ देव्युवाच ।।१।।

1. *oṁ devyuvāca*

एभिः स्तवैश्च मां नित्यं स्तोष्यते यः समाहितः ।
तस्याहं सकलां बाधां नाश[1]यिष्याम्यसंशयम् ।।2।।

2. *ebhiḥ stavaiśca māṁ nityaṁ stoṣyate yaḥ samāhitaḥ* ।
tasyāhaṁ sakalāṁ bādhāṁ nāṣa[1]yiṣyāmyasaṁśayam ।।

Oṁ. The Goddess said

He who regularly propitiates me, with concentration, with these hymns, all his troubles shall I, without doubt, destroy.

मधुकैटभनाशं च महिषासुरघातनम् ।
कीर्तयिष्यन्ति ये तद्वद् वधं च शुम्भनिशुम्भयोः ।।३।।

3. *madhukaiṭabhanāśaṁ ca mahiṣāsuraghātanam* ।
kīrtayiṣyanti ye tadvad vadhaṁ ca śumbhaniśumbhayoḥ ।।

अष्टम्यां च चतुर्दश्यां नवम्यां चैकचेतसः ।
श्रोष्यन्ति चैव ये भक्त्या मम माहात्म्यमुत्तमम् ।।४।।

4. *aṣṭamyāṁ ca caturdaśyāṁ navamyāṁ caikacetasaḥ* ।
śroṣyanti caiva ye bhaktyā mama māhātmyamuttamam ।।

न तेषां दुष्कृतं किञ्चिद् दुष्कृतोत्था न चापदः ।
भविष्यति न दारिद्र्यं न चैवेष्टवियोजनम् ।।५।।

5. *na teṣāṁ duṣkṛtaṁ kiñcid duṣkṛtotthā na cāpadaḥ* ।
bhaviṣyati na dāridryaṁ na caiveṣṭaviyojanam ।।

Those who shall recite the annihilation of *Madhu* and *Kaiṭabha*, killing of Mahiṣāsura, as well as slaying of *Śumbha* and *Niśumbha* and/ or listen with single-minded devotion to my exalted glory on the eighth, fourteenth and ninth days of a lunar fort-night, will not be subjected to any evil or the resultant adversity; they will suffer neither from indigence nor separation of the dear ones.

[1]AR: शम śama

शत्रुतो न भयं तस्य दस्युतो वा न राजतः ।
न शस्त्रानलतोयौघात्कदाचित्सम्भविष्यति ॥६॥

6. *śatruto na bhayaṁ tasya dasyuto vā na rājataḥ* ।
na śastrānalatoyaughātkadācitsambhaviṣyati ॥

They will have no fear of foes, robbers or the king; nor of weapons, fire and flood.

तस्मान्ममैतन्माहात्म्यं पठितव्यं समाहितैः ।
श्रोतव्यं च सदा भक्त्या परं स्वस्त्ययनं हि तत् ॥७॥

7. *tasmānmamaitanmāhātmyaṁ paṭhitavyaṁ samāhitaiḥ* ।
śrotavyaṁ ca sada bhaktyā paraṁ svastyayanam hi tat ॥

Therefore, this glory of mine should be recited and listened to attentively and with devotion for this is the most auspicious.

उपसर्गानशेषांस्तु महामारीसमुद्भवान् ।
तथा त्रिविधमुत्पातं माहात्नं शमयेन्मम ॥८॥

8. *upasargānaśeṣāṁstu mahāmārīsamudbhavān* ।
tathā trividhamutpātaṁ māhātmyaṁ śamayenmama ॥

My glory is capable of quelling all calamities arising from epidemics and the three types of evil portents.*

यत्रैतत्पठ्यते सम्यङ्नित्यमायतने मम ।
सदा न तद्विमोक्ष्यामि सांनिध्यं तत्र मे स्थितम् ॥९॥

9. *yatraitatpaṭhyate samyaṅnityamāyatane mama*।
sadā na tadvimokṣyāmi sāṁnidhyaṁ tatra me sthitam॥

My shrine, where it is recited regularly according to the prescribed method, shall never be forsaken by me and my presence will always be there.

---

* These are (i) दैहिक, *daihika:* corporeal (ii) दैविक, *daivika:* supernatural and भौतिक, *bhautika:* elemental

बलिप्रदाने पूजायामग्निकार्ये महोत्सवे।
सर्वं ममैतच्चरितमुच्चार्यं श्राव्यमेव च॥१०॥

10. *balipradāne pūjāyāmagnikārye mahotsave* ।
sarvaṁ mamaitaccaritamucāryaṁ śrāvyameva ca ॥

At the time of offering oblations, in performing ritualistic worship, in fire-sacrifice, in grand festivals, in all places and on all occasions this hymn of mine is to be recited and listened to in full.

जानताऽजानता वापि बलिपूजां तथा कृताम्।
प्रतीच्छिष्याम्यहं[2] प्रीत्या वह्निहोमं तथा कृतम्॥११॥

11. *jānatā'jānatā vāpi balipūjāṁ tathā kṛtām* ।
pratīcchiṣyāmyahaṁ[2] *prītyā vahnihomaṁ tathā kṛtam* ॥

I shall lovingly accept the worship, offering of ablutions and fire-sacrifice performed with or without knowledge of the procedure.

शरत्काले महापूजा क्रियते या च वार्षिकी।
तस्यां ममैतन्माहात्म्यं श्रुत्वा भक्तिसमन्वितः॥१२॥

12. *śaratkāle mahāpūjā kriyate yā ca vārṣikī* ।
tasyāṁ mamaitanmāhātmyaṁ śrutvā bhaktisamanvitaḥ ॥

सर्वाबाधा[3]विनिर्मुक्तो धनधान्यसुतान्वितः।
मनुष्यो मत्प्रसादेन भविष्यति न संशयः॥१३॥

13. *sarvābādhā*[3] *vinirmukto dhanadhānyasutānvitaḥ* ।
manuṣyo matprasādena bhaviṣyati na saṁśayaḥ ॥

He who, on the occasion of the great annual worship in autumnal season, will listen to my glory with devotion, shall, with my blessings, be delivered, without doubt, from all troubles and endowed with wealth, grains and children.

---

[2]AR: प्रतीक्षिष्याम्यहं *pratīkṣiṣyāmyahaṁ*

[3]AR: सर्वबाधा *sarvabādhā*

श्रुत्वा ममैतन्माहात्म्यं तथा चोत्पत्तयः शुभाः ।
पराक्रमं च युद्धेषु जायते निर्भयः पुमान् ।।१४।।

14. *śrutvā mamaitanmāhātmyaṁ tathā cotpattayaḥ śubhāḥ* ।
parākramaṁ ca yuddheṣu jāyate nirbhayaḥ pumān ॥

By listening to this glory of mine, the propitious episodes of my incarnations and the narratives of my valour in battles, a man becomes fearless

रिपवः संक्षयं यान्ति कल्याणं चोपपद्यते ।
नन्दते च कुलं पुंसां माहात्म्यं मम शृण्वताम् ।।१५।।

15. *ripavaḥ saṁkṣayaṁ yānti kalyāṇaṁ copapadyate* ।
nandate ca kulaṁ puṁsāṁ māhātmyaṁ mama śṛṇvatām ॥

Enemies of men who listen to my glory, perish. Listeners to it, attain auspiciousness and their clan rejoices.

शान्तिकर्माणि सर्वत्र तथा दुःस्वप्नदर्शने ।
ग्रहपीडासु चोग्रासु माहात्म्यं शृणुयान्मम ।।१६।।

16. *śāntikarmāṇi sarvatra tathā duḥsvapnadarśane* ।
grahapīḍāsu cogrāsu māhātmyaṁ śṛnuyānmama ॥

At all propitiatory functions, on seeing nightmares and to alleviate the afflictions caused by severe adverse planetary conditions, this glory of mine should be listned to.

उपसर्गाः शमं यान्ति ग्रहपीडाश्च दारुणाः ।
दुःस्वप्नं च नृभिर्दृष्टं सुस्वप्नमुपजायते ।।१७।।

17. *upasargāḥ śamaṁ yānti grahapīḍāśca dāruṇāḥ* ।
duḥsvapnaṁ ca nṛbhirdṛṣṭaṁ susvapnamupajāyate ॥

(By listening to it) misfortunes are mitigated, so are serious planentary afflictions. A nightmare seen by men is transformed into a propitious dream.

बालग्रहाभिभूतानां बालानां शान्तिकारकम् ।
संघातभेदे च नृणां मैत्रीकरणमुत्तमम् ।।१८।।

18. *bālagrahābhibhūtānāṁ bālānāṁ śāntikārakam* ।
saṅghātabhede ca nṛṇāṁ maitrīkaraṇamuttamam ।।

It pacifies the children seized by the child-teasing planets or demons. It is the best means of restoring friendship in the event of disunity.

दुर्वृत्तानामशेषाणां बलहानिकरं परम् ।
रक्षोभूतपिशाचानां पठनादेवनाशनम् ।।१९।।

19. *durvṛttānāmaśeṣāṇāṁ balahānikaraṁ param* ।
rakṣobhūtapiśācānāṁ paṭhanādevanāśanam ।।

It completely destroys the strength of a whole lot of evil portents. Just by its recitation, demons, ghosts and goblins perish.

सर्वं ममैतन्माहात्म्यं मम सन्निधिकारकम् ।
पशुपुष्पार्घ्यधूपैश्च गन्धदीपैस्तथोत्तमैः ।।२०।।

20. *sarvaṁ mamaitanmāhātmyaṁ mama sannidhikārakam* ।
paśupuṣpārghyadhūpaiśca gandhadīpaistathottamaiḥ ।।

विप्राणां भोजनैर्होमैः प्रोक्षणीयैरहर्निशम् ।
अन्यैश्च विविधैर्भोगैः प्रदानैर्वत्सरेण या ।।२१।।

21. *viprāṇāṁ bhojanairhomaiḥ prokṣaṇīyairaharniśam* ।
anyaiśca vividhairbhogaiḥ pradānairvatsareṇa yā ।।

प्रीतिर्मे क्रियते सास्मिन् सकृत्सुचरिते श्रुते ।
श्रुतं हरति पापानि तथाऽऽरोग्यं प्रयच्छति ।।२२।।

22. *prītirme kriyate sāsmin sakṛtsucarite śrute* ।
śrutaṁ harati pāpāni tathā ''rogyaṁ prayacchati ।।

This entire glory of mine facilitates my proximity. The felicity that I derive from the year-long offerings of the finest varieties of animals, flowers, oblations, incenses, perfumes and lamps or feeding the *brāhmaṇas*, sacrifices, sprinkling of consecrated waters on me and offerings of other enjoyable objects every day, is equally derived by me just by hearing these auspicious acts of mine. All evils are mitigated and freedom from diseases obtained by hearing it.

रक्षां करोति भूतेभ्यो जन्मनां कीर्तनं मम ।
युद्धेषु चरितं यन्मे दुष्टदैत्यनिबर्हणम् ।।२३।।

23. *rakṣāṁ karoti bhūtebhyo janmanāṁ kīrtanaṁ mama* ।
yuddheṣu caritaṁ yanme duṣṭadaityanibarhaṇam ।।

Chanting of the episodes of my incarnation protects from evil spirits and those of my acts in the battlefield annihilates wicked demons.

तस्मिञ्छ्रुते वैरिकृतं भयं पुंसां न जायते ।
युष्माभिः स्तुतयो याश्च याश्च ब्रह्मर्षिभिः कृता ।।२४।।

24. *tasmiñchrute vairikṛtaṁ bhayaṁ puṁsāṁ na jāyate* ।
yuṣmābhiḥ stutayo yāśca yāśca brahmarṣibhiḥ kṛtā ।।

ब्रह्मणा च कृतास्तास्तु प्रयच्छन्ति शुभां मतिम् ।
अरण्ये प्रान्तरे वापि दावाग्निपरिवारितः ।।२५।।

25. *brahmaṇā ca kṛtāstāstu prayacchanti śubhāṁ matim* ।
araṇye prāntare vāpi dāvāgniparivāritaḥ ।।

दस्युभिर्वा वृतः शून्ये गृहीतो वापि शत्रुभिः ।
सिंहव्याघ्रानुयातो वा वने वनहस्तिभिः ।।२६।।

26. *dasyubhirvā vṛtaḥ śūnye gṛhīto vāpi śatrubhiḥ* ।
siṁhavyāghrānuyāto vā vane vanahastibhiḥ ।।

राज्ञाक्रुद्धेन चाज्ञप्तो वध्यो बन्धगतोऽपि वा ।
आघूर्णितो वा वातेन स्थित:पोते महार्णवे ।।२७।।

27. *rajñā kruddhena cājñapato vadhyo bandhagato 'pi vā* ।
āghūrṇito vā vātena sthitaḥ pote mahārṇave ।।

पतत्सु चापि शस्त्रेषु संग्रामे भृशदारुणे ।
सर्वाबाधासु घोरासु वेदनाभ्यर्दितोऽपि वा ।।२८।।

28. *patasu cāpi śastreṣu saṅgrāme bhṛśadāruṇe* ।
sarvābādhāsu ghorāsu vedanābhyardito 'pi vā ।।

स्मरन्ममैतच्चरितं नरो मुच्येत संकटात् ।
ममप्रभावात्सिंहाद्या दस्यवो वैरिणस्तथा ।।२९।।

29. *smaranmamaitaccaritaṁ naro mucyeta saṅkaṭāt* ।
mamaprabhāvātsiṁhādyā dasyavo vairiṇastathā ।।

दूरादेव पलायन्ते स्मरतश्चरितं मम ।।३०।।

30. *dūrādeva palāyante smarataścaritaṁ mama* ।।

Hearing those deeds of mine, men suffer no more from the fear caused by enemies. Eulogies that have been offered by all of you, the brāhmaṇical sages and *Brahmā* bestow felicitious intellect. A person who recalles these deeds of mine in the forest, on the deserted path; when caught in forest fire, surrounded by robbers in a secluded place, captured by enemies, followed by tigers, lions and wild elephants in the wilderness, arrested or sent to the gallows under the order of an angry king, tossed about in a boat by a tempest on the high seas, struck by weapons in the intensely hard battle or tormented by severe pain, shall attain to freedom from all types of crises. Just by recalling my deeds, lions and the other beasts, robbers and enemies flee to a distance; such is the impact of (recalling, reciting and/or listening to) my acts.

ऋषिरुवाच ।।३१।।

31. *ṛṣiruvāca*

इत्युक्त्वा सा भगवती चण्डिका चण्डविक्रमा ।।३२।।

32. *ityuktvā sā bhagavatī caṇḍikā caṇḍavikramā* ।।

पश्यतामेव देवानां[1] तत्रैवान्तरधीयत ।
तेऽपि देवा निरातङ्काः स्वाधिकारान् यथा पुरा ।।३३।।

33. *paśyatāmeva devānāṁ*[1] *tatraivāntaradhīyata* ।
te 'pi devā nirātaṅkāḥ svādhikārān yathā purā ॥

यज्ञभागभुजः सर्वे चक्रुर्विनिहतारयः ।
दैत्याश्च देव्या निहते शुम्भे देवरिपौ युधि ।।३४।।

34. *yajñabhāgabhujaḥ sarve cakrurvinihatārayaḥ* ।
daityāśca devyā nihate śumbhe devaripau yudhi ॥

जगद्विध्वंसिनि तस्मिन् महोग्रेऽतुलविक्रमे ।
निशुम्भे च महावीर्ये शेषाः पातालमाययुः ।।३५।।

35. *jagadvidhvaṁsini tasmin mahogre 'tulavikrame* ।
niśumbhe ca mahāvīrye śeṣāḥ pātālamāyayuḥ ॥

The Seer said

Saying this, that Supreme Goddess *Caṇḍikā* of immense might, disappeared there itself even as the gods looked on. Those gods too, with their enemies annihilated, attained freedom from terror. Their share of oblations in sacrifice having been restored, they resumed their respective authority as in the past. When the demons, including *Śumbha* and *Niśumbha* of incomparable might, who were bent upon destroying the world, were slayed, the remaining ones retired to *pātāla*, the lowest abyss.

एवं भगवती देवी सा नित्यापि पुनः पुनः ।
सम्भूय कुरुते भूप जगतः परिपालनम् ।।३६।।

36. *evaṁ bhagavatī devī sā nityāpi punaḥ punaḥ* ।
sambhūya kurute bhūpa jagataḥ paripālanam ॥

In this manner, O king! the venerable Goddess, though eternal, manifests herself again and again and sustains this world.

---

[1]AR: पश्यतां सर्वदेवानां *paśyatāṁ sarvadevānāṁ*

तयैतन्मोह्यते विश्वं सैव विश्वं प्रसूयते ।
सा याचिता च विज्ञानं तुष्टा ऋद्धिं प्रयच्छति ।।३७।।

37. *tayaitanmohyate viśvaṁ saiva viśvaṁ prasūyate* ।
sā yācitā ca vijñānaṁ tuṣṭā ṛddhiṁ prayacchati ।।

By her is this world deluded. She verily creates this world. On entreaty, when appeased, she bestows supreme knowledge and blesses with great fortune.

व्याप्तं तयैतत्सकलं ब्रह्माण्डं मनुजेश्वर ।
महाकाल्या महाकाले महामारी स्वरूपया ।।३८।।

38. *vyāptaṁ tayaitatsakalaṁ brahmāṇḍaṁ manujeśvara* ।
mahākālyā mahākāle mahāmārī svarūpayā ।।

O Lord of men! When the time comes for the great dissolution of this universe, that *Mahākāli*, pervades it in the form of great epidemic.

सैव काले महामारी सैव सृष्टिर्भवत्यजा ।
स्थितिं करोति भूतानां सैव काले सनातनी ।।३९।।

39. *saiva kāle mahāmārī saiva sṛṣṭirbhavatyajā* ।
sthitiṁ karoti bhūtānāṁ saiva kāle sanātanī ।।

In time, she verily is the Great Epidemic; in time she alone, though Unborn, becomes the Creation and, in time, she, the Eternity, sustains the beings.

भवकाले नृणां सैव लक्ष्मीर्वृद्धिप्रदा गृहे ।
सैवाभावे तथाऽलक्ष्मीर्विनाशायोपजायते ।।४०।।

40. *bhavakāle nṛṇāṁ saiva lakṣmīrvṛddhipradā gṛhe* ।
saivābhāve tathā 'lakṣmīrvināśāyopajāyate ।।

When it is time of ascendance for men, she verily is *Lakṣmī*, the Bestower of Affluence in homes. Again, in times of penury, it is she who becomes *Alakṣmī*, the Evil Fortune, for destruction.

स्तुता सम्पूजिता पुष्पैर्धूपगन्धादिभिस्तथा ।
ददाति वित्तं पुत्रांश्च मतिं धर्मे गतिं[5] शुभाम् ॥ॐ॥४१॥

41. *stutā sampūjitā puṣpairdhūpagandhādibhistathā* ।
dadāti vittaṁ putrāṁśca matiṁ dharme gatiṁ[5] *śubhām* ॥oṁ॥

Adored and worshipped with flowers, incense, perfume etc., she blesses with wealth and children, a righteous mind and felicitous finale. oṁ

इति श्रीमार्कण्डेयपुराणे सावर्णिके मन्वन्तरे देवीमाहात्म्ये फलस्तुतिर्नाम द्वादशोऽध्यायः ॥१२॥

iti śrīmārkaṇḍeyapurāṇe sāvarṇike manvantare devīmāhātmye phalastutirnāma dvādaśo 'dhyāyaḥ ॥12॥

Thus ends the twelfth chapter called 'Merits of Reciting the Eulogies' during the era of *Sāvarṇi Manu* in the 'Glory of the Goddess', (narrated) in the *Mārkaṇḍeya Purāṇa.*

उवाच २, अर्धश्लोकौ: २, श्लोका: ३७, एवम् ४१, एवमादित: ६७१
uvāca 2, *ardhaślokau* 2, *ślokāḥ* 37, *evam* 41 *evamāditaḥ* 671

uvāca 2, half ślokas 2, ślokās 37, total 41,
from beginning up to here 671.

[5]AR: तथा tathā

त्रयोदशोऽध्यायः

trayodaśo 'dhyāyaḥ

Chapter Thirteen

The Goddess Blesses *Suratha* and the Merchant with Boons.

ध्यानम्

dhyānam

Meditation

ॐ बालार्कमण्डलाभासां चतुर्बाहुं त्रिलोचनाम् ।
पाशाङ्कुशवराभीतीर्धारयन्तीं शिवां भजे ।।

Oṁ Bālārkamaṇḍalābhāsāṁ caturbāhuṁ trilocanām ।
pāśāṅkuśavarābhītīrdhārayantīṁ śivām bhaje ।।

OṀ. I MEDITATE UPON *ŚIVĀ*, THE ABODE OF AUSPICIOUSNESS. HER LUSTRE MATCHES THE EFFULGENCE OF THE RISING SUN. SHE HAS FOUR ARMS AND THREE EYES. SHE WIELDS A SNARE, A HOOK AND SIGNALS BOON AND FEARLESSNESS.

ॐ ऋषिरुवाच ।।१।।

1. *oṁ. ṛṣiruvāca*

एतत्ते कथितं भूप देवीमाहात्म्यमुत्तमम् ।
एवंप्रभावा सा देवी ययेदं धार्यतेजगत् ।।२।।

2. *etatte kathitaṁ bhūpa devīmāhātmyamuttamam* ।
evaṁprabhāvā sā devī yayedaṁ dhāryatejagat ।।

Oṁ. The Seer said

I have, O king! narrated to you this exalted 'Glory of the Goddess.' Such indeed is the power of the Goddess by whom this world is supported.

विद्या तथैव क्रियते भगवद्विष्णुमायया ।
तया त्वमेष वैश्यश्च तथैवान्ये विवेकिनः ।।३।।

3. *vidyā tathaiva kriyate bhagavadviṣṇumāyayā* ।
tayā tvameṣa vaiśyaśca tathaivānye vivekinaḥ ।।

मोह्यन्ते मोहिताश्चैव मोहमेष्यन्ति चापरे ।
तामुपैहि महाराज शरणं परमेश्वरीम् ।।४।।

4. *mohyante mohitāścaiva mohameṣyanti cāpare* ।
tāmupaihi mahārāja śaraṇaṁ parameśvarīm ।।

By that Illusive Power of Lord *Viṣṇu* is knowledge created. It is by her that you, this merchant and the others (even) possessing the faculty of discrimination, are deluded, were deluded and shall be deluded. O Monarch! seek refuge in that Supreme Empress.

आराधिता सैव नृणां भोगस्वर्गापवर्गदा ।।५।।

5. *ārādhitā saiva nṛṇāṁ bhogasvargāpavargadā* ।।

It is she who, on being worshipped, grants worldly enjoyments, heaven and the final beatitude to men.

मार्कण्डेय उवाच ।।६।।

6. *mārkaṇḍeya uvāca* ।।

इति तस्य वचः श्रुत्वा सुरथः स नराधिपः ।।७।।

7. *iti tasya vacaḥ śrutvā surathaḥ sa narādhipaḥ* ।।

प्रणिपत्य महाभागं तमृषिं शंसितव्रतम् ।।
निर्विण्णोऽतिममत्वेन राज्यापहरणेन च ।।८।।

8. *praṇipatya mahābhāgaṁ tamṛṣiṁ śaṁsitavratam* ।
nirviṇṇo 'timamatvena rājyāpaharaṇena ca ।।

जगाम सद्यस्तपसे स च वैश्यो महामुने ।
संदर्शनार्थमम्बाया नदीपुलिनसंस्थितः ।।९।।

9. *jagāma sadyastapase sa ca vaiśyo mahāmune* ।
saṁdarśanārthamambāyā nadīpulinasaṁsthitaḥ ।।

Mārkaṇḍeya said

After hearing these words of his, the king *Suratha* who was frustrated owing to excessive attachment and loss of his kingdom, prostrated before the noble seer who had been strictly observing the vow of penance. O great sage! he along with the merchant, *Samādhi,* instantly repaired to the sand-bank of a river for practising penance with the objective of having a vision of the Mother.

स च वैश्यस्तपस्तेपे देवीसूक्तं परं जपन् ।
तौ तस्मिन् पुलिने देव्याः कृत्वा मूर्तिं महीमयीम् ।।१०।।

10. *sa ca vaiśyastapastepe devīsūktaṁ paraṁ japan* ।
tau tasmin puline devyāḥ kṛtvā mūrtiṁ mahīmayīṁ ।।

Having formed the earthen image of the Goddess at that sand-bank, he and the merchant practised penance reciting the holy Hymn to the Goddess.

अर्हणां चक्रतुस्तस्याः पुष्पधूपाग्नितर्पणैः ।
निराहारौ यताहारौ तन्मनस्कौ समाहितौ ।।११।।

11. *arhaṇāṁ cakratustasyāḥ puṣpadhūpāgnitarpaṇaiḥ* ।
nirāhārau yatāhārau tanmanaskau samāhitau ।।

With full concentration of the mind, they worshipped her with flowers, incense and fire-sacrifice, now going without food, now taking restricted diet.

ददतुस्तौ बलिं चैव निजगात्रासृगुक्षितम् ।
एवं समाराधयतोस्त्रिभिर्वर्षैर्यतात्मनोः ।।१२।।

12. *dadatustau baliṁ caiva nijagātrāsṛgukṣitam* ।
evaṁ samārādhayatostribhirvarṣairyatātmanoḥ ।।

परितुष्टा जगद्धात्री प्रत्यक्षं प्राह चण्डिका ।।१३।।

13. *parituṣṭā jagaddhatrī pratyakṣaṁ prāha caṇḍikā* ।।

The two also offered oblation by sprinkling blood drawn from their bodies. When, worshipping in this manner with concentrated minds, three years had passed, *Caṇḍikā*, the nurturer of the universe, appeared before them and said:

देव्युवाच ।।१४।।

14. *devyuvāca*

यत्प्रार्थ्यते त्वया भूप त्वया च कुलनन्दन ।
मत्तस्तत्प्राप्यतां सर्वं परितुष्टा ददामि तत् ।।१५।।

15. *yatprārthyate tvayā bhūpa tvayā ca kulanandana* ।
mattastatprāpyatāṁ sarvaṁ parituṣṭā dadāmi tat ।।

The Goddess said

Get from me, O king, and you too, O merchant, the joy of your clan! all that you have been praying for. I am completely satisficd and shall grant you all.

मार्कण्डेय उवाच ।।१६।।

16. *mārkaṇḍeya uvāca*

ततो वव्रे नृपो राज्यमविभ्रंश्यन्यजन्मनि ।
अत्रैव च निजं राज्यं हतशत्रुबलं बलात् ।।१७।।

17. *tato vavre nṛpo rājyamavibhraṁśyanyajanmani* ।
atraiva ca nijam rājyaṁ hataśatrubalaṁ balāt ।।

Mārkaṇḍeya said

Then the king opted for an undecaying kingship in his other life and, for the present life, reclamation of his kingdom by force from the army of his enemies.

सोऽपि वैश्यस्ततो ज्ञानं वव्रे निर्विण्णमानसः ।
ममेत्यहमिति प्राज्ञः सङ्गविच्युतिकारकम् ।।१८।।

18. *so 'pi vaiśyastato jñānam vavre nirviṇṇamānasaḥ* ।
mametyahamiti prājñaḥ saṅgavicyutikārakam ।।

That wise merchant, whose mind had become apathetic to the wordly affairs, asked for the higher knowledge which would result in complete deviation from attachment to 'I' and 'mine'.

देव्युवाच ।।१९।।

19. *devyuvāca*

स्वल्पैरहोभिर्नृपते स्वं राज्यं प्राप्स्यते भवान् ।।२०।।

20. *svalpairahobhirnṛpate svaṁ rājyaṁ prāpsyate bhavān* ।।

हत्वा रिपूनस्खलितं तव तत्र भविष्यति ।।२१।।

21. *hatvā ripūnaskhalitaṁ tava tatra bhaviṣyati* ।।

The Goddess said

You will, o king! get back your kingdom in a few days by slaying your enemies and then it would remain secure with you.

मृतश्च भूयः संप्राप्य जन्म देवाद्विवस्वतः ।।२२।।

22. *mṛtaśca bhūyaḥ saṁprāpya janma devādvivasvataḥ* ।।

सावर्णिको नाम मनुर्भवान्[1] भुवि भविष्यति ।।२३।।

23. *sāvarṇiko nāma manurbhavān*[1] *bhuvi bhaviṣyati* ।।

After death you will be born again from the Sun god when your name on earth will be *Sāvarṇika Manu.*

वैश्यवर्य त्वया यश्च वरोऽस्मत्तोऽभिवाञ्छितः ।।२४।।

24. *vaiśyavarya tvaya yaśca varo 'smatto 'bhivāñchitaḥ* ।।

तं प्रयच्छामि संसिद्धयै तव ज्ञानं भविष्यति ।।२५।।

25. *taṁ prayacchāmi saṁsiddhyai tava jñānam bhaviṣyati*

O good merchant! I grant the boon that has been desired by you. You will be endowed with the knowledge by which you will attain to the final liberation.

मार्कण्डेय उवाच ।।२६।।

26. *mārkaṇḍeya uvāca*

इति दत्त्वा तयोर्देवी यथाभिलषितं वरम् ।।27।।

27. *iti dattvā tāyordevī yathābhilaṣitaṁ varam* ।।

बभूवान्तर्हिता सद्यो भक्त्या ताभ्यामभिष्टुता ।
एवं देव्या वरं लब्ध्वा सुरथः क्षत्रियर्षभः ।।२८।।

28. *babhūvāntarhitā sadyo bhaktyā tābhyāmabhiṣṭutā* ।
evaṁ devyā varaṁ labdhvā surathaḥ kṣatriyarṣabhaḥ ।।

सूर्याज्जन्म समासाद्य सावर्णिर्भविता मनुः ।।२९।।

29. *sūryājjanma samāsādya sāvarṇirbhavitā manuḥ* ।।

Markaṇḍeya said

Propitiated by the two and granting them the boons as desired by them, the Goddess instantly disappeared.

---

[1]AR मनुर्नाम *manurnāma*

Having, thus, received the boon from the Goddess, *Suratha,* the excellent *kṣatriya,* will obtain birth from the Sun and become *Sāvarṇi Manu.*

एवं देव्या वरं लब्ध्वा सुरथः क्षत्रियर्षभः ।
सूर्याज्जन्म समासाद्य सावर्णिर्भविता मनुः ॥ क्लीं ॐ ॥

evaṁ devyā varaṁ labdhvā surathaḥ kṣatriyarṣabhaḥ ।
sūryājjanma samāsādya sāvarṇirbhavitā manuḥ ॥klīm॥oṁ॥

Having thus recieved the boon from the Goddess, *Suratha,* the excellent *kṣatriya,* will obtain birth from the Sun and become *Sāvarṇi Manu.*॥*klīṁ*॥oṁ॥

इति श्री मार्कण्डेयपुराणे सावर्णिके मन्वन्तरे देवीमाहात्म्ये
सुरथवैश्ययोर्वरप्रदानं नाम त्रयोदशोऽध्यायः ॥१३॥

iti śrīmārkaṇḍeyapurāṇe sāvarṇike manvantare devī māhātmye surathavaiśyayorvarapradānaṁ nāma trayodaśo 'dhyāyaḥ ॥

Thus ends the thirteenth chapter called 'The Goddess Blesses *Suratha* and the Merchant with Boons' during the era of *Sāvarṇi Manu,* in the 'Glory of the Goddess', (narrated) in the *Mārkaṇḍeya Purāṇa.*

उवाच ६, अर्धश्लोकाः ११, श्लोकाः १२, एवम् २९, एवमादितः ७००
uvāca 6, *ardhaślokāḥ* 11, *ślokāḥ* 12, *evaṁ* 29 *evamāditaḥ* 700

uvāca 6, half ślokas 11, ślokās 12, total 29,
from beginning up to here 700.

इति श्रीदुर्गासप्तशती

iti śrīdurgāsaptaśatī
Śrīdurgāsaptaśatī concluded

उपसंहारः

12. *Upsaṁhāraḥ*

(conclusion)

Repetition of *Navārṇavidhiḥ*

After completing the recitation of the *Saptaśatī*, it is imperative to recite the *Navārṇa* and then follow it up with the recitation of the *Devīsūkta*. We, therefore, repeat it hereunder. All rituals are to be performed as is done in the *Navārṇa* before the recitation of the *Saptaśatī*.

For English translation, please see under the text of *Navārṇa* already given before the beginning of the *Saptaśatī*.

विनियोगः

श्री गणपतिर्जयति । ॐ अस्य श्री नवार्णमन्त्रस्य ब्रह्मविष्णुरुद्रा ऋषयः, गायत्र्युष्णिगनुष्टुभशछन्दांसि, श्रीमहाकालीमहालक्ष्मीमहासरस्वत्यो देवताः, ऐं बीजम्, ह्रीं शक्तिः, क्लीं कीलकम्, श्री महाकालीमहालक्ष्मीमहासरस्वती-प्रीत्यर्थे जपे विनियोगः।

viniyogaḥ

śrī gaṇapatirijayati । *oṁ asya śrīnavārṇamantrasya brahmaviṣṇurudrā ṛṣayaḥ, gāyatruṣṇiganuṣṭubhaśachandāṁsi, śrī mahākalīmahālakṣmīmahāsarasvatyo devatāḥ, aiṁ bījam, hrīṁ śaktiḥ, klīṁ kīlakam, śrīmahākālī mahālakṣmīmahāsarasvatī-prītyarthe jape viniyogaḥ* ।

ऋष्यादिन्यासः

ब्रह्मविष्णुरुद्रऋषिभ्यो नमः, शिरसि । गायत्र्युष्णिगनुष्टुपछन्दोभ्यो नमः, मुखे । महाकालीमहालक्ष्मीमहासरस्वतीदेवताभ्यो नमः, हृदि । ऐं बीजाय नमः, गुह्ये। ह्रीं शक्तये नमः, पादयोः । क्लीं कीलकाय नमः, नाभौ ।

ṛṣyādinyāsaḥ

brahmaviṣṇurudrarṣibhyo namaḥ, śirasi । *gāyatryuṣṇiganuṣṭupchandobhyo namaḥ, mukhe* । *mahākalīmahālakṣmīmahāsa-*

rasvatīdevatābhyo namaḥ hṛdi । aiṁ bijāya namaḥ, guhye । hrīm śaktaye namaḥ, pādayoḥ । klīm kīlakāya namaḥ, nābhau ।

ॐ ऐं ह्रीं क्लीं चामुण्डायै विच्चे-इति मूलेन करौ संशोध्य-

oṁ aiṁ hrīṁ klīṁ cāmundāyai vicce–iti mūlena karau saṁśodhya-

Perform *karanyāsa* after purifying hands while reciting the above basic *mantra.*

करन्यासः

ॐ ऐं अङ्गुष्ठाभ्यां नमः। ॐ ह्रीं तर्जनीभ्यां नमः। ॐ क्लीं मध्यमाभ्यां नमः। ॐ चामुण्डायै अनामिकाभ्यां नमः। ॐ विच्चे कनिष्ठिकाभ्यां नमः। ॐ ऐं ह्रीं क्लीं चामुण्डायै विच्चे करतलकरपृष्ठाभ्यां नमः।

karanyāsaḥ

oṁ aim aṅguṣṭhābhyaṁ namaḥ । oṁ hrīm tarjanībhyāṁ namaḥ । oṁ klīṁ madhyamābhyāṁ namaḥ । oṁ cāmuṇḍāyai anāmikābhyāṁ namaḥ। oṁ vicce kaniṣṭhikābhyāṁ namaḥ । oṁ aiṁ hrīṁ klīṁ cāmuṇḍāyai vicce karatalakarapṛṣṭhābhyāṁ namaḥ ।

हृदयादिन्यासः

ॐ ऐं हृदयाय नमः। ॐ ह्रीं शिरसे स्वाहा। ॐ क्लीं शिखायै वषट्। ॐ चामुण्डायै कवचाय हुम्। ॐ विच्चे नेत्रत्रयाय वौषट्। ॐ ऐं ह्रीं क्लीं चामुण्डायै विच्चे अस्त्राय फट्।

hṛdayādinyāsaḥ

oṁ aiṁ hṛdayāya namaḥ। oṁ hrīṁ śirase svāhā । oṁ klīṁ śikhāyai vaṣaṭ । oṁ cāmuṇḍāyai kavacāya hum । om vicce netratrayāya vauṣaṭ ⁝ aiṁ hrīṁ klīṁ cāmuṇḍāyai vicce astrāya phaṭ ।

अक्षरन्यास:

ॐ ऐं नमः, शिखायाम्। ॐ ह्रीं नमः, दक्षिणनेत्रे। ॐ क्लीं नमः, वामनेत्रे। ॐ चां नमः, दक्षिणकर्णे। ॐ मुं नमः, वामकर्णे। ॐ डां नमः, दक्षिणनासापुटे। ॐ यैं नमः, वामनासापुटे। ॐ विं नमः, मुखे। ॐ च्चें नमः, गुह्ये।

akṣaranyāsaḥ

oṁ aiṁ namaḥ, śikhāyām। oṁ hrīṁ namaḥ, dakṣiṇanetre। oṁ klīṁ namaḥ, vāmanetre। oṁ cāṁ namaḥ, dakṣiṇakarṇe। oṁ muṁ namaḥ, vāmakarṇe। oṁ ḍāṁ namaḥ, dakṣiṇanāsāpuṭe। oṁ yaiṁ namaḥ, vāmanāsāpuṭe। oṁ viṁ namaḥ, mukhe। oṁ cceṁ namaḥ, guhye।

एवं विन्यस्याष्टवारं मूलेन व्यापकं कुर्यात्

evaṁ vinyasyāṣṭavāraṁ mūlena vyāpakaṁ kuryāt

Thus entrusting, it should be extended all over by chanting the basic *mantra* eight times.

दिङ्न्यास:

ॐ ऐं प्राच्यै नमः। ॐ ऐं आग्नेय्यै नमः। ॐ ह्रीं दक्षिणायै नमः। ॐ ह्रीं नैर्ऋत्यै नमः। ॐ क्लीं प्रतीच्यै नमः। ॐ क्लीं वायव्यै नमः। ॐ चामुण्डायै उदीच्यै नमः। ॐ चामुण्डायै ऐशान्यै नमः। ॐ ऐं ह्रीं क्लीं चामुण्डायै विच्चे भूम्यै नमः।

diṅnyāsaḥ

oṁ aiṁ prācyai namaḥ। oṁ aiṁ āgneyyai namaḥ। oṁ hrīṁ dakṣiṇāyai namaḥ। oṁ hrīm nairṛtyai namaḥ। oṁ klīm pratīcyai namaḥ। oṁ klīṁ vāyavyai namaḥ। oṁ cāmuṇḍāyai udīcyai namaḥ। oṁ cāmuṇḍāyai aiśānyai namaḥ। oṁ aiṁ hrīm klīm cāmuṇḍāyai vicce bhūmyai namaḥ।

ध्यानम्

dhyānam

खड्गं चक्रगदेषुचापपरिघाञ्छूलं भुशुण्डीं शिरः
शङ्खं संदधतीं करैस्त्रिनयनां सर्वाङ्गभूषावृताम् ।
नीलाश्मद्युतिमास्यपाददशकां सेवे महाकालिकां
यामस्तौत्स्वपिते हरौ कमलजो हन्तुं मधुं कैटभम् ॥१॥

1 *khaḍgaṁ cakragadeṣucāpaparighāñchūlaṁ bhuśuṇḍīṁ śiraḥ*
śaṅkhaṁ saṁdadhatīṁ karaistrinayanāṁ sarvāṅgabhūṣāvṛtām ।
nīlāśmadyutimāsyapādadaśakāṁ seve mahākālikāṁ
yāmastautsvapite harau kamalajo hantuṁ madhuṁ kaiṭabham ॥

अक्षस्रक्परशुं गदेषुकुलिशं पद्मं धनुः कुण्डिकां
दण्डं शक्तिमसिं च चर्म जलजं घण्टां सुराभाजनम् ।
शूलं पाशसुदर्शने च दधतीं हस्तैः प्रसन्नाननां
सेवे सैरिभमर्दिनीमिह महालक्ष्मीं सरोजस्थिताम् ॥२॥

2 *akṣasrakparaśuṁ gadeṣukuliśaṁ padmaṁ dhanuḥ kuṇḍikāṁ*
daṇḍaṁ śaktimasiṁ ca carma jalajaṁ ghaṇṭāṁ surābhājanam ।
śūlaṁ pāśasudarśane ca dadhatīm hastaiḥ prasannānanāṁ
seve sairibhamardinīmiha mahālakṣmīṁ sarojasthitām ॥

घण्टाशूलहलानि शङ्खमुसले चक्रं धनुः सायकं
हस्ताब्जैर्दधतीं घनान्तविलसच्छीतांशुतुल्यप्रभाम् ।
गौरीदेहसमुद्भवां त्रिजगतामाधारभूतां महा-
पूर्वामत्र सरस्वतीमनुभजे शुम्भादिदैत्यार्दिनीम् ॥३॥

3 *ghaṇṭāśūlāhalāni śaṅkhamusale cakraṁ dhanuḥ sāyakaṁ*
hastābjairdadhatīṁ ghanāntavilasacchītāṁśutulyaprabhām ।
gaurīdehasamudbhavāṁ trijagatāmādhārabhūtāṁ mahā-
pūrvāmatra sarasvatīmanubhaje śumbhādidaityārdinīm ॥

In this way, following न्यास (*nyāsa*) and meditation, worship of the Goddess should be performed with mental equipment (*mānasika upacāra*). Thereafter, the *Navārṇa Mantra* should be repeated 108 or 1008 times. Before, however, the commencement of the repetition of this *Mantra*, worship of the rosary should be performed with this *Mantra*: *aim hrīm akṣamālikāyai namaḥ* and the following prayer should be recited:

ॐ मां माले महामाये सर्वशक्तिस्वरूपिणि ।
चतुर्वर्गस्त्वयि न्यस्तस्तस्मान्मे सिद्धिदाभव ।।
ॐ अविघ्नं कुरु माले त्वं गृह्णामि दक्षिणे करे ।
जपकाले च सिद्ध्यर्थं प्रसीद मम सिद्धये ।।

ॐ अक्षमालाधिपतये सुसिद्धिं देहि देहि सर्वमन्त्रार्थसाधिनि साधय
साधय सर्वसिद्धिं परिकल्पय परिकल्पय मे स्वाहा ।

oṁ māṁ māle mahāmāye sarvaśaktisvarūpiṇi ।
caturvargastvayi nyastastasmānme siddhidābhava ।।
oṁ avighnaṁ kuru māle tvaṁ gṛhṇāmi dakṣine kare ।
japakāle ca siddhyartham prasīda mama siddhaye ।।

oṁ akṣamālādhipataye susiddhiṁ dehi dehi
sarvamantrārthasādhini sādhaya sādhaya sarvasiddhim
parikalpaya parikalpaya me svāhā ।

After the prayer, *japa* should be performed which, on completion, should be offered to the Goddess with the following *śloka*.

गुह्यातिगुह्यगोप्त्री त्वं गृहाणास्मत्कृतं जपम् ।
सिद्धिर्भवतु मे देवि त्वत्प्रसादान्महेश्वरि ।।

guhyātiguhyagoptrī tvam gṛhāṇāsmatkṛtam japam ।
siddhirbhavatu me devi tvatprasādānmahesvari ।।

Thereafter करन्यासः (*karanyāsaḥ*) as follows:

ॐ ह्रीं अङ्गुष्ठाभ्यां नमः। ॐ चं तर्जनीभ्यां नमः। ॐ डिं मध्यमाभ्यां नमः। ॐ कां अनामिकाभ्यां नमः। ॐ यै कनिष्ठिकाभ्यां नमः। ॐ ह्रीं चण्डिकायै करतलकरपृष्ठाभ्यां नमः।

oṁ hrīṁ anguṣṭhābhyāṁ namaḥ । *oṁ caṁ tarjanībhayāṁ namaḥ* । *oṁ ḍiṁ madhyamābhyāṁ namaḥ* । *oṁ kāṁ anāmikābhyāṁ namaḥ* । *oṁ yai kaniṣṭhikābhyāṁ namaḥ* । *oṁ hrīm caṇḍikāyai karatalakarapṛṣṭhābhyāṁ namaḥ*।

हृदयादिन्यासः

hṛdayādinyāsaḥ

ॐ खड्गिनी शूलिनी घोरा गदिनी चक्रिणी तथा।
शंखिनी चापिनी बाणभुशुण्डीपरिघायुधा॥ हृदयाय नमः।

ॐ शूलेन पाहि नो देवि पाहि खड्गेन चाम्बिके।
घण्टास्वनेन नः पाहि चापज्यानिःस्वनेन च॥ शिरसे स्वाहा।

ॐ प्राच्यां रक्ष प्रतीच्यां च चण्डिके रक्ष दक्षिणे।
भ्रामणेनात्मशूलस्य उत्तरस्यां तथेश्वरि॥ शिखायै वषट्।

ॐ सौम्यानि यानि रूपाणि त्रैलोक्ये विचरन्ति ते।
यानि चात्यर्थघोराणि तै रक्षास्मांस्तथा भुवम्॥ कवचाय हुम्।

ॐ खड्गशूलगदादीनि यानि चास्त्राणि तेऽम्बिके।
करपल्लवसङ्गीनि तैरस्मान् रक्ष सर्वतः॥ नेत्रत्रयाय वौषट्।

ॐ सर्वस्वरूपे सर्वेशे सर्वशक्तिसमन्विते।
भयेभ्यस्त्राहि नो देवि दुर्गे देवि नमोऽस्तु ते॥ अस्त्राय फट्।

oṁ khaḍginī śūlinī ghorā gadinī cakriṇī tathā ।
śaṅkhinī cāpīnī bāṇabhuśuṇḍīparighāyudhā ।
hṛdayāya namaḥ ।

oṁ śūlena pāhi no devi pāhi khaḍgena cāmbike ।
ghaṇṭāsvanena naḥ pāhi cāpajyāniḥsvanena ca ॥
śirase svāhā ।

oṁ *prācyāṁ rakṣa pratīcyāṁ ca caṇḍike rakṣa dakṣiṇe* ।
bhrāmaṇenātmaśūlasya uttarasyāṁ tatheśvari ॥
śikhāyai vaṣaṭ

oṁ *ṣaumyāni yāni rūpāṇi trailokye vicaranti te* ।
yāni cātyarthaghorāṇi tai rakṣāsmāṁstathā bhuvam ॥
kavacāya hum ।

oṁ *khaḍgaśūlagadādīni yānī cāstrāṇi te 'mbike* ।
karapallavasaṅgīni tairasmān rakṣā sarvataḥ ॥
netratrayāya vauṣaṭ ।

oṁ *sarvasvarūpe sarveśe sarvaśaktisamanvite* ।
bhayebhyastrāhi no devi durge devi namo 'stu te ॥
astrāya phaṭ ।

ध्यानम्

dhyānam

ॐ विद्युद्दामसमप्रभां मृगपतिस्कन्धस्थितां भीषणां
कन्याभिः करवालखेटविलसद्धस्ताभिरासेवितास् ।
हस्तैश्चक्रगदासिखेटविशिखांश्चापं गुणं तर्जनीं
बिभ्राणामनलात्मिकां शशिधरां दुर्गां त्रिनेत्रां भजे ॥

oṁ *vidyuddāmasamaprabhāṁ mṛgapatiskandhasthitāṁ bhīṣaṇāṁ*
kanyābhiḥ karavālakheṭavilasaddhastābhirāsevitām ।
hastaiścakragadāsikheṭaviśikhāṁścāpaṁ guṇaṁ tarjanīṁ ॥
bibhrāṇāmanalātmikāṁ śaśidharāṁ durgāṁ trinetrāṁbhaje ॥

ऋग्वेदोक्तं देवीसूक्तम्

13. *Ṛgvedoktaṁ Devīsūktam*

Ṛgvedic Hymn to the Goddess

(X. 10. 125)

ॐ अहमित्यष्टर्चस्य सूक्तस्य वागाम्भृणी ऋषिः, सच्चित्सुखात्मकः सर्वगतः परमात्मा देवता, द्वितीयाया ऋचो जगती, शिष्टानां त्रिष्टुप् छन्दः, देवी-माहात्म्यपाठे विनियोगः ॥

oṁ. ahamityaṣṭarcasya sūktasya vāgāmbhṛṇī ṛṣiḥ, saccitsukhātmakaḥ. sarvagataḥ paramātmā devatā, dvitīyāyā ṛco jagatī, śiṣṭānāṁ triṣṭup chandaḥ, devīmāhātmyapāṭhe viniyogaḥ ॥

Om. Of this hymn comprising eight verses, I, *Vāk*, daughter of *Ambhṛṇa*, am the seer; *Paramātmā* (the Supreme Soul), Existence, Consciousness and Bliss that is omnipresent, is the deity. *Jagatī* is the metre for the second verse and *Triṣṭup* for the rest. Presented here in the context of the 'Glory of the Goddess.'

ध्यानम्

dhyānam

Meditation

ॐ सिंहस्था शशिशेखरा मरकतप्रख्यैश्चतुर्भिर्भुजैः
शङ्खं चक्रधनुःशरांश्च दधती नेत्रैस्त्रिभिः शोभिता ।
आमुक्ताङ्गदहारकङ्कणरणत्काञ्चीरणन्नूपुरा
दुर्गा दुर्गतिहारिणी भवतु नो रत्नोल्लसत्कुण्डला ॥

oṁ. siṁhasthā śaśiśekharā markataprakhyaiścaturbhirbhujaiḥ
śaṅkhaṁ cakradhanuḥśarāṁśca dadhatī netraistribhiḥ śobhitā ।
āmuktāṅgadahārakaṇkaṇaraṇatkāñcīraṇannūpurā
durgā durgatihāriṇī bhavatu no ratnollasatakuṇḍalā ॥

Oṁ. May *Durgā* be the destroyer of our misfortune. She is saddled on the Lion, wears the crown of Moon. In her four arms which shine like emerald, she wields the Conch, Discus, Bow and Arrow. With Three Eyes, she looks beautiful. Her limbs are adorned with bracelets, necklace, tinkling ornaments, girdle and anklets; bejewelled earrings shimmer in her ears.

देवीसूक्तम् (ऋग्वेद 10.10.125)

devīsūktam (Ṛgveda X. 10.125)

ॐ अहं रुद्रेभिर्वसुभिश्चराम्यहमादित्यैरुत विश्वदेवैः ।
अहं मित्रावरुणोभा बिभर्म्यहमिन्द्राग्नी अहमश्विनोभा ।।१।।

1. *oṁ. ahaṁ rudrebhirvasubhiścarāmyahamādityairuta viśvadevaiḥ* ।
ahaṁ mitrāvaruṇobhā bibharmyahamindrāgnī ahmaśvinobhā ।।

Hymn to the Goddess

Oṁ. I move with *Rudras, Vasus, Ādityas* and *Viśva-devas.* I support both *Mitra* and *Varuṇa,* (as well as) *Indra, Agni* and the two *Aśvinīkumāras.*

अहं सोममाहनसं बिभर्म्यहं त्वष्टारमुत पूषणं भगम् ।
अहं दधामि द्रविणं हविष्मते सुप्राव्ये यजमानाय सुन्वते ।।२।।

2. *ahaṁ somamāhanasaṁ bibharmyahaṁ tvaṣṭāramuta pūṣaṇaṁ bhagam* ।
ahaṁ dadhāmi draviṇaṁ haviṣmate suprāvye yajamānāya sunvate ।।

I support *Soma,* the slayer of enemies; *Tvaṣṭā, Pūṣā* and *Bhaga.* I grant blessings and riches to the sacrificer who, equipped with oblations, humbly offers them to the gods.

अहं राष्ट्री संगमनी वसूनां चिकितुषी प्रथमा यज्ञियानाम् ।
तां मा देवा व्यदधुः पुरुत्रा भूरिस्थात्रां भूर्य्यावेशयन्तीम् ।।३।।

3. *ahaṁ rāṣṭrī saṅgamanī vasūnāṁ cikituṣī prathamā*
yajñiyānām ।
tāṁ mā devā vyadadhuḥ purutrā bhūristhātrāṁ
bhūryyāveśayantīm ।।

I am the ruler of the universe. All *Vasus,* the guardians of treasures, are united in me. I am the foremost among those to whom sacrifice is addressed and the first among the gods who are worshipped. They have diffused me in all directions. I abide in many places and reveal myself in many ways.

मया सो अन्नमत्ति यो विपश्यति यः प्राणिति य ईं शृणोत्युक्तम् ।
अमन्तवो मां त उप क्षियन्ति श्रुधि श्रुत श्रद्धिवं ते वदामि ।।४।।

4. *mayā so annamatti yo vipaśyati yaḥ*
prāṇiti ya īṁ ṣṛṇotyuktam ।
amantavo māṁ ta upa ksiyanti śrudhi
śruta śraddhivaṁ te vadāmi ।।

Through me all mortals eat, see, breathe and hear what is uttered. Though they know it not, they abide in me. O Learned One! hear me as I speak to you the Truth that is accessible through Reverential Faith.

अहमेव स्वयमिदं वदामि जुष्टं देवेभिरुत मानुषेभिः ।
यं कामये तं तमुग्रं कृणोमि तं ब्रह्माणं तमृषिं तं सुमेधाम् ।।५।।

5. *ahameva svayamidaṁ vadāmi juṣṭaṁ*
devebhiruta mānuṣebhiḥ ।
yaṁ kāmaye taṁ tamugraṁ kṛnomi
taṁ brahmāṇam tamṛṣiṁ taṁ sumedhām ।।

I myself speak this truth which gratifies the gods as well as men. Him I make powerful whom I want to be so; him I make the seer, the knower of *Brahman* and highly intelligent.

अहं रुद्राय धनुरा तनोमि ब्रह्मद्विषे शरवे हन्तवा उ ।
अहं जनाय समदं कृणोम्यहं द्यावापृथिवी आ विवेश ॥६॥

6. *ahaṁ rudrāya dhanurā tanomi brahmadviṣe śarave hantavā u* ।
ahaṁ janāya samadaṁ kṛṇoymyahaṁ dyāvāpṛthivī ā viveśa ॥

To slay the antagonists of the Vedic lore, I draw the bow for *Rudra*; I delight my devotees. I pervade heaven and earth.

अहं सुवे पितरमस्य मूर्धन्मम योनिरप्स्वन्तः समुद्रे ।
ततो वि तिष्ठे भुवनानु विश्वोतामूं द्यां वर्ष्मणोप स्पृशामि ॥७॥

7. *ahaṁ suve pitaramasya mūrdhanmama*
yonirapsvantaḥ samudre ।
tato vi tiṣṭhe bhuvanānu viśvo-
tāmūṁ dyāṁ varṣmaṇopa spṛśāmi ॥

On top of this creation, I credit the Supreme Father. My creative power fills the waters of the infinite ocean. From these I spread into all the worlds of the universe and with my sublimity touch the heaven beyond.

अहमेव वात इव प्रवाम्यारभमाणा भुवनानि विश्वा ।
परो दिवा पर एना पृथिव्यैतावती महिना संबभूव ॥८॥

8. *ahameva vāta iva pravāmyārabhamāṇā bhuvanāni viśvā* ।
paro divā para enā pṛthivyaitāvatī mahinā saṁbabhūva ॥

I verily blow intensely like the wind and set the worlds of the universe into motion. In my own majesty, I have become so great that I shine forth beyond heaven and earth.

अथ तन्त्रोक्तं देवीसूक्तम्

14. *Atha Tantroktaṁ Devīsūktam*

Hymn to the Goddess from *Tantra*

After the Ṛgvedic Hymn to the Goddess, Hymn to the Goddess from the *Tantra* is to be recited. It has thirty *mantras.*

नमो देव्यै महादेव्यै शिवायै सततं नमः ।
नमः प्रकृत्यै भद्रायै नियताः प्रणताः स्म ताम् ॥१॥

1. *namo devyai mahādevyai śivāyai satataṁ namaḥ* ।
namaḥ prakṛtyai bhadrāyaī niyatāḥ praṇatāḥ sma tām ॥

Obeisance to the Goddess, the Supreme Goddess. Obeisance forever to *Śivā*, the Goddess of Felicity. Obeisance to *Prakṛti,* the Primordial Nature. Obeisance to *Bhadrā,* the Laudable. We bow in salutation to her unfailingly.

रौद्रायै नमो नित्यायै गौर्यै धात्र्यै नमो नमः ।
ज्योत्स्नायै चेन्दुरूपिण्यै सुखायै सततं नमः ॥२॥

2. *raudrāyai namo nityāyai gauryai dhātryai namo namaḥ* ।
jyotsnāyai cendurūpiṇyai sukhāyai satataṁ namaḥ ॥

Obeisance to *Raudrā,* the Formidable. Obeisance to *Nityā,* the Eternal. Obeisance to *Gaurī,* the Fair-complexioned. Obeisance to *Dhātrī,* the Nurturer. Obeisance to *Jyotsnā,* the Effulgence and Intrinsic Nature of the Moon. Obeisance always to *Sukhā,* the Felicity.

कल्याण्यै प्रणतां वृद्ध्यै सिद्ध्यै कुर्मो नमो नमः ।
नैर्ऋत्यै भूभृतां लक्ष्म्यै शर्वाण्यै ते नमो नमः ॥३॥

3. *kalyāṇyai praṇatāṁ vṛddhyai siddhyai kurmo namo namaḥ* ।
nairṛtyai bhūbhṛtāṁ lakṣmyai śarvāṇyai te namo namaḥ ॥

Obeisance again and again to *Vṛddhi,* the Augmentation and *Siddhi,* the Accomplishment, engaged in the welfare of those who seek refuge in her. Obeisance, obeisance to

Nairṛti, the Fortune of the demons; *Lakṣmī*, the Prosperity of the kings and *Sarvāṇī*, the consort of Lord *Śiva*.

दुर्गायै दुर्गपारायै सारायै सर्वकारिण्यै ।
ख्यात्यै तथैव कृष्णायै धूम्रायै सततं नमः ॥४॥

4. *durgāyai durgapārāyai sārāyai sarvakāriṇyai* ।
khyātyai tathaiva kṛṣṇāyai dhūmrāyai satataṁ namaḥ ॥

Repeated obeisance to *Durgā*, the Impassable; *Durgapārā*, the Deliverer from Calamity; *Sārā*, the Quintessence of All; *Sarvakāriṇī*, the Cause of All; *Khyāti*, the Fame; *Kṛṣṇā*, the Dark-complexioned (or the Consort of *Viṣṇu*) and *Dhūmrā*, the One Risen from the Smoke of the Sacrificial Fire).

अतिसौम्यातिरौद्रायै नतास्तस्यै नमो नमः ।
नमो जगत्प्रतिष्ठायै देव्यै कृत्यै नमो नमः ॥५॥

5. *atisaumyātiraudrāyai natāstasyai namo namaḥ* ।
namo jagatpratiṣṭhāyai devyai kṛtyai namo namaḥ ॥

We bow before and pay obeisance to *Atisaumyā*, Extremely Gentle and Charming and *Atiraudrā*, Extremely Wrathful. Obeisance again and again to the Goddess *Kṛti*, the Substratum of the World.

या देवी सर्वभूतेषु विष्णुमायेतिशब्दिता ।
नमस्तस्यै नमस्तस्यै नमस्तस्यै नमो नमः ॥६॥

6. *yā devī sarvabhūteṣu viṣṇumāyeti śabditā* ।
namastasyai namastasyai namastasyai namo namaḥ ॥

To the Goddess who is known among all beings as *Viṣṇumāyā*, the Illusive Power of Lord *Viṣṇu*: obeisance, obeisance, obeisance again and again.

या देवी सर्वभूतेषु चेतनेत्यभिधीयते ।
नमस्तस्यै नमस्तस्यै नमस्तस्यै नमो नमः ॥७॥

7. *yā devī sarvabhūteṣu cetanetyabhidhīyate* ।
namastasyai namastasyai namastasyai namo namaḥ॥

To the Goddess who is known as *Cetanā*, the Consciousness, in all beings: obeisance, obeisance, obeisance again and again.

या देवी सर्वभूतेषु बुद्धिरूपेण संस्थिता ।
नमस्तस्यै नमस्तस्यै नमस्तस्यै नमो नमः ॥८॥

8. *yā devī sarvabhūteṣu buddhirūpeṇa saṁsthitā* ।
namastasyai namastasyai namastasyai namo namaḥ ॥

To the Goddess who abides in all beings as *Buddhi*, the Intellect: obeisance, obeisance, obeisance again and again.

या देवी सर्वभूतेषु निद्रारूपेण संस्थिता ।
नमस्तस्यै नमस्तस्यै नमस्तस्यै नमो नमः ॥९॥

9. *yā devī sarvabhūteṣu nidrārūpeṇa saṁsthitā* ।
namastasyai namastasyai namastasyai namo namaḥ ॥

To the Goddess who abides in all beings as *Nidrā*, Sleep: obeisance, obeisance, obeisance again and again.

या देवी सर्वभूतेषु क्षुधारूपेण संस्थिता ।
नमस्तस्यै नमस्तस्यै नमस्तस्यै नमो नमः ॥१०॥

10. *yā devī sarvabhūteṣu kṣudhārūpeṇa saṁsthita* ।
namastasyai namastasyai namastasyai namo namaḥ ॥

To the Goddess who abides in all beings as *Kṣudhā*, Hunger: obeisance, obeisance, obeisance again and again.

या देवी सर्वभूतेषुच्छायारूपेण संस्थिता।
नमस्तस्यै नमस्तस्यै नमस्तस्यै नमो नमः ॥११॥

11. *yā devī sarvabhūteṣucchāyārūpeṇa saṁsthitā* ।
namastasyai namastasyai namastasyai namo namaḥ ॥

To the Goddess who abides in all beings as *Chāyā*, Reflection: obeisance, obeisance, obeisance again and again.

या देवी सर्वभूतेषु शक्तिरूपेण संस्थिता ।
नमस्तस्यै नमस्तस्यै नमस्तस्यै नमो नमः ॥१२॥

12. *yā devī sarvabhūteṣū śaktirupeṇa saṁsthitā* ।
namastasyai namastasyai namastasyai namo namaḥ ॥

To the Goddess who abides in all beings as *Śaktī*, Energy: obeisance, obeisance, obeisance again and again.

या देवी सर्वभूतेषु तृष्णारूपेण संस्थिता ।
नमस्तस्यै नमस्तस्यै नमस्तस्यै नमो नमः ॥१३॥

13. *yā devī sarvabhūteṣu tṛṣnānrūpeṇa saṁsthitā* ।
namastasyai namastasyai namastasyai namo namaḥ ॥

To the Goddess who abides in all beings as *Tṛṣṇā*, Desire: obeisance, obeisance, obeisance again and again.

या देवी सर्वभूतेषु क्षान्तिरूपेण संस्थिता ।
नमस्तस्यै नमस्तस्यै नमस्तस्यै नमो नमः ॥१४॥

14. *yā devī sarvabhūteṣu kṣāntirūpeṇa saṁsthitā* ।
namastasyai namastasyai namastasyai namo namaḥ ॥

To the Goddess who abides in all beings as *Kṣānti*, Forgiveness: obeisance, obeisance, obeisance again and again.

या देवी सर्वभूतेषु जातिरूपेण संस्थिता ।
नमस्तस्यै नमस्तस्यै नमस्तस्यै नमो नमः ॥१५॥

15. *yā devī sarvabhūteṣu jātirūpeṇa saṁsthitā* ।
namastasyai namastasyai namastasyai namo namaḥ ॥

To the Goddess who abides in all beings as *Jāti*, Lineage: obeisance obeisance, obeisance, again and again.

या देवी सर्वभूतेषु लज्जारूपेण संस्थिता ।
नमस्तस्यै नमस्तस्यै नमस्तस्यै नमो नमः ॥१६॥

16. *yā devī sarvabhūteṣu lajjārūpeṇa saṁsthitā* ।
namastasyai namastasyai namastasyai namo namaḥ ॥

To the Goddess who abides in all beings as *Lajjā*, Modesty : obeisance, obeisance, obeisance again and again.

या देवी सर्वभूतेषु शान्तिरूपेण संस्थिता।
नमस्तस्यै नमस्तस्यै नमस्तस्यै नमो नमः ॥१७॥

17. *yā devī sarvabhūteṣu śāntirūpeṇa saṁsthitā* ।
namastasyai namastasyai namastasyai namo namaḥ ॥

To the Goddess who abides in all beings as *Śānti*, Tranquility : obeisance, obeisance, obeisance again and again.

या देवी सर्वभूतेषु श्रद्धारूपेण संस्थिता।
नमस्तस्यै नमस्तस्यै नमस्तस्यै नमो नमः ॥१८॥

18. *yā devī sarvabhūteṣu śraddhārūpeṇa saṁsthitā* ।
namastasyai namastasyai namastasyai namo namaḥ ॥

To the Goddess who abides in all beings as *Śraddhā*, Reverential Faith : obeisance, obeisance, obeisance again and again.

या देवी सर्वभूतेषु कान्तिरूपेण संस्थिता।
नमस्तस्यै नमस्तस्यै नमस्तस्यै नमो नमः ॥१९॥

19. *yā devī sarvabhūteṣu kāntirūpeṇa saṁsthitā* ।
namastasyai namastasyai namastasyai namo namaḥ ॥

To the Goddess who abides in all beings as *Kānti*, Brilliance : obeisance, obeisance, obeisance again and again.

या देवी सर्वभूतेषु लक्ष्मीरूपेण संस्थिता।
नमस्तस्यै नमस्तस्यै नमस्तस्यै नमो नमः ॥२०॥

20. *yā devī sarvabhūteṣu lakṣmīrūpeṇa saṁsthitā* ।
namastasyai namastasyai namastasyai namo namaḥ ॥

To the Goddess who abides in all beings as *Lakṣmī*, Prosperity and Fortune : obeisance, obeisance, obeisance again and again.

या देवी सर्वभूतेषु वृत्तिरूपेण संस्थिता ।
नमस्तस्यै नमस्तस्यै नमस्तस्यै नमो नमः ॥२१॥

21. *yā devī sarvabhūteṣu vṛttirūpeṇa saṁsthitā* ।
namastasyai namastasyai namastasyai namo namaḥ ॥

To the Goddess who abides in all beings as *Vṛtti*, Occupation : obeisance, obeisance, obeisance again and again.

या देवी सर्वभूतेषु स्मृतिरूपेण संस्थिता ।
नमस्तस्यै नमस्तस्यै नमस्तस्यै नमो नमः ॥२२॥

22. *yā devī sarvabhūteṣu smṛtirūpeṇa saṁsthitā* ।
namastasyai namastasyai namastasyai namo namaḥ ॥

To the Goddess who abides in all beings as *Smṛti*, Recollection : obeisance, obeisance, obeisance again and again.

या देवी सर्वभूतेषु दयारूपेण संस्थिता ।
नमस्तस्यै नमस्तस्यै नमस्तस्यै नमो नमः ॥२३॥

23. *yā devī sarvabhūteṣu dayārūpeṇa saṁsthitā* ।
namastasyai namastasyai namastasyai namo namaḥ ॥

To the Goddess who abides in all beings as *Dayā*, Compassion : obeisance, obeisance, obeisance again and again.

या देवी सर्वभूतेषु तुष्टिरूपेण संस्थिता ।
नमस्तस्यै नमस्तस्यै नमस्तस्यै नमो नमः ॥२४॥

24. *yā devī sarvabhūteṣu tuṣṭirūpeṇa saṁsthitā* ।
namastasyai namastasyai namastasyai namo namaḥ ॥

To the Goddess who abides in all beings as *Tuṣṭi*, Contentment : obeisance, obeisance, obeisance again and again.

या देवी सर्वभूतेषु मातृरूपेण संस्थिता ।
नमस्तस्यै नमस्तस्यै नमस्तस्यै नमो नमः ॥२५॥

25. *yā devī sarvabhūteṣu matṛrūpeṇa saṁsthitā* ।
namastasyai namastasyai namastasyai namo namaḥ ॥

To the Goddess who abides in all beings as *Mātā*, the Mother : obeisance, obeisance, obeisance again and again.

या देवी सर्वभूतेषु भ्रान्तिरूपेण संस्थिता ।
नमस्तस्यै नमस्तस्यै नमस्तस्यै नमो नमः ॥२६॥

26. *yā devī sarvabhūteṣu bhrāntirūpeṇa saṁsthitā* ।
namastasyai namastasyai namastasyai namo namaḥ ॥

To the Goddess who abides in all beings as *Bhrānti*, Confusion : obeisance, obeisance, obeisance again and again.

इन्द्रियाणामधिष्ठात्री भूतानां चाखिलेषु या ।
भूतेषु सततं तस्यै व्याप्तिदेव्यै नमो नमः ॥२७॥

27. *indriyāṇāmadhiṣṭhātrī bhūtānāṁ cakhileṣu yā* ।
bhūteṣu satataṁ tasyai vyāptidevyai namo namaḥ ॥

We pay obeisance again and again and continually to the Goddess *Vyāpti*, thc Pcrmcating Spirit, who as the substratum of senses, abides in all beings and elements.

चितिरूपेण या कृत्स्नमेतद्व्याप्य स्थिता जगत् ।
नमस्तस्यै नमस्तस्यै नमस्तस्यै नमो नमः ॥२८॥

28. *citirūpeṇa yā kṛtsnametadvyāpya sthitā jagat* ।
namastasyai namastasyai namastasyai namo namaḥ ॥

To the Goddess who as *Citi*, Wisdom, pervades as the abiding spirit in the entire world: obeisance, obeisance, obeisance again and again.

स्तुता सुरैः पूर्वमभीष्टसंश्रया-
त्तथा सुरेन्द्रेण दिनेषु सेविता ।
करोतु सा नः शुभहेतुरीश्वरी
शुभानि भद्राण्यभिहन्तु चापदः ॥२६॥

29. *stutā suraiḥ pūrvamabhīṣṭasaṁśrayāt-*
tathā surendreṇa dineṣu sevitā ।
karotu sā naḥ śubhaheturīśvarī
śubhāni bhadrāṇyabhihantu cāpadaḥ ॥

May the Supreme Goddess, the Sovereign Empress, the Instrument of Fortune, whom the gods, led by *Indra* eulogised and served for many days in the olden times, bestow auspiciousness and blessings upon us and obliterate all calamities.

या साम्प्रतं चोद्धतदैत्यतापितै-
रस्माभिरीशा च सुरैर्नमस्यते ।
या च स्मृता तत्क्षणमेव हन्ति नः
सर्वापदो भक्तिविनम्रमूर्तिभिः ॥३०॥

30. *yā sāṁpratam coddhatadaityatāpitair-*
asmābhirīśā ca surairnamasyate ।
yā ca smṛta tatkṣaṇameva hanti naḥ
sarvāpado bhaktivinamramūrtibhiḥ ॥

We, the gods, now tormented by the impudent demons, pay obeisance to that Supreme Empress who, on being remembered by the persons with bowed heads and with devotion, humility and reverence, instantly destroys all calamities.

श्रीसप्तशतीरहस्यत्रयम्

15. *Śrīsaptaśatīrahasyatrayam*

Trilogy of Secrets of the *Saptaśatī*

ॐ अस्य श्रीसप्तशतीरहस्यत्रयस्य नारायण ऋषिरनुष्टुप्छन्दः महाकाली-
महालक्ष्मीमहासरस्वत्यो देवता यथोक्तफलावाप्त्यर्थं जपे विनियोगः ।

oṁ. asya śrīsaptaśatīrahasyatrayasya nārāyaṇa
ṛṣiranuṣṭupchandaḥ mahākālīmahālakṣmīmahāsarasvatyo
devatā yathoktaphalāvāptyarthaṁ jape viniyogaḥ ।

Oṁ. Of this Trilogy of Secrets of the Seven Hundred *ślokas* celebrating *Durgā, Nārāyaṇa* is the seer, *Anuṣṭup* is the metre, *Mahākālī, Mahālakṣmī, Mahāsarasvatī* are the deities. Here presented is this recital for attaining to the fruits as mentioned.

अथ प्राधानिकं रहस्यम्

15.1 *Atha Prādhānikaṁ Rahasyam*

The Pre-eminent Secret

राजोवाच

rājovāca

भगवन्नवतारा मे चण्डिकायास्त्वयोदिताः ।
एतेषां प्रकृतिं ब्रह्मन् प्रधानं वक्तुमर्हसि ॥१॥

1. *bhagavannavatārā me caṇḍikāyāstvayoditāḥ* ।
eteṣāṁ prakṛtiṁ brahman pradhānaṁ vaktumarhasi ॥

The king said

You have, O noble seer! explained to me the incarnations of *Caṇḍikā*. O *Brahman*! tell me about their pre-eminent nature now.

आराध्यं यन्मया देव्याः स्वरूपं येन च द्विज ।
विधिना ब्रूहि सकलं यथावत्प्रणतस्य मे ॥२॥

2. *ārādhyaṁ yanmayā devyāḥ svarūpam yena ca dvija* ।
vidhinā brūhi sakalaṁ yathāvatpraṇatasya me ॥

O sage! to me who has sought refuge in you, please reveal in detail the form of the Goddess I have to worship and the procedure to be followed by me.

ऋषिरुवाच

ṛṣiruvāca

इदं रहस्यं परममनाख्येयं प्रचक्षते ।
भक्तोऽसीति न मे किञ्चित्तवावाच्यं नराधिप ॥३॥

3. *idaṁ rahasyaṁ paramamanākhyeyaṁ pracakṣate* ।
bhakto 'sīti na me kiñcittavāvācyaṁ narādhipa ॥

This, it is said, is the highest secret not to be narrated. But o king! since you are my devotee, there is nothing that cannot be shared with you.

सर्वास्याद्या महालक्ष्मीस्त्रिगुणा परमेश्वरी ।
लक्ष्यालक्ष्यस्वरूपा सा व्याप्य कृत्स्नं व्यवस्थिता ।।४।।

4. *sarvāsyādyā mahālakṣmīstriguṇā parameśvarī* ।
lakṣyālākṣyasvarūpā sā vyāpya kṛtsnaṁ vyavasthitā ।।

Foremost among all is *Mahālakṣmī*, the Great Fortune. She is the Supreme Empress. In her rest three modes (*Sāttvika* – good or lightness; *Rājasika* – passion or activity and *Tāmasika* – stupor or darkness). She is of visible as well as invisible forms. She pervades the entire universe.

मातुलुङ्गं गदां खेटं पानपात्रं च बिभ्रती ।
नागं लिङ्गं च योनिं च बिभ्रती नृप मूर्धनि ।।५।।

5. *mātuluṅgaṁ gadāṁ kheṭaṁ pānapātraṁ ca bibhratī*।
nāgaṁ liṅgaṁ ca yoniṁ ca bibhratī nṛpa mūrdhani।।

She holds a citron, a mace, a shield and a drinking vessel in her hands. On her head, o king! she bears a serpent, a liṅga (phallus) and a yoni (uterus) [symbols of creation].

तप्तकाञ्चनवर्णाभा तप्तकाञ्चनभूषणा ।
शून्यं तदखिलं स्वेन पूरयामास तेजसा ।।६।।

6. *taptakāñcanavarṇābhā taptakāñcanabhūṣaṇā* ।
śūnyaṁ tadakhilaṁ svena pūrayāmāsa tejasā ।।

The lustre of her body resembles heated gold. Of the heated gold are her ornaments. She has filled the entire space with her effulgence.

शून्यं तदखिलं लोकं विलोक्य परमेश्वरी ।
बभार परमं रूपं तमसा केवलेन हि ।।७।।

7. *śūnyaṁ tadakhilaṁ lokaṁ vilokya parameśvarī* ।
babhāra paramaṁ rūpaṁ tamasā kevalena hi ।।

When that Supreme Empress looked at the entire void, she assumed another excellent form through her power of darkness.

सा भिन्नाञ्जनसंकाशा दंष्ट्राङ्कितवरानना ।
विशाललोचना नारी बभूव तनुमध्यमा ॥८॥

8. *sā bhinnāñjanasaṁkāśā daṁṣṭrāṅkitavarānanā* ।
viśālalocanā nārī babhūva tanumadhyamā ॥

She became a woman whose complexion matched the colour of shining collyrium. Her mouth with conspicuous teeth, was lovely. She was wide eyed and had a slender waist.

खड्गपात्रशिरः खेटैरलंकृतचतुर्भुजा ।
कबन्धहारं शिरसा बिभ्राणा हि शिरःस्रजम् ॥९॥

9. *khaḍgapātraśiraḥ kheṭairalaṁkṛtacaturbhujā* ।
kabandhahāraṁ śirasā bibhrāṇā hi śiraḥsrajam ॥

She had four arms adorned with the Sword, Vessel, Skull and Shield. She wore a garland of headless trunks around her neck and necklace of skulls around her head.

सा प्रोवाच महालक्ष्मीं तामसी प्रमदोत्तमा ।
नाम कर्म च मे मातर्देहि तुभ्यं नमो नमः ॥१०॥

10. *sā provāca mahālakṣmīṁ tāmasī pramadottamā* ।
nāma karma ca me mātardehi tubhyaṁ namo namaḥ ॥

That most elegant lady of dark complexion, spoke to *Mahālakṣmī:* obeisance to you, O Mother, again and again; give me my name and assign me my functions.

तां प्रोवाच महालक्ष्मीस्तामसीं प्रमदोत्तमाम् ।
ददामि तव नामानि यानि कर्माणि तानि ते ॥११॥

11. *tāṁ provāca mahālakṣmīstāmasīṁ pramadottamām* ।
dadāmi tava nāmāni yāni karmāṇi tāni te ॥

To that most elegant lady of dark complexion, *Mahālakṣmī* said: I give you your names and assign ycu whatever your functions are.

महामाया महाकाली महामारी क्षुधा तृषा ।
निद्रा तृष्णा चैकवीरा कालरात्रिर्दुरत्यया ।।१२।।

12. *mahāmāyā mahākālī mahāmārī kṣudhā tṛṣā* ।
nidrā tṛṣṇā caikavīrā kālarātrirduratyayā ।।

इमानि तव नामानि प्रतिपाद्यानि कर्मभिः ।
एभिः कर्मणि ते ज्ञात्वा योऽधीते सोऽश्नुते सुखम् ।।१३।।

13. *imāni tava nāmāni pratipādyāni karmabhiḥ* ।
ebhiḥ karmaṇi te jñatvā yo 'dhīte so 'śnute sukham ।।

Mahāmāyā, the Great Illusion; *Mahākālī*, the Great Darkness; *Mahāmarī*, the Great Epidemic; *Kṣudhā*, Hunger; *Tṛṣā*, Thirst; *Nidrā*, Sleep; *Tṛṣṇā*, Desire; *Ekavīrā*, the Sole Heroine; *Kālarātri*, the Night of Death and *Duratyayā*, the Most Invincible: these are your names which are indicative of your functions.

तामित्युक्त्वा महालक्ष्मीः स्वरूपमपरं नृप ।
सत्त्वाख्येनातिशुद्धेन गुणेनेन्दुप्रभं दधौ ।।१४।।

14. *tāmityuktvā mahālakṣmīḥ svarūpamaparaṁ nṛpa* ।
sattvākhyenātiśuddhena guṇenenduprabhaṁ dadhau ।।

Having told her thus, O king, *Mahālakṣmī* assumed another form by her unsurpassably pure power, called *sattva*, which in its quality of lustre, matched the moon.

अक्षमालाङ्कुशधरा वीणापुस्तकधारिणी ।
सा बभूव वरा नारी नामान्यस्यै च सा ददौ ।।१५।।

15. *akṣamālāṅkuśadharā vīṇāpustakadhāriṇī* ।
sā babhūva varā nārī nāmānyasyai ca sā dadau ।।

She became another excellent woman sporting a rosary of beads, a curved sword and holding a hook and a lute in her hands. To her she gave (the following) names :

महाविद्या महावाणी भारती वाक् सरस्वती ।
आर्या ब्राह्मी कामधेनुर्वेदगर्भा च धीश्वरी ।।१६।।

16. *mahāvidyā mahāvāṇī bhāratī vāk sarasvatī* ।
āryā brāhmī kāmadhenurvedagarbhā ca dhīśvarī ।।

Mahāvidyā, the Great Knowledge; *Mahāvāṇī,* the Great Speech; *Bhāratī,* Eloquence; *Vāk,* Voice; *Sarasvatī,* the Elegant Learning; *Āryā,* the Noble One; *Brāhmī, Brahmā's* Consort; *Kāmadhenu,* Wish-fulfilling Cow; *Vedagarbhā,* the Source of the *Vedas* and *Dhīśvarī,* the Ruler of Intellect.

अथोवाच महालक्ष्मीर्महाकालीं सरस्वतीम् ।
युवां जनयतां देव्यौ मिथुने स्वानुरूपतः ।।१७।।

17. *athovāca mahālakṣmīrmahākālīṁ sarasvatīm* ।
yuvāṁ janayatāṁ devyau mithune svānurūpataḥ ।।

Then *Mahālakṣmī* said to *Mahākālī* and *Mahāsarasvatī,* "Both of you goddesses now produce couples that accord with your respective natures."

इत्युक्त्वा ते महालक्ष्मीः ससर्ज मिथुनं स्वयम् ।
हिरण्यगर्भौ रुचिरौ स्त्रीपुंसौ कमलासनौ ।।१८।।

18. *ityuktvā te mahālakṣmīḥ sasarja mithunaṁ svayam* ।
hiraṇyagarbhau rucirau strīpuṁsau kamalāsanau ।।

After telling them this, *Mahālakṣmī* herself produced a beautiful couple of *Hiraṇyagarbhas* – a female and a male – born of the golden womb; they were seated on a lotus.

ब्रह्मन् विधे विरञ्चेति धातरित्याह तं नरम् ।
श्रीः पद्मे कमले लक्ष्मीत्याह माता च तां स्त्रियम् ।।१९।।

19. *brahman vidhe virañceti dhātarityāha taṁ naram*।
śrīḥ padme kamale lakṣmītyāha mātā ca tāṁ striyam।।

To that male, the Mother addressed as *Brahmā,* the repository of the *Vedas*; *Vidhi,* the Rule Maker and

Regulator and *Dhātā,* the Supporter. The female, she called *Śrī,* Fortune; *Padmā,* Seated on Lotus; *Kamalā,* the Lotus Blossom and *Lakṣmī,* Wealth.

महाकाली भारती च मिथुने सृजतः सह ।
एतयोरपि रूपाणि नामानि च वदामि ते ॥२०॥

20. *mahākālī bhāratī ca mithune sṛjataḥ saha* ।
etayorapi rūpāṇi nāmāni ca vadāmi te ॥

Then *Mahākalī* and *Bhāratī* produced a couple each. Let me tell you their forms and names.

नीलकण्ठं रक्तबाहुं श्वेताङ्गं चन्द्रशेखरम् ।
जनयामास पुरुषं महाकाली सितां स्त्रियम् ॥२१॥

21. *nīlakaṇṭhaṁ raktabāhuṁ śvetāṅgaṁ candraśekharam* ।
janayāmāsa puruṣaṁ mahākālī sitāṁ striyam ॥

स रुद्रः शंकरः स्थाणुः कपर्दी च त्रिलोचनः ।
त्रयी विद्या कामधेनुः सा स्त्री भाषाक्षरा स्वरा ॥२२॥

22. *sa rudraḥ śaṅkaraḥ sthāṇuḥ kapardī ca trilocanaḥ* ।
trayī vidyā kāmadhenuḥ sā strī bhāṣākṣarā svarā ॥

Mahākālī gave birth to a male with a blue throat, red arms and white limbs, with moon on his forehead and to a white-complexioned female. The male was (known as) *Rudra,* the Formidable; *Śaṅkara,* the Propitious; *Sthāṇu,* the Unchangeable; *Kapardī,* One with Matted Hair and *Trilocana,* Three-Eyed. That female was (called) *Trayī,* Embodiment of the *Vedic* Knowledge; *Vidyā,* Science; *Kāmadhenu,* the Wish-fulfilling Cow; *Bhāṣā,* the Language, *Akṣarā,* the Imperishable Letter and *Svarā,* the Utterance.

सरस्वती स्त्रियं गौरीं कृष्णं च पुरुषं नृप ।
जनयामास नामानि तयोरपि वदामि ते ॥२३॥

23. *sarasvātī striyaṁ gaurīṁ kṛṣṇam ca puruṣaṁ nṛpa* ।
janayāmāsa nāmāni tayorapi vadāmi te ॥

Sarasvatī gave birth to a white-complexioned female and a dark-complexioned male. Their names too I shall tell you.

विष्णुः कृष्णो हृषीकेशो वासुदेवो जनार्दनः ।
उमा गौरी सती चण्डी सुन्दरी सुभगा शिवा ।।२४।।

24. *viṣṇuḥ kṛṣṇo hṛṣīkeśo vāsudevo janārdanaḥ* ।
umā gaurī satī caṇḍī sundarī subhagā śivā ।।

(The male was known as) *Viṣṇu*, the All-pervading; *Kṛṣṇa*, Who Draws the Evil Out and Draws People unto Him; *Hṛṣīkeśa*, the Controller of Senses; *Vāsudeva*, the Son of *Vasudeva* and *Janārdana*, Master of the Beings. (The female was called) *Umā*,* *Śiva's* Prosperity; *Gaurī*, the White-complexioned; *Satī*, the Chaste; *Caṇḍī*, Slayer of *Caṇḍa* or the Ferocious One; *Sundarī*, the Beautiful One; *Subhagā*, Illustrious and *Śivā*, the Bestower of Felicity and Consort of *Śiva*.

एवं युवतयः सद्यः पुरुषत्वं प्रपेदिरे ।
चक्षुष्मन्तो नु पश्यन्ति नेतरेऽतद्विदोजनाः ।।२५।।

25. *evaṁ yuvatayaḥ sadyaḥ puruṣatvaṁ prapedire* ।
cakṣuṣmanto nu paśyanti netare 'tadvidojanāḥ ।।

In this way, the three maidens instantly attained to the male form. Only those endowed with the discerning eye see it, other persons can never know it.

ब्रह्मणे प्रददौ पत्नीं महालक्ष्मीर्नृपत्रयीम्।
रुद्राय गौरीं वरदां वासुदेवाय च श्रियम्।।२६।।

26. *brahmaṇe pradadau patnīṁ mahālakṣmīrnṛpatrayīm* ।
rudrāya gaurīṁ vardāṁ vāsudevāya ca śriyam ।।

---

* According to Kālidāsa, Umā is derived as follows: उ(u) मेति(meti): oh! do not go for penance. When at a very young age, Pārvatī goes to the forest for penance so that she can secure Śiva as her husband, her mother cried उ मा (u ma): don't go.

O king! *Mahālakṣmī* presented *Trayī* (*Sarasvatī*) to *Brahmā* for a wife, *Gaurī*, the Bestower of Boons, to *Rudra* and *Śrī* to *Vāsudeva* (*Viṣṇu*)

स्वरया सह सम्भूय विरिञ्चोऽण्डमजीजनत् ।
बिभेद भगवान् रुद्रस्तद् गौर्या सह वीर्यवान् ॥२७॥

27. *svarayā saha sambhūya viriñco 'ṇḍamajījanat* ।
bibheda bhagavān rudrastad gauryā sahavīryavān ॥

In association with *Svarā* (*Sarasvatī*), *Viriñci* (*Brahmā*) produced *brahmāṇḍā*, the primordial egg. It was broken by the mighty Lord *Rudra* in association with *Gaurī*.

अण्डमध्ये प्रधानादि कार्यजातमभून्नृप ।
महाभूतात्मकं सर्वं जगत्स्थावरजङ्गमम् ॥२८॥

28. *aṇḍamadhye pradhānādi kāryajātamabhūnnṛpa* ।
mahābhūtātmakaṁ sarvaṁ jagatsthāvarajaṅgamam ॥

In the centre of that egg, O king! was born all the primary matter from which evolved the entire world of animates and inanimates consisting of the five elements.

पुपोष पालयामास तल्लक्ष्म्या सह केशवः ।
संजहार जगत्सर्वं सह गौर्या महेश्वरः ॥२९॥

29. *pupoṣa pālayāmāsa tallakṣmyā saha keśavaḥ* ।
saṁjahāra jagtsarvaṁ saha gauryā maheśvaraḥ ॥

Keśava (*Viṣṇu*), along with *Lakṣmī* nurtured and sustained the entire world which the Supreme Lord *Śiva*, along with *Gaurī*, dissolved.

महालक्ष्मीर्महाराज सर्वसत्त्वमयीश्वरी ।
निराकारा च साकारा सैव नानाभिधानभृत् ॥३०॥

30. *mahālakṣmīrmahārāja sarvasattvamayīśvarī* ।
nirākārā ca sākārā saiva nānābhidhānabhṛt ॥

नामान्तरैर्निरूप्यैषा नाम्ना नान्येन केनचित् ॥ॐ॥३१॥

31. *nāmāntarairnirūpyaiṣā nāmnā nānyena kenacit* ॥*oṁ*॥

O Emperor! The Supreme Sovereign *Mahālakṣmī* is the True Nature of all. She is without form as well as with form and she bears many names. She ought to be determined by several other names, not just by this (*Mahālakṣmī*).

इति प्राधानिकं रहस्यं सम्पूर्णम् ।

iti prādhānikaṁ rahasyaṁ sampūrṇam ।

Thus concludes The Pre-eminent Secret.

अथ वैकृतिकं रहस्यम्

15.2 *Atha Vaikṛtikaṁ Rahasyam*

The Modified Secret

ऋषिरुवाच

ṛṣiruvāca

ॐ त्रिगुणा तामसी देवी सात्त्विकी या त्रिधोदिता ।
सा शर्वा चण्डिका दुर्गा भद्रा भगवतीर्यते ॥१॥

1. *oṁ. triguṇā tāmasī devī sāttvikī yā tridhoditā* ।
sā śarvā caṇḍikā durgā bhadrā bhagavatīryate ॥

The seer said

Oṁ. The Goddess (*Mahālakṣmī*), primarily endowed with the mode of purity and lightness who was earlier described in three ways as *Tāmasī*, etc., is also called *Śarvā*, the Destroyer; *Caṇḍikā*, Frightfully Powerful; *Durgā*, the Remover of Obstruction, *Bhadrā*, the Gracious and *Bhagavatī*, the Illustrious.

योगनिद्रा हरेरुक्ता महाकाली तमोगुणा ।
मधुकैटभनाशार्थं यां तुष्टावाम्बुजासनः ॥२॥

2. *yoganidrā hareruktā mahākālī tamoguṇā* ।
madhukaiṭabhanāśārthaṁ yāṁ tuṣṭāvāmbujāsanaḥ ॥

Mahākāli of deep stupor and darkness whom the lotus-seated *Brahmā* propitiated for slaying *Madhu* and *Kaiṭabha* is called *Yoganidrā*, the Mystic Sleep of Lord *Viṣṇu.*

दशवक्त्रा दशभुजा दशपादाञ्जनप्रभा ।
विशालया राजमाना त्रिंशल्लोचनमालया ॥३॥

3. *daśavaktrā daśabhujā daśapādāñjanaprabhā* ।
viśālayā rājamānā triṁśallocanamālayā ॥

She is of the hue of collyrium, has ten visages, ten arms and ten feet. She looks beautiful with the spacious row of thirty eyes.

स्फुरद्दशनदंष्ट्रा सा भीमरूपापि भूमिप ।
रूपसौभाग्यकान्तीनां सा प्रतिष्ठा महाश्रियः ॥४॥

4. *sphuraddaśanadaṁṣṭrā sā bhīmarūpāpi bhūmipa* ।
rūpasaubhāgyakāntīnāṁ sā pratiṣṭhā mahāśriyaḥ ॥

O king! although she is of ferocious looks with shining teeth and fangs, she is the substratum of all beauty, fortune, lustre and great affluence.

खड्गबाणगदाशूलचक्रशङ्खभुशुण्डिभृत् ।
परिघं कार्मुकं शीर्षं निश्च्योतद्रुधिरं दधौ ॥५॥

5. *khaḍgabāṇagadāśūlacakraśaṅkhabhuśuṇḍibhṛt* ।
parighaṁ kārmukaṁ śīrṣaṁ niścyotadrudhiraṁ dadhau ॥

She holds a sword, an arrow, a mace, a pike, a discus, a conch, a missile, a club, a bow and a head dripping with blood.

एषा सा वैष्णवी माया महाकाली दुरत्यया ।
आराधिता वशीकुर्यात् पूजाकर्तुश्चराचरम् ॥६॥

6. *eṣā sā vaiṣṇavī māyā mahākālī duratyayā* ।
ārādhitā vaśīkuryāt pūjākartuścarācaram ॥

This *Mahākālī*, the Illusive and the Impassable Power of Lord *Viṣṇu*, gets the entire world of animates and inanimates under the control of the worshipper who propitiates her.

सर्व देवशरीरेभ्यो याऽऽविर्भूतामितप्रदा ।
त्रिगुणा सा महालक्ष्मीः साक्षान्महिषमर्दिनी ॥७॥

7. *sarva devaśarīrebhyo yā ''virbhūtāmitapradā* ।
triguṇā sā mahālakṣmīḥ sākṣānmahiṣamardinī ॥

This *Mahālakṣmī* of three modes who became manifest from the bodies of all the gods is the purveyor of boundless fortune and is the vertiable slayer of *Mahiṣa.*

श्वेतानना नीलभुजा सुश्वेतस्तनमण्डला ।
रक्तमध्या रक्तपादा नीलजङ्घोरुरुन्मदा ॥८॥

8. *śveatānanā nīlabhujā suśvetastanamaṇḍalā* ।
raktamadhyā raktapādā nīlajaṅghorurunmadā ॥

Her face is fair, arms blue, orbs of breasts glowing white. She has red waist, red feet and blue shanks and thighs and is intoxicated.

सुचित्रजघना चित्रमाल्याम्बरविभूषणा ।
चित्रानुलेपना कान्ति रूपसौभाग्यशालिनी ॥९॥

9. *sucitrajaghanā citramālyāmbaravibhūṣanā* ।
citrānulepanā kānti rūpasaubhāgyaśālinī ॥

Of varied hues and attractive are her hips and loins. She wears garlands, garments and ornaments of variegated colours. She is an embodiment of lustre, beauty and fortune.

अष्टादशभुजा पूज्या सा सहस्रभुजा सती ।
आयुधान्यत्र वक्ष्यन्ते दक्षिणाधःकरक्रमात् ॥१०॥

10. *aṣṭādaśabhujā pūjyā sā sahasrabhujā satī* ।
āyudhānyatra vakṣyante dakṣiṇādhaḥkarakramāt ॥

Although she has thousands of arms, she is to be worshipped as of eighteen arms. Elsewhere are being described her weapons in the order from her lowest right hand (up to the lowest left hand).

अक्षमाला च कमलं बाणोऽसिः कुलिशं गदा ।
चक्रं त्रिशूलं परशुः शङ्खो घण्टा च पाशकः ॥११॥

11. *akṣamālā ca kamalaṁ bāṇo 'si kuliśaṁ gadā* ।
cakraṁ triśūlaṁ paraśuḥ śaṅkho ghaṇṭā ca pāśakaḥ ॥

शक्तिर्दण्डश्चर्म चापं पानपात्रं कमण्डलुः ।
अलंकृतभुजामेभिरायुधैः कमलासनाम् ॥१२॥

12. *śaktirdaṇḍaścarma cāpaṁ pānapātraṁ kamaṇḍaluḥ* ।
alaṁkṛtabhujāmebhirāyudhaiḥ kamalāsanām ॥

सर्व देवमयीमीशां महालक्ष्मीमिमां नृप ।
पूजयेत्सर्वलोकानां स देवानां प्रभुर्भवेत् ।।१३।।

13. *sarvadevamayīmīśāṁ mahālakṣmīmimām nṛpa* ।
pūjayetsarvalokānāṁ sa devānaṁ prabhurbhavet ।।

A rosary of beads, a lotus, an arrow, a sword, a thunderbolt, a mace, a discus, a trident, a battle-axe, a conch, a bell, a snare, a missile, a staff, a shield, a bow, a drinking vessel and a water pot. He, o king! who worships this *Mahālakṣmī*, whose arms are adorned with these weapons, who is seated on a lotus and in whom all the gods abide, becomes the lord of all the gods.

गौरीदेहसमुद्भूता या सत्त्वैकगुणाश्रया ।
साक्षात्सरस्वती प्रोक्ता शुम्भासुरनिबर्हिणी ।।१४।।

14. *gaurīdehasamudbhūtā yā sattvaikaguṇāśrayā* ।
sākṣātsarasvatī proktā śumbhāsuranibarhiṇī ।।

Manifested from the body of *Gaurī*, settled only in the *sattvaguṇa,* total purity, she is known as the veritable *Sarasvatī* who slayed *Śumbha,* the demon.

दधौ चाष्टभुजा बाणमुसले शूलचक्रभृत् ।
शङ्खं घण्टां लाङ्गलं च कार्मुकं वसुधाधिप ।।१५।।

15. *dadhau cāṣṭabhujā bāṇamusale śūlacakrabhṛt* ।
śaṅkhaṁ ghaṇṭāṁ lāṅgalaṁ ca kārmukaṁ vasudhādhipa ।।

O lord of earth! She has eight arms in which she has an arrow, a club, a pike, a discus, a conch, a bell, a plough and a bow.

एषा सम्पूजिता भक्त्या सर्वज्ञत्वं प्रयच्छति ।
निशुम्भमथिनी देवी शुम्भासुरनिबर्हिणी ।।१६।।

16. *eṣā sampūjitā bhaktyā sarvajñatvaṁ prayacchati* ।
niśumbhamathinī devī śumbhāsuranibarhiṇī ।।

This Goddess who trampled *Niśumbha* and slayed the demon *Śumbha*, makes him omniscient who worships her with devotion.

इत्युक्तानि स्वरूपाणि मूर्तीनां तव पार्थिव ।
उपासनं जगन्मातुः पृथगासां निशामय ।।१७।।

17. *ityuktāni svarūpāṇi mūrtīnāṁ tava pārthiva* ।
upāsanaṁ jaganmātuḥ pṛthagāsāṁ niśāmaya ।।

Heretofore, o king! I have described to you the true forms of the Goddess. Now listen to the individual procedure of worship of each of these forms of the Mother of the universe.

महालक्ष्मीर्यदा पूज्या महाकाली सरस्वती ।
दक्षिणोत्तरयोः पूज्ये पृष्ठतो मिथुनत्रयम् ।।१८।।

18. *mahālakṣmīryadā pūjyā mahākālī sarasvatī* ।
dakṣiṇottaryoḥ pūjye pṛṣṭhato mithunatrayam ।।

When *Mahālakṣmī* is to be worshipped, then *Mahākālī* and *Mahāsarasvatī* should be installed in the southern and northern directions respectively and behind them the three couples.

विरञ्चिः स्वरया मध्ये रुद्रो गौर्या च दक्षिणे ।
वामे लक्ष्म्या हृषीकेशः पुरतो देवतात्रयम् ।।१९।।

19. *virañciḥ svarayā madhye rudro gauryā ca dakṣiṇe* ।
vāme lakṣmyā hṛṣīkeśaḥ purato devatātrayam ।।

Virañci (*Brahmā*) with *Svarā* (*Sarasvatī*) (exactly behind *Mahālakṣmī*) should be in the centre, *Rudra* and *Gaurī* to their right and *Lakṣmī* and *Viṣṇu* to the left. In front of the three Goddesses, including *Mahālakṣmi*, the following three Goddesses should also be worshipped.

अष्टादशभुजामध्ये वामे चास्यादशानना ।
दक्षिणेऽष्टभुजा लक्ष्मीर्महतीति समर्चयेत् ।।२०।।

20. *aṣṭādaśabhujāmadhye vāme cāsyādaśānanā* ।
dakṣiṇe 'ṣṭabhujā lakṣmīrmahatīti samarcayet ।।

Mahālakṣmī of eighteen arms in the centre, (*Mahākālī*) of ten visages to her left and (*Mahāsarasvatī*) of eight arms should be worshipped to her right. Thus *Mahālakṣmī* is to be elaborately worshipped.

अष्टादशभुजा चैषा यदा पूज्या नराधिप ।
दशानना चाष्टभुजा दक्षिणोत्तरयोस्तदा ।।२१।।

21. *aṣṭādaśbhujā caiṣā yadā pūjyā narādhipa* ।
daśānanā cāṣṭabhujā dakṣiṇottarayostadā ।।

कालमृत्यू च सम्पूज्यौ सर्वारिष्टप्रशान्तये ।
यदा चाष्टभुजा पूज्या शुम्भासुरनिबर्हिणी ।।२२।।

22. *kālamṛtyū ca sampūjyau sarvāriṣṭapraśāntaye* ।
yadā cāṣṭabhujā pūjyā śumbhāsuranibarhiṇī ।।

नवास्याः शक्तयः पूज्यास्तदा रुद्रविनायकौ ।
नमो देव्या* इति स्तोत्रैर्महालक्ष्मीं समर्चयेत् ।।२३।।

23. *navāsyāḥ śaktayaḥ pūjyāstadā rudravināyakau* ।
namo devyā iti stotrairmahālakṣmīṁ samarcayet* ।।

When, O ruler of men! this Goddess of eighteen arms (*Mahālakṣmī*) or the one with ten faces (*Mahākalī*) or the one with eight arms (*Mahāsarasvatī*) is to be exclusively worshipped, then, to pacify all evil portents, *Kāla* (Time) and *Mṛtyu* (Death) should be worshipped on right and left. When the Goddess of Eight Arms, the Slayer of the demon *Śumbha*, is to be worshipped, her nine Energies (*Brāhmī, Māheśvarī, Kaumarī, Vaiṣṇavī, Vārāhī, Nārasiṁhī, Aindrī, Śivadūtī* and *Cāmuṇḍā*) and *Rudra* and *Vināyaka*

---

*Refers to *mantras* 9-32, Ch. V of the 'Glory of the Goddess'.

(*Gaṇeśa*) should also be worshipped. The Goddess *Mahālakṣmī* should be worshipped with the hymns 'Obeisance to the Goddess',* etc.!

अवतारत्रयार्चायां स्तोत्रमन्त्रास्तदाश्रयाः ।
अष्टादशभुजा चैषा पूज्या महिषमर्दिनी ।।२४।।

24. *avatāratrayārcāyāṁ stotramantrāstadāśrayāḥ* ।
aṣṭādaśabhujā caiṣā pūjyā mahiṣamardinī ।।

महालक्ष्मीर्महाकाली सैव प्रोक्ता सरस्वती ।
ईश्वरी पुण्यपापानां सर्वलोकमहेश्वरी ।।२५।।

25. *mahālakṣmīrmahākālī saiva proktā sarasvatī* ।
īśvarī puṇyapāpānāṁ sarvalokamaheśvarī ।।

While worshipping the three incarnations, hymns and *mantras* pertaining to them should be recited. (In the main) worship of this Goddess of Eighteen Arms, the Slayer of *Mahiṣāsura,* is to be performed. She is herself called *Mahalakṣmī, Mahākālī* and *Mahāsarasvatī*@. She is the Arbiter of Virtue and Vice and the Supreme Empress of all the worlds.

महिषान्तकरी येन पूजिता स जगत्प्रभुः ।
पूजयेज्जगतां धात्री चण्डिकां भक्तवत्सलाम् ।।२६।।

26. *mahiṣāntakarī yena pūjitā sa jagatprabhuḥ* ।
pūjayejjagatāṁ dhātrī caṇḍikāṁ bhaktavatsalām ।।

He who has worshipped the Destroyer of *Mahiṣa,* becomes the master of this world. Worship, therefore, *Caṇḍikā,* the Substratum of the World, who loves her devotees as their Mother.

---

*Refers to *mantras* 9-82, Ch. V of the 'Glory of the Goddess'.

@ It means that, in different forms, with different names, the Mother Goddess is essentially one and the same.

अर्घ्यादिभिरलंकारैर्गन्धपुष्पैस्तथाक्षतैः ।
धूपैर्दीपैश्च नैवेद्यैर्नानाभक्ष्यसमन्वितैः ।।२७।।

27. *arghyādibhiralaṁkārairgandhapuṣpaistathākṣataiḥ* ।
dhūpairdīpaiśca naivedyairnānābhakṣyasamanvitaiḥ ।।

रुधिराक्तेन बलिना मांसेन सुरया नृप ।
(बलिमांसादिपूजेयं विप्रवर्ज्या मयेरिता ।।
तेषां किल सुरामांसैर्नोक्ता पूजा नृप क्वचित् ।)
प्रणामाचमनीयेन चन्दनेन सुगन्धिना ।।२८।।

28. *rudhirāktena balinā māṁsena surayā nṛpa* ।
(balimāṁsādipūjeyaṁ vipravarjyā mayeritā ।।
teṣāṁ kila surāmāṁsairnoktā pūjā nṛpa kvacit ।)
praṇāmācamanīyena candanena sugandhinā ।।

सकर्पूरैश्च ताम्बूलैर्भक्तिभावसमन्वितैः ।
वामभागेऽग्रतो देव्याश्छिन्नशीर्षं महासुरम् ।।२९।।

29. *sakarpūraiśca tāmbūlairbhaktibhāvasamanvitaiḥ* ।
vāmabhāge 'grato devyāśchinnaśīrṣaṁ mahāsuram ।।

पूजयेन्महिषं येन प्राप्तं सायुज्यमीशया ।
दक्षिणे पुरतः सिंहं समग्रं धर्ममीश्वरम् ।।३०।।

30. *pūjayenmahiṣaṁ yena prāptaṁ sāyujyamīśayā* ।
dakṣiṇe purataḥ siṁhaṁ samagraṁ dharmamīśvaram ।।

वाहनं पूजयेद्देव्या धृतं येन चराचरम् ।
कुर्याच्च स्तवनं धीमांस्तस्या एकाग्रमानसः ।।३१।।

31. *vāhanaṁ pūjayeddevyā dhṛtaṁ yena carācaram* ।
kuryācca stavanaṁ dhīmāṁstasyā ekāgramānasaḥ ।।

(The Goddess may be worshipped with) the offering of oblations, etc., ornaments, perfumes, flowers and whole grains, with incenses, lamps and several varieties of food; sacrifice of blood, meat and wine (worship with sacrificial blood and meat, etc., is, however, prescribed for non-

brāhmaṇas; for *brāhmaṇas* O king! worship with meat and wine is not prescribed anywhere); with obeisance, ritual sipping of water, offering of sandal perfume, camphor and betel nut, with complete devotion. On the left, in front of the Goddess, *Mahiṣa* of chopped head, who attained *sāyujya*, complete union with her, should be worshipped. On her right, in the front, the Lion, the mount of the Goddess, the embodiment of righteousness, the sovereign who upholds the world of the animates and inanimates, should be worshipped. Then, the wise person should, with completely attentive mind, recite the eulogy of the Goddess.

ततः कृताञ्जलिर्भूत्वा स्तुवीत चरितैरिमैः ।
एकेन वा मध्यमेन नैकेनेतरयोरिह ॥३२॥

32. *tataḥ kṛtañjalirbhūtva stuvīta caritairimaiḥ* ।
ekena vā madhyamena naikenetarayoriha ॥

Thereafter, with folded hands, he should propitiate her with all these Acts. If one opts for reciting only one Act, he should recite the Middle act but not either the First or the Final act.

चरितार्धं तु न जपेज्जपञ्छिद्रमवाप्नुयात् ।
प्रदक्षिणानमस्कारान् कृत्वा मूर्ध्नि कृताञ्जलिः ॥३३॥

33. *caritārdhaṁ tu na japejjapañchidramavāpnuyāt* ।
pradakṣiṇānamaskārān kṛtvā mūrdhni kṛtāñjaliḥ ॥

क्षमापयेज्जगद्धात्रीं मुहुर्मुहुरतन्द्रितः ।
प्रतिश्लोकं च जुहुयात्पायसं तिलसर्पिषा ॥३४॥

34. *kṣamāpayejjagaddhātrīṁ muhurmuhuratandritaḥ* ।
pratiślokaṁ ca juhuyātpāyasaṁ tilasarpiṣā ॥

A half Act must never be recited. Recitation of the Half-Act renders it deficient. Placing folded hands on the head and circumambulating, the fully alert devotee should seek pardon of the Goddess again and again. With each *śloka* (of Glory of the Goddess), an offering of milk, sesame and ghee should be made in the sacrificial fire.

जुहुयात्स्तोत्रमन्त्रैर्वा चण्डिकायै शुभं हविः ।
भूयो नामपदैर्देवीं पूजयेत्सुसमाहितः ।।३५।।

35. *juhuyātstotramantrairvā caṇḍikāyai śubhaṁ haviḥ* ।
bhūyo nāmapadairdevīṁ pūjayetsusamāhitaḥ ।।

Or, he should perform sacrifice for *Caṇḍikā* with auspicious oblations, chanting the *mantras.* After this, he should again, with full concentration, chant the *mantras* comprising the names of the Goddess.

प्रयतः प्राञ्जलिः प्रह्वः प्रणम्यारोप्य चात्मनि ।
सुचिरं भावयेदीशां चण्डिकां तन्मयो भवेत् ।।३६।।

36. *prayataḥ prāñjaliḥ prahvaḥ praṇamyāropya cātmani* ।
suciraṁ bhāvayedīśāṁ caṇḍikāṁ tanmayo bhavet ।।

Thereafter, controlling mind and senses, with his hands folded and head bowed in obeisance, he should meditate upon *Caṇḍikā* within his heart fully absorbed in her.

एवं यः पूजयेद्भक्त्या प्रत्यहं परमेश्वरीम् ।
भुक्त्वा भोगान् यथाकामं देवीसायुज्यमाप्नुयात् ।।३७।।

37. *evaṁ yaḥ pūjayedbhaktyā pratyahaṁ parameśvarīm* ।
bhuktvā bhogān yathākāmaṁ devīsāyujyamāpnuyāt ।।

He who, thus, worships the Sovereign Goddess every day with devotion, attains to *Devī- sāyujya* (gets united with her) after enjoying all the desired pleasures.

यो न पूजयते नित्यं चण्डिकां भक्तवत्सलाम् ।
भस्मीकृत्यास्य पुण्यानि निर्दहेत्परमेश्वरी ।।३८।।

38. *yo na pūjayate nityaṁ caṇḍikāṁ bhaktavatsalām* ।
bhasmīkṛtyāsya puṇyāni nirdahetparameśvarī ।।

He who does not worship *Caṇḍikā*, the affectionate Mother to her devotees, every day, his good deeds are burnt and reduced to ashes by the Supreme Goddess.

तस्मात्पूजय भूपाल सर्वलोकमहेश्वरीम् ।
यथोक्तेन विधानेन चण्डिकां सुखमाप्स्यसि ।।३६।।

39. *tasmātpūjaya bhūpala sarvalokamaheśvarīm* ।
yathoktena vidhānena caṇḍikāṁ sukhamāpsyasi ।।

Worship therefore, o king, *Caṇḍikā*, the great ruler of all the worlds, in accordance with the procedure as described and you will attain to happiness.

इति वैकृतिकं रहस्यं सम्पूर्णम् ।

iti vaikṛtikaṁ rahasyaṁ sampūrṇam.

Thus concludes The Modified Secret.

अथ मूर्तिरहस्यम्

15.3 *Atha Mūrtirahasyam*

The Secret of Personifications

ऋषिरुवाच

ṛṣiruvāca

The seer said

ॐ नन्दा भगवती नाम या भविष्यति नन्दजा ।
स्तुता सा पूजिता भक्त्या वशीकुर्याज्जगत्त्रयम् ।।१।।

1. *oṁ. nandā bhagavatī nāma yā bhaviṣyati nandajā* ।
stutā sā pūjitā bhaktyā vaśīkuryājjagattrayam ।।

Oṁ. The name of the Goddess who shall be born as the daughter of *Nanda,* is *Nandā.* Eulogised and worshipped with devotion, she grants the devotee control over the three worlds.

कनकोत्तमकान्तिः सा सुकान्तिकनकाम्बरा ।
देवी कनकवर्णाभा कनकोत्तमभूषणा ।।२।।

2. *kanakottamakantiḥ sā sukāntikanakāmbarā* ।
devī kanakavarṇābhā kanakottamabhūṣaṇā ।।

She Glows like the Finest Gold and Wears clothes of Golden colour. Her Lustre matches the Glistening Gold. The Goddess has a Shining Golden hue and wears Ornaments of the Finest Gold.

कमलाङ्कुशपाशाब्जैरलंकृतचतुर्भुजा ।
इन्दिरा कमला लक्ष्मीः सा श्री रुक्माम्बुजासना ।।३।।

3. *kamalāṅkuśapāśābjairalaṁkṛtacaturbhujā* ।
indirā kamalā lakṣmīḥ sā śrī rukmāmbujāsanā ।।

A lotus, a hook, a snare and a conch adorn her Four Arms. She sits on a golden lotus and her names are *Indirā,* the Ruler; *Kamalā,* Seated on the Lotus; *Lakṣmī,* Affluence and *Śrī,* Majesty.

या रक्तदन्तिका नाम देवी प्रोक्ता मयानघ ।
तस्याः स्वरूपं वक्ष्यामि शृणु सर्वभयापहं ।।४।।

4. *yā raktadantikā nāma devī proktā mayānagha* ।
tasyāḥ svarūpaṁ vakṣyāmi śṛṇu sarvabhayāpaham ।।

O noble king! of the Goddess whom I called by the name *Raktadantikā*, I shall presently narrate the true nature. (Hearing this) all fears are eradicated. Now listen.

रक्ताम्बरा रक्तवर्णा रक्तसर्वाङ्गभूषणा ।
रक्तायुधा रक्तनेत्रा रक्तकेशातिभीषणा ।।५।।

5. *raktāmbarā raktavarṇā raktasarvāṅgabhūṣaṇā* ।
raktāyudhā raktanetrā raktakeśātibhīṣaṇā ।।

रक्ततीक्ष्णनखा रक्तदशना रक्तदन्तिका ।
पतिं नारीवानुरक्ता देवी भक्तं भजेज्जनम् ।।६।।

6. *raktatīkṣṇanakhā raktadaśanā raktadantikā* ।
patiṁ nārīvānuraktā devī bhaktaṁ bhajejjanam ।।

She wears Red Clothes, her Complextion is Red, she Wears Red Ornaments on all her limbs. Her Weapons are Red, Red her Eyes and with her Red Hair, she looks ferocious. Her Nails are Sharp and Red, her Fangs are Red; she has red teeth. The Goddess loves the devotee who worships her, as a wife loves her husband.

वसुधेव विशाला सा सुमेरुयुगलस्तनी ।
दीर्घौ लम्बावतिस्थूलौ तावतीव मनोहरौ ।।७।।

7. *vasudheva viśālā sā sumeruyugalastanī* ।
dīrghau lambāvatisthūlau tāvatīva manoharau ।।

Her figure is Expansive like Earth. Her two Breasts are like the *Sumeru* hills. They are long, full and very heavy and most attractive.

कर्कशावतिकान्तौ तौ सर्वानन्दपयोनिधी ।
भक्तान् सम्पाययेद्देवी सर्वकामदुघौ स्तनौ ॥८॥

8. *karkaśāvatikāntau tau sarvānandapayonidhī* ।
bhaktān sampāyayeddevī sarvakāmadughau stanau ॥

Those two breasts are firm, extremely charming and two oceans of perfect bliss. They fulfil all the desires of the devotees. The Goddess feeds her devotees with them.

खड्गं पात्रं च मुसलं लाङ्गलं च बिभर्ति सा ।
आख्याता रक्तचामुण्डा देवी योगेश्वरीति च ॥९॥

9. *khaḍgaṁ pātraṁ ca musalaṁ lāṅgalaṁ ca bibharti sā* ।
ākhyātā raktacāmuṇḍā devī yogeśvarīti ca ॥

She carries a sword, a vessel, a pestle and a plough in her hands. She is known as *Raktacāmuṇḍā*, the Red Hued Divine Slayer of *Caṇḍa* and *Muṇḍa* and *Yogeśvarī*, the Controller of *yoga*.

अनया व्याप्तमखिलं जगत्स्थावरजङ्गमम् ।
इमां यः पूजयेत्भक्त्या स व्याप्नोति चराचरम् ॥१०॥

10. *anayā vyāptamakhilaṁ jagatsthāvarajaṅgamam* ।
imāṁ yaḥ pūjayetbhaktyā sa vyāpnoti carācaram ॥

This entire world of stationary as well as movable entities is filled by her. He who worships her with devotion, also pervades the entire world of animates and inanimates.

(भुक्त्वा भोगान् यथाकामं देवी सायुज्यमाप्नुयात्।)
(bhuktvā bhogān yathākāmaṁ devī sāyujyamāpnuyāt।)

(After enjoying the desired pleasures, he attains
to *Devī-sāyujya*, i.e., unity with the Goddess)

अधीते य इमं नित्यं रक्तदन्त्या वपुःस्तवम् ।
तं सा परिचरेद्देवी पतिं प्रियमिवाङ्गना ।।११।।

11. *adhīte ya imaṁ nityaṁ raktadantyā vapuḥstavam* ।
taṁ sā paricareddevī patiṁ priyamivāṅganā ।।

He who reads this eulogy of *Raktadantikā's* body, is adored by the Goddess as a beautiful woman adores her husband.

शाकम्भरी नीलवर्णा नीलोत्पलविलोचना ।
गम्भीरनाभिस्त्रिवलीविभूषिततनूदरी ।।१२।।

12. *śākambharī, nīlavarṇā nīlotpalavilocanā* ।
gambhīranābhistrivalīvibhūṣitatanūdarī ।।

Śākambharī, the One Who Nourishes with Vegetation, is of blue complexion and blue eyes. Her navel is deep around which there are three beautifying folds and her waist is slender.

सुकर्कशसमोत्तुङ्गवृत्तपीनघनस्तनी ।
मुष्टिं शिलीमुखापूर्णं कमलं कमलालया ।।१३।।

13. *sukarkaśasamottuṅgavṛttapīnaghanastanī* ।
muṣṭiṁ śilīmukhāpūrṇaṁ kamalaṁ kamalālayā ।।

पुष्पपल्लवमूलादिफलाढ्यं शाकसञ्चयम् ।
काम्यानन्तरसैर्युक्तं क्षुत्तृण्मृत्युभयापहम् ।।१४।।

14. *puṣpapallavamūlādiphalāḍhyaṁ śākasañcayam* ।
kāmyānantarasairyuktaṁ kṣuttṛṇmṛtyubhayāpaham ।।

कार्मुकं च स्फुरत्कान्ति बिभ्रती परमेश्वरी ।
शाकम्भरी शताक्षी सा सैव दुर्गा प्रकीर्तिता ।।१५।।

15. *kārmukaṁ ca sphuratkānti bibhratī parameśvarī* ।
śākambharī śatākṣī sā saiva durgā prakīrtitā ।।

Her beautiful breasts are firm, even, full, round, corpulent and compact. She dwells in the lotus. In her hands, she has a handful of arrows, a lotus, flowers, plants, roots, fruits and a rich collection of very desirable and highly succulent vegetables, which remove the fear of hunger, thirst and death. That Supreme Goddess, is known as *Śākambharī*, the One Who Nourishes with Vegetables; *Śatākṣī*, of Hundred Eyes and also *Durgā*, the Impassable One, wielding a shining bow.

विशोका दुष्टदमनी शमनी दुरितापदाम् ।
उमा गौरी सती चण्डी कालिका सा च पार्वती ।।१६।।

16. *viśokā duṣṭadamanī śamanī duritāpadām* ।
umā gaurī satī caṇḍī kālikā sā ca pārvatī ।।

She, who Alleviates Grief, Subdues the Wicked and Quells Evils and Calamities, is *Umā, Gaurī, Satī, Caṇḍī, Kālikā* and also *Pārvatī.*

शाकम्भरीं स्तुवन् ध्यायञ्जपन् सम्पूजयन्नमन् ।
अक्षय्यमश्नुते शीघ्रमन्नपानामृतं फलम् ।।१७।।

17. *śākambharīm stuvan dhyāyñjapan sampūjayannaman* ।
akṣayyamaśnute śighramannapānāmṛtaṁ phalam ।।

He who propitiates, meditates upon, remembers, worships and reverences *Śākambharī*, is soon blessed with nectar in the form of inexhaustible food, drinks and fruits.

भीमापि नीलवर्णा सा दंष्ट्रादशनभासुरा ।
विशाललोचना नारी वृत्तपीनपयोधरा ।।१८।।

18. *bhīmāpi nīlavarṇā sā daṁṣṭrādaśanabhāsurā* ।
viśālalocanā nārī vṛttapīnapayodharā ।।

The colour of the Goddess *Bhīmā*, the Formidable One, is also Blue. She has Shining Fangs and Teeth. She is a Wide-Eyed woman and her Breasts are Round and Full.

चन्द्रहासं च डमरुं शिरः पात्रं च बिभ्रती ।
एकवीरा कालरात्रिः सैवोक्ता कामदा स्तुता ।।१६।।

19. *candrahāsaṁ ca ḍamaruṁ śiraḥ pātraṁ ca bibhratī* ।
ekavīra kālaratriḥ saivoktā kāmadā stutā ।।

She wields a glittering sword, an hour-glass drum, a severed head and a vessel. She is propitiated as *Ekavīrā,* the Pre-eminent Warrior and *Kālarātri,* the Night of Dissolution and is also called *Kāmadā,* the Granter of Desires.

तेजोमण्डलदुर्धर्षा भ्रामरी चित्रकान्तिभृत् ।
चित्रानुलेपना देवी चित्राभरणभूषिता ।।२०।।

20. *tejomaṇḍaladurdharṣā bhrāmarī citrakāntibhṛt*।
citrānulepanā devī citrābharaṇabhūṣitā।।

Goddess *Bhrāmarī* of Variegated Hues, appears Inviolable owing to the Lustrous Halo around her. She is Anointed with a Variety of Unguents and wears Ornaments of Different Varieties.

चित्रभ्रमरपाणिः सा महामारीति गीयते ।
इत्येता मूर्तयो देव्या याः ख्याता वसुधाधिप ।।२१।।

21. *citrabhramarapāṇiḥ sā mahāmārīti gīyate* ।
ityetā mūrtayo devyā yāḥ khyātā vasudhādhipa ।।

She is extolled as *Citrabhramarapāṇi,* One with Multi-hued Bees in Hand, and *Mahāmārī,* the Great Epidemic. These, O king! are the personifications of the Goddess.

जगन्मातुश्चण्डिकायाः कीर्तिताः कामधेनवः ।
इदं रहस्यं परमम् न वाच्यं कस्यचित्त्वया ।।२२।।

22. *jaganmātuścaṇḍikāyāḥ kīrtitāḥ kāmadhenavaḥ* ।
idaṁ rahasyaṁ paramaṁ na vācyaṁ kasycittvayā ।।

Thus have been explained the personifications of *Caṇḍikā*, which if recited, are like wish-fulfilling cows. This great secret is not to be shared by you (with anyone).

व्याख्यानंदिव्यमूर्तीनामभीष्टफलदायकम् ।
तस्मात् सर्वप्रयत्नेन देवीं जप निरन्तरम् ॥२३॥

23. *vyākhyānaṁdivyamūrtīnāmabhīṣṭaphaladāyakam* ।
tasmāt sarvaprayatnena devīṁ japa nirantaram ॥

This narrative of the divine personifications yields the desired fruits. Therefore, O king! keep quietly repeating the names of the Goddess perpetually with unstinted effort.

सप्तजन्मार्जितैर्घोरैर्ब्रह्महत्यासमैरपि ।
पाठमात्रेण मन्त्राणां मुच्यते सर्वकिल्बिषैः ॥२४॥

24. *saptajanmārjitairghorairbrahmahatyāsamairapi* ।
pāṭhamātreṇa mantrāṇāṁ mucyate sarvakilbiṣaiḥ ॥

Of all the horrible sins and heinous acts, including slaying of a *brāhmaṇa*, accumulated over seven births, a person is absolved if only he recites the *mantras*.

देव्या ध्यानं मया ख्यातं गुह्याद् गुह्यतरं महत् ।
तस्मात् सर्वप्रयत्नेन सर्वकामफलप्रदम् ॥२५॥

25. *devyā dhyānaṁ mayā khyātam guhyād guhyataraṁ mahat* ।
tasmāt sarvaprayatnena sarvakāmaphalapradam ॥

I have, therefore, narrated to you the meditation of the Goddess with all-out effort. It is a greater secret than the highest secrets and bestower of all the desired fruits.

(एतस्यास्त्वं प्रसादेन सर्वमान्यो भविष्यसि ।
सर्वरूपमयी देवी सर्वं देवीमयं जगत् ।
अतोऽहं विश्वरूपां तां नमामि परमेश्वरीम् ।)

(etasyāstvaṁ prasādena sarvamānyo bhaviṣyasi ।
sarvarūpamayī devī sarvaṁ devīmayaṁ jagat ।
ato 'haṁ viśvarūpāṁ tāṁ namāmi parameśvarīm ।)

(With her blessings, you will be universally respected. All forms are the forms of the Goddess. The whole world is pervaded by the Goddess. I, therefore, pay obeisance to that Form of the Universe and the Supreme Empress of all).

इति मूर्तिरहस्यं सम्पूर्णम् ।

iti mūrtirahasyaṁ sampūrṇam.

Thus concludes 'The Secret of Personifications'.

दुर्गाद्वात्रिंशन्नाममाला

16. *Durgādvātriṁśannāmamālā*

Rosary of the Thirty-two Names of *Durgā*

दुर्गा दुर्गार्तिशमनी दुर्गापद्विनिवारिणी ।
दुर्गमच्छेदिनी दुर्गसाधिनी दुर्गनाशिनी ॥१॥

1. 1 *durgā* 2 *durgārtiśamanī* 3 *durgāpadvinivāriṇī* ।
4 *durgamacchedinī* 5 *durgasādhinī* 6 *durganāśinī* ॥

1 Impassable 2 Queller of terrible distress 3 Who Defends from terrible calamities 4 Who Tears Apart difficulties 5 Facilitator for overcoming obstructions 6 Killer of troubles.

दुर्गतोद्धारिणी दुर्गनिहन्त्री दुर्गमापहा ।
दुर्गमज्ञानदा दुर्गदैत्यलोकदवानला ॥२॥

2. 7 *durgatoddhārinī* 8 *durganihantrī* 9 *durgamāpahā*।
10 *durgamajñānadā* 11 *durgadaityalokadavānalā*॥

7 Who rescues from misfortunes 8 Slayer of the demon *Durga* 9 Alleviator of approaching difficulties 10 Who makes diffculties infructuous 11 Forest Fire to burn the world of demons.

दुर्गमा दुर्गमालोका दुर्गमात्मस्वरूपिणी ।
दुर्गमार्गप्रदा दुर्गमविद्या दुर्गमाश्रिता ॥३॥

3. 12 *durgamā* 13 *durgamālokā* 14 *durgamātmasvarūpiṇī* ।
15 *durgamārgapradā* 16 *durgamavidyā* 17 *durgamāśritā* ॥

12 Inaccessible 13 Of Dazzling Lustre 14 Impassable Intrinsic Nature of the soul 15 Who Shows the Path through difficulties 16 Knowledge of difficulties or, Knowledge attainable with difficulty. 17 Recourse in difficulties.

दुर्गमज्ञानसंस्थाना दुर्गमध्यानभासिनी ।
दुर्गमोहा दुर्गमगा दुर्गमार्थस्वरूपिणी ॥४॥

4. 18 *durgamajñānasaṁsthānā* 19 *durgamadhyānabhāsinī* ।
20 *durgamohā* 21 *durgamagā* 22 *durgamārthasvarūpiṇī* ॥

18 Abiding in the Impassable Knowledge (knowledge not in the reach of intellect) 19 Who, in meditation, sheds Inaccessible Effulgence 20 Who causes Impenetrable delusion 21 Difficult to Access 22 The Inherent Nature of difficult purport.

दुर्गमासुरसंहन्त्री दुर्गमायुधधारिणी ।
दुर्गमाङ्गी दुर्गमता दुर्गम्या दुर्गमेश्वरी ॥५॥

5. 23 *durgamāsurasaṁhantrī* 24 *durgamāyudhadhāriṇī* ।
25 *durgamāṅgī* 26 *durgamatā* 27 *durgamyā* 28 *durgameśvarī* ॥

23 Slayer of invincible demons 24 Wielder of unfailing weapons 25 Of Difficult Parts 26 Difficult to Attain 27 Accessible with Difficulty 28 Controller of Difficulties.

दुर्गभीमा दुर्गभामा दुर्गभा दुर्गदारिणी ।
नामावलिमिमां यस्तु दुर्गाया मम मानवः ॥६॥

6. 29 *durgabhīmā* 30 *durgabhāmā* 31 *durgabhā* 32 *durgadāriṇī* ।
nāmāvalimimāṁ yastu durgāyā mama mānavaḥ ॥

पठेत् सर्वभयान्मुक्तो भविष्यति न संशयः ॥७॥

7. *paṭhet sarvabhayānmukto bhaviṣyati na saṁśayaḥ* ॥

29 Ferocious for Difficulties 30 Mistress of Difficulties 31 Enlightens Difficulties 32 Tears apart Difficulties.

A person who recites this range of my – *Durgā's* – names shall, beyond doubt, be free from all fears.

इति दुर्गाद्वात्रिंशन्नाममाला
iti durgādvātriṁśannāmamālā

Durgādvatriṁśannāmamālā concluded.

अथ देव्यपराधक्षमापनस्तोत्रम्

17. *Atha Devyaparādhakṣamāpanastotram*

Hymn Seeking Pardon of the Goddess for Committing Offences

न मन्त्रं नो यन्त्रं तदपि च न जाने स्तुतिमहो
न चाह्वानं ध्यानं तदपि च न जाने स्तुतिकथाः ।
न जाने मुद्रास्ते तदपि च न जाने विलपनं
परं जाने मातस्त्वदनुसरणं क्लेशहरणम् ।।१।।

1. *na mantraṁ no yantraṁ tadapi ca na jāne stutimaho*
na cāhvānaṁ dhyānaṁ tadapi ca na jāne stutikathāḥ ।
na jāne mudrāste tadapi ca na jāne vilapanam
paraṁ jāne mātastvadanusaraṇaṁ kleśaharaṇam ।।

I do not know the *mantras* or the *yantras*, nor do I know how to eulogise you. I do not know invocation or meditation, nor do I know the accounts of your glory. I know not (the significance of) the mystic signs of your hands nor do I know how to cry in distress. I do, however, know, O Mother! that all afflictions are destroyed by following after you.

विधेरज्ञाने द्रविणविरहेणालसतया
विधेयाशक्यत्वात्तव चरणयोर्या च्युतिरभूत् ।
तदेतत् क्षन्तव्यं जननि सकलोद्धारिणि शिवे
कुपुत्रो जायेत क्वचिदपि कुमाता न भवति ।।२।।

2. *vidherajñānena draviṇavirahenālasatayā*
vidheyāśakyatvāttava caraṇayoryā cyutirabhūt ।
tadetat kṣantavyaṁ janani sakaloddhāriṇi śive
kuputro jāyeta kvacidapi kumātā na bhavati ।।

On account of my ignorance of the procedure, lack of wealth, my lethargy and want of capability to appropriately perform the worship of your feet, whatever deviation may have occured, may, O Auspicious Mother, Redeemer of All! be pardoned, for a son may be bad but the Mother can never be so.

पृथिव्यां पुत्रास्ते जननि बहवः सन्ति सरलाः
परं तेषां मध्ये विरलतरलोऽहं तव सुतः ।
मदीयोऽयं त्यागः समुचितमिदं नो तव शिवे
कुपुत्रो जायेत क्वचिदपि कुमाता न भवति ॥३॥

3. *pṛthivyāṁ putrāste janani bahavaḥ santi saralāḥ*
paraṁ teṣāṁ madhye viralataralo 'haṁ tava sutaḥ ।
madīyo 'yaṁ tyāgaḥ samucitamidaṁ no tava śive
kuputro jāyeta kvacidapi kumātā na bhavati ॥

O Mother! you have many simple children on earth but among them I am a rarer fickle son. O Mother Auspicious! it does not behove you to forsake me, for a son may be bad but the Mother can never be so.

जगन्मातर्मातस्तव चरणसेवा न रचिता
न वा दत्तं देवि द्रविणमपि भूयस्तव मया ।
तथापि त्वं स्नेहं मयि निरुपमं यत्प्रकुरुषे
कुपुत्रो जायेत क्वचिदपि कुमाता न भवति ॥४॥

4. *jaganmātarmātastava caraṇasevā na racitā*
na vā dattaṁ devi draviṇamapi bhūyastava mayā ।
tathapi tvaṁ snehaṁ mayi nirupamaṁ yatprakuruṣe
kuputro jāyeta kvacidapi kumātā na bhavati ॥

O Mother of the Universe! O my Mother! I have never performed service at your feet, nor O Goddess! have I offered enough wealth to you. Even then you shower your incomparable affection on this unworthy child, because a son may be bad but the Mother can never be so.

परित्यक्ता देवा विविधविधसेवाकुलतया
मया पञ्चाशीतेरधिकमपनीते तु वयसि ।
इदानीं चेन्मातस्तव यदि कृपा नापि भविता
निरालम्बो लम्बोदरजननि कं यामि शरणम् ।।५।।

5. *parityaktā devā vividhavidhasevākulatayā*
mayāpañcāśīteradhikamapanīte tu vayasi ।
idānīṁ cenmātastava yadi kṛpā nāpi bhavitā
nirālambo lambodarajanani kaṁ yāmi śaraṇam ।।

After remaining distracted in a variety of services to several gods for more than eighty five years of age, I have given them up now. Now, O Mother of the Pot-Bellied Gaṇeśa! if I, bereft of all shelters, do not receive even your grace, in whose refuge shall I go?

श्वपाको जल्पाको भवति मधुपाकोपमगिरा
निरातङ्को रङ्को विहरति चिरं कोटिकनकैः ।
तवापर्णे कर्णे विशति मनुवर्णे फलमिदं
जनः को जानीते जननि जपनीयं जपविधौ ।।६।।

6. *śvapāko jalpāko bhavati madhupākopamagirā*
nirātaṅko raṅko viharati ciraṁ koṭikanakaiḥ ।
tavāparṇe karṇe viśati manuvarṇe phalamidaṁ
janaḥ ko jānīte janani japanīyaṁ japavidhau ।।

The impact of even a syllable of your *mantra* entering the ears is that a pariah becomes an eloquent orator of sonorous speech and a pauper, rich with multi-million gold coins, fearlessly moves about for a long time. Who knows the impact of the silent repetition of your names (*japa*) by those who do so as per the prescribed procedure?

चिताभस्मालेपो गरलमशनं दिक्पटधरो
जटाधारी कण्ठे भुजगपतिहारी पशुपतिः ।
कपाली भूतेशो भजति जगदीशैकपदवीं
भवानी त्वत्पाणिग्रहणपरिपाटीफलमिदम् ॥७॥

7. *citābhasmālepo garalamaśanaṁ dikpaṭadharo*
jaṭādhārī kaṇṭhe bhujagapatihārī paśupatiḥ ।
kapālī bhūteśo bhajati jagadīśaikapadavīṁ
bhavāni tvatpāṇigrahaṇaparipāṭīphalamidam ॥

O *Bhavānī*! it is the result of taking your hand (in marriage) that he (Lord *Śiva*), whose body is smeared with the ashes of the pyre, whose food is poison, who remains naked, who has a braid of matted hair on his head, who wears the king of snakes (*Vāsuki*) around his neck, who holds a skull in his hand, is the lord of animals and ghosts, has attained to the stature of the Lord of the Universe.

न मोक्षस्याकाङ्क्षा भवविभववाञ्छापि च न मे
न विज्ञानापेक्षा शशिमुखि सुखेच्छापि न पुनः ।
अतस्त्वां संयाचे जननि जननं यातु मम वै
मृडानी रुद्राणी शिव शिव भवानीति जपतः ॥८॥

8. *na mokṣasyākāṅkṣā bhavavibhavavāñchāpi ca na me*
na vijñānāpekṣā śasimukhi sukhechāpi na punaḥ ।
atastvāṁ saṁyāce janani jananaṁ yātu mama vai
mṛḍāni rudrāṇī śiva śiva bhavānīti japataḥ ॥

O Beauteous Mother with moonlike face! I don't desire the final beatitude, I do not want all the luxuries of the earth, I do not have expectation of possessing knowledge of material sciences nor do I have the desire of worldly pleasure. I beg of you, O Mother! that I may spend my life constantly and quietly repeating (the names) *Mṛḍānī*, the Gracious; *Rudrāṇi*, the Formidable; *Śiva, Śiva*, your Auspicious Spouse and *Bhavānī*.

नाराधितासि विधिना विविधोपचारैः
किं रुक्षचिन्तनपरैर्न कृतं वचोभिः ।
श्यामे त्वमेव यदि किञ्चन मय्यनाथे
धत्से कृपामुचितमम्ब परं तवैव ॥९॥

9. *nārādhitāsi vidhinā vividhopacāraiḥ*
kiṁ rukṣacintanaparairna kṛtaṁ vacobhiḥ ।
śyāme tvameva yadi kiñcana mayyanāthe
dhatse kṛpāmucitamamba paraṁ tavaiva ॥

O *Śyāmā* (of the Dark Complexion)! I have not worshipped you according to the many prescribed rites. What acts of omission my uncouth speech, involved in vicious thoughts, has not committed? If you still, O Mother! look at me with graceful indulgence, it only behoves you.

आपत्सु मग्नः स्मरणं त्वदीयं करोमि दुर्गे करुणार्णवेशि ।
नैतच्छठत्वं मम भावयेथाः क्षुधातृषार्ता जननीं स्मरन्ति ॥१०॥

10. *āpatsu magnaḥ smaraṇaṁ tvadīyaṁ*
karomi durge karuṇārṇaveśi ।
naitacchaṭhatvaṁ mama bhāvayethāḥ
kṣudhātṛṣārtā jananīṁ smaranti ॥

O Mother *Durgā*! do not consider it to be my wickedness that I remember you only now when I am merged in distress, for children remember their mother when they are troubled by hunger.

जगदम्ब विचित्रमत्र किं परिपूर्णा करुणास्ति चेन्मयि ।
अपराधपरम्परापरं न हि माता समुपेक्षते सुतम् ॥११॥

11. *jagadamba vicitramatra kiṁ paripurṇā karuṇāsti cenmayi* ।
aparādhaparamparāparaṁ na hi mātā samupekṣate sutam ॥

O Mother of the Universe! What is unusual about the overwhelming compassion that you continue to extend to me? A mother never neglects her child even if he commits offences again and again.

मत्समः पातकी नास्ति पापघ्नी त्वत्समा न हि ।
एवं ज्ञात्वा महादेवि यथायोग्यं तथा कुरु ।।१२।।

12. *matsamaḥ pātakī nāsti pāpaghnī tvatsamā na hi* ।
evaṁ jñātvā mahādevi yathāyogyaṁ tathā kuru ।।

A sinner like me there is none. None like you is the slayer of sins. Knowing this, O Great Goddess! do as you deem fit.

इति श्रीशङ्कराचार्यविरचितं देव्यपराधक्षमापनस्तोत्रं सम्पूर्णम् ।

iti śrīśaṅkarācāryaviracitaṁ devyaparādhakṣamāpana stotraṁ sampūrṇam ।

Thus concludes 'The Hymn Seeking Pardon of the Goddess for Committing Offences' composed by Śrī Śaṅkarācārya.*

*With reference to the fifth *śloka* of this *stotra* where the author's age has been mentioned as eighty-five years, it is likely that he is one of the Masters in the Śaṅkarācārya tradition since it is well known that the Ādi Śaṅkara left his mortal frame when he was thirty-two years.

सिद्धकुञ्जिकास्तोत्रम्

18. *Siddhakuñjikāstotram*

The Hymn of the Key to Accomplishment

शिव उवाच

śiva uvāca

Śiva said

शृणु देवि प्रवक्ष्यामि कुञ्जिकास्तोत्रमुत्तमम् ।
येन मन्त्रप्रभावेण चण्डीजापः शुभो भवेत् ॥१॥

1. *śṛṇu devi pravakṣyāmi kuñjikāstotramuttamam* ।
yena mantraprabhāveṇa caṇḍījāpaḥ śubho bhavet ॥

Listen O Goddess! I shall narrate the excellent 'Hymn of the Key'. With the impact of its *mantras*, the recitation of *Caṇḍī* becomes auspicious.

न कवचं नार्गलास्तोत्रं कीलकं न रहस्यकम् ।
न सूक्तं नापि ध्यानं च न न्यासो न च वार्चनम् ॥२॥

2. *na kavacaṁ nārgalāstotraṁ kīlakaṁ na rahasyakam* ।
na sūktaṁ nāpi dhyānaṁ ca na nyāso na ca vārcanam ॥

कुञ्जिकापाठमात्रेण दुर्गापाठफलं लभेत् ।
अति गुह्यतरं देवि देवानामपि दुर्लभम् ॥३॥

3. *kuñjikāpāṭhamātreṇa durgāpāṭhaphalaṁ labhet* ।
ati guhyataraṁ devi devānāmapi durlabham ॥

Neither the Armour, nor the Hymn of the Bolt, nor the Pin; neither (three) Secrets, nor the Hymns; neither meditation, nor entrustment of various limbs, nor even worshipping, but only the recitation of (the Hymn of) the Key, yields the fruit of recitation of *Durgāsaptaśatī* (Glory of the Goddess). O Goddess! it is highly confidential and inaccessible even to the gods.

गोपनीयं प्रयत्नेन स्वयोनिरिव पार्वति ।
मारणं मोहनं वश्यं स्तम्भनोच्चाटनादिकम् ।
पाठमात्रेण संसिद्ध्येत् कुञ्जिकास्तोत्रमुत्तमम् ।।४।।

4. *gopanīyaṁ prayatnena svayoniriva pārvati* ।
māraṇaṁ mohanaṁ vaśyaṁ stambhanoccāṭanādikam ।
pāṭhamātreṇa saṁsiddhyet kuñjikāstotramuttamam ।।

O Pārvatī! it is to be kept concealed with utmost effort like a woman keeps her generative organ. Just the recitation of the excellent Hymn of the Key accomplishes the objective of *Māraṇa* (incantation to kill enemies), *Mohana* (incantation to cause bewilderment), *Vaśya* (incantation to subdue) and *uccāṭana* (incantation to extirpate), etc.

अथ मन्त्रः

atha mantraḥ

Now the *Mantra*

ॐ ऐं ह्रीं क्लीं चामुण्डायै विच्चे।। ॐ ग्लौं हुं क्लीं जूं सः ज्वालय
ज्वालय ज्वल ज्वल प्रज्वल प्रज्वल ।।
ऐं ह्रीं क्लीं चामुण्डायै विच्चे ज्वल हं सं लं क्षं फट् स्वाहा ।।
।।इति मन्त्रः*।।

oṁ. aiṁ hrīṁ klīṁ cāmuṇḍāyai vicce ।। *oṁ. glauṁ huṁ klīṁ jūṁ saḥ jvālaya jvālaya jvala jvala prajvala prajvala.*
oṁ. aiṁ hrīṁ klīṁ cāmuṇḍāyai vicce jvala haṁ saṁ laṁ kṣaṁ phaṭ svāhā.

iti mantraḥ

Mantra Concluded.*

*It is beleived that it is neither desirable nor necessary, nor possible to translate or decode these *mantras*. Only *japa* is sufficient. However, see some notes in parenthesis [ ] on pages 76-78 in the *Devyatharvaśirṣam*.

नमस्ते रुद्ररूपिण्यै नमस्ते मधुमर्दिनि ।
नमः कैटभहारिण्यै नमस्ते महिषार्दिनि ॥१॥

1. *namaste rūdrarūpiṇyai namaste madhumardini* ।
namaḥ kaiṭabhahāriṇyai namaste mahiṣārdini ॥

Obeisance to the Form of *Rudra*; obeisance to the Crusher of *Madhu*; obeisance to the Slayer of *Kaiṭabha*; obeisance to the Tormentor of *Mahiṣa*.

नमस्ते शुम्भहन्त्र्यै च निशुम्भासुरघातिनि ॥२॥

2. *namaste śumbhahantryai ca niśumbhāsuraghātini* ॥

Obeisance to the Slayer of *Śumbha* and to the Destroyer of the demon *Niśumbha*.

जाग्रतं हि महादेवि जपं सिद्धं कुरुष्व मे ।
ऐंकारी सृष्टिरूपायै ह्रींकारी प्रतिपालिका ॥३॥

3. *jāgrataṁ hi mahādevi japaṁ siddhaṁ kuruṣva me* ।
aiṁkārī sṛṣṭirūpāyai hrīṁkārī pratipālikā ॥

O Great Goddess! awaken my repetitive chants of the *mantra* and grant it accomplishment. In the form of *aiṁ*, you are the intrinsic nature of creation; in the form of *hrīṁ*, you are its sustainer;

क्लींकारी कामरूपिण्यै बीजरूपे नमोऽस्तु ते ।
चामुण्डा चण्डघाती च यैकारी वरदायिनी ॥४॥

4. *klīṁkārī kāmarūpiṇyai bījarūpe namo 'stu te* ।
cāmuṇḍā caṇḍaghātī ca yaikārī varadāyinī ॥

In the form of *klīṁ*, you are the seed of desire. Obeisance to you in the seed form. You are *Cāmuṇḍā*, the slayer of *Caṇḍa*. In the form of *yai*, you are the dispenser of boons.

विच्चे चाभयदा नित्यं नमस्ते मन्त्ररूपिणि ॥५॥

5. *vicce cābhayadā nityaṁ namaste mantrarūpiṇi* ॥

As *vicce*, you are the eternal bestower of freedom from fear. Obeisance to you in the form of the *mantra.*

धां धीं धूं धूर्जटेः पत्नी वां वीं वूं वागधीश्वरी ।
क्रां क्रीं क्रूं कालिका देवी शां शीं शूं मे शुभं कुरु ।।६।।

6. *dhāṁ dhīṁ dhūṁ dhūrjaṭeḥ patnī vāṁ vīṁ vūṁ vāgadhīśvarī* ।
krāṁ krīṁ krūṁ kālikā devī śāṁ śīṁ śūṁ me śubhaṁ kuru ।।

As *dhāṁ dhīṁ dhūṁ*, you are the consort of *Śiva* of the matted hair; as *vāṁ vīṁ vūṁ* you are *Sarasvatī*, the Ruler of Speech; as *krāṁ krīṁ krūṁ* you are Goddess *Kālikā*, the Ruler of Time. *śāṁ, śīṁ śūṁ*, grant me auspiciousness, O Goddess!

हुं हुं हुंकाररूपिण्यै जं जं जं जम्भनादिनी ।
भ्रां भ्रीं भ्रूं भैरवी भद्रे भवान्यै ते नमो नमः ।।७।

7. *huṁ huṁ huṁkārarūpiṇyai jaṁ jaṁ jaṁ jambhanādinī* ।
bhrāṁ bhrīṁ bhrūṁ bhairavī bhadre bhavānyai te namo namaḥ ।।

huṁ, huṁ, you are the sound of *huṁ*; *jaṁ jaṁ jaṁ* you are the devourer of demons; *bhrāṁ bhrīṁ bhrūṁ* you are the noble *Bhairavī*. Obeisance to you again and again, O *Bhavānī!*

अं कं चं टं तं पं यं शं वीं दुं ऐं वीं हं क्षं ।
धिजाग्रं धिजाग्रं त्रोटय त्रोटय दीप्तं कुरु कुरु स्वाहा ।।
पां पीं पूं पार्वती पूर्णा खां खीं खूं खेचरी तथा ।।८।।

8. *aṁ kaṁ caṁ ṭaṁ taṁ paṁ yaṁ śaṁ vīṁ duṁ aiṁ vīṁ haṁ kṣaṁ*
dhijāgraṁ dhijāgraṁ troṭaya troṭaya dīptaṁ kuru kuru svāhā ।।
pāṁ pīṁ pūṁ pārvatī pūrṇā khāṁ khīṁ khūṁ khecarī tathā ।।

Rise up, rise up. Tear asunder, tear asunder. Illumine. *Svāhā*, I offer this oblation. *pāṁ, pīṁ, pūṁ*; You are *Pārvatī*, the Perfect One. *Khāṁ khīṁ khūṁ* you are the Traverser of the Sky.

सां सीं सूं सप्तशती देव्या मन्त्रसिद्धिं कुरुष्व मे ।

sāṁ sīṁ sūṁ saptaśatī devyā mantrasiddhim kurūṣva me

In the flow of *sāṁ sīṁ sūṁ*, grant complete perfection to the *mantras* of *Devīsaptaśatī* for me.

इदं तु कुञ्जिकास्तोत्रं मन्त्रजागर्तिहेतवे ।
अभक्ते नैव दातव्यं गोपितं रक्ष पार्वति ॥

idaṁ tu kuñjikāstotraṁ mantrajāgartihetave ।
abhakte naiva dātavyaṁ gopitaṁ rakṣa pārvati ॥

This 'Hymn of the Key', meant to awaken the (inherent power of the) *mantra*, is not to be imparted to a non-devotee. O *Pārvatī*! treat and protect this as secret.

यस्तु कुञ्जिकया देवि हीनां सप्तशतीं पठेत् ।
न तस्य जायते सिद्धिररण्ये रोदनं यथा ॥

yastu kuñjikayā devi hīnāṁ saptaśatīṁ paṭhet ।
na tasya jāyate siddhiraraṇye rodanaṁ yathā ॥

He who recites 'Glory of the Goddess' without (reciting) the 'Hymn of the Key', does not receive accomplishment. It is like crying in the wilderness.

इति श्रीरुद्रयामले गौरीतन्त्रे शिवपार्वतीसंवादे कुञ्जिकास्तोत्रं सम्पूर्णम् ।

iti śrīrudrayāmale gaurītantre śivapārvatīsaṁvāde kuñjikāstotraṁ sampūrṇam.

Thus is concluded the 'Hymn of the Key' as part of the conversation of *Śiva* and *Pārvatī* in the *Gaurītantra* of *Śrīrudrayamala.*

क्षमा-प्रार्थना

19. *Kṣamā-Prārthanā*

Seeking Forgiveness

अपराधसहस्राणि क्रियन्तेऽहर्निशं मया ।
दासोऽयमिति मां मत्वा क्षमस्व परमेश्वरि ॥१॥

1. *aparādhasahasrāṇi kriyante 'harniśaṁ mayā* ।
dāso 'yamiti māṁ matvā kṣamasva parameśvari ॥

Thousands of offences are committed by me day and night. Considering that 'this one is my servitor', forgive me, O Supreme Ruler!

आवाहनं न जानामि न जानामि विसर्जनम् ।
पूजां चैव न जानामि क्षम्यतां परमेश्वरि ॥२॥

2. *āvāhanaṁ na jānāmi na jānāmi visarjanam* ।
pūjāṁ caiva na jānāmi kṣamyatāṁ parameśvari ॥

I do not know how to invoke you, nor do I know how to bid farewell; nor even do I know how to worship you. Grant me forgivenes, O Supreme Ruler!

मन्त्रहीनं क्रियाहीनं भक्तिहीनं सुरेश्वरि ।
यत्पूजितं मया देवि परिपूर्णं तदस्तु मे ॥३॥

3. *mantrahīnaṁ kriyāhīnāṁ bhaktihīnaṁ sureśvari*।
yatpūjitaṁ mayā devi paripūrṇaṁ tadastu me॥

Even though it is without the appropriate *mantras,* without the appropriate rites and without sincere devotion; may it, O Ruler of the gods, become perfect.

अपराधशतं कृत्वा जगदम्बेति चोच्चरेत् ।
यां गतिं समवाप्नोति न तां ब्रह्मादयः सुराः ॥४॥

4. *aparādhaśataṁ kṛtvā jagadambeti coccaret* ।
yāṁ gatiṁ samavāpnoti na tāṁ brahmādayaḥ surāḥ ॥

Even after committing hundreds of offences, if a person pronounces *Jagadambā*, 'Mother of the World', he attains to the status which the gods *Brahmā* and others do not get.

सापराधोऽस्मि शरणं प्राप्तस्त्वां जगदम्बिके ।
इदानीमनुकम्प्योऽहं यथेच्छसि तथा कुरु ॥५॥

5. *sāparādho 'smi śaraṇaṁ prāptastvāṁ jagadambike* ।
idānīmanukampyo 'haṁ yathecchasi tathā kuru ॥

Although I am a sinner, yet O Mother of the world! I have sought refuge in you and, therefore, deserve your compassion. Do as you wish.

अज्ञानाद्विस्मृतेर्भ्रान्त्या यन्न्यूनमधिकं कृतम् ।
तत्सर्वं क्षम्यतां देवि प्रसीद परमेश्वरि ॥६॥

6. *ajñānādvismṛterbhrāntyā yannyūnamadhikaṁ kṛtam* ।
tatsarvaṁ kṣamyatāṁ devi prasīda parameśvari ॥

All the acts of omission and commission that I may have committed out of ignorance, loss of memory or confusion, may kindly be forgiven. O Supreme Goddess! be gracious.

कामेश्वरि जगन्मातः सच्चिदानन्दविग्रहे ।
गृहाणार्चामिमां प्रीत्या प्रसीद परमेश्वरि ॥७॥

7. *kāmeśvari jaganmātaḥ saccidānandavigrahe* ।
gṛhāṇārcāmimāṁ prītyā prasīda parameśvari ॥

O Supreme Goddess! O Bestower of Desires! O Mother of the Universe! O Embodiment of Existence, Consciousness and Bliss! Be gracious and accept this worship of mine.

गुह्यातिगुह्यगोप्त्री त्वं गृहाणास्मत्कृतं जपम् ।
सिद्धिर्भवतु मे देवि त्वत्प्रसादात्सुरेश्वरि ॥८॥

8. *guhyātiguhyagoptrī tvaṁ gṛhāṇāsmatkṛtaṁ japam* ।
siddhirbhavatu me devi tvatprasādātsureśvari ॥

You are the Preserver of the Innermost Secrets. O Sovereign Goddess! accept the recitation I have offered. With your blessing, may I attain to perfection.

श्री दुर्गार्पणमस्तु

śrī durgārpaṇamastu

Offered to *Śrī Durgā*

20. Āratī

आरती

जगजननी जय ! जय !!

(मा! जगजननी जय ! जय !!)

भयहारिणि, भवतारिणि, भवभामिनि जय ! जय !!

जगजननी जय ! जय !!

तू ही सत-चित-सुखमय शुद्ध ब्रह्मरूपा ।
सत्य सनातन सुन्दर पर-शिव सुर-भूपा ।।१।।

जगजननी जय ! जय !!

आदि अनादि अनामय अविचल अविनाशी ।
अमल अनन्त अगोचर अज आनँदराशी ।।२।।

जगजननी जय ! जय !!

अविकारी, अघहारी, अकल, कलाधारी ।
कर्त्ता विधि, भर्त्ता हरि, हर सँहारकारी ।।३।।

जगजननी जय ! जय !!

तू विधिवधू, रमा, तू उमा, महामाया ।
मूलप्रकृति विद्या तू, तू जननी, जाया ।।४।।

जगजननी जय ! जय !!

राम, कृष्ण तू, सीता, व्रजरानी राधा ।
तू वाञ्छाकल्पद्रुम, हारिणि सब बाधा ।।५।।

जगजननी जय ! जय !!

दश विद्या, नव दुर्गा, नानाशस्त्रकरा ।
अष्टमातृका, योगिनि, नव नव रूप धरा ।।६।।

जगजननी जय ! जय !!

तू परधामनिवासिनी, महाविलासिनि तू ।
तू ही श्मशानविहारिणी, ताण्डवलासिनि तू ।।७।।

जगजननी जय ! जय !!

सुर-मुनि-मोहिनि सौम्या तू शोभाऽऽधारा ।
विवसन विकट-सरूपा, प्रलयमयी धारा ।।८।।
जगजननी जय ! जय !!

तू ही स्नेह-सुधामयि, तू अति गरलमना ।
रत्नविभूषित तू ही, तू ही अस्थि-तना ।।९।।
जगजननी जय ! जय !!

मूलाधारनिवासिनी, इह-पर-सिद्धिप्रदे ।
कालातीता काली, कमला तू वरदे ।।१०।।
जगजननी जय ! जय !!

शक्ति शक्तिधर तू ही नित्य अभेदमयी ।
भेदप्रदर्शिनि वाणी विमले! वेदत्रयी ।।११।।
जगजननी जय ! जय !!

हम अति दीन दुखी मा! विपत जाल घेरे ।
हैं कपूत अति कपटी, पर बालक तेरे ।।१२।।
जगजननी जय ! जय !!

निज स्वभाववश जननी! दयादृष्टि कीजै ।
करुणा कर करुणामयि! चरण-शरण दीजै ।।१३।।
जगजननी जय! जय!!

jagajananī jaya! jaya!!
(*mā! jagajananī jaya! jaya!!*)
bhayahāriṇi, bhavatāriṇi, bhavabhāmini jaya! jaya !
jagajananī jaya! jaya!!

1. *tū hī sata-cita-śukhamaya śuddha brahmarūpā* ।
satya sanātana sundara para-śiva-sura -bhūpā ।।
jagajananī jaya! jaya!!

2. *ādi anādi anāmaya avicala avināśī* ।
amala ananta agocara aja ānandarāśī ।।
jagajananī jaya! jaya!!

3. *avikārī, aghahārī, akala kalādhārī* ।
karttā vidhi, bharttā hari, hara saṁhārakārī ॥
jagajananī jaya! jaya!!

4. *tū vidhivadhū, ramā, tū umā, mahāmāyā* ।
mūlaprakṛti vidyā tū, tū jananī, jāyā ॥
jagajananī jaya! jaya!!

5. *rāma, kṛṣṇa tū, sītā, vrajarānī rādhā* ।
tū vāñchākalpadruma, hāriṇi saba bādhā ॥
jagajananī jaya! jaya!!

6. *daśa vidyā, nava durgā, nānāśaśtrakarā* ।
aṣṭamātṛkā, yogini, nava nava rūpa dharā ॥
jagajananī jaya! jaya!!

7. *tū paradhāmanivāsini, mahāvilāsini tū* ।
tū hī śmśānavihāriṇi, tāṇḍavalāsini tu ॥
jagajananī jaya! jaya!!

8. *sura-muni-mohini saumyā tū śobhā "dhārā* ।
vivasana vikaṭa-sarūpā pralayamayī dhārā ॥
jagajananī jaya! jaya!!

9. *tū hī sneha-sudhāmayi, tū ati garalamanā* ।
ratnavibhūṣita tū hī, tū hī asthi-tanā ॥
jagajananī jaya! jaya!!

10. *mūlādhāranivāsini, iha-para-siddhiprade* ।
kālātītā kālī, kamalā tū varade ॥
jagajananī jaya! jaya!!

11. *śakti śaktidhara tū hī nitya abhedamayī* ।
bhedapradarśini vāṇī vimale! vedatrayī ॥
jagajananī jaya! jaya!!

12. *hama ati dīna dukhī mā! vipata jāla ghere* ।
hain kapūta ati kapaṭī, para bālaka tere ॥
jagajananī jaya! jaya!!

13. *nija svabhāvavāśa jananī! dayādṛṣṭi kījai* ।
karuṇā kara karuṇāmayi! caraṇa śaraṇa dījai ॥
jagajananī jaya! jaya!!

Victory! Victory!! to You, O Mother of the Universe. You alleviate fear and redeem from metempsychosis; You are the Consort of Lord *Śiva*. Victory! Victory!! to You.

1. You are Existence, Consciousness and Bliss. You are pure *Brahman*. You are Truth, Eternity and Beauty. You O Divine Empress! are the highest form of Auspiciousness. Victory! Victory!! to You.
2. You are Primordial, Without Beginning, Without Name, Unswerving, Indestructible. You are Unstained, Infinite, Beyond Senses, Beyond Birth (and Death), the Veritable Treasure of Bliss. Victory! Victory!! to You.
3. You are Immutable, Remover of Sins, Without Parts, yet Comprising All Parts. You are *Brahmā*, the Creator; *Viṣṇu*, the Protector; and *Śiva*, the Destroyer. Victory! Victory!! to You.
4. You are *Sarasvatī*, the Consort of *Brahmā*; You are *Lakṣmī*, the Consort of *Viṣṇu*; You are *Pārvatī*, the Consort of *Śiva*. You are the Great Illusive Force; you are the Primal Nature, you are Knowledge, you are the Mother. You are the Wife. Victory! Victory!! to You.
5. You are *Rāma* and *Kṛṣṇa*. You are *Sītā* and *Rādhā*, the princess of *Vraja*. You are the Wish-Fulfilling-Tree and Remover of All Impediments. Victory! Victory!! to You.
6. You are Ten Forms of Knowledge; Nine Forms of *Durgā*, Alleviator of Difficulties. You wield a variety of weapons. You are the Mother in Eight Forms. You are *Yoginī*. You attain to new and ever new forms. Victory! Victory!! to You.

7. In the Highest Abode you reside. You rejoice in a vast variety of sports. You roam in the crematoriums and perform the *tāṇḍava* and *lāsya* dances*. Victory! Victory!! to You.
8. You delude the gods and ascetics. You are Gentle and Beautiful. You are the Basis of all Elegance. In your starkness, you are Horrifying. You are the Torrential Wave of Deluge. Victory! Victory!! to You.
9. You verily are the Ambrosia of Love. You are the Deadly Poison too. You are adorned with jewels and you are also the Skeletal Frame of Bones. Victory! Victory!! to You.
10. You, (as *Kuṇḍalinī*) reside at the root of existence. You are the Bestower of Terrestrial as well as Transcendental Accomplishments. You are the Timeless *Kālī* and you verily are *Kamalā*, the Bestower of Boons. Victory! Victory!! to You.
11. You are Energy. You are the Wielder of Energy too. You are the Indivisible Eternity. And as Speech, you are the Displayer of all Divisions too. You are the Pristine Trilogy of the *Vedas*. Victory! Victory!! to You.
12. We, O Mother! are in dire distress, tangled in the web of calamities. Crooked and wicked though we are, we are still your children. Victory! Victory!! to You.
13. O Mother! spare a merciful glance at us, in keeping with your nature. O Compassionate Mother! be compassionate and grant us refuge in your feet.

---

*Two types of dance. *Tāṇḍava* is the frantic or violent form whereas *Lāsya* is accompanied with singing and instrumental music, expressing emotions of love.

21. And Finally, this Prayer......

जय महेश-भामिनी, अनेक-रूप-नामिनी,

समस्त-लोक-स्वामिनी, हिमशैल-बालिका ।

रघुपति-पद परम प्रेम, तुलसी यह अचल नेम,

देहु ह्वै प्रसन्न पाहि प्रणत-पालिका ।।

jaya maheśa-bhāminī, aneka-rūpa-nāminī,

samasta-loka-svāminī, himaśaila-bālikā ।

raghupati-pada parama prema, tulasī yaha acala nema,

dehu hvai prasanna pāhi praṇata-pālikā ।।

Glory to *Śiva's* Consort having countless forms and names. O Daughter of the *Himālaya*! you are the Empress of All the Worlds. Tulasī prays, O Protector of those in your refuge! grant me unshakable love of the highest order in the feet of Raghupati.

गोस्वामी तुलसीदास (विनय पत्रिका १६.३)

Gosvāmī Tulasīdāsa (*Vinaya Patrikā* 16.3)

APPENDICES
I to IV

APPENDIX

I. Names, Adjectives, Epithets, Incarnations and Associates of the Mother Goddess Appearing in the Text

Countless are the names, epithets, incarnations and associates of the Mother. Some of them appear in the *Caṇḍīpātha* which we have endeavoured to list below. It is possible that even from there, some may have been omitted through oversight. Meanings and interpretations of each of these names, epithets, incarnations and associates, may, likewise, be many. It depends upon the context and, even more, the *śraddhā* of the devotee to give meaning or interpretation to each of them. We have, in great humility, tried to provide such meanings and interpretations with contextual variations, at the appropriate places while translating the text without, however, any claims to finality.

	अ	A
1.	अम्बा	Ambā
2.	अहंकारा	Ahaṁkārā
3.	अनन्ता	Anantā
4.	अभव्या	Abhavyā
5.	अपर्णा	Aparṇā
6.	अनेकवर्णा	Anekavarṇā
7.	अमेयविक्रमा	Ameyavikramā
8.	अनेकशस्त्रहस्ता	Anekaśastrahastā
9.	अनेकास्त्रधारिणी	Anekāstradhāriṇī
10.	अप्रौढा	Apraudhā
11.	अग्निज्वाला	Agnijvālā
12.	अग्निदेवता	Agnidevatā
13.	अजिता	Ajitā
14.	अपराजिता	Aparājitā

15.	अमृतकला	Amṛtakalā
16.	अम्बिका	Ambikā
17.	अभेद्या	Abhedyā
18.	अचिन्त्यरूपचरिता	Acintyarūpacaritā
19.	अर्धमात्रास्थिता	Ardhamātrāsthitā
20.	अशेषसौम्येभ्यस्त्वतिसुन्दरी	Aśeṣasaumyebhyastvatisundarī
21.	अखिलात्मिका	Akhilātmikā
22.	अनानन्दा	Anānandā
23.	अविज्ञाना	Avijñānā
24.	अब्रह्म	Abrahma
25.	अपञ्चीकृतमहाभूता	Apañcīkṛtamahābhūtā
26.	अखिलंजगत्	Akhilaṁjagat
27.	अवेद	Aveda
28.	अविद्या	Avidyā
29.	अजा	Ajā
30.	अनजा	Anajā
31.	अधा	Adhā
32.	अग्निवर्णा	Agnivarṇā
33.	असुरनाशयित्री	Asuranāśayitrī
34.	अदिति	Aditi
35.	अभयहस्तका	Abhayahastakā
36.	अज्ञेया	Ajñeyā
37.	अलक्ष्या	Alakṣyā
38.	अनलात्मिका	Analātmikā
39.	अनायतस्तानना	Anāyatastānanā
40.	अरुणक्षौमा	Aruṇakṣaumā
41.	अरविन्दस्थिता	Arvindasthitā
42.	अरुणलोचना	Aruṇalocanā
43.	अरिकुलभयदा	Arikulabhayadā

44.	अखिलदेवमहर्षिपूज्या	Akhiladevamaharṣipūjyā
45.	अव्याकृता	Avyākṛtā
46.	अचिन्त्यमहाव्रता	Acintyamahāvratā
47.	अखिलशास्त्रसारा	Akhilaśāstrasārā
48.	असङ्गा	Asaṅgā
49.	अभ्युदयदा	Abhyudayadā
50.	अतिसौम्या	Atisaumyā
51.	अतिरौद्रा	Atiraudrā
52.	असिपाशिनी	Asipāśinī
53.	अतिभैरवा	Atibhairavā
54.	अतिविस्तारवदना	Ativistāravadanā
55.	अरुणा	Aruṇā
56.	अणिमादिभिरावृता	Aṇimādibhirāvṛtā
57.	अर्धाम्बिकेशा	Ardhāmbikeṣā
58.	अपांस्वरूपस्थिता	Apāṁsvarūpasthitā
59.	अलङ्घ्यवीर्या	Alaṅghyavīryā
60.	अनघा	Anaghā
61.	अयोनिजा	Ayonijā
62.	अक्षमालाङ्कुशधरा	Akṣamālāṅkuśadharā
63.	अक्षरा	Akṣarā
64.	अञ्जनप्रभा	Añjanaprabha
65.	अमितप्रभा	Amitaprabhā
66.	अष्टादशभुजा	Aṣṭādaśabhujā
67.	अष्टभुजा	Aṣṭabhujā
	आ	**Ā**
68.	आर्द्रचित्ता	Ārdracittā
69.	आर्तपरित्राणपरायणा	Ārtaparitrāṇaparāyaṇā
70.	आर्या	Āryā
71.	आद्या	Ādyā

72.	आनन्दा	Ānandā
73.	आत्मशक्ति	Ātmaśakti
74.	आमुक्ताङ्गदहारकङ्कण-रणत्काञ्चीरणन्नूपुरा	Āmuktāṅgadahārakaṅk-aṇaraṇtkāñcīraṇannūpurā
	इ	**I**
75.	इन्द्राणी	Indrāṇī
76.	इन्द्राणीपतिसद्भावपूजिता	Indrāṇīpatisadbhāvapūjitā
77.	इन्दुरूपिणी	Indurūpiṇi
78.	इन्द्रियाणामधिष्ठात्री	Indriyāṇāmadhiṣṭhātrī
79.	इन्द्रशक्ति	Indraśakti
80.	इन्दुलेखाधृता	Indulekhādhṛtā
81.	इन्दुकिरीटा	Indukirīṭā
82.	इन्दिरा	Indirā
	ई	**Ī**
83.	ईश्वरी	Īśvarī
84.	ईषद्धासा	Īṣaddhāsā
	उ	**U**
85.	उत्कर्षिणी	Utkarṣiṇī
86.	उद्योतिनी	Udyotinī
87.	उमा	Umā
88.	उषा	Uṣā
89.	उद्यद्भानुसहस्रकान्ति	Udyadbhānusahasrakānti
90.	उत्तप्तहेमरुचिरा	Uttaptahemarucirā
91.	उन्मदा	Unmadā
	ऊ	**Ū**
92.	ऊर्ध्वकेशिनी	Ūrdhvakeśinī
93.	ऊर्ध्वा	Ūrdhvā

	ए	E
94.	एककन्या	Ekakanyā
95.	एका	Ekā
96.	एकवीरा	Ekavirā
	ऐ	**Ai**
97.	ऐन्द्री	Aindrī
98.	ऐंकारी	Aiṁkārī
	क	**Ka**
99.	कमलानना/कमला	Kamalānanā/Kamalā
100.	कलमञ्जीररञ्जिनी	Kalamañjīrarañjinī
101.	क्रूरा	Krūrā
102.	कौमारी	Kaumārī
103.	क्रिया	Kriyā
104.	कुमारी	Kumārī
105.	कैशोरी	Kaiśorī
106.	कालरात्रि	Kālarātri
107.	कराली	Karālī
108.	कात्यायनी	Kātyāyanī
109.	कूष्माण्डा	Kūṣmāṇḍā
110.	क्रोधसमाकुला	Krodhasamākulā
111.	कालिका	Kālikā
112.	कामाक्षी	Kāmākṣī
113.	कुलेश्वरी	Kuleśvarī
114.	कामिनी	Kāminī
115.	कामिका	Kāmikā
116.	कौबेरी	Kauberī
117.	कल्याणशोभना	Kalyāṇaśobhanā
118.	काली	Kālī

119.	कपालिनी	Kapālinī
120.	कर्मफलेषुजुष्टा	Karmaphaleṣujuṣṭā
121.	कृष्णेनसंस्तुता	Kṛṣṇenasaṁstutā
122.	कालाभ्रा	Kālābhrā
123.	कैटभारिहृदयैककृताधिवासा	Kaiṭabhārihṛdayaikakṛtādhivāsā
124.	कल्याणी	Kalyāṇī
125.	कृष्णा	Kṛṣṇā
126.	कृत्या	Kṛtyā
127.	कान्ति	Kānti
128.	कौशिकी	Kauśikī
129.	कल्हाराबद्धमाला	Kalhārābaddhamālā
130.	करालवदना	Karālavadanā
131.	करालवक्त्रा	Karālavaktrā
132.	करुणातरङ्गिताक्षी	Karuṇātaraṅgitākṣī
133.	कामेश्वरी	Kāmeśvarī
134.	कलाकाष्ठादिरूपा	Kalākāṣṭhādirūpā
135.	कौशाम्भःक्षरिका	Kauśāmbhaḥkṣarikā
136.	किरीटिनी	Kiriṭinī
137.	कामधेनु	Kāmadhenu
138.	कान्तिरूपसौभाग्यशालिनी	Kāntirūpasaubhāgyaśālinī
139.	कनकोत्तमकान्ति	Kanakottamakānti
140.	कनकाम्बरा	Kanakāmbarā
141.	कनकवर्णाभा	Kanakavarṇābhā
142.	कनकोत्तमभूषणा	Kanakottamabhūṣaṇā
143.	कामदा	Kāmadā
144.	करुणार्णवा	Karuṇārṇavā
145.	कैटभहारिणी	Kaiṭabhahāriṇī
146.	क्लींकारी	Klīṁkārī
147.	कामरूपिणी	Kāmarūpiṇī

ख	**Kha**
148. खड्गधारिणी	Khaḍgadhāriṇī
149. खड्गिनी	Khaḍginī
150. ख्याति	Khyāti
ग	**Ga**
151. गौरी	Gaurī
152. गजसमारूढा	Gajasamārūḍhā
153. गरुडासना	Garuḍāsanā
154. गुह्येश्वरी	Guhyeśvarī
155. गुणत्रयविभाविनी	Guṇatrayavibhāvinī
156. गदिनी	Gadinī
157. गौरीदेहसमुद्भवा	Gaurīdehasamudbhavā
158. गुणाश्रया	Guṇāśrayā
159. गुणमया	Guṇamayā
160. गृहीतोग्रमहाचक्रा	Gṛhītogramahācakrā
161. गुह्यातिगुह्यगोप्त्री	Guhyātiguhyagoptrī
घ	**Gha**
162. घोरा	Ghorā
163. घोररूपिणी	Ghorarūpiṇī
164. घोररूपा	Ghorarūpā
च	**Ca**
165. चण्डघण्टा	Caṇḍaghaṇṭā
166. चित्रा	Citrā
167. चित्तरूपा	Cittarūpā
168. चिता	Citā
169. चिति	Citi
170. चिन्ता	Cintā
171. चामुण्डा	Cāmuṇḍā

172.	चण्डमुण्डविनाशिनी	Caṇḍamuṇḍavināśinī
173.	चण्डी	Caṇḍī
174.	चण्डिका	Caṇḍikā
175.	चर्चिका	Carcikā
176.	चित्रघण्टा	Citraghaṇṭā
177.	चूडामणि	Cūḍāmaṇi
178.	चक्रिणी	Cakriṇī
179.	चतुर्भुजा	Caturbhujā
180.	चतुर्वक्त्रा	Caturvaktrā
181.	चापिनी	Cāpinī
182.	चिन्मयातीता	Cinmayātītā
183.	चिन्मयानन्दा	Cinmayānandā
184.	चेतना	Cetanā
185.	चितिरूपा	Citirūpā
186.	चार्वङ्गी	Cārvaṅgī
187.	चन्द्रार्धचूडा	Candrārdhacūḍā
188.	चित्रकोद्भासिमाला	Citrakodbhāsimālā
189.	चन्द्ररेखाविभूषणा	Candrarekhāvibhūṣaṇā
190.	चण्डविक्रमा	Caṇḍavikramā
191.	चित्रमाल्याम्बरविभूषणा	Citramālyāmbaravibhūṣanā
192.	चित्रानुलेपना	Citrānulepanā
193.	चित्रकान्तिभृत्	Citrakāntibhṛt
194.	चित्राभरणभूषिता	Citrābharaṇabhūṣitā
195.	चित्रभ्रमरपाणि	Citrabhramarapāṇi
196.	चण्डघाती	Caṇḍaghāti
	छ	**Ch**
197.	छत्रेश्वरी	Chatreśvarı
198.	छाया	Chāyā

ज	Ja
199. जया	Jayā
200. जलोदरी	Jalodarī
201. जगदम्बा	Jagadambā
202. ज्वालामुखी	Jvālāmukhī
203. जयन्ती	Jayantī
204. जगद्धात्री	Jagaddhātrī
205. जगन्मूर्ति	Jaganmūrti
206. जगन्माता	Jaganmātā
207. जगदात्मशक्ति	Jagadātmaśakti
208. जगत्त्रयहितैषिणी	Jagattrayahitaiṣiṇī
209. ज्योत्स्ना	Jyotsnā
210. जगत्प्रतिष्ठा	Jagatpratiṣṭhā
211. जाति	Jāti
212. जिह्वाललनभीषणा	Jihvālalanabhīṣaṇā
213. जगदाधारभूता	Jagadādhārabhūtā

त	Ta
214. तपस्विनी	Tapasvinī
215. तैजसी	Taijasī
216. तलवासिनी	Talavāsinī
217. तुष्टि	Tuṣṭi
218. तिर्यक्	Tiryak
219. तपसा ज्वलन्ती	Tapasā jvalantī
220. तामसी	Tāmasī
221. तृष्णा	Tṛṣṇā
222. तुङ्गकुचा	Tuṅgakucā
223. तप्तकाञ्चनवर्णाभा	Taptakāñcanavarṇābhā
224. तप्तकाञ्चनभूषणा	Taptakāñcanabhūṣaṇā
225. तनुमध्यमा	Tanumadhyamā

226.	तृषा	Tṛṣā
227.	तनूदरी	Tanūdarī
228.	तेजोमण्डलदुर्धर्षा	Tejomaṇḍaladurdharṣā
	द	**Da**
229.	देवी	Devī
230.	दुर्गा	Durgā
231.	दारिद्र्यदुःखभयहारिणी	Dāridryaduḥkhabhayahāriṇī
232.	दीनार्तपरित्राणपरायणा	Dīnārtaparitrāṇaparāyaṇā
233.	देवमाता	Devamātā
234.	दक्षकन्या	Dakṣakanyā
235.	दक्षयज्ञविनाशिनी	Dakṣayajñavināśinī
236.	देवेशी	Deveśī
237.	दुष्प्रेक्ष्या	Duṣprekṣyā
238.	दण्डिनी	Daṇḍinī
239.	दंष्ट्राकराली	Daṁṣṭrākarālī
240.	दुरितापहा	Duritāpahā
241.	दक्षदुहिता	Dakṣaduhitā
242.	दुर्गमा	Durgamā
243.	दुराचारविघातिनी	Durācāravighātinī
244.	देवानामुपकारिणी	Devānāmupakāriṇī
245.	दुर्गपारा	Durgapārā
246.	दया	Dayā
247.	दिवाकरनिभा	Divākaranibhā
248.	द्वीपिचर्मपरीधाना	Dvīpicarmaparīdhānā
249.	दशनोज्ज्वला	Daśanojjvalā
250.	दुर्गार्तिनाशिनी	Durgārtināśinī
251.	दंष्ट्रोद्धृतवसुंधरा	Daṁṣṭroddhṛtavasuṁdharā
252.	दंष्ट्राकरालवदना	Daṁṣṭrākarālavadanā

253. दुर्गार्तिहारिणी	Durgārtihāriṇī
254. दंष्ट्राङ्कितवरानना	Daṁṣṭrāṅkitavarānanā
255. दुरत्यया	Duratyayā
256. दशवक्त्रा	Daśavaktrā
257. दशभुजा	Daśabhujā
258. दशपादा	Daśapādā
259. दंष्ट्रादशनभासुरा	Daṁṣṭrādaśanabhāsurā
260. दुर्गार्तिशमनी	Durgārtiśamanī
261. दुर्गापद्विनिवारिणी	Durgāpadvinivāriṇī
262. दुर्गमच्छेदिनी	Durgamacchedinī
263. दुर्गसाधिनी	Durgasādhinī
264. दुर्गनाशिनी	Durganāśinī
265. दुर्गतोद्धारिणी	Durgatoddhāriṇī
266. दुर्गनिहन्त्री	Durganihantrī
267. दुर्गमापहा	Durgamāpahā
268. दुर्गमज्ञानदा	Durgamajñānadā
269. दुर्गदैत्यलोकदवानला	Durgadaityalokadavānalā
270. दुर्गमा	Durgamā
270(a). दुर्गमालोका	Durgamālokā
271. दुर्गमात्मस्वरूपिणी	Durgamātmasvarūpiṇī
272. दुर्गमज्ञानसंस्थाना	Durgamajñānasaṁsthānā
273. दुर्गमध्यानभासिनी	Durgamadhyānabhāsinī
274. दुर्गमोहा	Durgamohā
275. दुर्गमगा	Durgamagā
276. दुर्गमार्थस्वरूपिणी	Durgamārthasvarūpiṇī
277. दुर्गमासुरसंहन्त्री	Durgamāsurasaṁhantrī
278. दुर्गमायुधधारिणी	Durgamāyudhadhāriṇī
279. दुर्गमाङ्गी	Durgamāṅgī
280. दुर्गमता	Durgamatā
281. दुर्गम्या	Durgamyā

282. दुर्गमेश्वरी Durgameśvarī
283. दुर्गभीमा Durgabhīmā
284. दुर्गभामा Durgabhāmā
285. दुर्गभा Durgabhā
286. दुर्गदारिणी Durgadāriṇī

ध **Dha**

287. धनुर्धरी Dhanurdharī
288. धर्मधारिणी Dharmadhāriṇī
289. धात्री Dhātrī
290. धूम्रा Dhūmrā
291. धनुश्शराङ्कुशपाशशूलयुता Dhanuśśarāṅkuśapāśaśūlayutā
292. ध्रुवा Dhruvā
293. धीश्वरी Dhīśvarī

न **Na**

294. नारायणी Nārāyaṇī
295. नित्या Nityā
296. निशुम्भशुम्भहननी Niśumbhaśumbhahananī
297. नानाभरणशोभाढ्या Nānābharaṇaśobhāḍhyā
298. नानारत्नोपशोभिता Nānāratnopaśobhitā
299. नीलग्रीवा Nīlagrīvā
300. नलकूबरी Nalakūbari
301. नारसिंही Nārasiṁhī
302. निद्रा Nidrā
303. नित्येऽक्षरेत्रिधामात्रास्थिता Nitye 'kṣaretridhāmātrāsthitā
304. नित्यार्धमात्रास्थिता Nityārdhamātrāsthitā
305. नैका Naikā
306. नीलास्यद्युतिमास्यपाददशका Nilāsyadyutimāsyapādadaśakā
307. नन्दा Nandā

308. निजशस्त्रास्त्रवर्षिणी Nījaśastrāstravarṣiṇī
309. निश्शेषदेवगुणशक्तिसमूहमूर्ति Niśśeṣadevaguṇaśaktisamūha-mūrti
310. नैर्ऋति Nairṛti
311. नागाधीश्वरविष्टरा Nāgādhīśvaraviṣṭarā
312. नेत्रत्रयोद्भासिता Netratrayodbhāsitā
313. नियमितविलसच्चोलिका Niyamitavilasaccolikā
314. नरमालाविभूषणा Naramālāvibhūṣaṇā
315. निमग्नारक्तनयना Nimagnāraktanayanā
316. नादापूरितदिङ्मुखा Nādāpūritadiṅmukhā
317. निराधारा Nirādhārā
318. नयनत्रययुक्ता Nayanatrayayuktā
319. नियता Niyatā
320. नारी Nārī
321. निराकारा Nirākārā
322. नीलभुजा Nīlabhujā
323. नीलजङ्घोरु Nīlajaṅghoru
324. नन्दजा Nandajā
325. नीलवर्णा Nīlavarṇā
326. नीलोत्पलविलोचना Nīlotpalavilocanā
327. निशुम्भासुरघातिनी Niśumbhāsuraghātinī

प **Pa**

328. पिनाकधारिणी Pinākadhāriṇī
329. पाटला Pāṭalā
330. पाटलावती Pāṭalāvatī
331. पट्टाम्बरपरीधाना Paṭṭāmbaraparīdhānā
332. पुरुषाकृति Puruṣākṛti
333. प्रौढा Prauḍhā
334. परमेश्वरी Parameśvarī

335.	प्रत्यक्षा	Pratyakṣā
336.	पार्वती	Pārvatī
337.	प्रेतसंस्था	Pretasaṁsthā
338.	पद्मासना	Padmāsanā
339.	पद्महस्ता	Padmahastā
340.	पूतना	Pūtanā
341.	पद्मावती	Padmāvatī
342.	पापनाशिनी	Pāpanāśinī
343.	प्रचण्डदैत्यदर्पघ्ना	Pracaṇḍadaityadarpaghnā
344.	प्रचण्डदोर्दण्डदैत्यदर्प-विनाशिनी	Pracaṇḍadordaṇḍadaityadarp-vināśinī
345.	पराजननी	Parājananī
346.	प्रकृति	Prakṛti
347.	पुष्टि	Puṣṭi
348.	परापराणां परमा	Parāparāṇāṁ Paramā
349.	पञ्चीकृतमहाभूता	Pañcīkṛtamahābhūtā
350.	पावना	Pāvanā
351.	पाशाङ्कुशबाणधरा	Pāśāṅkuśabāṇadharā
352.	पापहारिणी	Pāpahāriṇī
353.	प्रात:सूर्य समप्रभा	Prātaḥsūryasamaprabhā
354.	पाशाङ्कुशधरा	Pāśāṅkuśadharā
355.	प्रसन्नानना	Prasannānanā
356.	परमाविद्या	Paramāvidyā
357.	पापात्मनामलक्ष्मी	Pāpātmanāmalakṣmī
358.	परमाप्रकृति	Paramāprakṛti
359.	परमार्तिहन्त्री	Paramārtihantrī
360.	प्रसादसुमुखी	Prasādasumukhī
361.	परा	Parā
362.	पाशाङ्कुशवराभीतिधारयन्ती	Pāśāṅkuśavarābhītidhārayantī

363.	प्रमदोत्तमा	Pramadottamā
364.	पूज्या	Pūjyā
365.	पीनघनस्तनी	Pinaghanastanī
366.	पापघ्नी	Pāpaghnī
367.	प्रतिपालिका	Pratipālikā
	ब	**Ba**
368.	बुद्धि	Buddhi
369.	ब्राह्मी	Brāhmī
370.	बुद्धिदा	Buddhidā
371.	बहुला	Bahulā
372.	बहुलप्रेमा	Bahulapremā
373.	बलप्रदा	Balapradā
374.	ब्रह्मवादिनी	Brahmavādinī
375.	ब्रह्मचारिणी	Brahmacāriṇī
376.	ब्रह्माणी	Brahmāṇī
377.	बोधलक्षणाबुद्धि	Bodhalakṣaṇābuddhi
378.	बाणभुशुण्डीपरिघायुधा	Bāṇabhuśuṇḍīparighāyudhā
379.	ब्रह्मस्वरूपिणी	Brahmasvarūpiṇī
380.	ब्रह्म	Brahma
381.	ब्रह्मस्तुता	Brahmastutā
382.	बद्धहिमांशुरत्नमुकुटा	Baddhahimāṁśuratnamukuṭā
383.	बन्धूककाञ्चननिभा	Bandhūkakāñcananibhā
384.	बालरविद्युतिः	Bālaravidyutiḥ
385.	बाभ्रवी	Bābhravī
386.	बालार्कमण्डलाभासा	Bālārkamaṇḍalābhāsā
387.	बीजरूपा	Bījarūpā
	भ	**Bha**
388.	भक्तसुलभा	Bhaktasulabhā

389. भगवती Bhagavatī
390. भवप्रीता Bhavaprītā
391. भवानी Bhavānī
392. भवमोचनी Bhavamocanī
393. भाविनी Bhāvinī
394. भाव्या Bhāvyā
395. भव्या Bhavyā
396. भद्रकाली Bhadrakālī
397. भैरवी Bhairavī
398. भूतार्तिहारिणी Bhūtārtihāriṇī
399. भुक्तिमुक्तिप्रदायिनी Bhuktimuktipradāyinī
400. भक्तजनोद्दामदत्तानन्दोदया Bhaktajanoddāmadattāna-ndodayā
401. भक्तकामदुघा Bhaktakāmadughā
402. भवती Bhavatī
403. भीमा Bhīmā
404. भ्रामरी Bhrāmarī
405. भद्रा Bhadrā
406. भ्रान्ति Bhrānti
407. भीमाक्षी Bhīmākṣī
408. भैरवनादिनी Bhairavanādinī
409. भुवनेशी/भुवनेश्वरी Bhuvaneśī/Bhuvaneśvarī
410. भिन्नाञ्जनसंकाशा Bhinnāñjanasaṁkāśā
411. भारती Bhāratī
412. भाषा Bhāṣā
413. भीमरूपा Bhīmarūpā
414. भक्तवत्सला Bhaktavatsalā

म **Ma**

415. महाकाली Mahākālī

416. महालक्ष्मी	Mahālakṣmī
417. महांसरस्वती	Mahāsarasvtī
418. महामाया	Mahāmāyā
419. महातपा	Mahātapā
420. मनस्	Manas
421. मातङ्गी	Mātaṅgī
422. मतङ्गमुनिपूजिता	Mātaṅgamunipūjitā
423. माहेश्वरी	Māheśvarī
424. महिषासुरमर्दिनी	Mahiṣāsuramardinī
425. मधुकैटभहन्त्री	Madhukaiṭabhahantrī
426. महोदरी	Mahodarī
427. मुक्तकेशी	Muktakeśī
428. महाबला	Mahābalā
429. महागौरी	Mahāgaurī
430. महिषासना	Mahiṣāsanā
431. महारौद्रा	Mahāraudrā
432. महाघोरपराक्रमा	Mahāghoraparākramā
433. महोत्साहा	Mahotsāhā
434. महाभयविनाशिनी	Mahābhayavināśinī
435. मृगवाहिनी	Mṛgavāhinī
436. मालाधरी	Mālādharī
437. महादेवी	Mahādevī
438. मनःशोकविनाशिनी	Manaḥśokavināśinī
439. महिषवाहिनी	Mahiṣavāhinī
440. मुकुटेश्वरी	Mukuṭeśvarī
441. मङ्गला	Maṅgalā
442. मधुकैटभविद्रावी	Madhukaiṭabhavidrāvī
443. महिषासुरनिर्णाशी	Mahiṣāsuranirṇāṣī
444. महाविद्या	Mahāvidyā

445.	महामेधा	Mahāmedhā
446.	महास्मृति	Mahāsmṛti
447.	महामोहा	Mahāmohā
448.	महासुरी	Mahāsurī
449.	महारात्रि	Mahārātri
450.	मोहरात्रि	Moharātri
451.	महादुर्गप्रशमनी	Mahādurgapraśamanī
452.	महाकारुण्यरूपिणी	Mahākāruṇyarūpiṇī
453.	मातृका	Mātṛkā
454.	महापूर्वा	Mahāpūrvā
455.	मृगपतिस्कन्धस्थिता	Mṛgapatiskandhasthitā
456.	मुक्तेर्हेतुभूता	Mukterhetubhūtā
457.	मौलिबद्धेन्दुरेखा	Maulibaddhendurekhā
458.	मेधा	Medhā
459.	महेश्वरी	Maheśvarī
460.	माता	Mātā
461.	मालाकुम्भकपालनीरजकरा	Mālākumbhakapālanīrajakarā
462.	मधुरमधुमदा	Madhuramadhumadā
463.	महाहिवलया	Mahāhivalayā
464.	मयूरवरवाहना	Mayūravaravāhanā
465.	महीस्वरूपा	Mahīsvarūpā
466.	महावृषभवाहिनी	Mahāvṛṣabhavāhinī
467.	मयूरकुक्कुटवृता	Mayūrkukkuṭavṛtā
468.	महाशक्तिधरा	Mahāśaktidharā
469.	महावज्रा	Mahāvajrā
470.	महारावा	Mahārāvā
471.	मुण्डमथना	Muṇḍamathanā
472.	महाऽविद्या	Mahā 'vidyā
473.	महीमयी	Mahīmayī

474.	मरकतप्रख्यैश्चतुर्भुजैः- शङ्खंचक्रधनुःशरांश्चदधती	Marakataprakhyaiścaturbhujaiḥ-śaṅkhaṁcakradhanuḥśarāṁś-cadadhatī
475.	महावाणी	Mahāvāṇī
476.	महाश्री	Mahāśrī
477.	महिषमर्दिनी	Mahiṣamardinī
478.	महिषान्तकारी	Mahiṣāntakārī
479.	मृडानी	Mṛḍānī
480.	मधुमर्दिनी	Madhumardinī
481.	महिषार्दिनी	Mahiṣārdinī
482.	मन्त्ररूपिणी	Mantrarūpiṇī

य **Ya**

483.	युवती	Yuvatī
484.	यति	Yati
485.	यशस्विनी	Yaśasvinī
486.	यमघण्टा	Yamghaṇṭā
487.	योगिनी	Yoginī
488.	योगनिद्रा	Yoganidrā
489.	यशोदागर्भसम्भवा	Yaśodāgarbhasambhavā
490.	यज्ञियानां प्रथमाचिकितुषी	Yajñiyānāṁ prathamācikituṣī
491.	योगेश्वरी	Yogeśvarī
492.	यैकारी	Yaikārī

र **Ra**

493.	रत्नप्रिया	Ratnapriyā
494.	रौद्रमुखी	Raudramukhī
495.	रथमारूढा	Rathamārūḍhā
496.	रक्तबीजवधा	Raktabījavadhā
497.	रात्रि	Rātri

498.	राष्ट्री	Rāṣṭrī
499.	रक्तवसना	Raktvasanā
500.	रक्तदन्तिका	Raktadantikā
501.	रक्तालिप्तपयोधरा	Raktāliptapayodharā
502.	रौद्रा	Raudrā
503.	रक्तवस्त्रा	Raktavastrā
504.	रुचिराक्षमाला	Rucirākṣamālā
505.	रविचन्द्रवह्निनेत्रा	Ravicandravahninetrā
506.	रत्नोल्लसत्कुण्डला	Ratnollasatkuṇḍalā
507.	रूपसौभाग्यकान्तीनांप्रतिष्ठा	Rūpasaubhāgyakāntīnāṁpratiṣṭhā
508.	रक्तमध्या	Raktamadhyā
509.	रक्तपादा	Raktapādā
510.	रुक्माम्बुजासना	Rukmāmbujāsanā
511.	रक्ताम्बरा	Raktāmbarā
512.	रक्तवर्णा	Raktavarṇā
513.	रक्तसर्वाङ्गभूषणा	Raktasarvāṅgabhūṣaṇā
514.	रक्तायुधा	Raktāyudhā
515.	रक्तनेत्रा	Raktanetrā
516.	रक्तकेशा	Raktakeśā
517.	रक्ततीक्ष्णनखा	Raktatīkṣṇanakhā
518.	रक्तदशना	Raktadaśanā
519.	रक्तचामुण्डा	Raktacāmuṇḍā
520.	रुद्ररूपिणी	Rudrarūpiṇī

ल **La**

521.	लक्ष्मी	Lakṣmī
522.	लज्जा	Lajjā
523.	ललितादेवी	Lalitādevī
524.	लोचनत्रयभूषिता	Locanatrayabhūṣitā

525. लक्ष्यालक्ष्यस्वरूपा	Lakṣyālakṣyasvarūpā
526. लम्बोदरजननी	Lambodarajananī
व	**Va**
527. वनदुर्गा	Vanadurgā
528. वैष्णवी	Vaiṣṇavī
529. वाराही	Vārāhī
530. विमला	Vimalā
531. वृद्धमाता	Vṛddhamātā
532. विष्णुमाया	Viṣṇumāyā
533. वृषारूढा	Vṛṣārūḍhā
534. वृषवाहना	Vṛṣavāhanā
535. वारुणी	Vāruṇī
536. वज्रधारिणी	Vajradhārinī
537. विन्ध्यवासिनी	Vindhyavāsinī
538. वागीश्वरी	Vāgīśvarī
539. वज्रहस्ता	Vajrahastā
540. विधातृवरदा	Vidhātṛvaradā
541. वन्दिताङ्घ्रियुगला	Vanditāṅghriyugalā
542. व्याधिनाशिनी	Vyādhināśinī
543. विजया	Vijayā
544. विज्ञाना	Vijñānā
545. वेदितव्या	Veditavyā
546. वेदा	Vedā
547. विद्या	Vidyā
548. वैरोचनी	Vairocanī
549. वाक्	Vāk
550. विश्वमोहिनी	Viśvamohinī
551. वरदा	Varadā

552. विश्वरूपिणी Viśvarūpiṇī
553. विद्युद्दामसमप्रभा Vidyuddāmasamaprabhā
554. वार्ता Vārtā
555. वृद्धि Vṛdhi
556. वृत्ति Vṛtti
557. व्याप्तिदेवी Vyāptidevī
558. वल्लकीं वादयन्ती Vallakīṁ Vādayantī
559. विचित्रखट्वाङ्गधरा Vicitrakhaṭvāṅgadharā
560. वरदाङ्कुशपाशाभीतिकरा Varadāṅkuśapāśābhītikarā
561. विश्वेश्वरी Viśveśvarī
562. वषट्कार Vaṣaṭkāra
563. वृत्रप्राणहरा Vṛtraprāṇaharā
564. विश्वात्मिका Viśvātmikā
565. विश्वार्तिहारिणी Viśvavārtihāriṇī
566. विन्ध्याचलनिवासिनी Vindhyācalanivāsinī
567. वसूनां सङ्गमनी Vasūnāṁ saṅgamanī
568. विशाललोचना Viśālalocanā
569. वीणापुस्तकधारिणी Vīṇāpustakadhāriṇī
570. वेदगर्भा Vedagarbhā
571. विशाला Viśālā
572. विच्चे Vicce

श **Śa**

573. शिवा Śivā
574. शरण्या Śaraṇyā
575. शरणागतपरित्राणपरायणा Śaraṇāgataparitrāṇaparāyaṇā
576. शूलधारिणी Śūladhāriṇī
577. शाम्भवी Śāmbhavī
578. शिवदूती Śivadūtī

579.	शैलपुत्री	Śailaputrī
580.	शिखिवाहना	Śikhivāhanā
581.	श्वेतरूपधरा	Śvetarūpadharā
582.	शत्रूणां भयवर्धिनी	Śatrūṇāṁ bhayavardhinī
583.	शववाहना	Śavavāhanā
584.	शङ्खिनी	Śaṅkhinī
585.	शाङ्करी	Śāṅkarī
586.	शूलेश्वरी	Śūleśvarī
587.	श्री	Śrī
588.	शुम्भनिशुम्भधूम्राक्षमर्दिनी	Śumbhaniśumbhadhūmrākṣa-mardinī
589.	शूलिनी	Śūlinī
590.	श्रीमहाविद्या	Śrīmahāvidyā
591.	शुद्धा	Śuddhā
592.	शिवदा	Śivadā
593.	शङ्खं संदधती	Śaṅkhaṁ saṁdadhatī
594.	शून्यसाक्षिणी	Śūnyasākṣiṇī
595.	शीतांशुतुल्यप्रभा	Śītāṁśutulyaprabhā
596.	शुम्भादिदैत्यार्दिनी	Śumbhādidaityārdinī
597.	शशिधरा	Śaśidharā
598.	शिरोमालिका	Śiromālikā
599.	श्रद्धा	Śraddhā
600.	शब्दात्मिका	Śabdātmikā
601.	शशिमौलिकृताप्रतिष्ठा	Śaśimaulikṛtāpratiṣṭhā
602.	शर्वाणी	Śarvāṇī
603.	शक्ति	Śakti
604.	शान्ति	Śānti
605.	शुककलपठितं शृण्वती	Śukakalapaṭhitaṁ śṛṇvatī
606.	श्यामलाङ्गी	Śyāmalāṅgī

607.	शशिशकलधरा	Śaśiśakaladharā
608.	शङ्खपात्रा	Śaṅkhapātrā
609.	शुष्कमांसा	Śuṣkamāṁsā
610.	शिवाशतनिनादिनी	Śivāśataninādinī
611.	शिवशक्तिरूपा	Śivaśaktirūpā
612.	शक्तिभूता	Śaktibhūtā
613.	शङ्खचक्रगदाशार्ङ्ग-गृहीतपरमायुधा	Śaṅkhacakragadāśārṅga-gṛhitaparamāyudhā
614.	शिरोमालाविभूषणा	Śiromālāvibhūṣaṇā
615.	शताक्षी	Śatākṣī
616.	शाकम्भरी	Śākambharī
617.	शशिशेखरा	Śaśiśekharā
618.	श्वेतानना	Śvetānanā
619.	शुम्भहन्त्री	Śumbhahantrī

स **Sa**

620.	सर्वकार्यविधायिनी	Sarvakāryavidhāyinī
621.	सर्वमङ्गलमङ्गल्या	Sarvamaṅgalamaṅgalyā
622.	सर्वार्थसाधिका	Sarvārthasādhikā
623.	सर्वस्यार्तिहरा	Sarvasyārtiharā
624.	सर्वस्वरूपा	Sarvasvarūpā
625.	सर्वेशा	Sarveśā
626.	सर्वशक्तिसमन्विता	Sarvaśaktisamanvitā
627.	सती	Satī
628.	साध्वी	Sādhvī
629.	सर्वमन्त्रमयी	Sarvamantramayī
630.	सत्ता	Sattā
631.	सत्यानन्दस्वरूपिणी	Satyānandasvarūpiṇī
632.	सद्गति	Sadgati

633. सर्वविद्या	Sarvavidyā
634. सुन्दरी	Sundarī
635. सुरसुन्दरी	Surasundarī
636. सर्ववाहनवाहना	Sarvavāhanavāhanā
637. सर्वासुरविनाशा	Sarvāsuravināśā
638. सर्वदानवघातिनी	Sarvadānavaghātinī
639. सर्वशास्त्रमयी	Sarvaśāstramayī
640. सत्या	Satyā
641. सर्वास्त्रधारिणी	Sarvāstradhāriṇī
642. सावित्री	Sāvitrī
643. सुरेश्वरी	Sureśvarī
644. स्कन्दमाता	Skandamātā
645. सिद्धिदात्री	Siddhidātrī
646. सर्वाभरणभूषिता	Sarvābharaṇabhūṣitā
647. सर्वयोगसमन्विता	Sarvayogasamanvitā
648. सुगन्धा	Sugandhā
649. सरस्वती	Sarasvatī
650. सर्वमङ्गला	Sarvamaṅgalā
651. सर्वकामप्रदायिनी	Sarvakāmapradāyinī
652. सुपथा	Supathā
653. स्वाहा	Svāhā
654. स्वधा	Svadhā
655. सर्वगता	Sarvagatā
656. सर्वसौभाग्यदायिनी	Sarvasaubhāgyadāyinī
657. सर्वशत्रुविनाशिनी	Sarvaśatruvināśinī
658. सुरासुरशिरोरत्नघृ- ष्टचरणाम्बिका	Surāsuraśiroratna- ghṛṣṭacaraṇāmbikā
659. सुतरा	Sutarā
660. स्थितिसंहारकारिणी	Sthitisaṁhārakāriṇī

661. स्वरात्मिका Svarātmikā
662. सुधा Sudhā
663. संध्या Sandhyā
664. सृष्टिरूपा Sṛṣtirūpā
665. स्थितिरूपा Sthitirūpā
666. संहृतिरूपा Saṁhṛtirūpā
667. सौम्या Saumyā
668. सौम्यतरा Saumyatarā
669. सर्वशक्ति Sarvaśakti
670. संसारार्णवतारिणी Saṁsārārṇavatāriṇī
671. सर्वाङ्गभूषावृता Sarvāṅgabhūṣāvṛtā
672. सैरिभमर्दिनी Sairibhamardinī
673. सरोजस्थिता Sarojasthitā
674. सनातनी Sanātanī
675. सर्वे श्वरेश्वरी Sarveśvareśvarī
676. सिंहस्कन्धाधिरूढा Siṁhaskandhādhirūḍhā
677. सिद्धिकामैः सेविता Sidhikāmaiḥ sevitā
678. सुखा Sukhā
679. सिद्धि Siddhi
680. सारा Sārā
681. सर्वकारिणी Sarvakāriṇī
682. स्मृति Smṛti
683. सुमनोहरा Sumanoharā
684. स्त्रीरत्नम् Strīratnam
685. सर्वज्ञे श्वरभैरवाङ्कनिलया Sarvajñeśvarabhairavāṅkanilayā
686. स्मेरमुखी Smeramukhī
687. सर्वभूता Sarvabhūtā
688. स्वर्गमुक्तिप्रदायिनी Svargamuktipradāyinī
689. स्वर्गापवर्गदा Svargāpavargadā

690. सहस्रनयनोज्ज्वला — Sahasranayanojjvalā
691. सिंहस्था — Siṁhasthā
692. सर्वस्याद्या — Sarvasyādyā
693. स्त्री — Strī
694. स्वरा — Svarā
695. सुभगा — Subhagā
696. सर्वसत्त्वमयी — Sarvasattvamayī
697. साकारा — Sākārā
698. सात्त्विकी — Sāttvikī
699. सर्वदेवशरीरेभ्यः-आविर्भूता — Sarvadevaśarīrebhyaḥ-āvirbhūtā
700 सुश्वेतस्तनमण्डला — Suśvetastanamaṇḍalā
701. सुचित्रजघना — Sucitrajaghanā
702. सहस्रभुजा — Sahasrabhujā
703. सर्वदेवमयी — Sarvadevamayī
704. सत्त्वैकगुणाश्रया — Sattvaikaguṇāśrayā
705. सुकान्ति — Sukānti
706. सुमेरुयुगलस्तनी — Sumeruyugalastanī
707. सर्वरूपमयी — Sarvarūpamayī

ह — Ha

708. हरिप्रिया — Haripriyā
709. हंसमारूढा — Haṁsamārūḍhā
710. हिमाचलसुतानाथसंस्तुता — Himācalasutānāthasaṁstutā
711. ह्री — Hrī
712. हृत्पुण्डरीकमध्यस्था — Hṛtpuṇḍarīkamadhyasthā
713. हरिनेत्रकृतालया — Harinetrakṛtālayā
714. हिमाचलकृताश्रया — Himācalakṛtāśrayā

715. हंसयुक्तविमानस्था — Haṁsayuktavimānasthā
716. ह्रींकारी — Hrīṁkārī

क्ष — **Kṣa**

717. क्षेमकरी — Kṣemakarī
718. क्षमा — Kṣamā
719. क्षान्ति — Kṣānti
720. क्षुधा — Kṣudhā

त्र — **Tra**

721. त्र्यम्बका — Tryambakā
722. त्रैलोक्यस्याखिलेश्वरी — Trailokyasyākhileśvarī
723. त्रिनेत्रा — Trinetrā
724. त्रिजगदाधारभूता — Trijagadādhārabhūtā
725. त्रिदशपरिवृता — Tridaśaparivṛtā
726. त्रयी — Trayī
727. त्रिशूलवरधारिणी — Triśūlavaradhāriṇī
728. त्रिशूलचन्द्राहिधरा — Triśūlacandrāhidharā
729. त्रैलोक्यत्राणसहिता — Trailokyatrāṇasahitā
730. त्रिभिर्नेत्रैः शोभिता — Tribhirnetraiḥ śobhītā
731. त्रिगुणा — Triguṇā
732. त्रिंशल्लोचनमाला — Triṁśallocanamālā

ज्ञ — **Jña**

733. ज्ञाना — Jñānā
734. ज्ञानरूपिणी — Jñānarūpiṇī
735. ज्ञेया — Jñeyā

APPENDIX

II. Weapons Mentioned in the *Saptaśatī*

The generic Sanskrit term for a weapon is *Āyudha.* These are said to be of three types: (i) *Praharaṇa,* e.g., a sword; (ii) *Hastamukta,* e.g., a disc and (iii) *Yantramukta,* e.g., an arrow. Terms *śastra* and *astra* are also used for weapons. They are for striking and throwing. While a *śastra* is hand-held during attack or defence, an *astra* is thrown or released from a bow, like an arrow or from the finger or hand like a *disc.* This, however, is a broad distinction and not always adhered to. Both terms are, often, interchangeably used.

Apart from the physical weapons, there are powerful *mantras* which render water and even ordinary physical weapons potent enough to destroy the enemy. A shield (*carma*) is used to protect the person physically from the onslaught of an enemy.

1. अङ्कुश/*Aṅkuśa* : A hook, a goad. A hand-held weapon for striking. Generally an elephant-driver's instrument for controlling the elephant.
2. अर्गला/*Argalā* : A bolt, a bar or an obstruction used to barricade the enemy's passage. *Argalā stotram* in this book is a hymn to release any obstruction in the successful accomplishment of the objective of recitation of *Durgāsaptaśatī.*
3. असि/*Asi* : A sword, a scimitar, a sharp-edged shining weapon for striking at the enemy. Also, करवाल/ *Karavāla,* खड्ग/ *Khaḍga,* कृपाण/ *Kṛpāṇa,* चन्द्रहास/ *Candrahāsa:* these are different types of swords varying in size and strike-power. *Candrahāsa* is the name of the sword which Lord *Śiva* had presented to *Rāvaṇa.*

4. बाण/*Bāṇa* : An arrow, a shaft; other names for an arrow are सायक /*Sāyaka*, शर/*Śara*, इषु/*Iṣu*, तीर/*Tīra*, नाराच/*Nārāca*, शिलीमुख/*Śilīmukha*, विशिख/*Viśikha*, शर/*Śara*. Several types of arrows with varying functions have been mentioned in ancient literature: आग्नेय/*Āgneya* (fire-fuming); पर्जन्य/*Parjanya* (artificial clouds are caused by it resulting in rainfall and thunderstorm to thwart enemy-action or plans); वायव्य/*Vāyavya* (causes hurricane followed by complete darkness during the day); पन्नग/*Pannaga* (produces snakes); गरुड/*Garuḍa* (used for quelling the snakes, *Garuḍa* being an implacable enemy of snakes); ब्रह्मास्त्र/*Brahmāstra* (an unfailing weapon, only another *Brahmāstra* can counter it); पाशुपत/*Pāśupata* (It can destroy the whole world. Lord *Śiva* wields it. Only *Arjuna* had it in the *Mahābhārata*); नारायण/*Nārāyaṇa* (as lethal as *Brahmāstra*, cannot be countered by anything or any person. It follows the enemy/ies wherever he/they may run for escape or refuge. Only by surrendering himself can the enemy be saved).

5. भिन्दिपाल/*Bhindipāla* : A javelin thrown from hand. A kind of sling for throwing arrows or stones. An arrow shot through a tube from the hand.

6. भुशुण्डी/*Bhuśuṇḍī* : A missile; a fire-arm

7. चक्र/*Cakra* : A discus or a disc held on the forefinger of the hand. Thrown from a distance aiming at the enemy. A sharp circular missile. *Sudarśana Cakra* is the discus of Lord *Viṣṇu* and his incarnations *Nṛsiṁha* and Lord *Kṛṣṇa*.

8. चाप/*Cāpa* : A bow; used for shooting the arrows from. पिनाक/*Pināka* and शार्ङ्ग/*Śārṅga* are the famous bows of

Lord *Śiva* and Lord *Viṣṇu* respectively. *Śārṅga* was also the bow of *Śrī Rāma* and *Śrī Kṛṣṇa*, Lord *Viṣṇu's* incarnations. Other names for *Cāpa* : धनु/*Dhanu*; धनुष *Dhanuṣa*; कार्मुक/*Kārmuka*.

9. चापज्या/*Cāpajyā* : The string of a bow.

10. चर्म/*Carma* : A shield.

11. डमरु/*Ḍamaru* : A small drum, shaped like an hourglass. While it is also used for an auspicious purpose (Lord *Śiva* used it to pronounce the Sanskrit alphabet called माहेश्वर सूत्र/*Māheśvara Sūtras*), in battle or war, it is used to create panic in the enemy ranks by its sound. (Generally used by *Kāpālikas*.)

12. दण्ड/*Daṇḍa* : A staff or a heavy stick with one end thicker than the other; a cudgel. A sceptre.

13. गदा/*Gadā* : A mace; a club. Its lower end is very heavy. In size, it reaches from the floor to the chest. Its weight can be as much as 800 kg. Also खेट/*Kheṭa*; खेटक/*Kheṭaka*. (Kaumodikī is the name of Nārayaṇa's mace. In the Mahābhārata, Bhīma and Duryodhana were the master wielders of the mace).

14. घण्टा/*Ghaṇṭā* : A plate of dazzling metal struck as a clock in the battle-ground to create fear in the enemy-camp and demoralise the opponent.

15. हल/*Hala* : A plough. Also लाङ्गल/*Lāṅgala*. (Balarāma, Śrī Kṛṣṇa's elder brother, is also known as Haladhara).

16. इषुधि/*Iṣudhi* : A quiver.

17. कवच/*Kavaca* : An armour.

18. खट्वाङ्ग/*Khaṭvāṅga* : A club or a staff with a skull at the top; it is shaped like a foot or bedstead.

19. क्षुरप्र/ *Kṣurapra* : An arrow with horseshoe-shaped head with a razor–sharp edge.

20. कुलिश/ *Kuliśa* : The thunderbolt – *Indra*'s weapon, formed from the bones of the sage *Dadhīci.* Also वज्र/ *Vajra.* An axe, a hatchet.

21. कुण्टा/ *Kuṇṭā* : A five-yard long staff with a plough-shaped upper end. A lance; a barbed dart.

22. मुद्गर/ *Mudgara* : A hammer-like weapon with a long handle. A mallet; a club; a mace.

23. मुसल/ *Musala* : A pestle, shaped like a mace.

24. परशु/ *Paraśu* : A battle-axe. Its end is quadrangular and length about two yards. *Śrī Paraśurāma,* the sixth of the ten incarnations of Lord *Viṣṇu* and known to have wiped out the *kṣatriya* clans twenty-one times, wielded it.

25. परिघ/ *Parigha* : It has a vice-like grip; an iron bar; another type is an iron stick and the third type has a heavy upper end.

26. पटह/ *Paṭaha* : A war-drum to declare the start of battle/ war.

27. पाश/ *Pāśa* : A snare; a net; a fetter or a noose. It is said to be of two types : (i) *Varuṇa Pāśa* (ii) Ordinary *Pāśa.* It is made of steel-strings twisted into a rope. Its one end is shaped like a triangle with zinc tablets at the bottom. In antoher description, it is made of the threads of cotton, jute, grass or leather twisted into a rope. Its size is five yards. *Varuṇa,* the Regent of Ocean and of the Western Quarter, wields it.

28. पट्टिश/ *Paṭṭiśa* : A spear with three points; a sharp-edged spear.

29. ऋष्टि/*Ṛṣṭi* : A double-edged sword; a spear or a lance.

30. शक्ति/Śakti : A heavy, one-yard Long missile thrown with both hands. It has a large handle, very sharp, flaming tongue and claws. Its face resembles that of a lion. It is of blue colour and studded with small bells. One of the many varieties of *Śakti* is *Utkrāntidā*, a flying missile.

31. शङ्ख/*Śaṅkha* : A conch-shell. A martial drum declaring the commencement of war or battle. (In ancient times, wars or a day's battle began at sunrise with sounding of the conch-shell by both the warring camps. It also ended in the same way.) It was also customary for the chiefs of the battalions to assign proper names to their conches (See *Bhagavadgītā* I.15-16). Lord Viṣṇu and Lord Kṛṣṇa carry the *Pāñcajanya śaṅkha.*

32. शूल/*Śūla* : A pike; a dart; a sharp–pointed weapon.

33. तोमर/*Tomara* : An iron-club; it has a snake-like shape. Its front end is made of iron and the lower part is wooden. It is said to have two wings in the lower part so that, when shot, it may go flying fast.

34. त्रिशिख/*Triśikha* : Also त्रिशूल/*Triśūla* : A trident, famous as the weapon of Lord Śiva.

35. (महा) उल्का (Mahā) Ulkā: A fiery phenomenon in the sky; a meteor; a fire-brand; a torch; a fiery missile.

APPENDIX
III. Glossary

ॐ/*Oṁ* : Symbolises *Brahman*, the Infinite, Truth, Consciousness, Bliss. Has three syllables or sounds – ***a, u*** and *ṁ*. *Brahmā*, the creator; *Viṣṇu*, the sustainer and preserver; and *Śiva*, the annihilator, are present in it and are represented respectively by the forementioned three syllables. It is the *ādi-mantra* (primal chant). Also called *praṇava* or *udgītha*.

आदित्य/*Ādityas* : Sons of *Kaśyapa* from *Aditi*, the mother of the gods. Twelve in number, they represent the Sun in twelve months. Their names are – (i) *Dhātā* (ii) *Mitra* (iii) *Aryamā* (iv) *Rudra* (v) *Varuṇa* (vi) *Sūrya* (vii) *Bhaga* (viii) *Vivasvān* (ix) *Pūṣā* (x) *Savitā* (xi) *Tvaṣṭā* and (xii) *Viṣṇu*.

अभिचार/*Abhicāra* : Use of magical spells or incantations for causing harm to someone. It is one of the *upapātakas*, a sin of the lower degree. (See *Manusmṛti* XI.59-66 for a list of *upapātakas*. *Abhicāra* is mentioned in the 63rd *śloka* thereof).

अम्बा (जगदम्बा)/*Ambā* (*Jagadambā*) : The Mother. The Mother Goddess. The Mother of the Universe. *Lit. ambā* or *ambikā* also means mother.

अमृतबन्धु/*Amṛtabandhus* : The immortals, the gods. Friends/brothers of ambrosia or the immortal fraternity.

अनुष्टप् (अनुष्टुभ्)/*Anuṣṭup* (*Anuṣṭubh*) : One of the metres of Sanskrit prosody. The original *śloka*. It has several varieties but the most in use has eight syllables in each quarter but of variable quantity. Fifth syllable of each quarter should be short, the sixth long and the seventh alternately long and short. In terms of sanctity, it is next only to *Gāyatrī*.

अङ्गन्यास/***Aṅganyāsa*** **:** Touching the limbs of the body with the hand accompained by appropriate *mantras* for installing the deity/deities with multiple epithets/names.

अपर्णा/***Aparṇā*** **:** Name of *Pārvatī.* In the course of her penance following her birth in the house of *Himācala, Pārvatī,* to obtain Lord *Śiva* as her consort, gave up eating even the dry leaves (*parṇas*) falling from trees and, thus, earned the epithet *Aparṇā.*

अर्गला/***Argalā*** **:** *Lit.,* a bolt, a latch-bar for fastening a door. The term is used to suggest obstruction or impediment. It is indicated here that if, before reading the main hymn (*Durgāsaptaśatī*), this hymn is recited with faith and reverence, it shuts up all the obstructions, impediments and troubles. In other words, recitation of this hymn ensures a trouble-free worship of the Goddess with the seven hundred *ślokas* – *Saptaśatī* – and the Mother blesses the devotees with all the desired boons.

अश्विन्/***Aśvins*** **:** Twin gods, considered paragons of beauty. Physicians of the gods; sons of the Sun. They represent transition from darkness to light. Young, swift and bright.

अथर्वशीर्ष/***Atharvaśīrṣa*** **:** Head of the *Atharvaveda. Vedas* have three parts: *Samhitās, Brāhmaṇās* and *Āraṇyakas. Upaniṣads* are mainly part of the *Āraṇyakas* and considered to be the epitome of the *Vedic* knowledge, constituting the *Brahmavidyā,* the knowledge of the Ultimate Reality and, therefore, the essence of all *Vedic* wisdom. *Atharvaśīrṣas* are primarily five in number and they appear towards the end of *Atharvaveda.* They are, therefore, said to be the *Upaniṣadic* part of that *Veda. Devyatharvaśīrṣa* is considered to be the best of all of them. In the 26th verse of this hymn, it has been stated that by reciting this hymn, one reaps the fruit of reciting all the five *Atharvaśīrṣas.*

भग/*Bhaga* : One of the twelve forms of the Sun (see *Ādityas*). The Moon. A form of *Śiva.* Qualities such as *Jñāna* (knowledge), *Bala* (strength), *Aiśvarya* (majesty), *Vīrya* (Virility), *Śakti* (energy), *Teja* (lustre), affluence and prosperity, happiness and good fortune, fame, glory, excellence, etc. The word, in fact, denotes many meanings and the one who possesses some of these attributes is respectfully addressed as *Bhagavān.* God or His several forms or incarnations, too are, addressed as *Bhagavān.*

भगवती/*Bhagavatī* : Feminine of *Bhagavān. Bhagavatī* is the epithet of *Durgā, Lakṣmī, Sarasvatī* and their different incarnations or forms. A noble lady. A revered woman.

भारद्वाज/*Bhārdvāja* : Coming from or relating to *Bhardvāja. Bhārdvāja,* also associated with the sage *Yājñavalkya,* is a seer of many *Vedic* hymns and one of the seven stars (*saptarṣis*); sometimes mentioned as *Vālmiki's* disciple. An *āśrama* in his name is still there in *Prayāga. Śri Rāma* and also *Bharata,* on their way to the forest, had a short stay with him.

बीज/*Bīja* : The mystic seed, the root of a *mantra* representing the deity.

भैरव/*Bhairava* : One of the eight *Rudras* (see *Rudras*); a form of *Śiva.* Name of a classical *rāga* that generates emotions of fear/terror. *Lit.* fierce, formidable, horrible.

भुवनेशी/*Bhuvaneśī* : Ruler/Sovereign/Empress of *Bhuvana,* the whole world, the earth, heaven, water, etc.

ब्रह्मा/*Brahmā* : The creator. The first of the trinity of *Brahmā, Viṣṇu* and *Śiva.*

चण्डी/*Caṇḍī* : Name of the Goddess. Slayer of the demon *Caṇḍa.*

चण्डिका/***Caṇḍikā*** : Another name of the Goddess. *Lit.* violent, impetuous; proverbially seething with anger.

चामुण्डा/***Cāmuṇḍā*** : A fierce or a frightful form of the Goddess who slayed *Caṇḍa* and *Muṇḍa*

चतुरङ्गबल/***Caturaṅgabala*** : A complete army of four parts: elephants, chariots, cavalry and infantry.

दानव/***Dānavas*** : Sons of *Danu*, a daughter of *Dakṣa*, married to *Kaśyapa*. Demons

दैत्य/***Daityas*** : Sons of *Kaśyapa* from Diti, another daughter of *Dakṣa*. Another clan of demons.

दक्ष/***Dakṣa*** : See *Satī*

दक्षयज्ञविनाशिनी/***Dakṣayajñavināśinī*** : See *Satī*

दौहृद/***Dauhṛdas*** : A clan of demons. *Lit.* evil disposition of mind.

देव/***Devas*** : The gods. See *Tridaśa*

देवता/***Devatā*** : A deity. A god or a goddess

देवी/***Devī*** : A goddess. An honorific for a respected, virtuous, noble woman. Address of *Durgā*, the deity eulogised in various forms in the *Durgāsaptaśatī* or *Devīmāhātmya*. *Lit.* lustrous, luminous, shining, effulgent.

धौम्र/***Dhaumras*** : *Lit.* greyness, smoky. A clan of demons.

गायत्री/***Gāyatrī*** : A Vedic metre of 24 syllables and three *pādas*, each having eight syllables. Considered most sacred. Also the name of the most sacred *Vedic mantra* daily repeated by millions of Hindus during morning and evening prayers. The number of *mantras* in the *Rātri Sūkta* which are in Gāyatrī metre, is also eight.

गण/***Gaṇas*** : The troops of demi–gods who are attendants

of Lord *Śiva* or the Goddess. A *gaṇa* is a follower or an associate.

गन्धर्व/*Gandharva* : A celestial muscian. *Gandharvas* are a class of demigods regarded as singers or musicians of the gods.

गौरी/*Gaurī* : A white or fair-complexioned girl. Name of *Pārvatī*. An eight-year-old girl. Virgin maid.

गुह/*Guha* : One whose missile goes unimpeded and unrepulsed. An epithet of *Kārttikeya,* son of *Śiva* and commander-in-chief of the gods' army in their battle against demons led by *Tāraka* whom he killed. Also known as *Kumāra,* he restored to the gods their authority. *Guha* is also the name of a king of the *Niṣāda* (*cāṇḍāla*) clan and ruler of *Śriṅgverapura.* A horse. Also, the name of *Viṣṇu* and *Śiva.*

ईश्वरी/Īśvarī : The supreme and sovereign ruler. Supreme Controller possessing highest power and authority. *Śiva's* name is *Īśvara,* hence *Śiva's* consort.

कला/*Kalā* : Here, a division of time variously calculated (1/900 of a day or 1.6 minutes or 1/1800 of a day or 0.8 minutes or 2 minutes and $26\frac{54}{201}$ seconds or 1 minute and $35\frac{25}{301}$ seconds, or 8 seconds, a minute, 48 seconds, etc.)

Kalā is a small part of anything, a part or portion of the whole, sixteenth part (there are 16 *kalās*); a digit; a digit (16th pārt) of the moon; interest on capital. 60th part of one-thirtieth part of a Zodiacal sign. Any practical art, there being 64 such arts. A term for seven sub-strata of the elements of human body – *māṁsa* (flesh); *rakta* (blood); *meda* (fat); *śleṣma* (phlegm), *mala* (urine or secretion); *pitta* (bile) and *retas* (semen virile). Elesewhere, in place of phlegm, urine and bile, there are *rasa* (chyle), *asthi* (bone) and *majjā* (marrow). There are several other meanings also.

कालक/***Kālakas*** : A class of demons. A crane, a heron.

कालकेय/***Kālakeya*** : Progeny of *Kālakas.*

कलियुग/***Kaliyuga*** : The black or the dark age in which we are living. Literally, the age of strife. One of the four *yugas* or ages with a duration of 4,32,000 man-years. Other three are – *Kṛta* or *Satya* (17,28000 years), *Tretā* (12,96000 years) and *Dvāpara* (8,64,000 years).

कम्बु/***Kambu*** : A class of demons. Spotted; variegated; a shell; a conch.

काष्ठा/***Kāṣṭhā*** : A measure of time (1/30 *kalā*, 1/12 *kalā*, etc.) A quarter or a region of the world. A limit, boundary, the final frontier. The path of wind and clouds in the atmosphere. The Sun. A fixed place of a lunar mansion. Name of one of the wives of *Kaśyapa* and daughter of *Dakṣa.*

कात्यायनी/***Kātyāyanī*** : The Mother Goddess who manifested herself in the hermitage of the sage *Kātyāyana* in order to accomplish the task of the gods. *Kātyāyana* accepted her as his daughter. Hence *Kātyāyanī.* In the *Bhāgavata Purāṇa,* the *Gopikās* worshipped *Kātyāyanī* for obtaining *Śrī Kṛṣṇa* as their husband. Name of Pārvatī. Wife of the sage Yājñavalkya. Mother of Kārttikeya.

कुशिक/***Kuśika*** : Grandfather (or, according to some accounts, father) of the sage *Viśvāmitra.* Father of *Gādhi* who is regarded as the father of *Viśvāmitra.* From him, his successor (s) came to be known as *Kauśikas.*

कवच/***Kavaca*** : Armour; coat of mail. A *mantra* or a set of *mantras* promising protection of various parts of the body from ill-effects caused by natural phenomena and supernatural powers; from diseases, afflictions, enemies and traitors etc.

कीलक/*Kīlaka* : *Lit.* a pin or a wedge. It is supposed to be thick at one end and tapered to a thin edge at the other. It prevents free movement. Used for fixing or binding.

Contextually, the *Kīlaka* Hymn fixes the *Argalā* (Bolt) Hymn. To prevent misuse of the *Devīsaptaśatī* by undeserving or unscrupulous persons, Lord *Siva* has, in a manner of saying, bolted it and fixed it with a pin. *Mantras* of the Hymn of the Pin are not easy to interpret and open to different interpretations. This has been done intentionally. Only with the grace of Lord *Śiva,* the correct meanings of the *mantras* of this Hymn are realised by a deserving devotee. The first *mantra* where Lord *Śiva* has been reverenced as the embodiment of pure knowledge with the three *Vedas* – *Ṛk, Sāma* and *Yajuṣ* – as his three eyes, is a pointer to the necessity of invoking blessings with a prayer to open the devotee's eye of knowledge so that he may unfasten the pin and open the bolt.

कोलाविध्वंसी/*Kolāvidhvaṁsī* : Name of a clan of *kṣatriyas* who invaded and destroyed the capital city of *Kolā* in the South.

कोश एवं बल/*Kośa and Bala* : Treasure and the armed forces : two constituent members of State. The other five are *Svāmī* (the Master or the king); *Amātyas* (ministers or counsellors); *Suhṛt* (friends, allies and well-wishers); *Rāṣṭra* (territory, realm, kingdom or empire) and *Durga* (citadel or fort).

कृष्णा/*Kṛṣṇā* : *Kṛṣṇapakṣa,* the dark fortnight of a lunar month and one of the epithets of the Mother Goddess. Black, dark. Name of *Draupadī,* wife of *Pāṇḍavas.*

महाकाली/*Mahākālī* : An epithet of *Durgā* in her terrific form. Great *Kālī.* The dark or the black-complexioned Goddess. The Supreme Controller of Time. *Śiva's* consort.

महालक्ष्मी/*Mahālakṣmī* : Consort of *Viṣṇu* or *Nārāyaṇa.* Great *Lakṣmī,* the sustainer and preserver of the world. Goddess of fortune, prosperity, riches, wealth and affluence.

महासरस्वती/*Mahāsarasvatī* : Great *Sarasvatī.* Consort of *Brahmā,* the creator. Goddess of learning, wisdom and arts.

मन्त्र/*Mantra* : The mystic chant, consultation. Advising. Consecrating with sacred texts; enchanting with spells or charms.

A hymn or a prayer. A formula of prayer sacred to a particular deity.

A portion of the *Veda,* including the *Saṁhitā* and distinguished from the *Brāhmaṇa.*

मनु/*Manu* : Representative Man. Father of the human race. Fourteen in number, they are the successive progenitors or sovereigns of the earth. Their names are – 1) *Svāyambhuva,* 2) *Svārociṣa,* 3) *Auttami,* 4) *Tāmas* 5) *Raivata* 6) *Cākṣuṣa* 7) *Vaivasvata* 8) *Sāvarṇi* 9) *Dakṣasāvarṇi* 10) *Brahmasāvarṇi* 11) *Dharmasāvarṇi* 12) *Raudrasāvarṇi* 13) *Raucyadevasāvarṇi* 14) *Indrasāvarṇi.* The age or the period of a *Manu* is called *Manvantara.* Ours is the *Vaivasvata Manvantara.*

मार्कण्डेय/*Mārkaṇḍeya* : Name of the seer after whom the *Mārkaṇḍeya Purāṇa* is christened (*Durgāsaptaśatī* is a part of this *Purāṇa*). Son of the sage *Mṛkaṇḍu.* One of the *Chirañjīvīs* (long-living ones) who, though destined to die young, gained long life by propitiating Lord Śiva.

मतङ्गमुनिपूजिता/*Mataṅgmunipūjitā* : Name of the Goddess. *Lit.* worshipped by *Mataṅga,* the sage who, despite belonging to low caste, rose to high eminence and earned the title of a *Ṛṣi* (the seer). It was he who, in the face of opposition, initiated *Śabarī* of the *Bhīla* tribe. Before his death, he advised her to wait in her cottage for *Śrī Rāma* who would visit her whereafter she would attain to the final beatitude.

मातङ्गी/*Mātaṅgī:* Name of the Goddess. A female elephant.

मातृका/*Mātṛkā*: The mother-syllable. A *mātṛkā* is a syllable or a prosodial instant. *Matṛkā* is mother. It is an epithet of the divine mothers. They are seven or eight. Seven are – 1) *Brāhmī* 2) *Māheśvarī* 3) *Kaumārī* 4) *Vaiṣṇavī* 5) *Māhendrī* 6) *Vārāhī* and 7) *Cāmuṇḍā*. Eight include 1) *Brāhmī* 2) *Māheśvarī* 3) *Caṇḍī* 4) *Vārāhī* 5) *Vaiṣṇavī* 6) *Kaumārī* 7) *Cāmuṇḍā* and 8) *Carcikā*. Their number is, sometimes, extended to sixteen also.

मौर्य/*Mauryas*: Descendants of *Murā* or *Mura*. A class of demons.

मित्रावरुण/*Mitrāvaruṇas*: *Mitra* and *Varuṇa* : Two of the *Ādityas*, often mentioned together, especially in the *Vedic* literture. *Mitra* is Sun while *Varuṇa* is the Regent of the Seas.

नारसिंही/*Nārasimhī*: Energy or consort of *Narasiṁha* or *Nṛsiṁha*, the fourth incarnation of Lord *Viṣṇu*, in the form of Man-Lion. He slayed *Hiraṇyakaśipu*, the elder brother of *Hiraṇyākṣa* and father of *Prahlāda*, a great devotee of Lord *Viṣṇu*. The latter incarnated himself as *Narasiṁha* to protect *Prahlāda* from the demon's tyranny and redeem the gods from the terror perpetrated by him.

नैर्ऋति/*Nairṛti*: Belonging to *Nairṛtya*, the South-Western direction which being the nether region, is the abode of demons. *Narṛti* is the epithet of Goddess as regent of that direction and, therefore, represents the fortune of demons.

पदपाठ/*Padapāṭha* : Arrangement of the *Vedic* text in which each word is written and pronounced in its original form and independently of phonetic changes. This is as against the *Saṁhitāpāṭha*, i.e., the continuous text of the *Veda*.

पञ्चभूत/Pañcabhūta : Five elements – *Pṛthvī* (earth), *Jala* (water), *Vāyu* (air), *Agni* (Fire) and *Ākāśa* (space or ether).

प्रजापति/*Prajāpati* : The god presiding over creation. An epithet of ten lords of created beings. A king, a father, the progenitor.

पुरुष एवं प्रकृति/*Puruṣa & Prakṛti* : According to the *Sāṅkhya* school of philosophy, there are two principles : *Puruṣa* (spirit) and *Prakṛti* (matter). The entire phenomenal evolution, according to this school, is due to the latter. The former sets the latter in action by staying close to it as the conscious being but is neither concerned with nor affected by it. Matter has three modes or guṇas: *sattva* (goodness or lightness), *rajas* (passion, activity, restlessness) and tamas (darkness, stupor, ignorance, inertia, heaviness). All activity is the interplay of these modes.

पूषा/*Pūṣā* : The Sun.

रुद्र/*Rudras* : *Lit.* dreadful, frightful, formidable, great, large, praiseworthy. One who drives away evil. A group of the gods, eleven in number. According to the *Vāyu Purāṇa*, their names are – 1) *Ajaikapāda* 2) *Ahirbudhnya* 3) *Hara* 4) *Nirṛta* 5) *Īśvara* 6) *Bhuvana* 7) *Aṅgāraka* 8) *Ardhaketu* 9) *Mṛtyu* 10) *Sarpa* and 11) *Kapālī*. They are considered partial incarnations of *Śiva*. *Rudra* is also the epithet of *Śiva*. *Hanumān* is considered to be an incarnation of *Rudra*.

शक्ति/Śakti : As an epithet of the Goddess, it has several shades of meanings : power, will, capacity, energy, prowess, strength, capability, efficacy, effectiveness, etc. As a consort of any particular god or divine incarnation, *Śakti* is his energy or female divinity. She is the intrnisic power or potential of a man. In relation to *Puruṣa* of the *Sāṅkhya* school, *Śakti* is his *prakṛti*. As *Māyā* of the *Advaita* (non-dualistic) *Vedānta*, she is the Illusive Power of *Brahman* and as such *sadasadvilakṣaṇā* (beyond distinction as to existence or non-existence). As regal power, it has three elements – (i) *Prabhutva Śakti* (majesty or pre-eminence) (ii) *Mantra-Śakti* (Power of *mantra*, consultation) and (iii) *Utsāha Śakti* (Power of energy). *Śakti* also signifies *Kavitva śakti* (poetic power), *Vitta Śakti* (financial power), etc. *Śakti* is also a weapon (See *Śakti* – Appendix II). As power of speech, it is again of three types – (i) *Abhidhā* (the literal power or sense of a word) (ii) *Lakṣaṇā* (the indirect application or the secondary signification of a word) and (iii) *Vyañjanā*, the figurative or eliptical mode of expression.

शतभिषा/Śatabhiṣā : An asterism. The twenty-fourth lunar-mansion containing one hundred stars.

शब्दात्मिका/Śabdātmikā : The very spirit of the word. *Śabda* here denotes *Śabdabrahman*, i.e., the *Vedas*. The Goddess is the very spirit, the intrinsic meaning or essence as well as the substratum of the *Vedas*. As *Sarasvatī*, she also represents speech. *Śabda* is also sound, the object of the sense of hearing and a property of *ākāśa*. As such, the Goddess is the spirit that prevails in sound.

श्री/Śrī : Honorific signifying majesty, excellence, affluence, power, prosperity, fortune, virtuosity, etc. Also, the name of the Goddess *Lakṣmī/Durgā*.

सती/*Satī* : Daughter of *Prajāpati Dakṣa,* one of the ten lords of beings, first created by *Brahmā.* She was married to Lord *Śiva.* There was no love lost between *Śiva* and *Dakṣa.* On becoming *Prajāpati, Dakṣa* organised a great sacrifice, invited all the gods except *Śiva* and *Satī. Satī,* nonetheless insisted on going to her father's house against *Śiva's* wishes. He, therefore, sent her with an attendant. She was not welcomed there and observed that *Śiva's* share of oblations had not been kept aside. Angry, she burnt herself in the *Yoga*-fire. On hearing this, *Śiva* sent *Vīrabhadra,* a fierce attendant created by *Śiva* from his matted hair. He, along with his companions, destroyed the sacrifice. *Satī* was born again as *Pārvatī* in the house of *Himālaya,* practised severe penance and obtained Lord *Śiva* again as her husband.

सौभर/*Saubhara* : Relating to *Sobhari,* a patronymic of *Kuśika* (see *Kauśika*)

सायुज्य/*Sāyujya* : Identification; intimate union with the deity. Absorption. One of the four types of *Mukti* (final beatitude). Other three are – *sāmīpya* (proximity, vicinity, closeness), *sārūpya* (likeness, sameness of form); *sālokya* (being in the same sphere or world as the deity) or *sārṣṭi* (possessing the same station).

सिद्ध/*Siddha* : A semi-divine being of great purity and holiness; one possessing eight *siddhis* (accomplishments) – (i) *aṇimā* (the power to become small as an atom) (ii) *laghimā* (power to assume excessive lightness of weight) (iii) *Prāpti* (power to obtain anything) (iv) *prākāmya* (possession of irresistible will) (v) *mahimā* (power to increase size at will) (vi) *īśitva* (greatness, superiority, sovereignty, rulership) (vii) *vaśitva* (power to control, subjugate) (viii) *kāmavasāyitā* (power to suppress or enjoy passion at will).

शिवा/*Śivā* : The consort of Lord *Śiva.* Feminine form of *Śiva.* Felicity, Auspiciousness. Source of welfare and happiness. Also, a jackal.

शिवदूती/*Śivadūtī* : Appeared from the body of the Mother Goddess and deputed Lord *Śiva* as her ambassador to *Śumbha* and *Niśumbha* and the other demons to surrender or be prepared to be devoured by her attendants.

स्कन्दमाता/*Skandmātā* : Mother of *Skanda* or *Kārttikeya.* According to the *Chāndogya Upaniṣad, Skanda* is the name of *Sanatkumāra,* one of the four perennial child-sages.

सोम/*Soma:* A *Vedic* sacrifice (*Somayāga*). Name of a plant considered most important in the *Vedic*-sacrificial offering. The juice of *soma* plant, nectar; the beverage of the gods.

तंत्र/*Tantra* : *Tantra* is a treatise teaching mystical formularies for the worship of the deities or for the attainment of superhuman powers. Some scholars believe that the key to all religious or mystical practices of the Hindus is *Tantra.* There are three main divisions of *Tantric* works – *Brāhmaṇa Tantras, Jaina Tantras* and *Bauddha Tantras. Brāhmaṇa Tantras* include *Pañcarātra* (*Vaiṣṇava Tantras*), *Śaivāgama* (Śaiva *Tantras*) and *Śāktāgama* (*Śākta Tantras*). The spiritual *sādhanā* in accordance with the *Śāktāgama* demands strict discipline, ritualstic purification and devotion to *Jagadambā,* the Mother of the Universe.

त्रैलोक्य/*Trailokya* : Three worlds – heaven, earth and the nether or the lower region.

त्रयी/*Trayī* : Three *Vedas* – *Ṛk, Sāma* and *Yajuṣ* – taken together. Also, intellect or faculty of understanding.

त्रिदश/*Tridaśa* : *Liṭ* 30 (3x10) or 33 (3x10+3). A god, a goddess. Gods in general. Thirty-three *vedic* gods – 12 *Ādityas,* 8 *Vasus,* 11 *Rudras* and 2 *Aśvins.*

त्र्यम्बका/***Tryambakā*** : Having three eyes. *Śiva* is *Traymbaka*, so *Śivā* is *Tryambakā*. The third eye represents supreme knowledge. Its opening means attainment of the knowledge of the Supreme. The three eyes are also equated with the knowledge of the past, present and future and of the three worlds. Opening of the third eye by *Śiva* brings dissolution of the world. He destroyed *Kāma*, the god of love and passion, with the third eye.

त्वष्टा/***Tvaṣṭā*** : Viśvakarmā, architect of the gods. He manufactured the discus of *Viṣṇu*, the trident of *Śiva* and some other weapons of the gods with a part of the bright disc of the Sun.

उच्चाटन/***Uccāṭana*** : The magical incantation for eradication or extirpation of evil forces.

उदायुध/***Udāyudha*** : *Lit.* with uplifted or upraised weapons. A clan of demons.

उद्गीथ/***Udgītha*** : See Oṁ.

उष्णिक्/***Uṣṇik*** : A metre with seven syllables in a quarter.

वैप्रचित्त/***Vaipracitta*** : A clan of demons.

वाराही/***Vārāhī*** : *Varāha* or *Vārāha*, the Great Boar, is the third of the ten incarnations of Lord *Viṣṇu*. He slayed the demon *Hiraṇyākṣa* and retrieved the earth from the nether region. His Energy or Consort is *Vārāhī*.

वार्ता/वार्त्ता/***Vārtā/Vārttā*** : Occupation of a *Vaiśya* – agriculture, cattle-breeding or trade. A statement of mere facts without rhetoric.

वसु/***Vasus*** : *Lit.* Sweet, wealthy, rich, good. A class of deities, eight in number – (1) *Āpa* (2) *Dhruva* (3) *Soma* (4) *Dhara* (5) *Anila* (6) *Anala* (7) *Pratyūṣa* and (8) *Prabhāsa*.

वषट्कार/ *Vaṣaṭakāra* : A mystic/exclamatory chant used at the end of offering oblation to the deity. Represents power or energy.

विनियोग/ *Viniyoga* : Parting. Giving up – Assigning, entrustment or presentation to the deity after reading the *saṅkalpa,* i.e., the intention or purpose for which a hymn or a *mantra* is to be recited. Water taken in the right hand is dropped on earth. This is an act of reverence, propitiating the deity for granting the purpose for which the recitation is undertaken.

विष्णु-उरुक्रम/ *Viṣṇu-urukrama* : Viṣṇu is the second of the Divine Trinity, the sustainer and protector of the creation. *Urukrama* is his epithet; *lit.* taking wide strides. Refers to *Viṣṇu* as *Vāmana,* his fifth incarnation. He demanded three steps of land from the demon king *Vali* or *Bali* and in those steps measured the earth, heaven and the lower region with one step still remaining which, at *Vali's* request, he placed on his head and sent him to the nether world as its ruler. In the Vedic literature, Viṣṇu-urukrama sometimes refers to Sun who, in three strides covers three spheres or the entire day as morning, mid day and the evening.

विश्वेदेव/ *Viśvedeva* : Sons of *Viśva,* they are ten in number – (1) *Vasu* (2) *Satya* (3) *Kratu* (4) *Dakṣa* (5) *Kāla* (6) *Kāma* (7) *Dhṛti* (8) *Kuru* (9) *Pururavā* and (10) *Mādrava.*

यन्त्र/ *Yantra* : *Lit.*, a fetter or a throng, an appliance, a machine or an implement. Contextually, a mystical diagram used as an amulet. Some of the mystical *yantras* mentioned in the *Tantric* literature are – *yantrarāja, śrīyantra, sarvatobhadra, smarahara, muktiyantra,* etc. *Mantra, tantra* and *yantra* are, often, referred together.

APPENDIX

IV. First-line Index of Sanskrit Verses

1. *Saptaślokī Durgā*

(Hymn of Seven Verses to *Durgā*)

Pages 27 to 30

2. *Śrīdurgāṣṭottaraśatanāmastotram*

(Hymn of One Hundred and Eight Names of *Śrīdurgā*)

Pages 31 to 37

* no. not indicated, first verse before *viniyoga*

@ no. not indicated, second verse before *viniyoga*

3. *Devyāḥ Kavacam*

(Armour of the Goddess)

Pages 38 to 53

N

P

R

S

4. *Argalāstotram*
(Hymn of the Bolt)

Pages 54 to 60

5. *Kīlakam*

(Hymn of the Pin)

Pages 61 to 65

6. *Vedoktaṁ Rātrisūktam*

(Vedic Hymn of the Night)

Pages 66 to 68

7. *Tantroktaṁ Rātrisūktam*

(Hymn of the Night from *Tantra*)

Pages 69 to 71

8. *Śrīdevyatharvaśīrṣam*
(The Highest Meaning of the Goddess according to the *Atharvaveda*)
Pages 72 to 84

11. *Śrīdurgāsaptaśatī*

(Seven Hundred Verses to *Durgā*)

Chapter One

Pages 102 to 126

* concluding *mantra*, no. not indicated.

B

D

E

J

K

Chapter Two
Pages 128 to 147

Chapter Three
Pages 148 to 160

Chapter Four
Pages 161 to 177

Chapter Five
Pages 181 to 203

S

T

V

Y

Chapter Six
Pages 204 to 210

A

C

D

Chapter Seven
Pages 211 to 218

Chapter Eight
Pages 219 to 235

T

V

Y

Chapter Nine
Pages 236 to 247

Chapter Ten
Pages 248 to 256

Chapter Eleven
Pages 257 to 273

Chapter Thirteen
Pages 285 to 291

E

H

I

J

M

P

S

T

V

Y

13. *Ṛgvedoktaṁ Devīsūktam*
(Ṛgvedic Hymn to the Goddess)

Pages 299 to 302

14. *Tantroktaṁ Devīsūktam*
(Hymn to the Goddess from *Tantra*)

Pages 303 to 310

K

N

R

S

Y

15. *Śrīsaptaśatī Rahasyatrayam*
(Trilogy of Secrets of *Saptaśatī*)

15.1 *Prādhānikaṁ Rahasyam*
(The Pre-eminent Secret)

Pages 312 to 320

15.2 *Vaikṛtikaṁ Rahasyam* (The Modified Secret)

Pages 321 to 331

śaktirdaṇḍaścarma cāpaṁ pānapātraṁ kamaṇḍaluḥ 12

sarvadevamayīmīśāṁ mahālakṣmīmimāṁ nṛpa 13

sarvadevaśarīrebhyo yā ''virbhūtāmitaprabhā 7

sphuraddaśanadaṁṣṭrā sā bhīmarūpāpi bhūmipa 4

sucitrajaghanā citramālyāmbaravibhūṣaṇā 9

śvetānanā nīlabhujā suśvetastanamaṇḍalā 8

T

tataḥ kṛtāñjalirbhūtvā stuvīta caritairimaiḥ 32

tasmātpūjaya bhūpāla sarvalokamaheśvarīm 39

(॥ॐ॥) *triguṇā tāmasī devī sāttvikī yā tridhoditā* 1

V

vāhanaṁ pūjayeddevyā dhṛtaṁ yena carācaram 31

virañciḥ svarayā madhye rudro gauryā ca dakṣiṇe 19

Y

yoganidrā hareruktā mahākālī tamoguṇā 2

yo na pūjayate nityaṁ caṇḍikāṁ bhaktavatsalām 38

15.3 *Mūrti Rahasyam* (The Secret of Personfication)

Pages 332 to 339

A

adhīte ya imaṁ nityaṁ raktadantyā vapuḥstavam 11

anayā vyāptamakhilaṁ jagatsthāvarajaṅgamam 10

ato 'haṁ viśvarūpāṁ tāṁ namāmi parameśvarīm

last line; no. not given.

B

bhīmāpi nīlavarṇā sā daṁṣṭrādaśanabhāsurā 18

(bhuktvā bhogān yathākāmaṁ devīsāyujyamāpnuyat)

after 10th śloka,
no. not indicated.

16. *Durgādvātriṁśannāmamālā*

(Rosary of Thirty-two Names of *Durgā*)

Pages 340 to 341

17. *Devyaparādhakṣamāpanastotram*

(Hymn Seeking Pardon of the Goddess the committing Offences)

Pages 342 to 347

18. *Siddhakuñjikāstotram*

(Hymn of the Key to Accomplishment)

Pages 348 to 352

J

jāgrataṁ hi mahādevi japaṁ siddhaṁ kuruṣva me 3rd after mantra

K

klīṁkārī kāmarūpiṇyai bījarūpe namo 'stu te 4th after mantra

kuñjikāpāthamātreṇa durgāpāṭhaphalaṁ labhet 3rd before mantra

N

na kavacaṁ nārgalāstotraṁ kīlakaṁ na rahasyakam 2nd before mantra

namaste rudrarūpiṇyai namaste madhumardini 1st after mantra

namaste śumbhahantryai ca niśumbhāsuraghātini 2nd after mantra

S

ṣṛṇu devi pravakṣyāmi kuñjikāstotramuttamam 1st before mantra

sāṁ sīṁ sūṁ saptaśatī devyā mantrasiddhiṁ kuruṣva me no. not indicated, after eighth mantra

V

vicce cābhayadā nityaṁ namaste mantrarūpiṇi 5th after mantra

Y

yastu kuñjikayā devi hīnāṁ saptaśatīṁ paṭhet last, no. not indicated

19. *Kṣamā-Prārthanā*
(Seeking Forgiveness)

Pages 353 to 355

A

ajñanādvismṛterbhrāntyā yannyūnamadhikaṁ kṛtam 6

aparādhaśataṁ kṛtvā jagadambeti coccaret 4